Student Manual for
Theory and Practice of Counseling and Psychotherapy

NINTH EDITION

Gerald Corey

California State University, Fullerton

Diplomate in Counseling Psychology,

American Board of Professional Psychology

BROOKS/COLE
CENGAGE Learning·

Australia · Brazil · Canada · Mexico · Singapore · Spain
United Kingdom · United States

ISBN-13: 978-1-133-30934-5
ISBN-10: 1-133-30934-8

Brooks/Cole
20 Davis Drive
Belmont, CA 94002-3098
USA

Cengage Learning is a leading provider of customized learning solutions with office locations around the globe, including Singapore, the United Kingdom, Australia, Mexico, Brazil, and Japan. Locate your local office at: **www.cengage.com/global**

Cengage Learning products are represented in Canada by Nelson Education, Ltd.

To learn more about Brooks/Cole, visit **www.cengage.com/brookscole**

Purchase any of our products at your local college store or at our preferred online store **www.CengageBrain.com**

Printed in the United States of America
1 2 3 4 5 6 7 15 14 13 12 11

CONTENTS

PART 1

Basic Issues in Counseling Practice

Chapter **1**

Introduction and Overview

INTRODUCTION TO THIS MANUAL

This manual is designed to accompany *Theory and Practice of Counseling and Psychotherapy,* Ninth Edition, and *Case Approach to Counseling and Psychotherapy,* Eighth Edition (both Brooks/Cole, Cengage Learning, ©2013). The manual is aimed at helping you personalize the process by which you learn about counseling theories and therapeutic practice. It emphasizes the *practical application* of various therapeutic approaches to your personal growth. And it stresses the critical evaluation of each therapy as you are called on to use the skills of the approach in exercises, activities, and consideration of case examples and problems.

The manual is appropriate for courses in counseling theory and practice, intervention strategies, and human services; it is also useful for internship experiences. It is well suited to practicum courses during which you apply your knowledge of the helping process to specific, practical field experiences. Key features of the manual are:

- Self-inventories to assess your attitudes and beliefs about counseling theory and practice, the counselor as a person, and ethical issues
- A summary overview of each major theory of counseling
- A review of the highlights of each theory
- Questions for discussion and evaluation
- A prechapter self-inventory for each approach
- Sample forms and charts for some chapters
- Assessment forms for the appraisal of life patterns
- Case examples by experts illustrating their approaches to a client from their theoretical perspectives (for each theory chapter)
- The case of Stan for each of the theory chapters
- The case of Ruth for each of the theory chapters
- Activities for inside and outside of class
- Ethical and professional issues for exploration
- Issues basic to your personal development
- A glossary of key terms for each theory
- A comprehension check, or quiz, for each of Chapters 2 to 15

This ninth edition of the *Student Manual* has been updated to coordinate with the content changes in the ninth edition of the text, *Theory and Practice of Counseling and Psychotherapy.* For each of the theory chapters (Chapters 4 to 14), the following content has been updated: overview of the theory, glossary of key terms, questions for reflection and discussion, and quiz (comprehension check) for each theory. In addition, each theory chapter contains a new case example in which a professional with expertise in the given theory illustrates his or her way of applying the key concepts and techniques of the theory to a specific case.

Acknowledgments

I greatly appreciate the contributions made by the following people for demonstrating how their theoretical orientation can be applied to working with a client:

James Ruby, PhD, Assistant Professor of Human Services at California State University, Fullerton (Chapter 4: Working with a Client from a Psychodynamic Perspective).

Richard E. Watts, PhD, Distinguished Professor in Counselor Education, Sam Houston University (Chapter 5: Working with a Client from an Adlerian Therapist's Perspective).

David N. Elkins, PhD, Professor Emeritus, Graduate School of Education and Psychology, Pepperdine University (Chapter 6: Working with a Client from an Existential Therapist's Perspective; and Chapter 7: Working with a Client from a Person-Centered Approach).

Jon Frew, PhD, ABPP, Professor of Psychology, Pacific University School of Professional Psychology (Chapter 8: Working with a Client from a Gestalt Therapist's Perspective).

Arnold A. Lazarus, PhD, ABPP, Distinguished Professor Emeritus in the Graduate School of Applied and Professional Psychology at Rutgers University and President of the Lazarus Institute in Skillman, New Jersey (Chapter 9: Working with a Client from a Multimodal and Behavior Therapist's Perspective).

Caroline Bailey, PhD, Assistant Professor of Social Work at California State University, Fullerton (Chapter 9: Working with a Client from a Behavior Therapist's Perspective; and Chapter 10: Working with a Client from a Cognitive Behavioral Approach).

Robert E. Wubbolding, EdD, Professor Emeritus of Counseling at Xavier University and the Director of the Center for Reality Therapy in Cincinnati (Chapter 11: Working with a Client from a Reality Therapist's Perspective).

Mary M. Read, PhD, Director of Clinical Training in the Counseling Department at California State University, Fullerton (Chapter 12: Working with a Client from a Feminist Therapist's Perspective).

Kathy M. Evans, PhD, Associate Professor at the University of Southern Carolina and the Coordinator of the Counselor Education Program; **Elizabeth A. Kincade, PhD,** Chair of the Counseling Center at Indiana University of Pennsylvania; and **Susan Rachael Seem, PhD,** Professor in the Department of Counselor Education at The College of Brockport, State University of New York (Chapter 12: Drs. Evans, Kincade, and Seem collaborated on working with a client from a feminist therapy approach).

John J. Murphy, PhD, Professor of Psychology and Counseling at the University of Central Arkansas (Chapter 13: Working with a Client from a Solution-Focused Brief Therapist's Perspective).

John Winslade, PhD, Professor of Counseling at California State University at San Bernardino, and Associate Dean of the College of Education (Chapter 13: Working with a Client from a Narrative Therapist's Perspective).

Melanie Horn Mallers, PhD, is Assistant Professor of Human Services at California State University, Fullerton (Chapter 14: Working with a Client from a Family Systems Therapist's Perspective).

Jamie Bludworth, PhD, Licensed Psychologist, private practice, Phoenix, Arizona. (Contributed to various cases).

I also appreciate the input of **Michelle Muratori, PhD,** Johns Hopkins University, a colleague who assisted in the revision of this student manual in a number of other ways: She provided me with suggestions for revision, gave feedback on the new cases for this edition, reviewed the classroom exercises and activities, and went over all the quiz items and rewrote those items needing revision.

I would like to thank **Assistant Editor, Mia Dreyer,** for her input and coordination of the supplements and for copyediting this Student Manual. If you have any questions about this or any of the other supplementary materials, or would like to offer your input, please contact her directly at naomi.dreyer@cengage.com.

HOW TO USE THE MANUAL WITH THE TEXTBOOK

Let me suggest some ways of deriving the maximum benefit from the combined use of the textbook and the manual. These suggestions are based on student input and my experiences in teaching counseling courses.

1. Begin with the manual. Skim the entire manual to get some "feel" for the program.

2. Then complete the survey questionnaire in this chapter. (You may find it useful to take it again at the end of the course to assess any changes in your attitudes toward counseling and the helping process.)

3. Before you read and study a textbook chapter on one of the 11 theories, complete the manual's corresponding prechapter self-inventory, which is based on the key concepts of the approach discussed in the textbook. The purpose of the inventory is to assess your degree of agreement or disagreement with the concepts of the theory, *not* to seek the "right answer." My students have said that the inventories give them a clear focus as they read the chapter material.

4. Also before reading each theory chapter, carefully study the manual's overview of the theory treated in the chapter. The overview provides a framework, in capsule form, for the entire textbook chapter. A glossary of key terms and several questions for discussion and evaluation are also included in the manual to assist you in considering important issues before you read the textbook chapter. Students report that the overviews give an organizational framework from which to better grasp the textbook material.

5. After reading and studying a textbook chapter, turn again to the manual.

   a. Review the questions (for critique and personal applications).

   b. Retake (or at least review) the self-inventory.

   c. Look at the overview and focus on key ideas of the theory once again.

   d. Review the key terms defined in the glossary.

   e. Select a few key questions or exercises that are most meaningful to you, and clarify your position on the issues underlying the questions.

   f. Circle the questions or exercises you chose, write down additional questions you would like to pursue, and bring both sets to class for further discussion.

   g. Apply the list of questions in the "Reviewing the Highlights of a Theory" section of this chapter to the theory you are studying.

   h. Take a careful look at the questions and exercises for the case of Stan as a way to apply a given theory to one case throughout the text and this manual.

   i. Formulate your own critique of the approach, and think about aspects that you would most like to incorporate in your own personal style of counseling.

   j. Take the quizzes at the end of each theory chapter and score them, referring to the key in the Appendix.

6. For most of the chapters in this manual, I have intentionally provided an abundance of exercises and questions, more than are likely to be integrated within one course. Look over all the material in a chapter and select the questions and exercises that seem the most relevant, stimulating, and interesting to you. I hope that at the end of the course you will review the material in this manual. At that time you may want to consider questions or activities that you chose not to address in your initial reading.

7. In reading and thinking about Chapter 2, "The Counselor: Person and Professional", do your best to relate to the issues in a personal manner. This chapter will set the tone for the book by raising issues that you can explore as you study each of the theory chapters. Students have found that they get a lot more from this course (and from the textbook and manual) by relating to what they read in a *personal* way. Thus, in studying each theory you have some excellent opportunities to apply what you are learning about the theory to your own life. By bringing yourself into this reading, you make the course much more interesting than if you merely studied abstract theories in an impersonal and strictly academic manner.

8. As you read and study the chapters in both the textbook and this manual, compare the approaches. Look for common denominators among all the theories with respect to key concepts and practices. Look for major points of disagreement. And begin to think of selecting certain aspects of each approach that seem suited to your personality and style of counseling as well as to the type of work you expect to do.

9. Many students have found it valuable to keep a journal, writing about their experiences in the course or elaborating on particular activities, questions, and issues in the manual. Those who take the time to keep a journal typically say that doing so was well worth the effort.

10. Consider organizing and participating in a *study group* as a way of reviewing for tests and as a help in applying the material to yourself personally. If you meet with your small group at various times in the semester, members will have opportunities to learn from one another. A number of students have told me that by teaching or coaching fellow students they really learned the material. This process helped them crystallize key concepts and see differences and similarities among the approaches. A study group is particularly useful in exploring ethical, legal, and professional issues. Of course, this process of meeting for study sessions will be invaluable as a way to review for major tests and the final examination.

11. *Case Approach to Counseling and Psychotherapy,* Eighth Edition (Corey, 2013), is devoted to working with one client, named Ruth. With each therapy approach an expert in the particular theoretical orientation shows how he or she might work with Ruth. Following up on this, I then demonstrate my way of working with Ruth from each theoretical perspective and invite you to continue by applying ideas from each theory to Ruth. This book is designed for use as a combined package with the textbook and this manual.

12. *The Art of Integrative Counseling,* Third Edition (Corey, 2013), is designed to assist you in bringing together elements of the various theories in your own way. This book is an expansion of what you will find in Chapter 15, "An Integrative Perspective." Once you have completed the study of *Theory and Practice of Counseling and Psychotherapy,* if you want a more comprehensive discussion of psychotherapy integration, *The Art of Integrative Counseling* may be of value to you.

13. An educational self-study package entitled *DVD for Integrative Counseling: The Case of Ruth and Lecturettes* is available for student use as a home-study package with any of these textbooks. In this manual I make frequent reference to this student self-study DVD program in the event you are using the program with *Theory and Practice of Counseling and Psychotherapy.* For each of the various theories, you will find my brief version of working with Ruth (the client in the DVD program) from each theoretical perspective. In Chapter 15 I demonstrate my integrative approach to counseling Ruth and provide guidelines and an exercise aimed at helping you conceptualize how you might work with Ruth from an integrative perspective.

14. The "Case of Stan" is the subject of Chapter 16 (in the textbook and this manual) and aims at helping you see the application of a variety of techniques at various stages in the counseling process with the same client. This chapter illustrates an integrative approach that draws from all the therapies and applies a thinking, feeling, and behaving model in counseling Stan. This chapter offers a review of the various theories as applied to a single case example that allows for a comparison among the approaches. There is also a *DVD for Theory*

and Practice of Counseling and Psychotherapy: The Case of Stan and Lecturettes, where I show how I work with Stan from each of the various approaches covered in this book. For each of the 13 sessions in this program, I apply a few selected techniques designed to illustrate each theory in action. There are also brief lecturettes (about 15 minutes) for each chapter of *Theory and Practice of Counseling and Psychotherapy*.

 JERRY COREY BEGINS COUNSELING STAN

Session 1. Intake and Assessment (A simulated demonstration)

An important note. "Stan" is being role-played and does not represent an actual client. Although we both attempted to be as real as possible in these sessions, the specific themes portrayed all pertain to the single client (Stan) in each of the chapters of the textbook.

Before you view the first counseling session with Stan, read Chapter 1, pages 13–16, "Introduction to the Case of Stan" in the textbook. This background information will provide you with a basis for understanding how the different theories can be applied to working with Stan. This section of the text describes an intake interview, presents Stan's autobiography, and lists key themes in his life that will be addressed in the various theory chapters. Write down some of your impressions based on what you read in Chapter 1 before you view Session 1 on the DVD. What is your overall impression of Stan, and how do you think it would be for you to work with him?

After viewing Session 1, address these questions:

1. What are some of the topics that you would most want to address with Stan at the initial intake and assessment session?

2. Stan says, "I wonder what good talking is going to do." What would you say to him?

3. Stan tells you that he expects that you will give him answers to his problems. What would you tell him about your role as his counselor?

4. Stan informs you that he is nervous coming to his first counseling session. How you would explore his anxiety about being in counseling?

5. How would you begin to discuss Stan's spiritual background during his intake assessment?

6. When asked about his goals for counseling (what he wants to work on), Stan's response is: "I just want to feel better about myself. I feel nervous about everything." How could you help him make this goal more concrete and specific?

7. The therapist (Jerry) suggests to Stan that he talk about his anxiety in the session whenever he becomes aware that he is anxious. What do you think about this suggestion?

8. What would you tell Stan about yourself if you were to work with him as his therapist?

9. If you had to assign a tentative diagnosis for Stan, what would this be?

10. Would you want Stan for a client? Why or why not?

A Suggested In-Class Activity

If you are viewing the counseling sessions with Stan in class, after each session form small groups to discuss your reactions to the session. Your discussion could address your reactions to both Stan and to me as his therapist. If you can get experientially involved after viewing a session, this will enhance your learning about the counseling process and about applying theory to practice. Ideally, I suggest that you form groups of three people. One can "become Stan" and can do some further role playing as a continuation of the themes you saw demonstrated. Another person can become Stan's counselor and attempt to stay within the spirit of the theory that is being studied. The third person can function as a process observer. After you have had a few minutes to actually experience these roles, you can then debrief and talk about what it was like for each of you to be in a given role and what was learned from the exercise.

REVIEWING THE HIGHLIGHTS OF A THEORY

Directions: This set of questions has been designed to apply to each of the counseling theories after you have studied it. As a way to help you get the approach into clearer focus, give a few concise summary statements in your own words in answer to each question. Use this outline to write your *critical evaluation* of each of the therapeutic approaches. This outline (and the quizzes for each chapter) would be very helpful for either studying on your own or as a basis for discussion in a study group, should you decide to organize one. You might bring your critiques to class as a basis for active participation in discussion.

1. Key concepts of the theory
   a. What is the theory's *view of human nature,* and what are the *basic assumptions* underlying the approach?
   b. What primary characteristics distinguish the approach? What are its major areas of focus and emphasis?
   c. What are some of the most important concepts?
2. The therapeutic process
   a. What do you think are the most important therapeutic goals?
   b. What are the functions and role of the therapist?
   c. What is the client's role in the therapeutic process? What is expected of the client? What does the client do?
   d. What is the role of the therapeutic relationship in terms of therapy outcomes?
3. Applications: Techniques and procedures of the approach
   a. What are a few of the techniques and methods that you would most want to incorporate into your counseling practice?
   b. Where is the approach most applicable? To what types of clients? To what types of problems? In what settings?
   c. How can you apply some concepts and techniques of the approach to group counseling?
   d. How can this theory fit into the framework of brief therapy?
   e. What do you see as the major strength of this theory from a diversity perspective?
   f. What do you see as the major shortcoming of this theory from a diversity perspective?
   g. What is *your evaluation* of the approach? What do you consider to be the most significant contribution of this approach? What do you consider to be the most significant limitation of this approach?
   h. In what ways can you apply this approach to yourself *personally* as a basis for self-understanding and for making changes you desire?
   i. What are some of the most significant and personally meaningful questions that you would like to pursue further?

SURVEY OF ATTITUDES AND VALUES RELATED TO COUNSELING AND PSYCHOTHERAPY

A Self-Inventory and Pretest

Directions: This is *not* a traditional multiple-choice test in which you must select the correct answer. Instead, it is a survey of *your* basic beliefs, attitudes, and values related to counseling and psychotherapy. Circle the letter beside the response that most closely reflects *your viewpoint* at this time. *You may circle more than one response* for each item.

Notice that a blank line ("e") is included in each item. If none of the provided options seem appropriate or if you have what you consider a better answer, write your response (or responses) on the line. Bring the completed inventory to class during one of the beginning sessions of the course and compare your viewpoints with those of other students. *Take the inventory again at the end of the course* to see whether any of your beliefs, attitudes, and values have changed.

1. I think the *main* purpose of counseling and psychotherapy is to
   a. assist clients in creating solutions to their problems.
   b. tell others how best to organize their life.
   c. increase a client's awareness.
   d. always provide an answer to the client's problem.
   e. _____

2. Clients who seek counseling
   a. can be trusted to find creative solutions to their problems.
   b. are generally in need of advice on how to proceed.
   c. will progress only if I am highly active and structured.
   d. will generally be resistant to change unless doing so is easy.
   e. _____

3. Regarding the issue of human freedom, I believe that we
   a. create our own destiny by making choices.
   b. possess *limited* degrees of freedom.
   c. are almost totally the products of conditioning.
   d. are what our genetic makeup and environment make us.
   e. _____

4. I believe that setting the goals of counseling
   a. is primarily the client's responsibility.
   b. is primarily the therapist's responsibility.
   c. is a collaborative venture of client and therapist.
   d. can interfere with the spontaneity of counseling.
   e. _____

5. The goal of psychotherapy is
   a. assisting clients in creating a new life story.
   b. making the unconscious conscious.
   c. providing symptom relief in as brief a time as possible.
   d. learning realistic and responsible behavior.
   e. _____

6. Counseling should mainly focus on
   a. what people are thinking.
   b. what people are feeling.
   c. what people are doing.
   d. each of these, depending on the stage of therapy.
   e. _____

7. Counseling is a process of
   a. reeducation.
   b. helping clients make life decisions.
   c. learning to integrate one's feeling and thinking.
   d. learning more effective coping behaviors.
   e. _____

8. Counseling and therapy should focus on
   a. the client's past experiences.
   b. the client's experience in the here and now.
   c. the client's strivings toward the future.
   d. both the present and the future.
   e. _____

9. To be an effective counselor in working with diverse client populations, it is important to be knowledgeable about
   a. how gender roles are influenced by society.
   b. how oppression and discrimination affect people of color.
   c. how one's culture influences one's choices.
   d. areas such as sexual orientation, disability, and spirituality.
   e. _____

10. When practicing counseling in a multicultural society, it is essential to
    a. have specialized coursework on various cultures.

b. get fieldwork experience in multicultural settings.

c. understand a counselor's own culture.

d. develop skills in working with culturally different clients.

e. _____

11. Specific knowledge about cultural differences is

a. essential for effective counseling.

b. dangerous because of the tendency to stereotype.

c. impossible to acquire because of the number of cultures.

d. useful in providing a conceptual framework.

e. _____

12. A person's early childhood experiences are

a. not really important material for therapy.

b. the determinants of the person's present adjustments.

c. experiences that must be explored in therapy.

d. of interest but not of much significance for who one is today.

e. _____

13. The most important function of a therapist is

a. being present for and with the client.

b. interpreting the meaning of the client's symptoms.

c. creating trust that allows the client to freely explore feelings and thoughts.

d. giving the client specific suggestions for things to do outside the therapy sessions.

e. _____

14. I believe that counselors should be

a. active and directive.

b. relatively nondirective, allowing the client to direct.

c. whatever the client wants them to be.

d. directive or nondirective, depending on the client's capacity for self-direction.

e. _____

15. The power of a therapist

a. should be used to manipulate the client in the direction the therapist deems best for the client.

b. should be minimized because of its danger.

c. can be a vital force that the therapist can use in modeling for a client.

d. needs to be shared with the client toward the aim of client empowerment.

e. _____

16. To help a client, a therapist

a. needs to have had a problem similar to the client's problem.

b. must be free of any conflicts in the area he or she is exploring with the client.

c. must share many of the same life experiences and worldview with the client.

d. must like the client personally.

e. _____

17. For individuals wishing to become therapists, experiencing personal therapy

a. is an absolute necessity.

b. is not an important factor in a therapist's capacity to work with others.

c. is necessary only when a therapist has severe personal problems.

d. should be encouraged strongly, but not required.

e. _____

18. Regarding the client–therapist relationship, I think

a. the client is the expert on his or her own life.

b. the therapist should remain relatively anonymous.

c. it is of critical importance, regardless of one's theoretical orientation.

d. this is the most important factor related to therapeutic outcomes.

e. _____

19. A counselor should

a. select one theory and work strictly within that framework for the sake of consistency.

b. not be too concerned about theory, and instead trust his or her intuitions in working with the client.

c. strive to combine a couple of theoretical approaches.

d. borrow techniques from many different theories.

e. _____

20. Of the following, the most important feature of effective therapy is
   a. knowledge of the theory of counseling and behavior.
   b. skill in using techniques appropriately.
   c. genuineness and openness on the therapist's part.
   d. the therapist's ability to specify a treatment plan and evaluate the results.
   e. _____

Directions: For items 21 through 50, circle the answer (T = true, F = false, or both) that best fits your belief. Then, on the line provided, give a reason for your answer. Because these items are designed to sample your views, there are no "right" or "wrong" answers; hence, there is no answer key.

Example: T   F   Giving advice is an important function of therapists.

   This is the easy way out, but it is not therapy.

T   F   21. Therapists should work only with clients whom they really like and care for.
_____

T   F   22. As long as I counsel others, it is essential that I be open to the idea of receiving therapy myself.
_____

T   F   23. I expect to apply my theory to practice in much the same way with all my clients.
_____

T   F   24. It is critical that my values be kept out of the therapy process.
_____

T   F   25. To work with a client effectively, the therapist must first be aware of the person's cultural background.
_____

T   F   26. I should model certain behaviors that I expect my clients to learn.
_____

T   F   27. My own levels of self-awareness and psychological health are probably the most important variables that determine the success or failure of counseling.
_____

T   F   28. It is therapeutically useful for me to be completely open, honest, and transparent with my clients.
_____

T   F   29. It is appropriate for me to discuss my personal conflicts at length with my clients, for they can apply my solutions to problems they are facing.
_____

T   F   30. The kind of person I am is more important than my theoretical orientation and my use of techniques.
_____

T   F   31. Knowledge of my own cultural background is as important as knowing about the cultural background of my client.
_____

T F   32. Intellectual insight is enough to make change happen for clients.

_____

T F   33. Therapy must be aimed at social and political change if any real personal change is to occur.

_____

T F   34. My job as a therapist is basically that of a teacher, for I am reeducating clients and teaching them coping skills.

_____

T F   35. I view my client as being an expert in his or her own life.

_____

T F   36. Because confrontation might cause great pain or discomfort in a client, I think it is generally unwise to use this technique.

_____

T F   37. My own needs are really not important in the therapeutic relationship with a client.

_____

T F   38. Silences during a therapy session should be avoided.

_____

T F   39. It is essential that I form a collaborative relationship with my client.

_____

T F   40. The therapeutic relationship should be characterized by the same degree of sharing by both client and therapist.

_____

T F   41. I must be careful to avoid mistakes, for my clients will lose respect for me if they observe me faltering.

_____

T F   42. For effective counseling, technical skills are more important than the therapeutic relationship.

_____

T F   43. Therapy can have either a positive or a negative effect on a client.

_____

T F   44. There is no personal change or growth unless a person is open to anxiety and pain.

_____

T F   45. As a counselor, I want to be flexible and modify the techniques I use, especially in counseling culturally diverse clients.

_____

T F   46. As a counselor, I strive to be objective and not to become personally involved with my clients.

_____

T   F   47. As a therapist, I should not judge my client's behavior, for therapy and value judgments are incompatible.

_____

T   F   48. If I experience intense feelings toward my client (anger or sexual attraction, for example), I have lost my potential effectiveness to counsel that person, and I should end the relationship.

_____

T   F   49. It is inappropriate to touch clients in any way, under any circumstances.

_____

T   F   50. I would accept a client who was mandated to attend counseling.

_____

Chapter 2

The Counselor: Person and Professional

A SURVEY OF YOUR ATTITUDES AND BELIEFS ABOUT THE COUNSELOR AS PERSON AND PROFESSIONAL

Directions: This self-inventory is designed to clarify your thinking on issues raised in the textbook concerning the counselor as a person and a professional. You may want to select more than one answer; notice also that line "e" is for any qualifying responses you want to make or any other answer you would like to provide.

1. Which of the following is most important as a determinant of the outcome of therapy?
   a. skills and techniques the counselor possesses
   b. particular theoretical orientation of the counselor
   c. kind of person the counselor is
   d. quality of a collaborative client–therapist relationship
   e. _____

2. What is the most important component of therapist authenticity?
   a. respectful curiosity
   b. caring and compassion for the client
   c. willingness to confront the client when necessary
   d. modeling those qualities the therapist expects of the client
   e. _____

3. Which of the following is the most important attribute, or personal characteristic, of effective therapists?
   a. having an appreciation of their own culture
   b. being open to change
   c. being present and making connections

   d. having resolved any pressing personal problems
   e. _____

4. What is your position with respect to you receiving personal therapy before you begin working with clients?
   a. I don't feel the need because I have few pressing problems.
   b. I am very eager to get involved in my own therapy as a client.
   c. I am ethically obligated to experience my own therapy before I expect to counsel others.
   d. I would do it only if I were required to do so.
   e. _____

5. If you were to become a client, on what issue(s) might you most focus in your therapy sessions?
   a. reauthoring the story of my life
   b. unfinished situations from my past, especially relationships with my parents
   c. fears of overidentifying with my clients' problems
   d. anxieties over my ability to work effectively with various types of clients
   e. _____

6. Over which of the following issues do you have the greatest degree of *anxiety* when you think about beginning as a counselor?

    a. not having the knowledge or skills to be effective

    b. making a mistake (or mistakes) that will damage the client

    c. having clients demand too much from me and being unable to meet those demands

    d. finding that I was never really cut out to be a therapist in the first place

    e. _____

7. How would you determine what constitutes *appropriate* and *useful* self-disclosure as a counselor?

    a. by doing whatever feels comfortable to me at the time

    b. by observing the reactions of my client to my disclosures

    c. by observing the degree to which the client engages in deeper self-exploration

    d. by monitoring my motivations for engaging in self-disclosure

    e. _____

8. How does the issue of *perfectionism* apply to you as a counselor?

    a. I am sure that I will demand perfection of myself; I cannot tolerate making any mistakes in my sessions.

    b. I will view my mistakes as an opportunity and learn from them.

    c. If I failed with a client, I think I would be devastated.

    d. Although I will strive to be the best I can, I will not burden myself with the demand that I never make mistakes.

    e. _____

9. When do you think it is important to *disclose yourself* to your clients?

    a. when they ask for it or when I sense that this is what they need

    b. whenever I have persistent reactions, thoughts, perceptions, or feelings

    c. when I want to influence clients to choose a certain course of action

    d. when little seems to be happening in the sessions

    e. _____

10. What is your policy on engaging in *self-disclosure* with your clients?

    a. I believe in sharing my thoughts, feelings, and reactions when I sense they are getting in the way of my ability to be fully present.

    b. I believe I need to carefully weigh what I disclose for fear of damaging our relationship.

    c. I believe that sharing some of my life experiences with clients can strengthen our working relationship.

    d. If I expect clients to self-disclose, I should be willing to model this appropriately.

    e. _____

11. How do you think you would tend to deal with *silences* during a counseling session?

    a. I would be threatened and tend to think I had done something wrong.

    b. I would ask the client questions to get him or her going again.

    c. I would discuss with the client my own reactions to the silence.

    d. I would sit it out and wait for the client to take the initiative.

    e. _____

12. What is your view on the role of *giving advice* in counseling?

    a. Because I see the counseling process as guiding clients, I would freely give advice if I thought this was what the client wanted.

    b. I would rarely, if ever, give advice, for even if the advice was good, it may make the client dependent on me.

    c. Because I view the client as an expert on him- or herself, I would refrain from dispensing advice.

    d. I think I would give advice to a client when I had a strong preference for a direction I hoped he or she would choose.

    e. _____

13. What are your views concerning the use of *humor* in therapy?

    a. Whenever it is appropriate, I would use humor in a session because laughter is potentially very therapeutic.

    b. I would use humor only after I had established a solid relationship with a client.

c. I would avoid humor, as I think it can easily distract a client from dealing with the serious matters of therapy.

d. I would use humor when my client got into "heavy feelings" to lighten things up a bit so that neither of us would get depressed.

e. _____

14. How will you go about developing your own counseling style?

a. I will work within the framework of one theory initially.

b. I will model myself after a supervisor.

c. I will combine techniques from several therapeutic approaches.

d. I will keep a journal of what I do and experience as I work with clients.

e. _____

15. How do you think you can best stay vital *as a person* and *as a professional*?

a. by learning to leave my worries about work at the office

b. by taking the time to play and engage in hobbies

c. by making sure that my personal needs are being met in my life away from work

d. by quitting a job as soon as I find that I am losing interest or when I am feeling ineffective

e. _____

16. As a counselor, I expect that my values will affect the counseling process

a. when I have values that are strongly divergent from my client's.

b. only in cases in which I attempt to sway the client to my way of thinking.

c. at all times, because I cannot separate my values from my work as a counselor.

d. when I have strong negative reactions to certain behaviors or values of my client.

e. _____

17. My position on the role of values in therapy is that

a. therapists should never impose their values on a client.

b. therapists should teach the client proper values.

c. therapists should openly share their values when appropriate.

d. therapist values should be kept out of the relationship.

e. _____

18. Of the following motivations, the one that best expresses my reason for wanting to be in a helping profession is

a. my desire to nurture others.

b. my desire to give advice to those who have problems.

c. my desire to get confirmation of my value as a person.

d. my need to be needed and to feel that I am helping others.

e. _____

19. I won't feel ready to counsel others until

a. my own life is free of problems.

b. I've experienced counseling as a client.

c. I feel very confident and know that I'll be effective.

d. I've become a self-aware person and developed the ability to continually reexamine my own life and relationships.

e. _____

20. If a client evidenced strong feelings of attraction or dislike for me, I would

a. help the client work through these feelings and understand them.

b. enjoy these feelings if they were positive.

c. refer my client to another counselor.

d. direct the sessions into less emotional areas.

e. _____

Suggestions on How to Use This Inventory

1. Now that you have finished this inventory, go back over it and circle a few of the items that had the greatest meaning to you. Bring these issues to class and compare your reactions with those of fellow students. You might also discuss why these issues held special meaning for you.

2. Discuss with others in class (or in a small group in the class) what it was like for you to go through this inventory. What did it stir up in you? What did you learn about yourself?

3. Go back to the initial "Survey of Attitudes and Values Related to Counseling and Psychotherapy: A Self-Inventory and Pretest" in Chapter 1 of this manual. Look over your responses to determine the degree of consistency between these two surveys. I strongly recommend that you also circle several of the items that you would *most* like to bring up for class discussion. It is a good idea to review your initial responses at the end of the semester in small groups. This process can help you examine any shifts in your thinking.

 ## GLOSSARY OF KEY TERMS

Countertransference   The process of therapists seeing in their clients patterns of their own behavior, overidentifying with clients, or meeting their own needs through their clients.

Culture   The values and behaviors shared by a group of individuals.

Diversity-competent practitioner   An ongoing process that involves a practitioner developing awareness of beliefs and attitudes, acquiring knowledge about race and culture, and learning skills and intervention strategies necessary to work effectively with culturally diverse populations.

Professional burnout   A condition that occurs when helpers feel drained and depleted as a result of their work. Certain factors, such as constantly giving without expecting much in return, can sap helpers' vitality and motivation. Self-care can help to prevent this condition.

Self-monitoring   The ability to pay attention to what one is thinking, feeling, and doing. This is a crucial first step in self-care.

Value imposition   Refers to counselors' behavior in directly attempting to define a client's values, attitudes, beliefs, and behaviors.

 ## COUNSELOR VALUES AND THE THERAPEUTIC PROCESS

Read the section in Chapter 2 entitled "The Counselor as a Therapeutic Person" and reflect on your role as a change agent. When you think about what you most want to accomplish in counseling people, what do you hope for? I take the position that who you are as a person is the critical variable in determining the outcomes of your professional work with clients. Of course, you need to master theories of counseling, you need to have a wide range of knowledge, and you must acquire and hone many counseling skills. But being an effective counselor is far more than mastering a body of knowledge and possessing skills.

The Role of Values in Counseling

Read the section in Chapter 2 entitled "The Counselor's Values and the Therapeutic Process" and reflect on how certain of your values might be an asset or a liability in your work with clients. Which values are likely to help you connect with a client? Which of your values might make it difficult for you to objectively assist clients in finding their own way? These questions are designed to help you search yourself for answers about the role of values in counseling. After you have responded to these questions, talk with other students about your thoughts on these value issues.

- How important is it to keep your values to yourself to avoid biasing your client?

_____

_____

- What is one way that you can help clients clarify their own values?

_____

_____

■ To what degree is it possible for you to disagree with a client's values and still accept him or her as a person?

_____

_____

■ How would you deal with a situation in which you had a value conflict with a client?

_____

_____

■ What difference do you see between exposing your values or imposing your values on clients?

_____

_____

■ To what extent do you view counseling as a process of exploring values?

_____

_____

■ To what degree is it possible to separate a discussion of values from the therapeutic process?

_____

_____

■ What course of action might you take if a client asked you specific questions about your personal values?

_____

_____

Dealing With Value Conflicts

At times you and a client may experience value clashes that make it difficult for you to work together. To help you identify such circumstances, complete the following inventory, and determine when you might refer a client to someone else because of a conflict of value systems. Use this code:

1 = I would definitely work well with this type of person.

2 = I would probably find working with this type of person difficult or challenging.

3 = I am quite certain that I would not work well with this type of person.

_____ 1. an adolescent girl who wants to explore her feelings about whether to have an abortion

_____ 2. a gay or lesbian couple who want to explore their relationship problems

_____ 3. a lesbian couple who want to discuss their desire to adopt a child

_____ 4. a person who is deeply troubled over an extramarital affair but is not ready to give up this relationship

_____ 5. a person who has a great deal of hostility toward any form of religion and who wants to explore her negative feelings in this area

_____ 6. a person who has extremely strong fundamentalist religious beliefs

_____ 7. a man whose basic value system includes the attempt to use and exploit others for his own gain

_____ 8. a teenager who is having unsafe sex and sees no problem with this behavior

_____ 9. a high school student who thinks she may be lesbian and wants to explore her sexual orientation

_____ 10. an interracial couple wanting to adopt a child and being faced with their respective parents' opposition to the adoption

Some Questions You Might Explore

1. What specific kinds of clients might you have difficulty working with because of a clash of values?

2. How would you handle the situation if you discovered that you were not being effective with a client because of a difference in values?

3. What are some of your central values and beliefs, and how do you think they will either inhibit *or* facilitate your work as a counselor?

BECOMING AN EFFECTIVE MULTICULTURAL COUNSELOR

Working ethically with culturally diverse client populations requires that you possess the awareness, knowledge, and skills to deal effectively with their concerns. Although it is unrealistic to expect you to have an in-depth knowledge of all cultural backgrounds, it is feasible for you to have a comprehensive grasp of the general principles for working ethically and sensitively with clients who are different from you. Try to understand the worldview of the culturally different client, and develop appropriate intervention strategies and techniques to become an effective multicultural counselor.

Take an inventory of your current level of awareness, knowledge, and skills by completing the following self-examination of multicultural counseling competencies.

Multicultural Counseling Competencies: A Self-Examination

This self-examination on how well you are able to demonstrate multicultural counseling competencies is based on standards proposed by Sue, Arrendondo, and McDavis (1992). It is for your own use in evaluating how well you are doing in becoming competent as a counselor of clients whose cultural background differs from yours. This self-assessment is not intended as a research instrument and is certainly not intended to compete with other excellent research protocols.

Give yourself a grade for each question based on the following criteria.

A = always B = often C = sometimes D = seldom F = never

If you wish to use numbers to calculate an average to arrive at a grade, use the following scores: A = 4, B = 3, C = 2, D = 1, F = 0.

I. Counselor Awareness, Knowledge, and Skills

_____ 1. I actively work on becoming more aware of my own cultural heritage.

_____ 2. I constantly seek to become more aware of different cultural heritages.

_____ 3. I strive to understand and value cultural heritages that differ from my own.

_____ 4. I work at understanding how my own cultural background influences my beliefs, values, attitudes, and biases about psychological processes.

_____ 5. I regularly evaluate the limits of my competencies and expertise in counseling persons from different cultural backgrounds.

_____ 6. I question my comfort with differences that exist between me and my clients in regard to race, ethnicity, culture, and beliefs.

_____ 7. I strive to understand how my own racial and cultural heritage affects my personal and professional definitions and biases about what is normal and abnormal.

_____ 8. I seek to understand how oppression, racism, discrimination, and stereotyping affect me personally.

_____ 9. I regularly question how I may have benefited or been adversely affected directly or indirectly by individual, institutional, or cultural racism.

_____ 10. I diligently work at uncovering my own beliefs, attitudes, and feelings regarding racism.

_____ 11. I seek to gain greater knowledge about how I affect others.

_____ 12. I strive to become ever more knowledgeable about my communication style and how it may facilitate or hinder working with clients who are culturally different from me.

_____ 13. I regularly seek out educational, consultative, and training experiences that enrich my understanding of culturally different populations.

_____ 14. I constantly engage in the process of understanding myself as a racial and cultural being.

_____ 15. I actively strive to achieve a nonracist identity.

II. Understanding the Worldview of the Culturally Different Client

_____ 16. I work at becoming aware of my negative emotional reactions toward racial and ethnic groups that may prove detrimental to my clients.

_____ 17. I willingly and regularly contrast my own beliefs and attitudes with those of culturally different clients with whom I work in a way that is nonjudgmental.

_____ 18. I question myself constantly about any stereotypes and preconceived notions I hold toward other racial and ethnic minority groups.

_____ 19. I study to obtain specific knowledge and information about particular culturally different groups before trying to work with them individually or collectively.

_____ 20. I work to more thoroughly incorporate competencies that will help me in understanding the literature on minority identity developmental models.

_____ 21. I update myself regularly (at least every 3 months) in understanding how race, culture, and ethnicity may affect personality formation, vocational choices, manifestations of psychological disorders, help-

seeking behavior, and the appropriateness of counseling approaches.

_____ 22. I actively engage in processes (such as reading, supervision, and discussions) that help me gain a greater awareness of how sociopolitical influences impinge upon the life of racial and ethnic minorities.

_____ 23. I interact with people of different cultures in striving to understand how immigration issues, poverty, racism, stereotyping, and powerlessness all leave major scars that may influence the counseling process.

_____ 24. I familiarize myself as often as possible (but at least quarterly) with relevant and up-to-date research regarding the mental health and disorders of various ethnic and racial groups.

_____ 25. I actively seek out educational experiences that enrich my knowledge, understanding, and cross-cultural skills.

_____ 26. I am actively involved with individuals, outside of counseling settings, whose cultural heritage differs from mine in order to more fully appreciate and understand their lives and lifestyles.

III. Developing Appropriate Intervention Strategies and Techniques

_____ 27. I seek to recognize as well as respect my clients' religious and spiritual beliefs and values about physical and mental functioning.

_____ 28. I strive to understand and respect indigenous helping practices and minority community intrinsic help-giving networks.

_____ 29. I value and appreciate bilingualism.

_____ 30. I do not view another language as an impediment to counseling.

_____ 31. I seek to know and understand how generic characteristics of counseling (e.g., culture- or class-bound) may clash with cultural values of various minority groups.

_____ 32. I strive to recognize societal barriers that prevent minorities from using mental health services.

_____ 33. I examine potential bias in assessment instruments on a regular basis.

_____ 34. I use assessment procedures and interpret assessment findings in regard to the cultural and linguistic characteristics of my clients.

_____ 35. I regularly study about minority family structures, hierarchies, values, and beliefs.

_____ 36. I seek out knowledge about the community characteristics and resources where I live.

_____ 37. I make it my business to become aware of relevant discriminatory practices at the social and community level that may be affecting the psychological welfare of my clients and minority culture populations.

_____ 38. I work constantly at becoming skilled and able to engage in a variety of verbal and nonverbal helping responses, including the accurate and appropriate sending and receiving of verbal and nonverbal messages.

_____ 39. I resist becoming tied down to any one method or approach to helping.

_____ 40. When I sense that my helping style is limited and potentially inappropriate, I work at anticipating and addressing its negative impact.

_____ 41. I question myself periodically as to when I should exercise institutional intervention skills on behalf of clients.

_____ 42. I help clients determine whether a problem stems from racism or bias in others so that they do not inappropriately blame themselves.

_____ 43. I seek consultation from traditional leaders or religious and spiritual leaders and practitioners when it is appropriate in the treatment of culturally different clients.

_____ 44. I take responsibility for interacting in the language requested by my clients even if it means making a referral to outside resources, such as a bilingual counselor, or finding a translator with cultural knowledge and an appropriate professional background.

_____ 45. I regularly engage in training and becoming more of an expert in the use of traditional assessment and testing instruments and in understanding their technical aspects as well as their cultural limitations.

_____ 46. I work toward eliminating biases, prejudices, and discriminatory practices.

_____ 47. I strive to become increasingly aware of the sociopolitical contexts in conducting evaluations and providing interventions.

_____ 48. I sensitize myself through various means to issues of oppression, sexism, and racism.

_____ 49. I take responsibility in educating my clients about the processes of psychological intervention, such as goals, expectations, legal rights, and my counseling orientation.

Scores on this self-administered instrument range from "A" to "F." There are three areas in which to assess yourself:

1. Counselor Awareness, Knowledge, and Skills, Items 1–15

   My Grade _____

2. Understanding the Worldview of the Culturally Different Client, Items 16–26

   My Grade _____

3. Developing Appropriate Intervention Strategies and Techniques, Items 2–49

   My Grade _____

   My Total Grade _____

Since all three areas are related, a low grade in any one will affect the other two. Therefore, in evaluating your score, look at both your area grades and your total grade. Ways to constructively improve your grades include the following:

- Examining your own cultural heritage and background
- Attending workshops and classes on multicultural counseling

- Obtaining supervision from a skilled multicultural counselor
- Reading books and journal articles
- Joining a group that studies multicultural issues
- Viewing videos on multicultural counseling
- Participating in interactive computer software focused on multicultural counseling
- Becoming a member of a professional group that deals with multicultural counseling issues, such as the Association for Multicultural Counseling and Development
- Participating in minority culture events in your community, and working in the sociopolitical arena to bring about needed changes

Source: Adapted from S. T. Gladding, P. Pedersen, and D. Stone, "Multicultural Counseling Competencies: A Self-Examination," *ACES Spectrum Newsletter,* Winter, 1997, Vol. 58, No. 2. Reprinted with permission of authors.

SUGGESTED ACTIVITY

Cultural Diversity in Counseling Practice

Directions: Fill in the blanks with the answers you think are appropriate for you. Remember that in this kind of activity there are no "correct" answers and that the point of the exercise is to stimulate you to think about what it will take for you to become a culturally effective counselor.

1. How effective do you think you would be in counseling clients who are culturally different from you?

_____

_____

2. What is one specific way in which your cultural background could help you understand clients from different cultures?

_____

_____

3. What is an example of a belief, attitude, or assumption of yours that could block your effectiveness in working with diverse client populations?

_____

_____

4. What is an example of a belief, attitude, or assumption of yours that will enhance your effectiveness in working with diverse client populations?

_____

_____

5. What can you do to increase your *awareness and knowledge* in the area of cultural diversity?

_____

_____

6. What *specific knowledge* do you think you need to effectively counsel someone who is different from you in ethnic background, age, gender, sexual orientation, or socioeconomic status?

_____

_____

7. What is one *skill* that you would most like to acquire to make you more effective in counseling those from different cultures?

_____

_____

8. How could you encourage and allow a client who is culturally different from you to teach you about his or her culture?

_____

_____

9. When and why might you decide to refer a client who differs from you with respect to culture, ethnicity, socioeconomic background, religion or value system, age, sexual orientation, or gender?

_____

_____

10. What do you see as your major challenge in becoming a culturally skilled counselor?

_____

_____

A Suggested In-Class Activity

For an interactive exercise in class, after you have recorded your responses, join with one other classmate and interview each other using these same questions. Discuss the similarities and differences between your responses.

SUGGESTED ACTIVITY

Personal Issues in Counseling and Psychotherapy

Directions: Fill in the blanks with the answers you think are appropriate for you. Of course, there are no "correct" answers. Try to give your immediate response to each question. Bring your answers to class for discussion.

1. List two major personal qualities, or strengths, that you think will be assets for you as a counselor.

_____

_____

2. List two personal limitations, or areas that you need to examine, that might interfere with your effectiveness as a counselor.

_____

_____

3. What are a few of your specific concerns or anxieties regarding your work as a beginning counselor?

_____

_____

4. How would you respond if you were required to participate in personal psychotherapy as a basic part of your degree program?

_____

_____

5. Can you think of specific instances in which you would give your clients advice?

_____

_____

6. What would you do if one of your values sharply contrasted with your client's values?

_____

_____

7. How do you think you react if you suggested a technique and your client refused to participate?

_____

_____

8. If you were being interviewed for a counselor's position, how would you answer the question "How do you view your role as a counselor?"

_____

_____

9. Knowing yourself, what factors in your life and your personality might contribute most to your own burnout or loss of spirit?

_____

_____

10. What important steps would you be willing to take to prevent burnout?

_____

_____

Suggested In-Class Activity

Here is a suggestion for an interactive exercise in class after you have recorded your responses. Join with one other classmate and interview each other with these questions. Discuss the similarities and differences between your responses.

 # A SMALL GROUP EXERCISE

Personal Strategies for Self-Care and Managing Stress

Although you cannot always control stressful events, you do have a great deal of control over how you interpret and react to these events. In small groups, explore ways that you can best learn to manage stress in your life. What concrete steps can you take to prevent the negative impact of stress? Become attuned to the subtle signs of burnout rather than waiting for a full-blown condition of emotional and physical exhaustion to set in. Develop your own strategy for staying vital both personally and professionally. In your discussion group, identify a few specific self-care strategies that you would be willing to put into practice. Here are a few suggestions for self-care and managing stress that you might explore in your group:

■ Evaluate your goals, priorities, and expectations to see if they are realistic and if they are getting you what you want.

■ Learn to monitor the impact of stress, both on the job and at home.

■ Attend to your health through adequate sleep, an exercise program, proper diet, meditation, and relaxation.

■ Develop a few friendships that are characterized by a mutuality of giving and receiving.

■ Learn how to be internally motivated and to work for self-rewards as opposed to looking to others to confirm your worth.

■ Find meaning through play, travel, or new experiences.

■ Learn your own limits, and learn to set limits with others.

■ Learn to accept yourself with your imperfections, including being able to forgive yourself when you make a mistake or do not live up to your ideals.

■ Seek counseling as an avenue of personal development.

This is not an exhaustive list, but it does provide a few ideas for thinking about ways you can take better care of yourself. Which of the above self-care strategies most appeals to you? Are there any not on this list that you would add?

_____

_____

_____

_____

QUIZ ON THE COUNSELOR: PERSON AND PROFESSIONAL

A Comprehension Check

Score _____%

Note: Please refer to Appendix 1 for the scoring key.

True/false items: Decide if the following statements are "more true" or "more false" as they apply to The Counselor: Person and Professional.

T   F   1. If counselors hide behind the safety of their professional role, their clients will likely keep themselves hidden in therapy.

T   F   2. Empirical research strongly and consistently supports the centrality of the therapeutic relationship as a primary factor contributing to psychotherapy outcomes.

T   F   3. Clients place more value on the specific techniques used rather than on the personality of the therapist.

T   F   4. Meta-analyses of studies on therapeutic effectiveness have shown that techniques have relatively little effect on therapeutic outcome.

T   F   5. As a therapist, it is your function to persuade clients to accept or adopt your value system since it has been perfected through years of training.

T   F   6. It is impossible for human beings to maintain a sense of objectivity; thus, therapists who attempt to maintain objectivity are fooling themselves.

T   F   7. If clients express a desire for you to give them answers, you should do so.

T   F   8. It is a professional obligation, not an ethical obligation, for counselors to develop a sensitivity to their clients' cultural differences.

T   F   9. Most beginning counselors have ambivalent feelings when meeting their first clients.

T   F   10. Judging the appropriate amount of self-disclosure is only a problem for new counselors.

Multiple-choice items: Select the *one best answer* of those alternatives given.

_____ 11. Counselors who leave their reactions and selves out of their clinical work

  a. are likely to be ineffective counselors and merely technical experts.

  b. are most likely psychodynamic practitioners who are creating the analytic framework.

  c. are definitely practicing in an unethical manner and might be violating laws depending on the state in which they are practicing.

  d. have mastered setting good boundaries in therapy.

_____ 12. Which of the following statements about effective counselors is NOT true?

  a. Effective counselors have the courage to leave the security of the known if they are not satisfied with the way they are.

  b. Effective counselors feel adequate with others and allow others to feel powerful with them.

  c. Effective counselors are certain that their knowledge about human nature is correct and feel obligated to steer their clients away from making poor decisions.

  d. Effective counselors are committed to living fully rather than settling for mere existence.

_____ 13. _____ refer to aspects such as the alliance, the relationship, the personal and interpersonal skills of the therapist, client agency, and extra-therapeutic factors.

  a. Technical factors

  b. Contextual factors

  c. Subjective factors

  d. Phenomenological factors

_____ 14. There is considerable evidence indicating that the _____ of the psychotherapist is inextricably intertwined with the outcome of psychotherapy.

    a. décor of the office

    b. socioeconomic status

    c. person

    d. genetic makeup

    e. general attractiveness

_____ 15. Linda, a licensed therapist with strong negative opinions about homosexuality and gay marriage, believes that her clients Joe and Robert should dissolve their relationship and give heterosexuality a chance. Linda is

    a. being true to her own values; thus, her advice to Joe and Robert is ethical.

    b. behaving in an illegal manner.

    c. not maintaining an objective stance and seems to be encapsulated by her worldview.

    d. qualified to assess whether or not Joe and Robert should remain a couple because she is licensed.

_____ 16. Yi-Lung, a recent immigrant from Taiwan, has been encouraged by his American girlfriend to join her in couples counseling. During the first session, Yi-Lung seems reluctant to self-disclose and admits that he does not believe counseling is the best way for them to address their problems. The counselor should

    a. try to understand how Yi-Lung perceives the value of formal helping.

    b. realize that Yi-Lung may have different expectations about the helping process based on his cultural background.

    c. take Yi-Lung's degree of acculturation into account when working with him and his girlfriend.

    d. all of these.

_____ 17. Which of the following statements about therapeutic goals is true?

    a. Setting goals is inextricably related to values.

    b. Clients initially tend to have a clear sense of what they expect from therapy.

    c. The exploration of what a client wants from therapy should rarely be discussed during the first few sessions because it can feel overwhelming to him or her.

    d. A client who lacks therapeutic goals does not belong in therapy.

_____ 18. A counselor trainee makes the following comment in class: "I would never work with a counselor who has been a client in counseling! If they can't handle their own problems, how could they possibly be effective in helping others?" What would be an appropriate response on the part of the instructor?

    a. "Our own work as a client can teach us valuable lessons about how to creatively facilitate deeper levels of self-exploration in clients. And it tends to increase our appreciation for the courage our clients display in their therapeutic journeys.

    b. "You're right! Counselors who need counseling are probably unstable and should not interact with clients."

    c. "I can't believe we admitted you into this training program. You should be ashamed of yourself for saying that."

    d. "Well, I have been in counseling. Are you suggesting that I am ineffective?"

_____ 19. Yolanda, a therapist specializing in working with adolescents, told a young pregnant client to strongly consider giving her child up for adoption. In Yolanda's words: "Certainly you don't want to eliminate the possibility of going to college and ruin your future by having a child at such a young age, right?" Yolanda is

    a. doing the client a favor by being direct and offering her guidance.

    b. exerting influence and imposing her values on the client.

c. merely exposing her own values, and thus, is behaving ethically.

d. surely projecting her own life story onto the client.

_____ 20. Understanding the sociopolitical system of which clients are a part is

a. something that only social workers do.

b. a requirement only for those who want to specialize in social justice issues.

c. necessary in order to become multiculturally competent.

d. not important for therapists working in private practice.

_____ 21. Counselors _____ must examine their expectations, attitudes, biases, and assumptions about the counseling process and also about persons from diverse groups.

a. from all cultural groups

b. from oppressed cultural groups

c. residing in affluent areas

d. who received their training from non-accredited programs

_____ 22. Which of the following is NOT a guideline for increasing your effectiveness with clients from diverse backgrounds?

a. Learn more about how your own cultural background has influenced your thinking and behaving.

b. Learn to pay attention to the common ground that exists among people of diverse backgrounds.

c. Use a one-size-fits-all approach in your clinical work.

d. Examine where you obtained your knowledge about culture.

_____ 23. In determining the appropriateness of self-disclosure, consider

a. what to reveal.

b. when to reveal.

c. how much to reveal.

d. all of these.

_____ 24. Tom plans to work with clients who are mandated by the courts to receive counseling. Considering they will be involuntary clients, Tom should

a. not expect change to occur.

b. not be too concerned about the informed consent process, since confidentiality will not be an issue.

c. make sure that he prepares them well for the process.

d. plan to counter their resistance with promises of dramatic change in order to instill hope in them.

_____ 25. Students willing to risk making mistakes in supervised learning situations and willing to reveal their self-doubts

a. will find a direction that leads to growth.

b. will be perceived poorly by their clinical supervisor.

c. are probably too impulsive and should develop better boundaries.

d. will be stifled in the long run; thus, they should modify their approach to learning.

Ethical Issues in Counseling Practice

 ## ETHICAL ISSUES AND PROBLEMS FOR EXAMINATION

These groups of questions correspond to the sections in Chapter 3 of the textbook. Make a brief outline of your position on each of these ethical issues.

1. *Introduction*

   a. What one ethical issue would you most want to explore and talk about in class?

   b. In what sense are ethical issues an integral part of counseling practice regardless of one's theoretical orientation?

2. *Putting clients' needs before your own*

   a. What are some of your personal needs that you think will help you become a more effective counselor?

   b. What are some of your personal needs that you think may hinder you in effectively counseling clients?

3. *Ethical decision making*

   a. In what way can you make the ethics codes work for you? How might the codes be a catalyst for your thinking about ethical dilemmas?

   b. If you were faced with an ethical dilemma, what specific steps would you take in making a decision?

4. *The right of informed consent*

   a. The ethics codes of most professional organizations require that clients be presented with enough information to make informed choices about entering the client–therapist relationship. What are some matters you would explore with your clients at the first and second counseling sessions?

   b. Assume that during an initial session with a client you determine that this individual would best be helped by a referral. If there were no referral source available, what would you do?

5. *Dimensions of confidentiality*

   a. What information would you give your clients about the nature and purpose of confidentiality? What would you say if a client asked you under what circumstances you would break confidentiality? How would you explain the limits of confidentiality to your clients during the initial session?

   b. Some states allow children and adolescents to participate in psychological counseling without parental knowledge and consent. What particular factors do you think might justify minors receiving treatment without parental consent? Why? What would you tell minors about confidentiality as it pertains to talking about them to their parents?

   c. Assume that you are counseling an elementary school child in a community clinic and that the child's parents show up one day and want to know what is going on. How will you cope with your responsibility to the parents without divulging certain confidences revealed to you by the child?

   d. Court decisions make it clear that therapists have a duty to warn and protect. What guidelines can you think of to help you assess a situation in which you would feel responsible to warn and protect?

6. *Ethical issues in a multicultural perspective*

   a. What ethical questions, if any, should be raised if you counsel someone who differs from you with respect to race? Culture? Sexual orientation? Age? Disability? Gender? Socioeconomic status?

   b. What do you consider to be the most pressing challenge of becoming a culturally competent counselor?

   c. What life experiences have you had that would either aid or hinder you in working with clients from diverse ethnic and cultural backgrounds?

   d. In working with your clients, how will you focus on both individual and environmental factors that are influencing them?

7. *Ethical issues in the assessment process*

   a. What are the ethical issues involved in using a diagnostic category for a client?

   b. What ethical concerns might you have, if any, if you were expected to provide a *DSM-IV-TR* diagnosis for clients during the initial session?

   c. What are your thoughts about the values and limitations of diagnosis as a part of the assessment process?

8. *Ethical aspects of evidence-based practice*

   a. Evidence-based practice involves accountability to your clients by using interventions that have empirical support. What do you think of this practice?

   b. How would you deal with the pressure to use interventions that are both brief and standardized in your work setting?

   c. To what degree do you think that evidence-based practice will improve the effectiveness of client services?

9. *Managing multiple relationships in counseling practice*

   a. Do you think dual or multiple relationships are an inevitable part of practicing in any setting? Explain.

   b. As you read the text, consider what specific dual or multiple relationships you consider to be the most problematic. How would you determine if a relationship was either inappropriate or unethical?

   c. If you were involved in a dual relationship with a client, what procedures could you follow to minimize the risk of harm?

   d. Can you think of some ways you would deal differently with *avoidable* dual relationships than with those that were unavoidable?

GLOSSARY OF KEY TERMS

Aspirational ethics   A higher level of ethical practice that addresses doing what is in the best interests of clients.

Assessment   Evaluating the relevant factors in a client's life to identify themes for further exploration in the counseling process.

Boundary crossing   A departure from a commonly accepted practice that could *potentially* benefit a client (e.g., attending a client's wedding).

Boundary violation   A boundary crossing that takes the practitioner out of the professional role, which generally involves exploitation. It is a serious breach that harms the client and is therefore unethical.

Confidentiality   This is an ethical concept, and in most states therapists also have a legal duty not to disclose information about a client.

Diagnosis   The analysis and explanation of a client's problems. It may include an explanation of the causes of the client's difficulties, an account of how these problems developed over time, a classification of any disorders, a specification of preferred treatment procedure, and an estimate of the chances for a successful resolution.

Dual or multiple relationships   A counselor assumes two (or more) roles simultaneously or sequentially with a client. This may involve assuming more than one professional role or combining professional and nonprofessional roles.

Ethical decisions   To make ethical decisions, consult with colleagues, keep yourself informed about laws affecting your practice, keep up to date in your specialty field, stay abreast of developments in ethical practice, reflect on the impact your values have on your practice, and be willing to engage in honest self-examination.

Evidence-based practice (EBP)   Psychotherapists are required to base their practice on techniques that have empirical evidence to support their efficacy.

Informed consent   The right of clients to be informed about their therapy and to make autonomous decisions pertaining to it.

Mandatory ethics   The view of ethical practice that deals with the minimum level of professional practice.

Nonprofessional interactions   Additional relationships with clients other than sexual ones.

Positive ethics   An approach taken by practitioners who want to do their best for clients rather than simply meet minimum standards to stay out of trouble.

Practice-based evidence   Using data generated during treatment to inform the process and outcome of treatment.

Privileged communication   A legal concept that generally bars the disclosure of confidential communications in a legal proceeding.

 ## SELF-INVENTORY OF ATTITUDES RELATING TO ETHICS ISSUES

Directions: This inventory is designed to assess your attitudes and beliefs on specific ethics issues. Select the response that comes closest to your position, or write your own response in "e." Bring the completed inventory to class for discussion.

1. A therapist should terminate a therapeutic relationship when
   a. the client decides to terminate.
   b. the therapist judges that it is time to terminate.
   c. it is reasonably clear that the client is not benefiting from therapy.
   d. the client reaches an impasse.
   e. _____

2. Regarding confidentiality, I believe
   a. it is never ethical to disclose anything a client tells me under any circumstances.
   b. it is ethical to break a confidence when the therapist deems that the client might do harm to him- or herself or to others.
   c. confidences can be shared with the parents of the client if the parents request information.

   d. deciding when to break confidentiality ultimately will be left to my professional judgment.
   e. _____

3. My definition of an ethical therapist is one who
   a. devotes time to self-examination on matters of ethics.
   b. is careful not to take advantage of his or her position of power.
   c. follows all of the codes of ethics.
   d. knows the right course of action to take in each problem situation.
   e. _____

4. Regarding the issue of counseling friends, I think that
   a. it is acceptable to have a valued friend as a client.

b. it should be done rarely and then only if it is clear that the friendship will not interfere with the therapeutic relationship.

c. friendship and therapy should not be mixed.

d. a friend could be accepted as a client only when the friend asks to be.

e. _____

5. I would tend to refer a client to another professional if

a. it were clear that the client was not benefiting in the relationship with me.

b. I felt a strong sexual attraction to the person.

c. the client continually stirred up painful feelings in me (reminded me of my mother, father, ex-spouse, and so on).

d. I had a hard time caring for or being interested in the client.

e. _____

6. Regarding the ethics of social and personal relationships with clients, it is my position that

a. it is never wise to see or to get involved with clients on a social basis.

b. it is an acceptable practice to strike up a social relationship once the therapy relationship has ended if both want to do so.

c. with some clients a personal and social relationship might well enhance the therapeutic relationship by building trust.

d. it is ethical to combine a social and therapeutic relationship if both parties agree.

e. _____

7. One of the best ways to determine on what occasions and under what circumstances I would break confidentiality with a client is to

a. confer with a supervisor or a consultant.

b. check out my perceptions with several colleagues.

c. follow my own intuitions and trust my own judgment.

d. discuss the matter with my client and solicit his or her opinion.

e. _____

8. In terms of appreciating and understanding the value systems of clients who are culturally different from me,

a. I see it as my responsibility to learn about their values and not impose mine on them.

b. I would encourage them to accept the values of the dominant culture for survival purposes.

c. I would attempt to modify my counseling procedures to fit their cultural values.

d. it is imperative that I learn about the specific cultural values my clients hold.

e. _____

9. To be effective in counseling clients from a different culture, I will need to

a. possess specific knowledge about the particular group I am counseling.

b. be able to accurately "read" nonverbal messages.

c. have had direct contact with this group.

d. treat these clients no differently from clients from my own cultural background.

e. _____

10. My view of evidence-based practice is that it

a. is bound to improve counseling practice because it relies on empirical procedures.

b. has little relevance to what I consider to be effective counseling practice.

c. fits for some theories, but not for other theoretical orientations.

d. puts too much emphasis on techniques and not enough on the importance of the therapeutic relationship.

e. _____

Some Suggestions for Using This Self-Inventory

- On completing this inventory, look over the items, and circle those you would like to bring to class and discuss with others. Limit yourself to a few issues that have stimulated your thinking the most.

- Look over the initial inventory that you completed in Chapter 1 of this manual. Compare the general tone of your responses in the two surveys.

- Work in pairs on certain questions. Compare your positions on each issue.

- Divide the class into small groups, each group taking one of the issues for discussion: confidentiality, dual and multiple relationships, therapist responsibility, the client–therapist relationship, therapist competence, therapist values and needs, and so on.

- Next, each group can report a consensus to the rest of the class. Some good material for debates can be generated when divergent viewpoints are established within or between groups.

CASES INVOLVING ETHICAL DILEMMAS

Try your hand at dealing with these cases. Look for what you consider to be the core of the ethical dilemma in each case. Identify the issues, and clarify the position you would take in each situation. Working with these cases in class is an excellent way for you to expand your awareness of the ethical dimension of practice, and it will help you learn a process of ethical decision making. I suggest that you try role-playing these vignettes first. After you have had opportunities to be both the client and the counselor, discuss the issues involved in each situation.

Dealing With Sexual Attractions

You have been treating client A for 6 weeks and find that your sexual attraction to him or her has been growing as the counseling relationship develops. It is becoming more and more difficult to focus on the therapy process because of your attraction. You feel, in turn, that A is flirtatious, although you have begun to doubt your own judgment and objectivity. You find yourself thinking about your client often, and you would like to extend the time you have together beyond the counseling sessions. You have had two sexual dreams involving the client. Although you are concerned about A's best interests, it is difficult for you to really listen, and you are aware of being preoccupied with being liked and accepted by A. At this point you are feeling some guilt and wondering if these feelings are "normal" in this situation.

1. Does this attraction present both a personal and a professional problem? If so, how?

2. Might you be inclined to discuss your attraction with your client? Give your rationale for either doing so or not doing so.

3. Would you discuss this situation with another professional, such as a colleague? Your supervisor? Your therapist?

4. Would you continue working with A, or would you refer him or her to another counselor? If you chose the first course, how would you deal with both your feelings toward A and A's feelings toward you? If you took the latter course, what reasons would you give to A for wanting to make this referral?

Dealing With a Client's Initiative

Still considering the prior case, assume that before you had made a decision concerning the way you would proceed with A, he or she returned the next week and began the session by telling you:

> There is something I really need to talk about. Lately I've been thinking a lot about you, and I'd really like to spend more time with you—outside of this office. You are very exciting to me, not just sexually but as a person, and I'd so much like to get to know more about you. It's important for me to know how you feel about me.

1. What are your feelings and thoughts as you listen to A?

2. What might you tell A about your feelings for him or her?

3. How would you deal with A's request to spend some time with you out of the office?

4. What do you see as the ethical issues involved in the way you might proceed?

A Colleague Having an Affair With a Former Student

You have just found out that a psychologist who works in your student mental health clinic is having an affair with one of his former students. The affair began 10 months after the student completed therapy with him. The psychologist was teaching a counseling skills course on campus, and after the course ended, they began dating in earnest. There has been quite a lot of gossip and debate in the clinic about the relationship, but the psychologist refuses to discuss it. Your colleagues wonder if it violates professional ethics. There is also the question of whether it violates the ethics of the student–teacher relationship.

1. What are your thoughts about a psychologist who is an educator and on rare occasions dates a former student? Do you see any difference between a therapist–client relationship and an instructor–student relationship?

2. Given the fact that there is gossip, what might you say to your colleague? If your colleague refused to talk about the matter, what might you do?

3. What are your thoughts about the ethics of forming social or intimate relationships with *former* clients? Besides the amount of time that has elapsed since the end of therapy, what other factors need to be considered?

4. Assume that the psychologist in this situation approached you and *asked* for your reactions. For a start, what might you say? (This scenario would be a good one to role-play.)

Racism Among Your Colleagues

What do you do when sexism or racism is manifested by your colleagues? You work in the Psychiatry Department of a major metropolitan hospital and have become quite disturbed at the element of bias that you see around you. You have heard several therapists refer to clients in derogatory terms. In particular, you fear that the attitudes of one White male therapist who is counseling several African American women may be affecting his professional judgment. From some comments that you have heard from this therapist, it sounds to you as if he has definite prejudices against minorities and women.

1. Would you be likely to confront this therapist? Why or why not?

2. What would you want to ask him or tell him?

3. What ethics issues are involved in this situation?

Some Cases Pertaining to Confidentiality

After reading about the general guidelines for confidentiality in the textbook, reflect on your position if you were the counselor in each of these cases.

1. You have been seeing an adolescent girl in a community mental health clinic for 3 months. Lately she has complained of severe depression and says that life seems hopeless. She is threatening suicide and even wants details from you concerning how she can successfully go through with it. Are you obliged to disclose this information to her guardians because she is under legal age? What will you tell your client? What consultation might you seek?

2. A client reveals to you that he has stolen some expensive laboratory equipment from the college where you are a counselor. A week later the dean calls you into her office to talk with you about this particular client. What do you tell the dean? And what do you not tell her?

3. You are working in a community agency that provides testing and counseling services for those suspected of being infected by HIV. The legal and ethical problem your staff is debating is the duty to protect others from HIV infection by a client. What input would you give your staff on this question: Must counselors violate confidentiality and perhaps take coercive action when a client known to be HIV-positive is believed to be sexually active or sharing needles?

4. In the course of a counseling session, a youth tells you that he is planning to do serious physical harm to a fellow student. What would you tell your client? How would you proceed?

5. Your client is a 15-year-old girl sent to you by her parents. One day the parents request a session to discuss their daughter's progress and to see what they can do to help. What information can you share with the parents, and what can you not disclose? What might you discuss with the girl before you see her parents? What will you do if she makes it clear that she does not want you to see her parents or tell them anything?

Additional Cases to Consider

1. You have been meeting with a 30-year-old, biracial female (African American, Asian) for several sessions. She has two children and has generally been focusing on her difficult relationship with her former husband. Today she tells you that she has been withholding a disclosure that she finds shameful. She wants to tell you her secret, but is worried about how you might react.

   What would you say to this person?

   _____
   _____
   _____

2. A 25-year-old Caucasian male comes to your office for an assessment after he tests positive for cannabis in a random drug test at his place of employment. He tells you that he used to smoke cannabis frequently when he was in college but has stopped doing so because of his employer's drug policy. He states that he believes he tested positive for cannabis because he was at a party where others were smoking. Three weeks later he tests positive for cannabis again.

   What would you say to this person?

   _____
   _____
   _____

3. A 28-year-old, single, heterosexual, Asian female seeks assistance because she has had a long history of difficult relationships with male authority figures. She discloses that she was sexually abused while in middle school by a well-respected man in her small town. She informed her family of the abuse about two years ago and feels that they did not respond to her concerns at all. She further states that her father was particularly dismissive of her feelings of being violated by the person who abused her.

   What ethical issues does this case present for you, if any?

   Would you be inclined to explore with her this situation of abuse?

   _____
   _____
   _____

4. An 18-year-old bisexual female college student has been coming to you to assist with her depressed mood. She has not been doing well in school and informs you that her girlfriend recently broke up with her because the depressive symptoms had been interfering with their relationship. Your client then tells you that she cut herself last night

to cope with the emotional pain. She states that she felt better after cutting herself. She denies suicidal ideation and expresses concern and worry that she will become a "cutter."

Does this case present ethical concerns for you? If so, what are they?

Would you pursue the topic of self-harm with your client? Why or why not?

_____

_____

_____

5. A 32-year-old, married, African American male has been having difficulties in his marriage. He has been married for 8 years and is worried that his wife may be having an affair. He is embarrassed to tell you that he has been checking his wife's text messages and e-mail communications without her knowledge or permission. He feels ashamed about violating her privacy but says that he feels like he can't stop because it is the only way he can trust her. He becomes tearful when he tells you that he feels as if he is obsessed with the idea that his wife is having an affair (even though he has found no evidence of it).

If he asked you what you thought of what he has done, how would you respond?

_____

_____

_____

SUGGESTED ACTIVITIES AND EXERCISES

Here are some activities that you can do on your own, in small groups in the classroom, in pairs, or by contacting professional counselors to sample their reactions to some of these ethics issues. Because there are more activities than you can probably realistically complete, select those topics that have the most meaning for you.

1. Assume that you are in a field placement as a counselor in a community agency. The administrators tell you that they do *not* want you to inform your clients that you are a student intern. They explain that your clients might feel that they were getting second-class service if they found out that you were in training. The administrators contend that your clients are paying for the services they receive (on a sliding scale based on their ability to pay) and that it would not be psychologically good to give them any information that might cause them to conclude that they were not getting the best help available. What would you say and do if you found yourself as an intern in this situation? Would it be ethical to follow this directive and not inform your clients that you were a trainee and that you were receiving supervision? Do you agree or disagree with the rationale of the administrators? Might you accept the internship assignment under the terms outlined if you could not find any other field placements?

2. How might you proceed if you knew of the unethical practice of a colleague? What kinds of unethical behavior of your colleagues, if any, do you think you would report?

3. Discuss some ways in which you can prepare clients for issues pertaining to confidentiality. How can you teach them about its purposes and the legal restrictions on it? Think particularly about counseling minors.

4. What experiences have you had with people from a different cultural background? Did you learn anything about your potential prejudices? What prejudices, if any, did you feel directed at you? You might bring your experiences to class. Also, I suggest that you interview other students or faculty members who identify themselves as ethnically or culturally different from you. What might they teach you about differences that you as a counselor would need to take into consideration to work more effectively with them?

5. Assume that you are applying for a job or writing a résumé to be used in private practice. Write your own professional disclosure statement in a page or two. Consider writing the essence of your views about matters such as these: the nature and purpose of counseling; what clients might expect from the process; a division of responsibilities between your client and you; a summary of your theoretical position, including the main techniques you are likely to use; a statement of the kinds of clients and problems you are best qualified to work with; matters that might affect your relationship with your clients such as legal restrictions, agency policy, and limits of confidentiality; and any other topics that you think could help clients decide if they wanted to consult with you. This exercise can help you clarify your own positions and give you valuable practice for job interviews, licensure exams, and interviews for graduate school admission.

6. Write an *informed consent document* that you might give to clients. This could be in the form of a contract that outlines your responsibilities to clients. It can be considered an extension of the professional disclosure statement that you wrote in the previous exercise. The point of this exercise is to give you an opportunity to develop your own version of an information sheet that you might provide for your clients.

KNOW THE CODES OF ETHICS OF PROFESSIONAL ORGANIZATIONS

Each of the major mental health professional organizations has its own code of ethics, which can be obtained by contacting the particular organization. I strongly recommend that you obtain a copy of the ethics code of at least one mental health profession and familiarize yourself with the basic guidelines for ethical practice. Although ethics codes do not provide answers to ethical dilemmas you will encounter, they do offer general guidance. It is essential that you know the basic content of the codes of your profession.

All of the following codes of ethics and guidelines for practice are available in the booklet, *Codes of Ethics for the Helping Professions*, Fourth Edition (Brooks/Cole, Cengage Learning, 2011), which is sold at a nominal price when packaged with the textbook, *Theory and Practice of Counseling and Psychotherapy*. Alternatively, you may obtain particular codes of ethics by contacting the organizations directly or by downloading these ethics codes from the organizations' websites.

1. **American Counseling Association (ACA):** *Code of Ethics*, ©2005
   Visit www.counseling.org/ for more information on this organization.
2. **National Board for Certified Counselors (NBCC):** *Code of Ethics*, ©2005
   Visit www.nbcc.org/ for more information on this organization.
3. **Commission on Rehabilitation Counselor Certification (CRCC):** *Code of Professional Ethics for Rehabilitation Counselors*, ©2010
   Visit www.crccertification.com/ for more information on this organization.
4. **Association for Addiction Professionals (NAADAC):** *Code of Ethics*, ©2008
   Visit www.naadac.org/ for more information on this organization.
5. **Canadian Counselling Association (CCA):** *Code of Ethics*, ©2007
   Visit www.ccacc.ca/home.html for more information on this organization.
6. **American School Counselor Association (ASCA):** *Ethical Standards for School Counselors*, ©2004
   Visit www.schoolcounselor.org/ for more information on this organization.
7. **American Psychological Association (APA):** *Ethical Principles of Psychologists and Code of Conduct*, ©2002
   Visit www.apa.org/ for more information on this organization.
8. **American Psychiatric Association:** *The Principles of Medical Ethics With Annotations Especially Applicable to Psychiatry*, ©2009
   Visit www.psych.org/ for more information on this organization.
9. **American Group Psychotherapy Association (AGPA):** *Ethical Guidelines for Group Therapists*, ©2002
   Visit www.groupsinc.org/ for more information on this organization.

10. **American Mental Health Counselors Association (AMHCA):** *Code of Ethics,* ©2010
    Visit www.amhca.org/ for more information on this organization.
11. **American Association for Marriage and Family Therapy (AAMFT):** *Code of Ethics,* ©2001
    Visit www.aamft.org/ for more information on this organization.
12. **International Association of Marriage and Family Counselors (IAMFC):** *Ethical Code,* ©2005
    Visit www.iamfc.com/ for more information on this organization.
13. **Association for Specialists in Group Work (ASGW):** *Best Practice Guidelines,* ©2008
    Visit www.asgw.org/ for more information on this organization.
14. **National Association of Social Workers (NASW):** *Code of Ethics,* ©2008
    Visit www.socialworkers.org/ for more information on this organization.
15. **National Organization for Human Services:** *Ethical Standards of Human Service Professionals,* ©2000
    Visit www.nationalhumanservices.org/ for more information on this organization.
16. **Feminist Therapy Institute (FTI):** *Feminist Therapy Code of Ethics,* ©2000
    Visit www.feminist-therapy-institute.org/ for more information on this organization.
17. **American Music Therapy Association (AMTA):** *Code of Ethics,* ©2008
    Visit www.musictherapy.org/ for more information on this organization.

 ## QUIZ ON ETHICAL ISSUES IN COUNSELING PRACTICE

A Comprehension Check

Score _____ %

Note: Please refer to Appendix 1 for the scoring key.

True/false items: Decide if the following statements are "more true" or "more false" as they apply to ethical issues in counseling practice.

T   F   1. Mandatory ethics is a higher level of ethical practice that addresses doing what is in the best interests of clients.

T   F   2. It is unethical for us to meet our personal needs through our professional work.

T   F   3. Professional codes of ethics educate counseling practitioners and the general public about the responsibilities of the profession and provide a basis for accountability.

T   F   4. It is a mistake to equate behaving legally with being ethical.

T   F   5. Looking at the relevant ethics codes for general guidance is the last step one should take when faced with an ethical problem.

T   F   6. Informed consent is an ethical requirement that is an integral part of the therapeutic process; however, it is not a legal requirement.

T   F   7. Informed consent is a positive approach that helps clients become active partners and true collaborators in their therapy.

T   F   8. Privileged communication is a legal concept that generally bars the disclosure of confidential communications in a legal proceeding.

T   F   9. In reasoning through any ethical dilemma, there is usually just one course of action to follow.

T   F   10. The central aim of evidence-based practice is to require psychotherapists to base their practice on techniques that have empirical evidence to support their efficacy.

Multiple-choice items: Select the *one best answer* of those alternatives given.

_____ 11. Which of the following statements about diagnosis is NOT true?

 a. Diagnosis is the analysis and explanation of a client's problems.

 b. Diagnosis is always a part of the assessment process in counseling.

 c. Diagnosis consists of identifying a specific mental disorder based on a pattern of symptoms.

 d. None of these (they are all true).

_____ 12. What is the primary rationale for conducting a comprehensive assessment of the client as the initial step in the therapeutic process?

 a. Specific counseling goals cannot be formulated and appropriate treatment strategies cannot be designed until a client's past and present functioning is understood.

 b. Conducting a comprehensive assessment of the client offers inexperienced therapists a concrete framework from which to practice. Seasoned clinicians rarely use this approach since they can quickly assess the client's problem.

 c. Insurance companies require clinicians to submit a comprehensive assessment of the client in order to fully reimburse them for services.

 d. Those who conduct comprehensive assessments of their clients are protected from being sued for malpractice.

_____ 13. What does the acronym DSM stand for?

 a. Deviance and Sociopathy Manual

 b. Developmental and Statistical Measurement of Mental Disorders

 c. Diagnostic and Statistical Manual of Mental Disorders

 d. Diagnostic and Statistical Measurement Reference Guide

_____ 14. Kendra is a biracial client who presents as being reserved and passive and who makes minimal eye contact. Her therapist should

 a. consider that Kendra's behavior and mannerisms may reflect distinctive ethnic and cultural patterns.

 b. diagnose Kendra as being depressed.

 c. view Kendra's behavior as resistance to the therapeutic process.

 d. confront Kendra immediately to ensure that future sessions are more productive.

_____ 15. Generally speaking, the concept of privileged communication does NOT apply to

 a. group counseling.

 b. couples counseling and family therapy.

 c. child and adolescent therapy.

 d. all of these.

_____ 16. David is a counselor trainee who is working in a mental health center under the supervision of Dr. Garcia. In order to behave in an ethical manner, David should

 a. inform his clients at the outset of counseling that he plans to consult with his supervisor Dr. Garcia in order to ensure that he is providing them with high quality care.

 b. not reveal to his clients that he is a trainee under supervision so as to prevent them from questioning his competence, which could undermine the therapeutic process.

 c. ask Dr. Garcia to sit in on every session he conducts to ensure that he is developing competence.

 d. refuse to work with actual clients until he is a highly competent therapist.

_____ 17. Ethics codes

 a. are intended to provide ready-made answers for the ethical dilemmas that practitioners will encounter.

 b. are becoming so specific that they have nearly eliminated the need for practitioners to use critical thinking skills and clinical judgment when faced with ethical issues.

c. are best used as guidelines to formulate sound reasoning and serve practitioners in making the best judgments possible.

d. are so general that they are of little, if any, use to clinicians.

_____ 18. Paula recently discovered that two of her clients that she sees individually had a stormy relationship in the past. She is wondering whether she can remain objective in working with them. Paula should

a. look at the relevant ethics codes for general guidance on the matter.

b. brainstorm various possible courses of action.

c. discuss options with other professionals to get their perspectives.

d. all of these.

_____ 19. When the author uses the term multiple relationships, he is referring to

a. dual relationships and nonprofessional relationships.

b. the large caseloads of therapists.

c. the pattern that some clients have of cheating on their significant others and juggling several relationships at once.

d. serial monogamy.

_____ 20. In many mental health settings, clinicians are pressured to use interventions that

a. tap into unconscious dynamics.

b. are research-supported even if they are lengthy.

c. are brief and standardized.

d. focus on early childhood experiences.

_____ 21. Which of the following is NOT one of the three pillars of EBP?

a. looking for the best available research

b. relying on the best available legal advice

c. relying on clinical expertise

d. taking into consideration the client's characteristics, culture, and preferences.

_____ 22. Which of the following accounts for more of the treatment outcome?

a. the therapist's theoretical orientation

b. the therapeutic method employed

c. client factors

d. the duration of treatment

_____ 23. The *ACA Code of Ethics* stresses that counseling professionals must learn how to

a. manage multiple roles and responsibilities in an ethical way.

b. eliminate multiple roles altogether in order to keep boundaries from becoming blurred.

c. sensitively confront colleagues who are juggling multiple roles.

d. file ethics complaints when they witness a colleague engaging in various professional roles.

_____ 24. Except for _____, which is unequivocally unethical, there is not much consensus regarding the appropriate way to deal with multiple relationships.

a. socializing with clients

b. sexual intimacy with current clients

c. bartering with clients (e.g., goods for services)

d. sexual attraction to clients

e. all of these

_____ 25. Dr. Hernandez has been invited to the wedding of her client Cynthia. If she accepts the invitation,

a. Dr. Hernandez will be committing a boundary violation.

b. Dr. Hernandez will be engaging in a boundary crossing.

c. Dr. Hernandez will be acting unethically.

d. Dr. Hernandez will be breaking the law and could spend some time in jail.

PART 2

Theories and Techniques of Counseling

Chapter **4**

Psychoanalytic Therapy

 ## PRECHAPTER SELF-INVENTORIES

Directions: The purpose of this self-inventory scale is to identify and clarify your attitudes and beliefs related to the key concepts of and issues raised by each therapeutic approach.

- Complete the self-inventory before you read the corresponding textbook chapter.
- After reading the chapter and discussing it in class, take the self-inventory again to determine whether you have modified your position on any of the issues.
- Respond to each statement, giving the initial response that most clearly identifies how you really think.
- Remember that the idea is for you to express your view, not to decide which is the "correct" answer. Each statement is a true assumption of the particular approach. Thus, you are rating your degree of agreement or disagreement with the assumptions that are a part of each theory.

Using the following code, write the number of the response that most closely reflects your viewpoint on the line at the left of each statement:

> 5 = I *strongly agree* with this statement.
>
> 4 = I *agree*, in most respects, with this statement.
>
> 3 = I am *undecided* in my opinion about this statement.
>
> 2 = I *disagree*, in most respects, with this statement.
>
> 1 = I *strongly disagree* with this statement.

Compare your responses with those of your classmates, and use the statements as points for discussion in class sessions.

———— 1. Clients are ready to terminate therapy when they have clarified and accepted their current emotional problems, and also have understood the historical roots of their difficulties.

———— 2. Our infantile conflicts may never be fully resolved even though many aspects of transference are worked through with a therapist.

———— 3. We experience transference with many people, and our past is always a vital part of the person we are presently becoming.

———— 4. The transference situation is considered valuable in therapy because its manifestations provide clients with the opportunity to reexperience a variety of feelings that would otherwise be inaccessible.

———— 5. The key to understanding human behavior is understanding the unconscious.

———— 6. Most psychological conflicts are not open to conscious control because their source has been repressed and remains unconscious.

_____ 7. The unconscious, even though it is out of awareness, has a great influence on behavior.

_____ 8. Development during the first 6 years of life is a crucial determinant of the adult personality.

_____ 9. Most personality and behavior problems have roots in a failure to resolve some phase of psychosexual development in early childhood.

_____ 10. One learns the basic sense of trust in one's world during the first year of life.

_____ 11. To progress toward healthy development, one must learn how to deal with feelings of rage, hostility, and anger during the second and third years of life.

_____ 12. It is normal for children around the age of 5 to have concerns about their sexuality, their sex roles, and their sexual feelings.

_____ 13. Insight, understanding, and working through earlier, repressed material are essential aspects of therapy.

_____ 14. Therapists should engage in relatively little self-revelation and should remain anonymous.

_____ 15. For therapy to be effective, clients must be willing to commit themselves to an intensive and long-term therapeutic process.

_____ 16. Therapy is not complete until the client works through the transference process.

_____ 17. Analysis and interpretation are essential elements in the therapeutic process.

_____ 18. It is important that a client relive the past in the therapy process.

_____ 19. Effective therapy cannot occur unless the underlying causes of a client's problem are understood and treated.

_____ 20. The basic aim of therapy is to make the unconscious conscious.

OVERVIEW OF PSYCHOANALYTIC THERAPY

Key Figures and Major Focus

Original key figure: Sigmund Freud, father of psychoanalysis. Ego psychologist: Erik Erikson. Object relations: Margaret Mahler. Historically, psychoanalysis was the first system of psychotherapy. It is a personality theory, a philosophy of human nature, and a method of therapy.

Philosophy and Basic Assumptions

Although the Freudian view of human nature is basically deterministic and focuses on irrational forces, biological and instinctual drives, and unconscious motivation, later developments in psychoanalysis stressed social and cultural factors. Contemporary psychoanalytic thinking emphasizes the development of the ego and the differentiation and individuation of the self. The contemporary psychoanalytic approaches deviate significantly from traditional or Freudian psychoanalysis, yet these modern versions retain the emphasis on the unconscious, the role of transference and countertransference, and the importance of early life experiences.

Key Concepts

Key notions include the division of the personality into the id, ego, and superego; the unconscious; anxiety; the functioning of ego-defense mechanisms; an understanding of transference and countertransference; a focus on the past for clues to present problems; and the development of personality at various stages of life. Healthy personality development is based on successful resolution of both psychosexual and psychosocial issues at the appropriate stages throughout the life span. Psychopathology is the result of failing to meet some critical developmental task or becoming fixated at some early level of development. Freudian psychoanalysis is basically an id psychology, whereas the newer formulations of psychoanalytic therapy are based on an ego psychology. The contemporary psychoanalytic approaches include object-relations, self psychology, and relational psychoanalysis. These newer formulations concentrate on the development of the ego, and they pay more attention to the social and cultural factors that influence the differentiation of an individual from others. Contemporary psychoanalysis gives increased emphasis to the therapeutic relationship and views therapy as an interactive process between client and therapist.

Therapeutic Goals

A primary goal is to make the unconscious conscious. Both psychoanalysis and psychoanalytically oriented therapy seek the growth of the ego through analysis of resistance and transference, allowing the ego to solve the unconscious conflicts. The restructuring of personality is the main goal, rather than solving immediate problems. Contemporary analytically-oriented therapists are interested in their clients' pasts, but they intertwine that understanding with the present and with the future. The past is relevant to the extent that it sheds light on a client's present and future direction.

Therapeutic Relationship

In classical psychoanalysis the anonymity of the therapist is stressed, so that clients can project feelings onto the therapist. The focus is on resistances that occur in the therapeutic process, on interpretation of a client's life patterns, and on working through transference feelings. Through this process, clients explore the parallels between their past and present experience and gain new understanding that can be the basis for personality change.

With the modern psychoanalytic approaches, the therapist does not remain anonymous, emphasis is given to the here-and-now interactions between client and therapist, and therapists can decide when and what to disclose to clients. Both transference and countertransference are central aspects in the relationship that are addressed. Contemporary relational theorists have challenged the authoritarian nature of classical analysis and replaced it with a more egalitarian model.

Techniques and Procedures

All techniques are designed to help the client gain insight and bring repressed material to the surface so that it can be dealt with in a conscious way. Major techniques of traditional psychoanalysis include maintaining the analytic framework, free association, interpretation, dream analysis, analysis of resistance, and analysis of transference. These techniques are geared to increasing awareness, gaining intellectual insight, and beginning a working-through process that will lead to a reorganization of the personality. In contemporary psychoanalytic practice, more latitude is given to the therapist in using a diverse range of techniques and in developing the therapeutic relationship. In contemporary relational psychoanalysis, the therapist does not strive for a nonparticipating, detached, and objective stance, but is attuned to the nature of the therapeutic relationship, which is viewed as a key factor in bringing about change. The newer psychoanalytic theorists have enhanced, extended, and refocused classical analytic techniques.

Applications

Good candidates for analytic therapy include professionals who wish to become therapists as well as people who have been helped by intensive therapy and want to go further. This therapy demands sacrifices of time, money, and personal commitment and is typically a long-term process. Psychoanalytic concepts and techniques can be adapted to both time-limited therapy and group therapy.

Brief psychodynamic therapy makes use of these psychodynamic concepts: impact of stages of development, the unconscious and resistance, the usefulness of interpretation, stressing the working alliance, and the reenactment of past emotional issues in relationship to the therapist.

Psychodynamically oriented group therapy is based on many of the same concepts as brief therapy. Especially useful in group therapy are these facets: understanding transference and multiple transferences, understanding and monitoring leader countertransference, and exploring interpersonal relationships within the here-and-now context of the group. A basic tenet of psychodynamic therapy groups is the notion that group participants, through their interactions within the group, re-create their social situation, implying that the group becomes a microcosm of their everyday lives.

Multicultural Perspectives

The psychosocial approach that emphasizes turning points at various stages of life has relevance for understanding diverse client populations. As well as examining intrapsychic influences, therapists can assist clients in identifying and dealing with the influence of environmental situations on their personality development. Traditional psychoanalysis has many limitations from a multicultural perspective. However, the goals of brief psychodynamic therapy can provide new experiences and new understanding for clients. With this briefer form of psychoanalytically oriented therapy, clients can relinquish old patterns and establish new patterns in their present behavior.

Contributions

Many other models have developed as reactions against psychoanalysis. The theory provides a comprehensive and detailed system of personality. It emphasizes the legitimate place of the unconscious as a determinant of behavior, highlights the profound effect of early childhood development, and provides procedures for tapping the unconscious. Several factors can be applied by practitioners with nonanalytic orientations, such as understanding how resistance is manifested, how early trauma can be worked through so that a client is not fixated, the manifestations of transference and countertransference in the therapy relationship, and the functioning of ego-defense mechanisms.

Limitations

Classical psychoanalysis involves lengthy training for the therapist and a great amount of time and expense for clients. The approach stresses the role of insight but does not give due recognition to the importance of action methods. The model is based on the study of neurotic individuals, not of healthy people. The orthodox Freudian approach, with its stress on instinctual forces, does not give adequate attention to social, cultural, and interpersonal factors. The techniques of this long-term approach are of limited applicability to crisis counseling, working with many culturally diverse client populations, and social work.

 GLOSSARY OF KEY TERMS

Anal stage   The second stage of psychosexual development, when pleasure is derived from retaining and expelling feces.

Analytical psychology   An elaborate explanation of human nature that combines ideas from history, mythology, anthropology, and religion.

Animus (anima) The biological and psychological aspects of masculinity and femininity, which are thought to coexist in both sexes.

Anxiety A feeling of impending doom that results from repressed feelings, memories, desires, and experiences emerging to the surface of awareness. From a psychoanalytic perspective, there are three kinds of anxiety: reality, neurotic, and moral anxiety.

Archetypes The images of universal experiences contained in the collective unconscious.

Blank screen An anonymous stance assumed by classical psychoanalysts aimed at fostering transference.

Borderline personality disorder A disorder characterized by instability, irritability, self-destructive acts, impulsivity, and extreme mood shifts. Such people lack a sense of their own identity and do not have a deep understanding of others.

Brief psychodynamic therapy (BPT) An adaptation of the principles of psychoanalytic theory and therapy aimed at treating selective disorders within a preestablished time limit.

Classical psychoanalysis The traditional (Freudian) approach to psychoanalysis based on a long-term exploration of past conflicts, many of which are unconscious, and an extensive process of working through early wounds.

Collective unconscious From a Jungian perspective, the deepest level of the psyche that contains an accumulation of inherited experiences.

Compensation An ego-defense mechanism that consists of masking perceived weaknesses or developing certain positive traits to make up for limitations.

Contemporary psychoanalysis Newer formulations of psychoanalytic theory that share some core characteristics of classical analytic theory, but with different applications of techniques; extensions and adaptations of orthodox psychoanalysis.

Countertransference The therapist's unconscious emotional responses to a client that are likely to interfere with objectivity; unresolved conflicts of the therapist that are projected onto the client.

Crisis According to Erikson, a turning point in life when we have the potential to move forward or to regress. At these turning points, we can either resolve our conflicts or fail to master the developmental task.

Death instincts A Freudian concept that refers to a tendency of individuals to harbor an unconscious wish to die or hurt themselves or others; accounts for the aggressive drive.

Denial In denial there is an effort to suppress unpleasant reality. It consists of coping with anxiety by "closing our eyes" to the existence of anxiety-producing reality.

Dialectical behavior therapy (DBT) A blend of cognitive behavioral and psychoanalytic techniques that generally involves a minimum of one year of treatment.

Displacement An ego-defense mechanism that entails redirection of some emotion from a real source to a substitute person or object.

Dream analysis A technique for uncovering unconscious material and giving clients insight into some of their unresolved problems. Therapists participate with clients in exploring dreams and in interpreting possible meanings.

Dream work The process by which the latent content of a dream is transformed into the less threatening manifest content.

Ego The part of the personality that is the mediator between external reality and inner demands.

Ego-defense mechanisms Intrapsychic processes that operate unconsciously to protect the person from threatening and, therefore, anxiety-producing thoughts, feelings, and impulses.

Ego psychology The psychosocial approach of Erik Erikson, which emphasizes the development of the ego or self at various stages of life.

Fixation The condition of being arrested, or "stuck," at one level of psychosexual development.

Free association A primary technique, consisting of spontaneous and uncensored verbalization by the client, which gives clues to the nature of the client's unconscious conflicts.

Genital stage The final stage of psychosexual development, usually attained at adolescence, in which heterosexual interests and activities are generally predominant.

Id The part of personality, present at birth, that is blind, demanding, and insistent. Its function is to discharge tension and return to homeostasis.

Id psychology A theory stating that instincts and intrapsychic conflicts are the basic factors shaping personality development (both normal and abnormal).

Identification   As an ego defense, this may involve individuals identifying themselves with successful causes in the hope that they will be seen as worthwhile.

Identity crisis   A developmental challenge, occurring during adolescence, whereby the person seeks to establish a stable view of self and to define a place in life.

Individuation   The harmonious integration of the conscious and unconscious aspects of personality.

Interpretation   A technique used to explore the meanings of free association, dreams, resistances, and transference feelings.

Introjection   A process of taking in the values and standards of others.

Latency stage   A period of psychosexual development, following the phallic stage, that is relatively calm before the storm of adolescence.

Latent content   Our hidden, symbolic, and unconscious motives, wishes, and fears.

Libido   The instinctual drives of the id and the source of psychic energy; Freudian notion of the life instincts.

Life instincts   Instincts oriented toward growth, development, and creativity that serve the purpose of the survival of the individual and the human race.

Maintaining the analytic frame   Refers to a range of procedures, such as an analyst's anonymity, regularity, and consistency of meetings, as a structure for therapy.

Manifest content   The dream as it appears to the dreamer.

Moral anxiety   The fear of one's own conscience; people with a well-developed conscience tend to feel guilty when they do something contrary to their moral code.

Multiple transferences   A process whereby group members develop intense feelings for certain others in a group; an individual may "see" in others some significant figure such as a parent, life-partner, ex-lover, or boss.

Narcissism   Extreme self-love, as opposed to love of others. A narcissistic personality is characterized by a grandiose and exaggerated sense of self-importance and an exploitive attitude toward others, which hides a poor self-concept.

Narcissistic personality   Characterized by a grandiose and exaggerated sense of self-importance and an exploitive attitude toward others, which serve the function of masking a frail self-concept.

Neurotic anxiety   The fear that the instincts will get out of hand and cause one to do something for which one will be punished.

Object relatedness   Interpersonal relationships as they are represented intrapsychically.

Object relations   Interpersonal relationships as they are represented intrapsychically.

Object-relations theory   A newer version of psychoanalytic thinking, which focuses on predictable developmental sequences in which early experiences of self shift in relation to an expanding awareness of others. It holds that individuals go through phases of autism, normal symbiosis, and separation and individuation, culminating in a state of integration.

Oral stage   The initial phase of psychosexual development, during which the mouth is the primary source of gratification; a time when the infant is learning to trust or mistrust the world.

Persona   The mask we wear, or public face we present, as a way to protect ourselves.

Phallic stage   The third phase of psychosexual development, during which the child gains maximum gratification through direct experience with the genitals.

Pleasure principle   The idea that the id is driven to satisfy instinctual needs by reducing tension, avoiding pain, and gaining pleasure.

Projection   An ego-defense mechanism that involves attributing our own unacceptable thoughts, feelings, behaviors, and motives to others.

Psychodynamic psychotherapy   Psychoanalytically oriented psychotherapy involves a shortening and simplifying of the lengthy process of psychoanalysis.

Psychodynamics   The interplay of opposing forces and intrapsychic conflicts that provide a basis for understanding human motivation.

Psychosexual stages   The Freudian chronological phases of development, beginning in infancy. Each is characterized by a primary way of gaining sensual and sexual gratification.

Psychosocial stages   Erikson's turning points, from infancy through old age. Each presents psychological and social tasks that must be mastered if maturation is to proceed in a healthy fashion.

Rationalization   An ego-defense mechanism whereby we attempt to justify our behavior by imputing logical motives to it.

Reaction formation   A defense against a threatening impulse, involving actively expressing the opposite impulse.

Reality anxiety   The fear of danger from the external world; the level of such anxiety is proportionate to the degree of real threat.

Reality principle   The idea that the ego does realistic and logical thinking and formulates plans of action for satisfying needs.

Regression   An ego-defense mechanism whereby an individual reverts to a less mature form of behavior as a way of coping with extreme stress.

Relational analysis   An analytic model based on the assumption that therapy is an interactive process between client and therapist. The interpersonal analyst assumes that countertransference is a source of information about the client's character and dynamics.

Relational model   A model that characterizes therapy as an interactive process between client and therapist in which countertransference provides an important source of information about the client's character and dynamics.

Repression   The ego-defense mechanism whereby threatening or painful thoughts or feelings are excluded from awareness.

Resistance   The client's reluctance to bring to awareness threatening unconscious material that has been repressed.

Self psychology   A theory that emphasizes how we use interpersonal relationships (self objects) to develop our own sense of self.

Shadow   A Jungian archetype representing thoughts, feelings, and actions that we tend to disown by projecting them outward.

Sublimation   An ego defense that involves diverting sexual or aggressive energy into other channels that are socially acceptable.

Superego   That aspect of personality that represents one's moral training. It strives for perfection, not pleasure.

Time-limited dynamic psychotherapy (TLDP)   Through this form of psychoanalytically oriented therapy, clients gain a sense of what it is like to interact more fully and flexibly within the therapy situation. They are helped to apply to the outside world what they are learning in the office.

Transference   The client's unconscious shifting to the therapist of feelings and fantasies, both positive and negative, that are displacements from reactions to significant others from the client's past.

Transference relationship   The transfer of feelings originally experienced in an early relationship to other important people in a person's present environment.

Unconscious   That aspect of psychological functioning or of personality that houses experiences, wishes, impulses, and memories in an out-of-awareness state as a protection against anxiety.

Working through   A process of resolving basic conflicts that are manifested in the client's relationship with the therapist; achieved by the repetition of interpretations and by exploring forms of resistance.

QUESTIONS FOR REFLECTION AND DISCUSSION

1. Psychoanalytic psychotherapy is a dynamic, continually developing method of helping people solve psychological problems. As you think about this chapter, look for evidence to support this contention. What aspects of the Freudian revisionists and the contemporary psychoanalytic writers do you find of the most value to you personally?

2. The psychoanalytic approach underscores the importance of early psychosexual development. Do you see evidence that one's current problems are rooted in the significant events of one's first 6 years of life? When you apply this concept specifically to yourself, what connections between your childhood experiences and your present personality are you aware of? To what extent do you believe people can resolve their adult problems that stem from childhood experiences without exploring past events?

3. Contrast Carl Jung's view of human nature with Freud's view, especially with respect to the influence of the past on the development of present personality structure. What are the implications for counseling practice of these two perspectives of human development?

4. In your work as a counselor, many psychoanalytic techniques such as free association, dream interpretation, probing the unconscious, and interpretation and analysis of resistance and transference may not be appropriate, or they may be beyond your level of training. However, many of the concepts of the psychoanalytic approach can provide you with a useful framework in deepening your understanding of human behavior. What psychoanalytic concepts do you see as being potentially useful in your work as a counselor? Why?

5. The classical analyst tends to maintain warm detachment, objectivity, and anonymity so as to foster transference. What are your reactions to the therapeutic value of the therapist's assuming such a role? How do you think a self-disclosing stance on the therapist's part would alter the course of psychotherapy?

6. Compare and contrast classical psychoanalytic therapy with contemporary relational psychoanalysis. What are a few of the major differences between these approaches that you find most interesting?

7. This approach places considerable emphasis on therapists' awareness of their own needs and reactions toward clients (or awareness of countertransference). At this time, what kind of client behavior do you think you'd find most difficult? Are you aware of any of your vulnerabilities, unresolved personal concerns, or unmet needs that might interfere with your objectivity and effectiveness as a therapist? What are you willing to do to address any of these personal areas that could affect your professional work?

8. The psychoanalytic view of anxiety is that it is largely the result of keeping unconscious conflicts buried and that ego defenses develop to help the person curb anxiety. What implications does this view have for your work with people? Do you think defenses are necessary? What are the possible values of defense mechanisms? What do you think might happen if you were able to successfully strip away a client's defenses?

9. What are some of the main characteristics of brief psychodynamic therapy? How useful do you find this approach?

10. Can you apply any aspects of the psychoanalytic theory to your own personal growth? Mention a few specific areas of this approach that could help you deepen your self-understanding?

SUGGESTED ACTIVITIES AND EXERCISES

1. Write a letter to Freud. Tell him what you think of his contribution to psychology and how his theory applies to your life (or how it does not apply). Bring your letter to class, and share it with the other members.

2. Reread the section in the text that discusses the importance of the first 6 years of life. Then do the following:

   a. Write down a few key questions about your own psychosexual and psychosocial development from birth through age 6 that you would like to have answered.

   b. Seek out your relatives, and ask them some of the questions.

   c. Gather up any reminders of your early years.

   d. If possible, visit the place or places where you lived.

   e. Attempt to answer your own questions briefly in written form.

   f. Construct a chart showing key influences on your development during those early years.

   g. If the class wishes, bring the charts to class, and discuss in small groups the effects of each member's developmental history on his or her present life.

JERRY COREY COUNSELS STAN FROM A PSYCHOANALYTIC PERSPECTIVE

Session 2. Psychoanalytic Therapy Applied to the Case of Stan

The second session focuses mainly on Stan's resistance and dealing with transference. The assumption is being made that although Stan has had several sessions with me, he is still reluctant to trust me as his therapist. He is guarded and measures his responses, doing a good bit of censoring before he speaks. In the previous session Stan talked about how stern and critical his father was, and how he never had with him the kind of relationship he wanted. Stan is concerned that I will be critical of him much like his father was. Stan brings his history with his father into his perception of me and into our relationship.

Before viewing the session, read Chapter 4, pages 92–93 in the textbook and answer the questions in the text listed under the heading "Follow-Up: You Continue as Stan's Psychoanalytic Therapist." After reflecting on these questions, view the second session, and then address the following questions:

1. From a psychoanalytic perspective, how do you explain Stan's censoring and holding back?

2. From this theoretical perspective, what would be your main area of interest?

3. Stan says that he worries about what his therapist (Jerry) will think about him and that what he says in his sessions might come back to haunt him. Would you be inclined to reassure Stan that you would not use what he tells you against him? Why or why not?

4. Stan says that he does not think he is doing things the right way in his therapy sessions. How are you likely to intervene?

5. If Stan asked you (as his psychoanalytic therapist) what you are thinking about him, would you disclose your perceptions and reactions?

6. In free associating to the word "father," Stan says, "My father never saw me." How would you respond?

7. What are some potential therapeutic advantages of working with Stan's transference toward his therapist? As the therapist, how might you deal with your potential countertransference?

8. Toward the end of this session, Stan realizes how often he shuts himself off. As his therapist, what would you want to say to him about this?

9. To what extent is it important to focus on how Stan's past experiences are played out in his session with his psychoanalytic therapist?

10. What most interested you about this particular session? Why?

A Suggested In-Class Activity

In my classes, I make frequent use of small groups at most of the class meetings. I find that students are often willing to participate in a small group, and even get involved in role-playing activities, whereas in the entire class they are often hesitant to ask questions or share their thoughts. My hope is that you would find ways to share your reactions to the case of Stan with your classmates. If you are viewing the counseling sessions with Stan in class, it would be useful to form small groups to discuss your reactions to each session. Your discussion could address your reactions to both Stan and to me as his therapist. Specifically, the following three questions are suited for each of the counseling sessions with Stan:

1. What did you find most interesting in this session? Why?

2. If you were counseling Stan from this particular theoretical framework, what is one additional technique you might use? What would you hope to accomplish with this intervention?

3. If you were the client, how would you be likely to respond to the therapist's (Jerry's) comments and interventions in this particular session?

If you can get experientially involved after viewing a session, this will enhance your learning about the counseling process and about applying theory to practice. Ideally, I suggest that you form groups of three people. One can "become Stan" and can do some further role playing as a continuation of the themes you saw demonstrated. Another person can become Stan's counselor and attempt to stay within the spirit of the theory that is being studied. The third person can function as a process observer. After you have had a few minutes to experience these roles, spend some time debriefing; discuss what it was like for each of you to be in a given role and what you learned from the exercise. This is a useful structure to use for all of the theory chapters with the sections on counseling Stan.

JERRY COREY'S WORK WITH RUTH FROM A PSYCHOANALYTIC PERSPECTIVE

For each of the theory chapters in this manual, I describe my way of counseling Ruth from the perspective of the theory being considered. There are three resources in which I demonstrate the way I work with Ruth in detail: (1) *DVD for Integrative Counseling: The Case of Ruth and Lecturettes*; (2) *Case Approach to Counseling and Psychotherapy*; and (3) *The Art of Integrative Counseling*. If you are using the *DVD for Integrative Counseling*, these sections on Ruth will tie into what you are seeing. If you are not using this DVD program, the information given in each chapter in this manual will be sufficient for you to complete the exercises.

Some Background Data on Ruth

Because this is the first presentation of the case of Ruth, and because you will be exposed to Ruth's case from each of the following theoretical approaches, a brief description of data from her intake form is provided here.

Age: 39

Sex: Female

Race: Caucasian

Marital Status: Married

Socioeconomic Status: Middle class

Appearance: Dresses well, is slightly overweight, avoids eye contact, and speaks rapidly.

Living Situation: Recently graduated from college as an elementary education major, lives with husband (John, 45) and her four children (Rob, 19; Jennifer, 18; Susan, 17; and Adam, 16).

Presenting Problem

Client reports general dissatisfaction. She says her life is rather uneventful and predictable, and she feels some panic over reaching the age of 39. For 2 years she has been troubled with a range of psychosomatic complaints, including sleep disturbances, anxiety, dizziness, heart palpitations, and headaches. At times she has to push herself to leave the house. Client says that she cries easily, often feels depressed, and has a weight problem.

History of Presenting Problem

Client was as a housewife and mother until her children became adolescents. She then entered college part time and obtained a bachelor's degree. She has recently begun work toward a credential in elementary education. Through her contacts with others at the university, she became aware of how she has limited herself, how she has fostered her family's dependence on her, and how frightened she is of changing from her roles as mother and wife. Ruth is not clear at this point about who she is, apart from being mother, wife, and student. She realizes that she does not have a good sense of what she wants for herself and that she typically lived up to what others in her life wanted from her. Ruth has decided to seek individual counseling to explore her concerns in several areas:

■ Ruth is aware that she has lived a very structured and disciplined life, that she has functioned largely by taking care of the home and the needs of her four children and her husband, and that to some degree she is no longer content with this. Although she would like to get more involved professionally, the thought of doing so frightens her. She worries about how becoming more professionally involved might threaten her family.

■ Ruth's children range in age from 16 to 19, and all of them are now finding more of their satisfactions outside the family and are spending increasing time with their friends. Ruth sees these changes and is concerned about "losing" them. Ruth feels very much unappreciated by her children.

■ In thinking about her future, Ruth is not really sure who or what she wants to become. She would like to develop a sense of herself apart from the expectations of others. Ruth does not find her relationship with her husband, John, very satisfactory. She is anxious over the prospects of challenging this relationship, fearing that if she does she might end up alone.

All of these factors combined have provided the motivation for Ruth to take the necessary steps to initiate individual therapy. Perhaps the greatest catalyst for her coming to therapy is the increase of her physical symptoms and anxiety.

Psychosocial History

Client was the oldest of four children. Her father is a fundamentalist minister, and her mother is a housewife. She describes her father as distant, authoritarian, and rigid; her relationship with him was one of unquestioning adherence to his rules and standards. She remembers her mother as critical, and she felt that she could never do enough to please her. At other times her mother was supportive. The family showed little affection. In some ways Ruth took on the role of caring for her younger brother and sisters, largely in the hope of winning the approval of her parents. When she attempted to have any kind of fun, Ruth encountered her father's disapproval and outright scorn. To a large extent this pattern of taking care of others has extended throughout her life.

Exploring Psychoanalytic Themes With Ruth

Exploring Ruth's Transference

After Ruth has been in therapy for some time, she grows disenchanted with me because she does not see me as giving enough. She is beginning to resent my encouraging her to express more about the ways in which she sees me as ungiving. At this stage in her therapy she is experiencing some very basic feelings of wanting to be special and wanting proof of it, and we explore these feelings in her sessions.

Ruth is beginning to discover from the way she responds to me a connection between how she related to significant people in her life. She looks to me in some of the same ways that she looked to her father for approval and for love. I encourage her recollection of feelings associated with these past events so that she can work through the barriers that prevent her from functioning as a mature adult.

Exploring Past Experiences

Ruth internalized many of her father's strict views of sexuality. Because her father manifested a negative attitude toward her sexuality, she believed that her curiosity about sexual matters was unacceptable. Ruth's father caught her in an act of sexual experimentation (at the age of 6). Her sexual feelings were rigidly controlled. The denial of sexuality established at this age has been carried over into her adult life and gives rise to conflicts, guilt, remorse, and self-condemnation.

YOU CONTINUE WORKING WITH RUTH

1. Refer to *Case Approach to Counseling and Psychotherapy* (Chapter 2) for an illustration of how a psychoanalytically oriented therapist (Dr. William Blau) works with Ruth's case. In this chapter, I also demonstrate my version of counseling Ruth from a psychoanalytically oriented perspective.

2. See the *DVD for Integrative Counseling*: *The Case of Ruth and Lecturettes* (Session 4, on understanding and working with resistance; Session 10, on working with transference and countertransference; and Session 11, on understanding the past) and evaluate my way of incorporating psychoanalytic concepts with Ruth.

3. How would you react to Ruth's perception of you as distant and her feelings toward you of not sharing enough of yourself personally?

4. What are some ways you would work with Ruth's present sexual inhibitions based on her disclosure that she still feels guilty and ashamed over her sexual curiosity when she was a young girl?

5. If you were to continue counseling Ruth, what direction would you likely follow in exploring the themes described in questions 3 and 4 above?

A CASE FROM A PSYCHOANALYTIC PERSPECTIVE

Jonas: "A History of Unstable Relationships"
By **James R. Ruby, PhD**, Assistant Professor of Human Services, California State University at Fullerton

Background Information

Jonas is a 33-year-old Caucasian, gay male who was born in the back of a station wagon and became a ward of the state within 6 months of his birth. Jonas was in and out of foster care and group homes until he received a permanent foster placement at the age of 10. The family that took Jonas in was an affluent two-career family with one daughter, age 7. Jonas described the home as immaculate, strict, and in his opinion, "a bit neurotic." Corporal punishment was used in the home with great frequency and Jonas described his foster father as cold, brutal, and forbidding. Jonas described his relationship with his foster mother as less problematic, but he stated that he believed he could "never please her." Jonas' younger sister was described as "simply perfect."

At age 12, Jonas was sent to a military school because of his behaviors at home and at school. He described the military school setting as one he enjoyed, overall. The structure and the clearly defined expectations brought him "a sense of comfort." However, Jonas described an experience of sexual abuse that was perpetrated upon him by one of his military school instructors. This experience, he believed, had left an indelible mark on him.

Jonas came to counseling due to a series of unstable relationships with men, in combination with an inability to maintain employment. Jonas had been in a serious relationship with a man for two years that he described as incredibly passionate. In fact, Jonas described this man as the love of his life. When Jonas' partner began to lose interest in him and subsequently show interest in other men, Jonas became more and more agitated and angry. His attempts at maintaining the relationship became more desperate and volatile. When Jonas' partner decided to end the relationship, Jonas exploded with anger and a physical altercation ensued. After assaulting his partner, Jonas left the apartment and vandalized his partner's sports car by scratching curse words into it with his keys. The police were called and Jonas was arrested. As part of his sentence, Jonas was required to seek counseling.

During the counseling intake assessment, it was revealed that Jonas had a pattern of unstable relationships that carried over to the work environment. After being fired from a position, Jonas broke into his previous place of employment, erased files from computers, and vandalized property in the office. After both the relationship break-up and being fired, Jonas showed significant suicidal ideation.

Dr. James Ruby's Way of Working With Jonas From a Psychoanalytically Oriented Perspective

It became clear that the relational aspects of counseling would be key elements in working with Jonas. He would be very unlikely to simply trust his counselor in light of his tumultuous childhood history and his series of broken relationships. Additionally, the chaotic nature of his development gave rise to some common themes that emerged in his present-day relationships. In particular, it was useful to consider the connection between his current problems and significant events from earlier events in his life.

One key goal in counseling would be to foster a healthy transference, where Jonas could project feelings from earlier unstable relationships on to me, his counselor. From a psychoanalytic perspective, it is important for Jonas to feel safe enough with me to express his unresolved feelings of anxiety, anger, grief, and distrust. This is only brought about by my ability to establish an empathic relationship with him, one in which he is assured that whatever he says will not cause me to reject him or hurt him, as others have.

While Jonas tells his story, I would listen for themes, gaps, or inconsistencies, and when appropriate I would make interpretations. Some of these might be related to Jonas' expectations for relationships. I would explore how a person who has been routinely rejected and abused might find difficulty trusting others. It would be useful to know the unresolved conflicts within Jonas that inhibit his ability to move forward developmentally. In the midst of these conversations, I would need to listen for Jonas' readiness to change. If I tried to move too quickly, the work would be ineffective.

As Jonas tells his story and expresses his thoughts and feelings, I would listen for how he is incorporating defense mechanisms into his relationship with me. Hopefully, our relationship would be one in which he feels free to loosen his defenses and feel safe. Rather than challenge Jonas in a confrontational manner, I would simply focus on ways in which we might work through his resistance. In fact, I would hope that Jonas' time in counseling might be interpreted as a corrective experience, one in which he is not required to be anyone other than himself. It is through this nonjudgmental relationship that he might bolster his ego strength and feel more capable of being his true self with me. A consistent relationship with Jonas is needed to help bring this about. He must see me as someone who is willing to be the same with him today as I was yesterday. It is only then that he will believe that I will be the same tomorrow.

In our conversations, I would listen for how Jonas expresses his yearnings for a fulfillment of childhood desires and I would help him see the futility of expending energy doing so. Hopefully, Jonas would grow to recognize his own capabilities for being successful in loving relationships, the world of work, and caring for himself. It would be unhelpful to allow him to simply predict failure based on previous life experiences, but I would need to be careful not to allow my own feelings of countertransference to result in being overly paternal, for this would interfere with my own efforts at remaining objective.

A key process for Jonas will be termination. In light of his history of painful and turbulent relationships, he will need plenty of time to ready himself for the end of the counseling relationship. If it ends too abruptly, feelings of abandonment might be triggered within Jonas and the process of counseling could end up emulating his previous difficult relationships. However, if the process runs on too long, it could become a relationship built on dependence that does not help Jonas activate his own ego strength.

Follow-up: You Continue as Jonas' Psychoanalytically Oriented Therapist

1. What are some thoughts and feelings that stir within you surrounding hearing Jonas' story? How might these thoughts and feelings help, or hinder, your work with him?

2. Traditional psychoanalytic approaches focused on the counselor being a "blank slate," but Dr. Ruby focused on building an empathic, non-judgmental relationship with Jonas. Why do you suppose he focused on this?

3. Jonas described two events in his life in which he reacted in a rage-filled manner to the end of a relationship. Why do you suppose he reacted to those events in this way? Are there any defense mechanisms that might have been activated by Jonas during these times?

4. Based on the brief telling of Jonas' story, what developmental milestones might have been missed, or negatively impacted, in his life? How might this have influenced who he is today?

5. What other psychoanalytically-oriented therapeutic techniques might you have utilized with Jonas? How might they have been helpful in your work with him?

 ## QUIZ ON PSYCHOANALYTIC THERAPY

A Comprehension Check

Score _____%

Note: Refer to Appendix 1 for the scoring key for these quizzes. Count 4 points for each error, and subtract the total from 100 to get your percentage score. I recommend that you review these comprehension checks for midterm and final examinations. I also suggest that you bring to class questions that you would like clarified. If you get a wrong answer that you believe is right, bring it up for discussion. My classes have had some lively discussions, which have helped students learn to defend their positions.

True/false items: Decide if the following statements are "more true" or "more false" as they apply to psychoanalytic therapy.

T F   1. The psychosocial perspective is not at all compatible with the psychosexual view of development.

T F   2. Children who do not experience the opportunity to differentiate self from others may later develop a narcissistic personality disorder.

T F   3. The contemporary trends in psychoanalytic theory are reflected in object-relations theory, the self psychology model, and the relational model.

T F   4. Brief psychodynamic therapists assume a neutral therapeutic stance as a way to promote transference.

T F   5. Analytic therapy is oriented toward achieving insight.

T F   6. Working through is achieved almost totally by catharsis, including getting out deeply buried emotions.

T F   7. From the Freudian perspective, resistance is typically a conscious process.

T F   8. The contemporary psychoanalytic approaches place emphasis on the unconscious, the role of transference and countertransference, and the importance of early life experiences.

T   F   9. Object-relations theorists focus on symbiosis, separation, differentiation, and integration.

T   F   10. In object-relations theory there is an emphasis on early development as a decisive factor influencing later development.

Multiple-choice items: Select the *one best answer* of those alternatives given. Consider each question within the framework of psychoanalytic therapy.

_____ 11. Who of the following is **not** considered an object-relations theorist?

  a. Heinz Kohut

  b. Margaret Mahler

  c. Otto Kernberg

  d. Erik Erikson

_____ 12. Which of the following is **not** considered a contemporary psychoanalytic approach?

  a. object-relations theory

  b. self psychology

  c. relational psychoanalysis

  d. classical psychoanalysis

_____ 13. Which of the following is **not** a characteristic of the newer psychoanalytic thinking?

  a. Emphasis is on the origins, transformations, and organizational functions of the self.

  b. The contrasting experiences of others is highlighted.

  c. People are classified as compliant, aggressive, or detached types.

  d. Focus is on the differentiations between and integration of the self and others.

  e. Early development is seen as critical to understanding later development.

_____ 14. All of the following are concepts developed by Carl Jung except

  a. the shadow.

  b. normal infantile autism.

  c. animus and anima.

  d. collective unconscious.

  e. archetypes.

_____ 15. According to Erikson's psychosocial view, the struggle between industry and inferiority occurs during

  a. adolescence.

  b. old age.

  c. school age.

  d. infancy.

  e. middle age.

_____ 16. Erikson's preschool-age phase corresponds to which Freudian stage?

  a. oral

  b. anal

  c. phallic

  d. latency

  e. genital

_____ 17. Which term refers to the repetition of interpretations and the overcoming of resistance so that clients can resolve neurotic patterns?

  a. working through

  b. transference

  c. countertransference

  d. catharsis

  e. acting out

_____ 18. Analysis of transference is central to psychoanalysis because it

  a. keeps the therapist hidden and thus feeling secure.

  b. allows clients to relive their past in therapy and to gain insight.

  c. helps clients formulate specific plans to change behavior.

  d. is considered the only way to get at unconscious material.

  e. is the best way to understand one's lifestyle.

_____ 19. In brief psychodynamic therapy (BPT) the therapist

  a. assumes a nondirective and even passive role.

  b. deals exclusively with a single presenting problem.

  c. assumes an active role in quickly formulating a therapeutic focus that goes beyond the surface of presenting problems.

  d. avoids treating any underlying issue.

_____ 20. With respect to applying the psycho-analytic approach to group counseling, which statement(s) is (are) true?

a. In psychodynamic therapy groups, members re-create their social situations, implying that the group becomes a microcosm of their everyday lives.

b. Members can profit from identifying and exploring their transferences within the group.

c. Projections onto the therapist and other members provide a clue to a member's unresolved conflicts.

d. One's ways of relating within the group provides clues to patterns outside of the group.

e. all of the above.

_____ 21. Borderline and narcissistic disorders have been given much attention by

a. traditional psychoanalysis.

b. Jungian therapy.

c. object-relations theory.

d. Erikson's developmental approach.

_____ 22. During psychoanalytic treatment, clients are typically asked

a. to monitor their behavioral changes by keeping a journal that describes what they do at home and at work.

b. to make major changes in their lifestyle.

c. not to make radical changes in their lifestyle.

d. to give up their friendships.

_____ 23. Countertransference refers to

a. the irrational reactions clients have toward their therapists.

b. the irrational reactions therapists have toward their clients.

c. the projections of the client.

d. the client's need to be special in the therapist's eyes.

e. all except (a).

_____ 24. "Maintaining the analytic framework" refers to

a. the whole range of procedural factors in the treatment process.

b. the analyst's relative anonymity.

c. agreement on the payment of fees.

d. the regularity and consistency of meetings.

e. all of the above.

_____ 25. In psychoanalytic therapy (as opposed to classical analysis), which of the following procedures is *least* likely to be used?

a. the client lying on the couch

b. working with transference feelings

c. relating present struggles with past events

d. working with dreams

e. interpretation of resistance

Note: Another suggestion for feedback and for review is to retake the prechapter self-inventory. All 20 items are true statements as applied to the particular therapy, so thinking about them is a good way to review.

Chapter 5

Adlerian Therapy

 PRECHAPTER SELF-INVENTORY

Directions: Refer to page 43 for general directions. Use the following code:

5 = I *strongly agree* with this statement.

4 = I *agree*, in most respects, with this statement.

3 = I am *undecided* in my opinion about this statement.

2 = I *disagree*, in most respects, with this statement.

1 = I *strongly disagree* with this statement.

_____ 1. The social determinants of personality development are more powerful than the sexual determinants.

_____ 2. Humans can be understood by looking at where they are going and what they are striving toward.

_____ 3. People have a need to overcome inferiority feelings and strive for success.

_____ 4. Although we are not determined by our past, we are significantly influenced by our perceptions and interpretations of these past events.

_____ 5. People are best understood by seeing through the "spectacles" by which they view themselves in relation to the world.

_____ 6. Culture influences all of us, but individuals' expression of their culture differs due to their perception, evaluation, and interpretation.

_____ 7. It is therapeutically useful to ask clients to recall their earliest memories.

_____ 8. Each person develops a unique lifestyle, which should be a focal point of examination in counseling.

_____ 9. Clients in counseling should not be viewed as being "sick" and needing to be "cured"; it is better to see them as being discouraged and in need of reeducation.

_____ 10. Knowing about clients' position in their family of origin is important as a reference point for therapy.

_____ 11. Typically, clients come to therapy with mistaken assumptions or faulty beliefs about life.

_____ 12. Because emotions are integrated with our cognitive behavioral processes, it is appropriate that the counseling process be aimed at the exploration of the client's thoughts, goals, and beliefs.

_____ 13. Although establishing a good client–therapist relationship is essential for counseling to progress, this relationship alone will not bring about change.

_____ 14. One of a counselor's main tasks is to gather information about family relationships and then to summarize and interpret this material.

_____ 15. People tend to remember only those past events that are consistent with their current view of themselves.

_____ 16. Dreams are rehearsals for possible future courses of action.

_____ 17. Conscious factors should be given more attention than unconscious factors in the therapy process.

_____ 18. Although insight is a powerful adjunct to motivational change, it is not a prerequisite for change.

_____ 19. Insight can best be defined as translating self-understanding into constructive action.

_____ 20. At its best, counseling is a cooperative relationship geared toward helping clients identify and change their mistaken beliefs and goals.

 # OVERVIEW OF ADLERIAN THERAPY

Key Figures and Major Focus

Founder: Alfred Adler. Significant developer: Rudolf Dreikurs. Adler chose the name *Individual Psychology* (from the Latin, *individuum*, meaning indivisible) for his theoretical approach because he wanted to avoid reductionism. He used this name to describe his emphasis on the uniqueness and unity of the individual. The focus is on understanding whole persons within their socially embedded contexts of family, culture, school, and work. Dreikurs was the main figure responsible for transplanting Adlerian principles to the United States, especially in applying these principles to education, child guidance, and group work.

Philosophy and Basic Assumptions

More than any other theorist, Adler stresses social psychology and a positive view of human nature. He views human beings as influenced more by social than by biological forces. People are in control of their fate, not victims of it. Adler focuses on the person's past as perceived in the present and how his or her interpretation of early events has a continuing influence. Individuals create a distinctive lifestyle at an early age, rather than being merely shaped by childhood experiences. This lifestyle tends to remain relatively constant and defines one's beliefs about life and ways of dealing with its tasks.

Key Concepts

Consciousness, not the unconscious, is the center of personality. The Adlerian approach, based on a growth model, stresses the individual's positive capacities to live fully in society. It is characterized by seeing unity in the personality, understanding a person's world from a subjective vantage point, and stressing life goals that give direction to behavior. Humans are motivated by *social interest*, or a sense of belonging and having a significant place in society. While Adler considered social interest to be innate, he also believed that it must be learned, developed, and used. Feelings of inferiority often serve as the wellspring of creativity, motivating people to strive for competence, mastery, superiority, and perfection.

Therapeutic Goals

Adlerians are mainly concerned with helping clients identify and change their mistaken beliefs about self, others, and life. Adlerians do not decide for their clients what they should change or what their goals should be; rather, they work collaboratively with their clients in ways that enable them to reach their self-defined goals and assist clients in developing socially useful goals. Some specific goals include fostering social interest, helping clients overcome feelings of discouragement, changing faulty motivation, restructuring mistaken assumptions, and assisting clients to feel a sense of equality with others. Adlerians focus on reeducating individuals and reshaping society. Adlerian therapists educate clients in new ways of looking at themselves, others, and life. The aim of therapy is to assist clients in modifying their lifestyles so that they can more effectively navigate each of the life tasks they face.

Therapeutic Relationship

The client–therapist relationship is based on mutual respect, and both client and counselor are active. Clients are not viewed as passive recipients; rather, they are active parties in a relationship between equals. Through this collaborative partnership, clients recognize that they are responsible for their behavior. Attention is on examining the client's lifestyle, which is expressed in everything the client does. Therapists frequently interpret this lifestyle by demonstrating a connection between the past, the present, and the client's future strivings. Without initial trust and rapport, and sustained attention on the quality of the therapeutic relationship, the difficult work of changing one's style of living is not likely to occur.

Techniques and Procedures

Adlerians pay more attention to the subjective experiences of the client than they do to using techniques. They fit their techniques to the needs of each client. During the initial phase of counseling, the main techniques are attending and listening with empathy, following the subjective experience of the client as closely as possible, and identifying and clarifying goals. Adlerians have developed a variety of techniques and therapeutic styles to promote change, some of which have become common interventions in other therapeutic models. Techniques that go by the names of immediacy, advice, humor, silence, paradoxical intention, acting as if, spitting in the client's soup, catching oneself, the push-button technique, externalization, re-authoring, avoiding the traps, confrontation, use of stories and fables, early recollection analysis, lifestyle assessment, encouraging, task setting and commitment, giving homework, and terminating and summarizing have all been used. Adlerian practitioners typically begin the counseling process with a lifestyle assessment, which focuses on the family constellation and early recollections. Information gained from this comprehensive assessment of the individual guides the therapy process. A strength of Adlerian therapy is the variety of cognitive, behavioral, and experiential techniques that can be applied to a diverse range of clients in a variety of settings and formats. Therapists are not bound to follow a specific set of procedures; rather, they can tap their creativity by applying those techniques that they think are most appropriate for each client. Some of the specific techniques they often employ are empathic attending, encouragement, confrontation, the question, summarizing, interpretation of the family constellation, exploring early recollections, suggestion, and homework assignments. Most of these procedures were originally developed by Adler.

Applications

As a growth model, Adlerian theory is concerned with helping people reach their full potential. Its principles have been applied to a broad range of human problems and to alleviating social conditions that interfere with growth. The theory has been applied to areas such as education, parent education, couples counseling, family counseling, and group counseling. The approach has been widely adopted in elementary education, consultation groups with teachers, and child guidance work. Being grounded in the principles of social psychology, it is ideally suited for working with groups, couples, and families.

A *time-limited framework* can be applied to all forms of Adlerian therapy. Characteristics associated with *Adlerian brief group counseling* include initial establishment of a therapeutic alliance, identifying target problems and goal alignment, rapid assessment, active and directive inventions, a focus on strengths of group members, and an emphasis on both the present and the future. This time-limited framework conveys the expectation to group members that change will occur in a short period of time. Groups provide an ideal context for members to explore how their family-of-origin experiences have a current influence on their lives. Groups offer many opportunities to expand members' social interest.

Multicultural Perspectives

The interpersonal emphasis of Adlerian psychology is most appropriate for multicultural counseling. Adlerian therapy is well-suited to counseling diverse populations and doing social justice work because of the emphasis given to these key concepts: view of the person in a social context, social interest, the family constellation, striving toward purpose and goals, and the phenomenological nature of the approach on understanding the worldview of clients. The approach offers a range of cognitive and action-oriented techniques to help people explore their concerns in a cultural context. Adlerians are flexible in adapting their interventions to each client's unique life situation. Through this theory, a practitioner is able to find in different cultures many opportunities for viewing the self, others, and the world in multidimensional ways.

Contributions

Adler founded one of the major humanistic approaches to psychology, and his ideas have been integrated into many other therapies. The model is a forerunner of most current approaches to counseling. Adlerian therapy has a psychoeducational focus, a present and future orientation, and is a brief or time-limited approach. Adler's influence has extended into the community mental health movement. A major contribution of Adlerian psychology is its integrative nature and the fact that many other theories incorporate key concepts from the Adlerian approach. One of Adler's most important contributions is his influence on other therapy systems. Many of his basic ideas have found their way into most of the other psychological schools. There are significant linkages of Adlerian theory with most present-day theories, especially those that view the individual as purposive, self-determining, and striving for growth.

Limitations

Some of the approach's basic concepts are vague and not precisely defined, which makes it difficult to validate them empirically. Adlerian therapy does not lend itself to evidence-based practice. Critics contend that the approach oversimplifies complex human functioning and is based too heavily on a commonsense perspective.

 GLOSSARY OF KEY TERMS

Adlerian brief therapy   An intervention that is concise, deliberate, direct, efficient, focused, short-term, and purposeful.

Basic mistakes   Faulty, self-defeating perceptions, attitudes, and beliefs that may have been appropriate at one time but are no longer useful.

These are myths that are influential in shaping personality.

Birth order   Adler identified five psychological positions from which children tend to view life: oldest, second of only two, middle, youngest, and only. Actual birth order itself is less important than a person's interpretation of his or her place in the family.

Community feeling An individual's awareness of being part of the human community. Community feeling embodies the sense of being connected to all humanity and to being committed to making the world a better place.

Early recollections Childhood memories (before the age of 9) of one-time events. People retain these memories as capsule summaries of their present philosophy of life. From a series of early recollections, it is possible to understand mistaken notions, present attitudes, social interests, and possible future behavior.

Encouragement The process of increasing one's courage to face life tasks; used throughout therapy as a way to counter discouragement and to help people set realistic goals.

Family atmosphere The climate of relationships among family members.

Family constellation The social and psychological structure of the family system; includes birth order, the individual's perception of self, sibling characteristics and ratings, and parental relationships. Each person forms his or her unique view of self, others, and life through the family constellation.

Fictional finalism An imagined central goal that gives direction to behavior and unity to the personality; an image of what people would be like if they were perfect and perfectly secure.

Goal alignment A congruence between the client's and the counselor's goals and the collaborative effort of two persons working equally toward specific, agreed-on goals.

Guiding self-ideal Another term for fictional finalism, which represents an individual's image of a goal of perfection.

Holistic concept We cannot be understood in parts; all aspects of ourselves must be understood in relation to each other.

Individual psychology Adler's original name for his approach that stressed understanding the whole person, how all dimensions of a person are interconnected, and how all these dimensions are unified by the person's movement toward a life goal.

Inferiority feelings The early determining force in behavior; the source of human striving and the wellspring of creativity. Humans attempt to compensate for both imagined and real inferiorities, which helps them overcome handicaps.

Insight A special form of awareness that facilitates a meaningful understanding within the therapeutic relationship and acts as a foundation for change.

Interpretation Understanding clients' underlying motives for behaving the way they do in the here and now.

Life tasks Universal problems in human life, including the tasks of friendship (community), work (a division of labor), and intimacy (love and marriage).

Lifestyle The core beliefs and assumptions through which the person organizes his or her reality and finds meaning in life events. Our perceptions of self, others, and the world. Our characteristic way of thinking, acting, feeling, living, and striving toward long-term goals.

Lifestyle assessment The process of gathering early memories, which involves learning to understand the goals and motivations of the client.

Objective interview Adlerians seek basic information about the client's life as a part of the lifestyle assessment process.

Phenomenological approach Focus on the way people perceive their world. For Adlerians, objective reality is less important than how people interpret reality and the meanings they attach to what they experience.

Private logic Basic convictions and assumptions of the individual that underlie the lifestyle pattern and explain how behaviors fit together to provide consistency.

Reorientation The phase of the counseling process in which clients are helped to discover a new and more functional perspective and are encouraged to take risks and make changes in their lives.

Social interest A sense of identification with humanity; a feeling of belonging; an interest in the common good.

Striving for superiority A strong inclination toward becoming competent, toward mastering the environment, and toward self-improvement. The striving for perfection (and superiority) is a movement toward enhancement of self.

Style of life An individual's way of thinking, feeling, and acting; a conceptual framework by which the world is perceived and by which people are able to cope with life tasks; the person's personality.

Subjective interview The process whereby the counselor helps clients tell their life story as completely as possible.

The question Used in an initial assessment to gain understanding of the purpose that symptoms or actions have in a person's life. The question is, "How would your life be different, and what would you do differently, if you did not have this symptom or problem?"

QUESTIONS FOR REFLECTION AND DISCUSSION

1. Adlerians contend that first we think (and decide), then we feel, and then we act. Their emphasis is on cognition (thinking, beliefs, assumptions about life, attitudes). What are the strengths and limitations of this focus for a counselor?

2. Adlerians typically begin the counseling process with a lifestyle assessment, which focuses on the family constellation and early recollections. Within these areas, what information would you be most interested in gathering as you faced a new client?

3. When you think of yourself working with clients from diverse cultural and socioeconomic backgrounds, what are some of the most significant aspects of Adlerian therapy?

4. What are some major areas of contrast between Freud's and Adler's theories? Which perspective appeals to you more, and why?

5. When you look at Adler's life experiences and the development of his theory, what do you conclude? To what degree do you think it is possible to separate the theory from the theorist?

6. What are some ways that the Adlerian approach can be applied to group counseling? What are some advantages of using a group format with this approach?

7. The Adlerian notion of striving for superiority holds that we seek to change weakness into strength by excelling in a particular area as a compensation for perceived inferiority. What are some ways in which you strive for superiority? Does this process of compensation and striving work well for you?

8. Reread the descriptions of the oldest child, the second-born, the middle child, the youngest child, and the only child. What position did you occupy in your family? To what degree do you see your experiences as a child in your family as a factor shaping the person you are now?

9. In addition to focusing on the family constellation, Adlerians ask for a few early recollections. What is your earliest memory? What meaning does this recollection hold for you today?

10. Adlerians pay a lot of attention to "basic mistakes," or "private logic." In thinking about some of the conclusions you formed based on a series of life experiences, can you identify any mistaken assumptions you hold now or have held in the past? How do you think some of your basic mistakes affect the ways in which you think, feel, and act?

PERSONAL APPLICATION: THE LIFESTYLE ASSESSMENT

The lifestyle assessment is typically done at the initial phase of therapy as a way to obtain information about the client's family constellation, early recollections, dreams, and strengths as a person. This information is then summarized and interpreted, especially in light of the client's faulty assumptions about life (or "basic mistakes"). From the results of this assessment procedure, counselors make tentative interpretations about the client's lifestyle.

Although there are a number of formats for the lifestyle questionnaire, counselors may develop their own variation by focusing on information deemed most valuable for exploration in therapy. What follows is an example of a lifestyle questionnaire that has been modified and adapted from various sources, but especially from Mosak and

Shulman's *Life Style Inventory* (1988; Accelerated Development, Muncie, IN). To give you an experiential sense of the process of thinking and responding to this early life-history material, complete the following questionnaire as it applies to you. As much as possible, try to give your initial responses, without worrying about what you can and cannot remember or about any "correct" responses. I strongly encourage you to fill in the blanks and to make brief summaries after each section.

Family Constellation: Birth Order and Sibling Description

1. List the siblings from oldest to youngest. Give a brief description of each (including yourself). What most stands out for each sibling?

    _____

    _____

2. Do a rating of each of the siblings, from the highest to the lowest, on each of the following personality dimensions. Include your own position in relationship to your siblings.

Most to Least	*Most to Least*
intelligent _____	feminine _____
achievement-oriented _____	masculine _____
hardworking _____	easygoing _____
pleasing _____	daring _____
assertive _____	responsible _____
charming _____	idealistic _____
conforming _____	materialistic _____
methodical _____	fun-loving _____
athletic _____	demanding _____
rebellious _____	critical of self _____
spoiled _____	withdrawn _____
critical of others _____	sensitive _____
bossy _____	

3. Which sibling is the most different from you, and how? _____
    _____

4. Which is most like you, and how? _____
    _____

5. Which played together? _____

6. Which fought each other? _____

7. Who took care of whom? _____

8. Were there any unusual achievements by the siblings? _____

9. Any accidents or sickness? _____

10. What kind of child were you? _____

11. What was school like for you? _____

12. What childhood fears did you have? _____

13. What were your childhood ambitions? _____

14. What was your role in your peer group? _____

15. Were there any significant events in your physical and sexual development? _____

16. Any highlights in your social development? _____

17. What were the most important values in your family? _____

18. What stands out the most for you about your family life? _____

Family Constellation: Parental Figures and Relationships

1. Your father's current age. _____   Mother's age. _____

2. His occupation. _____   Her occupation. _____

3. What kind of person is he? _____   What kind of person is she? _____

_____   _____

_____   _____

4. His ambitions for the children. _____   Her ambitions for the children. _____

_____   _____

_____   _____

5. Your childhood view of your father. _____   Your childhood view of your mother. _____

_____   _____

_____   _____

6. His favorite child, and why? _____   Her favorite child, and why? _____

_____   _____

_____   _____

7. Relationship to children. _____   Relationship to children. _____

_____   _____

_____   _____

8. Sibling most like father. In what ways?   Sibling most like mother. In what ways?

_____   _____

9. Describe your parents' relationship with each other. _____

_____

10. In general, how did each of the siblings view and react to your parents? _____

_____

11. In general, what was your parents' relationship to the children? _____

_____

12. Besides your mother and father, were there any other significant adults in your life? Who were they? How did they affect you? _____

_____

Early Recollections and Dreams

1. What is your earliest single and specific memory? _____

_____

2. What are some other early recollections? Be as detailed as possible. _____

_____

3. What feelings are associated with any of these early memories? _____

_____

4. Can you recall any childhood dreams? _____

_____

5. Do you have any recurring dreams? _____

_____

Lifestyle Summary

1. Give a summary of your family constellation. (What stands out most about your role in your family? Are there any themes in your family history?) _____
   _____
   _____

2. Summarize your early recollections. (Are there any themes running through your early memories? Do you see any meaning in your early recollections?) _____
   _____

3. List your mistaken self-defeating perceptions. (What do you see as your "basic mistakes"?)
   _____
   _____

4. Summarize what you consider to be your strengths as a person. (What are your assets?)
   _____
   _____

Now that you have finished filling out this lifestyle questionnaire, answer the following questions:

- How much help is this questionnaire in getting you focused on what you might want from a therapeutic relationship?
- Assuming you will be a client in Adlerian therapy, based on the questionnaire, what theme(s) do you most want to address?
- Do you see connections between your past and the person you are today? What about any continuity from your past and present to your strivings toward the future?
- Do you see any patterns in your life? Are there any themes running through from child-hood to the present?

Consider bringing the results of your lifestyle summary to class. Form small groups and exchange with others what you learned from taking this self-assessment questionnaire.

LIFESTYLE ASSESSMENT OF STAN FROM AN ADLERIAN PERSPECTIVE

To provide more background material on Stan's developmental history, I will complete with him the lifestyle questionnaire that you just took.* (Now would be a good time to review Stan's background as presented in Chapter 1 of the text.)

FAMILY CONSTELLATION: BIRTH ORDER AND SIBLING DESCRIPTION

1. List all the siblings from oldest to youngest, giving a brief description of each.

Judy +7	*Frank* +4	*Stan* 25	*Karl* –2
attractive	athletic	immature	spoiled
brilliant	fun-loving	depressed a lot	devilish
out of my class	sociable	slow learner	demanding
highly capable	bright	a loner	overprotected
			accomplished

*This assessment is an adaptation of Mosak and Shulman's *Life Style Inventory* (1988).

masculine	scared	got his way	
mature	well-liked	self-critical	argued with me
hard worker	respected	not too accomplished	liked by mother responsible
made fun of me	the rejected child	daring	
sensitive	didn't like me	one who tried hard	sensitive

2. Rate the siblings on these traits, from most to least (*J* refers to Judy, *F* to Frank, *S* to Stan, and *K* to Karl).

intelligent	J F K S	feminine	J
achievement-oriented	F J K S	masculine	only F
hardworking	F J S K	easygoing	none of us
pleasing	J F K S	daring	K F J S
assertive	K F J S	responsible	J F S K
charming	K J F S	idealistic	J F S K
conforming	none	materialistic	K S F J
methodical	J F K S	fun-loving	F K J S
athletic	only F	demanding	K F S J
rebellious	S K F J	critical of self	S J F K
spoiled	only K	withdrawn	S J K F
critical of others	F K S J	sensitive	J K S F
bossy	K F S J		

3. Which sibling(s) is(are) the most different from you, and how? *Judy and Frank. They were both achievement-oriented, intelligent, respected by my parents, and liked by other kids. Whatever they did, they excelled in.*

4. Which sibling(s) is(are) most like you? *Really none. I always felt like the oddball in my family.*

5. Which played together? *Really nobody.*

6. Which fought each other? *Mainly my younger brother, Karl, and I.*

7. Who took care of whom? *Judy was responsible for taking care of me when I was a young kid.*

8. Any unusual achievements? *Judy won just about every award that was given out at school. Frank was at the top of his class and won athletic trophies.*

9. Any accidents or sickness? *I was hit by a car when I was 9 while I was riding my bicycle. My younger brother seemed sick a lot.*

10. What kind of child were you? *As a child I was lonely, felt hurt a lot, was withdrawn, felt as if I could never measure up to Frank and Judy, felt unwanted, and didn't feel the other kids wanted to play with me.*

11. What was school like for you? *For me, school was a real drag.*

12. What childhood fears did you have? *I was afraid of being picked on, afraid of being alone, and scared that I would fail at whatever I did.*

13. What were your childhood ambitions? *To build a race car and drive it!*

14. What was your role in your peer group? *The one who was chosen last.*

15. Any significant events in your physical and sexual development? *I was smaller than most other guys and didn't mature physically until late. I remember being scared of the sexual changes in my body—and confused!*

16. Any highlights in your social development? *I felt retarded. I always felt as if I was out of step, especially with girls.*

17. What were the most important values in your family? *To be honest, to work hard, and to get ahead.*

18. What stands out the most for you about your family life? *How I never really felt a part of the family, and how distant my older brother seemed to me.*

Family Constellation: Parental Figures and Relationships

Father	*Mother*
1. Current age. *55*	Current age. *53*
2. Occupation. *High school teacher*	Occupation. *Homemaker (part-time nurse)*
3. Kind of person. *Devoted to his work, detached, distant at home, passive.*	Kind of person. *Bossy, dominant, very hard to please, capable, aggressive. Demands her way.*
4. His ambitions for the children. *Strive and do well academically; never bring shame to the family.*	Her ambitions for the children. *To keep out of trouble, to succeed, to show respect for authority.*
5. Your childhood view of him. *Hard worker, dominated by my mother, passive and quiet, distant from me.*	Your childhood view of her. *Rejecting of me, depressed a lot, responsible. Expected too much of me.*
6. His favorite child. *Frank—he admired his academic and athletic accomplishments.*	Her favorite child. *Karl—she could see no wrong that the little brat could do.*
7. Relationship to children. *He really liked Frank and Judy and did a lot with Frank. He ignored me and didn't have much to do with Karl.*	Relationship to children. *She seemed to like and have time for all the kids, except for me.*
8. Sibling most like father. *Frank, in that he was smart and really loved school.*	Sibling most like mother. *Really none, except Judy might be most like her in that both are responsible and highly capable.*

9. Describe your parents' relationship to each other. *Horrible! She berated him and ran over him, and he would never stand up to her. He escaped into his work. They were never really affectionate or close with each other.*

10. Siblings' view of parents. *Frank and Judy thought a good deal of both my mother and my father; Karl respected Mom but had trouble with Dad; I didn't have much use for either of my parents and didn't want much to do with them.*

11. Parents' relationship to the children. *Good for Frank and Judy, OK for mother and Karl, and rotten for me.*

12. Besides your parents, who was another significant adult in your life? *My uncle, who seemed to take an interest in me and liked me.*

Early Recollections and Dreams

1. What is your earliest single and specific memory? *I was about 6. I went to school, and I was scared of the other kids and the teacher. When I came home, I cried and told my mother I didn't want to go back to school. She yelled at me and called me a baby.*

2. What are some other early recollections?

   a. *Age 6 1/2: My family was visiting my grandparents. I was playing outside, and some neighborhood kid hit me for no reason. We got in a big fight, and my mother came out and scolded me for being such a rough kid. She wouldn't believe me when I told her he had started the fight.*

   b. *Age 8: I stuck some nails in the neighbor's tires, and he caught me in the act. He took me by the neck to my folks. They both yelled at me and punished me. My father didn't talk to me for weeks.*

   c. *Age 9: I was riding my bike to school, and all of a sudden a car hit me from the side. I remember lying there thinking I might die. I went to the hospital with a broken leg and concussion. Being in that hospital was lonely and scary.*

3. What feelings are associated with these early memories? *I often felt that I could do no right. I was scared most of the time, felt lonely and never really felt understood or cared for.*

4. Can you recall any childhood dreams? *I recall going to bed late at night and dreaming that the devil was at my window. It scared the hell out of me, and I remember burying myself under the covers to hide.*

5. Any recurring dreams? *I'm alone in the desert, dying of thirst. I see people with water, but nobody seems to notice me, and nobody comes over to give me any water.*

Lifestyle Summary

1. Summary of Stan's family constellation: Stan was the third in a family of four children. Psychologically, he was a true middle child with two older children (one of each sex) in the family and a little brother who was the psychological youngest. The values of the family were achieving and doing well, yet he felt that he could never measure up to the standards of achievement of his older brother and sister. A central theme was that he felt excluded and unwanted. The attention was directed to his older siblings, and the only attention he could get was through negative means. He saw a cold war between his parents, and he learned to fear intimacy. Although he tried to make his parents feel proud of him, he was really never able to succeed. He kept to himself most of the time.

2. Summary of Stan's early recollections: "No matter what I do, I wind up being the fall guy and getting in trouble. Life is frightening, cruel, and punishing. I can't turn to either men or women for help or comfort: Women will be harsh and uncaring; men will withdraw from me for long periods."

3. Summary of Stan's basic mistakes: Stan's pattern and profile show a number of mistakes and self-defeating perceptions, some of which are:

   a. "Anything that can go wrong will go wrong, and I'll be blamed or punished for it."

   b. "Don't get close to people, especially women, because they will be harsh and uncaring."

   c. "If you can't do anything right, why try at all?"

   d. "Only perfect or near-perfect people make it in this world; I'm neither: I won't make it, I don't belong, and I'm not lovable."

   e. "If I don't let myself feel, I won't be hurt."

4. Summary of Stan's assets: Some of Stan's strengths that can be built on are:

   a. He has courage and is willing to look at his life.

   b. He is willing to question assumptions he has made that he did not question earlier.

   c. He realizes that he puts himself down a great deal, and he is determined to learn to accept and like himself.

   d. He has some clear goals—namely, to graduate and to work with kids as a counselor.

   e. He is motivated to work to feel equal to others, and he no longer wants to feel apologetic for his existence.

You proceed in working with Stan from an Adlerian perspective:

1. As you review Stan's lifestyle assessment, what stands out for you the most? What direction would you be inclined to pursue with him?

2. Stan has made several "basic mistakes." How would you work with him on correcting some of these mistaken perceptions? How would you work with him on a cognitive level, as a way of changing his behavior and his feelings?

3. Stan comes to counseling as a discouraged person who feels victimized. Do you have any ideas on applying encouragement in your counseling with him? What might you do if he persisted in his vision of himself as a victim who is powerless to make changes now?

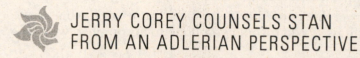

JERRY COREY COUNSELS STAN FROM AN ADLERIAN PERSPECTIVE

Session 3. Adlerian Therapy Applied to the Case of Stan

The assumption is that there is a link between this session and the prior one. Also, assume that I conducted a lifestyle assessment as a part of getting information about Stan as part of the initial intake. In the lifestyle assessment we focused mainly on his family constellation (including his relationship with parents and siblings). This session deals mainly with Stan reporting several of his early recollections.

Before viewing the session, read Chapter 5, pages 125–126, in the textbook and answer the questions in the text listed under "Follow-Up: You Continue as Stan's Adlerian Therapist." Also, before you view this session consider Stan's family constellation. Given Stan's position in his family as the third child, how might you expect this to influence the way he relates to his Adlerian therapist? How might Stan relate to authority figures? What area of his lifestyle might an Adlerian focus on in therapy? After reflecting on these questions, view the session. After doing so, reflect upon and discuss these questions:

1. What therapeutic value, if any, do you see in asking clients to report early recollections?

2. When Stan reports his early recollection about the kittens, he becomes sad and tears up. If you were counseling him, what intervention might you make at this point?

3. With respect to the events surrounding the early memory about the kittens, Stan claimed that he felt helpless and powerless. Can you speculate on how these feelings might be a theme in Stan's life today?

4. If you were the client, what do you imagine it would be like for you to report your own early recollections?

5. In discussing his reactions to his early memories, Stan sees a theme of being stupid. How might you work with Stan on his feeling of being stupid in so many areas of his life?

6. What is the relationship of early memories to basic mistakes?

7. In this session, Stan said, "I'll never quite get it right." What kind of intervention might you make?

8. What have you learned about working with emotion as it relates to timing and the therapeutic process in this session?

9. If you were to work within the Adlerian framework as a therapist, how would this be for you?

10. Can you identify with Stan in any ways in this session? If so, how?

A Suggested In-Class Activity

Spend some time in small groups going over Stan's lifestyle assessment, which is presented in some detail in the previous section. In what ways does this lifestyle assessment provide you with useful clues that you could use in counseling Stan? What are some specific areas you would most want to pursue in more depth if you were counseling Stan from an Adlerian perspective?

Small groups would be a useful follow-up for discussing your reactions to both the section in the text on Adlerian therapy with Stan and the video counseling session with Stan. Again, your discussion could address your reactions to both Stan and to me as his therapist. What shifts did you notice in Stan's demeanor during this session? What are some things you would want to say to Stan if you were counseling him? Do you see any ways to tie Stan's lifestyle assessment to his therapy? The following three other questions are useful to explore in small groups:

1. What did you find most interesting in this session? Why?

2. If you were counseling Stan from this particular theoretical framework, what is one additional technique you might use? What would you hope to accomplish with this intervention?

3. If you were the client, how would you be likely to respond to the therapist's (Jerry's) comments and interventions in this particular session?

JERRY COREY'S WORK WITH RUTH FROM AN ADLERIAN PERSPECTIVE

In the session dealing with termination (Session 13) in the *DVD for Integrative Counseling: The Case of Ruth and Lecturettes*, Ruth and I address her ambivalence about ending her therapy. The focus of this session is on specific changes she has made over the course of her therapy. In Adlerian terms, we are in the reorientation phase. In earlier sessions Ruth has made some new decisions and modified her goals. It was essential that she learn how to challenge her own thinking when she reverted to old patterns of self-criticism. My encouragement was important in her discovering her inner strength. Ruth has become more honest about what she is doing, and she is increasingly able to choose for herself instead of merely following the values she uncritically accepted from childhood.

A most important ingredient of the final stages of Ruth's therapy is commitment. She is finally persuaded that if she hopes to change she will have to set specific tasks for herself and take concrete action now that formal therapy is ending. In this reorientation stage the central task is to encourage Ruth to translate her insights into acting in new and more effective ways. Ruth has acquired a new appreciation for herself, yet she realizes it will be essential for her to continue practicing her new insights. In this final session there is considerable attention on Ruth's looking to the future and establishing revised goals. Where does she want to go from here? What concrete plans can she put into action? What are some contracts she can establish as a way to provide her with a useful direction?

You Continue Working With Ruth

1. Refer to *Case Approach to Counseling and Psychotherapy* (Chapter 3) for an illustration of how Adlerian therapists (Dr. Jim Bitter and Dr. Bill Nicoll) conduct a comprehensive lifestyle assessment with Ruth and engage her in exploring some of her life patterns. In this chapter, I also demonstrate my version of counseling Ruth from an Adlerian perspective.

2. See the *DVD for Integrative Counseling: The Case of Ruth and Lecturettes* (Session 13, the final session dealing with evaluation and termination) for a concrete illustration of assisting Ruth in the reorientation and action process.

3. Assume that you are counseling Ruth and that this is the termination phase of therapy. What are the major tasks you'd most want to accomplish?

4. During this reorientation phase of therapy, what kinds of encouragement would you give to Ruth?

5. How would you work with Ruth in helping her identify a new set of goals that she can continue working on now that the counseling sessions are ending?

 ## A CASE FROM AN ADLERIAN PERSPECTIVE

Jim: "I Need to Take a Hard Look at My Life"
By **Richard E. Watts**, PhD, Distinguished Professor in Counselor Education, Sam Houston University

Some Background Data

Jim, a 28-year-old assistant principal at a junior high school, came to counseling because he was having problems at work and because he was dissatisfied with the relationships he had had with women as an adult. He stated that he has been an assistant principal for two years. The first year he received a few complaints about being inflexible and overbearing, but he and his principal attributed it to inexperience. In his second year, the complaints increased from both faculty and parents, and recently the principal and superintendent of the school district met with Jim to discuss the complaints. He was scheduled to meet with them in a few weeks to develop a "growth plan." Jim stated that the meeting with the principal and superintendent was a "wake-up call," and having done some reflection over the past week, he realized that many of the comments from faculty and parents were similar to ones expressed by several of the women he had dated. Consequently, he now realized he needed to take a hard look at how he related to others, although he did not know what that would entail.

Dr. Richard Watts Works with Jim From an Adlerian Perspective

Developing and maintaining a strong, encouragement-focused counseling relationship with clients is crucial, and success in the subsequent phases of Adlerian counseling—assessment, insight, reorientation—is predicated on the development of this respectful and egalitarian relationship. I hoped to develop this kind of relationship with Jim so he would feel safe to explore and respond to what brought him to counseling.

As part of the assessment process, I discovered that Jim's father was an alcoholic and, although his parents stayed together until the father's death when Jim was 18, he remembered that his parents "fought constantly." In addition, when Jim's father was drunk, he was also verbally and physically abusive to Jim's mother, Jim, and his younger brother. Jim recalled that as early as first grade he experienced the expectation that he was to take care of his mother and, in many respects, parent his younger brother. All of Jim's early recollections centered on being scared about "out of control" situations and feeling safe when he was "in charge." Jim's style of life convictions could be summarized by the following syllogism: "I must be strong, others are not trustworthy or will let me down, the world is a scary place, and therefore I must be in charge or life will get out of control and overwhelm me." As I understood it, Jim developed a dysfunctional conviction (or "basic mistake") that, in order for his life to be manageable and for him to feel a sense of safety and security, he had to be in charge and be in control of his environment at all times.

In helping Jim gain insight or better understand this core conviction about control, I might ask, "Could it be you only feel safe or comfortable when you are in control or in charge of things?" I would seek to help him understand that some of his core beliefs may have enabled him to survive when he was younger but are not working very well for him as a young adult. Useful questions here might include: "What benefits do you gain from always having to be in control? What costs do you incur?" "How have people responded to you—both at work and in dating relationships—as you have interacted with them from an 'in control' and 'in charge' perspective?" "How do you think these beliefs will impact your future career and future relationships?"

The reorientation phase of counseling usually begins when clients have some understanding of their dysfunctional convictions and are ready to take action to put their understanding to work; however, an Adlerian therapist may also use the task-oriented interventions common to the reorientation phase earlier in the process to facilitate development of insight. Jim needs to consider alternative beliefs, behaviors, and, perhaps most importantly, motivations for his actions. Merely understanding the dynamics of his behavior would not be adequate for Jim. Instead, he not only needs to consider behavior changes, but implement some of them as well. Although several Adlerian interventions could be useful for Jim, I might consider asking him to use the time between sessions to "act as if" he were more like the person he wants to be, keep a journal of how he experiences the process, and discuss those experiences in subsequent sessions. Or, given his preference for structure, I might use the "Reflecting As If" (RAI) process that I developed. Using the RAI process, I would ask him to take a reflective step back before moving forward to act as if. To begin this process, I would ask him to reflect on and respond to the question: "How would you be different if you were acting as if you were the person you want to be?" We would then co-construct a list of 'as if' behaviors that manifest him acting as if, rank them from least to most difficult, and select a few for the coming week. Again, I would ask him to keep a journal and discuss his experiences in subsequent sessions. As he progressed to more difficult behaviors on the list, encouragement would be crucial because success would come less easily. Encouragement here would focus on affirming his effort and incremental growth—that is, helping him value the process of moving in a positive direction rather than viewing success only in terms of reaching a desired goal.

In addition to acting as if or reflecting as if, I might encourage Jim to "catch himself" in the process of repeating behaviors he is seeking to change. For example, when he encounters a situation in which he senses he needs to take charge—either at work or in a relationship—he can catch himself and reflect on the best course of action prior to responding. Throughout the reorientation phase, I would seek to demonstrate encouragement by having faith in Jim, seeking to engender hope for his continuing success, and affirming Jim's effort and progress rather than merely achievement of an outcome.

Follow-Up: You Continue as Jim's Therapist

1. What are your impressions and reactions to Dr. Watts' work with Jim? If you could work with Jim for 8-10 sessions, what would be your focus from an Adlerian perspective?

2. To what degree might your life experiences impact your work with Jim? To what degree might you use self-disclosure with him? How will you know if what you are sharing is for his benefit and not your own? What might be some indications that you are meaningfully using yourself as a person in counseling with Jim?

3. How might you work with Jim if he started manifesting control-oriented behaviors with you in counseling sessions? Would you discuss these behaviors with Jim? Why or why not? If so, how would you address them?

4. What Adlerian techniques not mentioned in the case study do you think might be useful for working with Jim? How might they be useful?

5. From an Adlerian counseling perspective, how might you work with Jim differently than the process explained in the case study? Explain why you chose this different course of action.

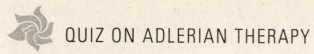

QUIZ ON ADLERIAN THERAPY

A Comprehension Check

Score _____ %

Note: Please refer to Appendix 1 for the scoring key.

True/false items: Decide if the following statements are "more true" or "more false" as they apply to Adlerian therapy.

T F 1. Adlerian therapy is well suited to a brief or time-limited approach.

T F 2. Adler chose the name Individual Psychology for his theoretical approach because he wanted to avoid reductionism.

T F 3. Striving for superiority is seen as a neurotic manifestation.

T F 4. Adler maintains that our style of life is not set until middle age.

T F 5. Adlerian therapy is flexible, and it can be tailored to work with culturally diverse clients.

T F 6. Adlerian counselors do not make interpretations.

T F 7. Adlerians place relatively little importance on the quality of the client–therapist relationship.

T F 8. Assessment is a basic part of the counseling process.

T F 9. Insight is best defined as understanding translated into action.

T F 10. Adlerians believe childhood experiences in themselves are the decisive factor in shaping personality.

Multiple-choice items: Select the *one best answer* of those alternatives given. Consider each question within the framework of Adlerian therapy.

_____ 11. According to Adler, childhood experiences

    a. are not relevant to the practice of counseling.

    b. determine the adult personality.

    c. passively shape us.

    d. in themselves are not as crucial as our attitude toward these experiences.

    e. are only necessary to discuss in the initial session.

_____ 12. The Adlerian point of view toward the role of insight in therapy is best stated in this way:

    a. Insight is a prerequisite to any personality change.

    b. To be of value, insight must be translated into a constructive action program.

    c. People will not make changes until they know the precise causes of their personality problems.

    d. Emotional insight must precede intellectual insight.

    e. Cognitive understanding is absolutely essential before significant behavior changes can occur.

_____ 13. Which of the following statements is **not** true as it is applied to Adlerian therapy?

    a. Consciousness, not the unconscious, is the center of personality.

    b. The approach is grounded on the medical model.

    c. It is a phenomenological and humanistic orientation.

    d. Feelings of inferiority can be the wellspring of creativity.

    e. Early influences can predispose the child to a faulty lifestyle.

_____ 14. Adler linked the recognition of inferiority feelings with striving for perfection or mastery. This notion is best captured by the saying

    a. A goal without a plan is just a wish.

    b. Goals are dreams with deadlines.

    c. Life is what happens to you while you're busy making other plans.

d. Inferiority and the quest for mastery are two sides of the same coin.

e. Success is not permanent. The same is also true of failure.

_____ 15. The lifestyle assessment includes information based on

a. the family constellation.

b. early recollections.

c. dreams.

d. mistaken, self-defeating perceptions.

e. all of the above.

_____ 16. Which is the correct sequence of human experiencing from an Adlerian perspective?

a. First we feel, then we think, then we act.

b. First we act, then we feel, then we think.

c. First we think, then we feel, then we act.

d. First we feel, then we act, then we think.

_____ 17. Adlerians could best be described as using which techniques?

a. They use strictly cognitive techniques.

b. They use emotive and behavioral techniques to get people to think.

c. They are bound by a clear set of therapeutic techniques.

d. They fit a variety of techniques to the needs of each client.

e. They have an aversion to using techniques because they see the therapeutic relationship alone as the healing factor.

_____ 18. How would the Adlerian therapist view the personal problems of clients?

a. as the result of cultural conditioning

b. as the end result of a process of discouragement

c. as living with problem-saturated stories

d. as the product of our innate tendencies toward self-destruction

_____ 19. Which of the following is **not** one of the four phases of the Adlerian therapeutic process?

a. establishing the proper therapeutic relationship

b. teaching the client the process of free association

c. conducting a comprehensive psychological assessment

d. encouraging the development of self-understanding

e. reorientation and reeducation

_____ 20. Which term does **not** fit Adlerian therapy?

a. holistic

b. social

c. teleological

d. deterministic

e. phenomenological

_____ 21. Which of the following does Adler **not** stress?

a. the unity of personality

b. biological and instinctual drives

c. direction in which people are headed

d. unique style of life that is an expression of life goals

e. feelings of inferiority

_____ 22. The phenomenological orientation pays attention to the

a. events that occur at various stages of life.

b. manner in which biological and environmental forces limit us.

c. way in which people interact with each other.

d. internal dynamics that drive a person.

e. way in which individuals perceive their world.

_____ 23. The concept of fictional finalism refers to

a. an imagined central goal that guides a person's behavior.

b. the hopeless stance that leads to personal defeat.

c. the manner in which people express their need to belong.

d. the process of assessing one's style of life.

e. the interpretation that individuals give to life events.

_____ 24. Adlerians consider which factor(s) to be influential in an individual's life?

a. psychological position in the family
b. birth order
c. interactions among siblings
d. parent–child relationships
e. all of the above

_____ 25. Adlerians value early recollections as an important clue to the understanding of

a. one's sexual and aggressive instincts.
b. the bonding process between mother and child.
c. the individual's lifestyle.
d. the unconscious dynamics that motivate behavior.
e. the origin of psychological trauma in early childhood.

Note: As regular practice, after completing these quizzes, retake the prechapter self-inventory. Each of the items in the self-inventory is true as applied to a given theory. It is useful to see if any of your ratings have changed after your study of the chapter.

Chapter 6

Existential Therapy

 PRECHAPTER SELF-INVENTORY

Directions: Refer to page 43 for general directions. Use the following code:

5 = I *strongly agree* with this statement.

4 = I *agree*, in most respects, with this statement.

3 = I am *undecided* in my opinion about this statement.

2 = I *disagree*, in most respects, with this statement.

1 = I *strongly disagree* with this statement.

_____ 1. A therapist has the job of challenging clients to discover ways that they are living a restricted existence.

_____ 2. The therapist's main task is to attempt to understand the subjective world of clients and help them come to new awareness and options.

_____ 3. One of the therapist's tasks is to encourage clients to develop the courage to face life squarely—by taking a stance, by making a decision, and by taking action.

_____ 4. Psychotherapy should be viewed as an approach to human relationships rather than as a set of techniques.

_____ 5. We are not victims of circumstance, but we are what we choose to become.

_____ 6. Regardless of past experiences, clients are challenged to take responsibility for how they are *now* choosing to be in their world.

_____ 7. Therapist authenticity and presence are crucial qualities in an effective therapeutic relationship.

_____ 8. The significance of our existence is never fixed once and for all; rather, we continue to re-create ourselves through our projects.

_____ 9. Responsibility is based on the capacity for awareness and self-reflection.

_____ 10. Freedom, self-determination, willingness, and decision making are qualities that form the very center of human existence.

_____ 11. The nature of freedom lies in the capacity to shape our own personal development by choosing among alternatives.

_____ 12. Even though there are limits to freedom (such as environment and genetic endowment), humans have the capacity to choose.

_____ 13. The major themes of psychotherapy are freedom and responsibility, isolation, alienation, death and its implications for living, and the continual search for meaning.

_____ 14. By refusing to give easy solutions or answers, therapists confront clients with the reality that they alone must find their own answers.

_____ 15. The failure to establish relatedness to others results in a condition marked by alienation, estrangement, and isolation.

_____ 16. Because there is no preordained design for living, people are faced with the task of creating their own meaning and purpose.

_____ 17. Guilt and anxiety do not necessarily need to be cured, for they are part of the human condition.

_____ 18. Anxiety can be the result of the person's awareness of his or her aloneness, finiteness, and responsibility for choosing.

_____ 19. The reality of death gives significance to living.

_____ 20. Therapists can help clients become less of a stranger to him- or herself by selectively disclosing their own responses at appropriate times.

OVERVIEW OF EXISTENTIAL THERAPY

Key Figures and Major Focus

Key figures in existential philosophy, which strives to define the nature of human existence, are Søren Kierkegaard, Friedrich Nietzsche, Martin Heidegger, Jean-Paul Sartre, Martin Buber, Ludwig Binswanger, and Medard Boss. Four prominent developers of existential psychotherapy are Viktor Frankl, Rollo May, Irvin Yalom, and James Bugental—all of whom developed their existential approaches to psychotherapy from strong backgrounds in both existential and humanistic psychology. In the United Kingdom, Emmy van Deurzen has made significant contributions to existential therapy through her writing and teaching. She founded the New School of Psychotherapy and Counselling, which focuses on training existential counselors. This approach examines the central concerns of the person's existence: death, freedom, existential isolation, and meaninglessness.

Philosophy and Basic Assumptions

Existential therapy reacts against the tendency to view therapy as a system of well-defined techniques; it affirms looking at those unique characteristics that make us human and building therapy on them. Existential therapy focuses on exploring themes such as mortality, meaning, choice, freedom, responsibility, self-determination, anxiety, and aloneness, as these relate to a person's current struggle.

The existential view of human nature is captured, in part, by the notion that the significance of our existence is never fixed once and for all; rather, we continually re-create ourselves through our projects. In essence, we are the authors of our lives. Thrust into a meaningless and absurd world, we are challenged to accept our aloneness and to create meaning in life. The awareness of our eventual nonbeing acts as a catalyst for finding meaning. Existential anxiety arises as we recognize the realities of our mortality, our confrontation with pain and suffering, our need to struggle for survival, and our basic fallibility. Existential anxiety is healthy and is a central part of the therapy process because anxiety can be used as a motivation to change. Anxiety arises from our awareness of freedom and responsibility.

Key Concepts

Existential therapy rests on six key propositions: (1) We have the capacity for self-awareness. (2) Because we are basically free beings, we must accept the responsibility that accompanies our freedom. (3) We have a concern to preserve our uniqueness and identity; we come to know ourselves in relation to knowing and interacting with others. (4) The significance of our existence and the meaning of our life are never fixed once and for all; instead, we re-create ourselves through our projects. (5) Anxiety is part of the human condition. (6) Death is also a basic human condition, and awareness of it gives significance to living. Clients in existential therapy are confronted with addressing ultimate concerns rather than coping with immediate problems. They are expected to put into action in daily life what they learn about themselves in therapy.

Therapeutic Goals

Existential therapy provides an invitation to clients to recognize the ways in which they are not living fully authentic lives and to make choices that will lead to their becoming what they are capable of being. The goal of existential therapy is to assist clients in their exploration of the existential "givens of life," how these are sometimes ignored or denied, and how addressing them can ultimately lead to a deeper, more reflective and meaningful existence. Rather than being concerned with solving problems of living, existential therapy is aimed toward removing roadblocks to meaningful living and helping clients assume responsibility for their actions. In existential therapy attention is given to clients' immediate, ongoing experience with the aim of helping them develop a greater presence in their quest for meaning and purpose. Some basic therapeutic goals are (1) to recognize factors that block freedom, (2) to challenge clients to recognize that they are doing something that they formerly thought was happening to them, (3) to widen clients' perspectives on choice, and (4) to accept the freedom and responsibility that go along with action.

Therapeutic Relationship

In existential therapy attention is given to the client's immediate, ongoing experience, especially what is going on in the interaction between the therapist and the client. The client–therapist relationship is of paramount importance because the quality of the I/Thou encounter offers a context for change. It is not the techniques a therapist uses that make a therapeutic difference; rather, it is the quality of the client–therapist relationship that heals. Instead of prizing therapeutic objectivity and professional distance, existential therapists value being fully present, and strive to create caring relationships with clients. Existential practitioners are willing to make themselves known through appropriate self-disclosure. Therapy is a collaborative relationship in which both client and therapist are involved in a journey of self-discovery.

Techniques and Procedures

The approach places primary emphasis on understanding the client's current experience, not on using techniques. Existential therapists are free to adapt their interventions to their own personality and style, and they pay attention to what each client requires. Therapists are *not* bound by any prescribed procedures and can use techniques from other schools. Interventions are used in the service of broadening the ways in which clients live in their world. Techniques are tools to help clients become aware of their choices and their potential for action. Therapists have a good deal of latitude in the methods they employ with a client at the different phases of the therapeutic process. Although existential practitioners may use techniques from other theoretical orientations, their interventions are guided by a philosophical framework about what it means to be human.

Applications

The approach is especially appropriate for those seeking personal growth. It can be useful for clients who are experiencing a developmental crisis (career or marital failure, retirement, grief work, transition from one stage of life to another). Clients experience anxiety rising out of existential conflicts, such as making key choices, accepting freedom and the responsibility that goes with it, struggling to find meaning in life, and facing the anxiety of their eventual death. These existential realities provide a rich therapeutic context.

As applied to *brief therapy,* the existential approach focuses on encouraging clients to examine issues such as assuming personal responsibility, expanding their awareness of their current situation, and making a commitment to deciding and acting. A time-limited framework can serve as a catalyst for clients to become maximally involved in their therapy sessions.

Existential group counseling requires an open attitude toward life and a willingness to explore unknown territory. Group members learn how others view them and how their behavior affects others. From what members learn about their interpersonal function in the group, they are able to take increased responsibility for making changes in their daily lives. Through an existential group, the participants can discover ways they may have lost their direction and can acquire more authentic ways of being.

Multicultural Perspectives

Because the existential approach is based on universal human themes, because it does not dictate a particular way of viewing reality, and because of its broad perspective, it is highly applicable in working in a multicultural context. Existential therapy is useful in working with culturally diverse clients because of its focus on universality, or the common ground that we all share. This approach emphasizes presence, the I/Thou relationship, and courage. As such, it can be effectively applied with diverse client populations with a range of specific problems and in a wide array of settings. For an approach to be labeled as existential, it is essential that the cultural, social, political, and ideological context be taken into account. Themes such as relationships, finding meaning, anxiety, suffering, and death are concerns that transcend the boundaries that separate cultures. Clients in existential therapy are encouraged to examine ways their present existence is being influenced by social and cultural factors. There is a great deal of international interest in the existential approach. The developments on the international scene indicate that existential therapy has wide appeal for diverse populations in many parts of the world.

Contributions

The essential humanity of the individual is highlighted. The person-to-person therapeutic relationship lessens the chances of dehumanizing therapy. The approach has something to offer counselors regardless of their theoretical orientation. It stresses self-determination, accepting the personal responsibility that accompanies freedom, and viewing oneself as the author of one's life. Further, it provides a perspective for understanding the value of anxiety and guilt, the role and meaning of death, and the creative aspects of being alone and choosing for oneself. The key concepts of the existential approach can be integrated into most of the other therapeutic orientations.

Limitations

The approach lacks a systematic statement of principles and practices of therapy. Many existential writers use vague and global terms or abstract concepts that are difficult to grasp. The model has not been subjected to scientific research as a way of validating its procedures. For those who value evidence-based practice, the existential approach has major limitations. In spite of the popularity of manualized therapy, existential therapy is based on the notion that every psychotherapy experience is unique, and thus this approach does not lend itself to matching techniques for specific problems. Existential therapy has limited applicability to lower-functioning clients, clients in extreme crisis who need direction, clients who are mostly concerned about meeting basic needs, and those who lack verbal skills.

GLOSSARY OF KEY TERMS

Angst   A Danish and German word whose meaning lies between the English words *dread* and *anxiety*. This term refers to the uncertainty in life and the role of anxiety in making decisions about how we want to live.

Anxiety   A condition that results from having to face choices without clear guidelines and without knowing what the outcome will be.

Authenticity   The process of creating, discovering, or maintaining the core deep within one's being; the process of becoming the person one is capable of becoming.

Existential analysis (dasein analyse)   The emphasis of this therapy approach is on the subjective and spiritual dimensions of human existence.

Existential anxiety   An outcome of being confronted with the four givens of existence: death, freedom, existential isolation, and meaninglessness.

Existential guilt   The result of, or the consciousness of, evading the commitment to choosing for ourselves.

Existential neurosis   Feelings of despair and anxiety that result from inauthentic living, a failure to make choices, and avoidance of responsibility.

Existential tradition   Seeks a balance between recognizing the limits and the tragic dimensions of human existence and the possibilities and opportunities of human life.

Existential vacuum   A condition of emptiness and hollowness that results from meaninglessness in life.

Existentialism   A philosophical movement stressing individual responsibility for creating one's ways of thinking, feeling, and behaving.

Freedom   An inescapable aspect of the human condition; we are the authors of our lives and therefore are responsible for our destiny and accountable for our actions.

"Givens of existence"   Core or universal themes in the therapeutic process: death, freedom, existential isolation, and meaninglessness.

Inauthenticity   Lacking awareness of personal responsibility and passively assuming that our existence is largely controlled by external forces.

Intersubjectivity   The fact of our interrelatedness with others and the need for us to struggle with this in a creative way.

Logotherapy   Developed by Frankl, this brand of existential therapy literally means "healing through reason." It focuses on challenging clients to search for meaning in life.

Neurotic anxiety   A response out of proportion to the situation. It is typically out of awareness and tends to immobilize the person.

Normal anxiety   An appropriate response to an event being faced.

Phenomenology   A method of exploration that uses subjective human experiencing as its focus. The phenomenological approach is a part of the fabric of existentially oriented therapies, Adlerian therapy, person-centered therapy, Gestalt therapy, and reality therapy.

Presence   Both a condition and goal of therapeutic change, which serves the dual functions of reconnecting people to their pain and attuning them to the opportunities to transform their pain.

Resistance   From an existential-humanistic perspective, resistance manifests as a failure to be fully present both during the therapy hour and in life.

Restricted existence   A state of functioning with a limited degree of awareness of oneself and being vague about the nature of one's problems.

Self-awareness   The capacity for consciousness that enables us to make choices.

QUESTIONS FOR REFLECTION AND DISCUSSION

1. What does personal freedom mean to you? Do you believe you are what you are now largely as a result of your choices, or do you believe you are the product of your circumstances?

2. As you reflect on some critical turning points in your life, what decisions appear to have been crucial to your present development?

3. Are you able to accept and exercise your own freedom and make significant decisions alone? Do you attempt to avoid living with freedom and responsibility? Are you inclined to give up some of your autonomy for the security of being taken care of by others?

4. Do you agree that each person is basically alone? What are the implications for counseling practice? In what ways might you have attempted to avoid your experience of aloneness? How has this concept been a source of strength for you?

5. What is your experience with anxiety? Does your anxiety result from the consideration that you must choose for yourself, the realization that you are alone, the fact that you will die, and the realization that you must create your own meaning and purpose in life? How have you dealt with anxiety in your own life?

6. To what extent do you believe that unless you take death seriously life has little meaning? What are the implications of this notion for the practice of therapy?

7. What specific things do you value most? What would your life be like without them? What gives your life meaning and a sense of purpose?

8. Have you experienced an "existential vacuum"? Is your life at times without substance, depth, and meaning? What is this experience of emptiness like for you, and how do you cope with it?

9. What are your reactions to the existential view of the importance of the client–therapist relationship? What strengths do you see in this view of the therapeutic relationship? To what degree are you open to challenging and changing your own life?

10. If you were working with a culturally diverse client population in a community agency, what existential concepts might you draw from, if any? What do you see as the major strengths and limitations of the existential approach as it is applied to multicultural counseling?

 ## SUGGESTED ACTIVITIES AND EXERCISES

Ways of Being "Dead" but Still Existing

In counseling situations I find it useful to ask people to examine parts of themselves that they feel are "dead." In what ways are you dead? How do you prevent yourself from experiencing life? What would happen if you chose to live fully instead of settling for your half-life/half-death existence?

Directions: As you read these comments that express some ways in which clients may choose "death" over "life," reflect on these questions: "How fully alive do I feel? When do I feel most alive? Least alive? What parts within me are 'dead' or 'dying'? What would it take for me to experience a new surge of vitality in these areas?" Then discuss in class, either in small groups or in dyads, the degree to which you feel fully alive. Also, share how the reality of death can give life a sense of meaning.

1. "I consistently choose to remain safe by avoiding any risks."
2. "I'll cut off all my feelings—that way I won't hurt. I've become a good computer, and I'll never experience pain."
3. "I'm dead, hollow, empty, with nothing inside. I can't find any real purpose for living. I just exist and wait for each day to pass."
4. "I live in isolation from people. I don't want to get close, so I keep myself distant from everyone."

Now list some possible ways in which parts of *you* are not fully "alive":

1. _____
2. _____
3. _____
4. _____

Will We Really Change?

According to the existentialists, the best means of understanding individuals is watching their striving for the future. Because humans are always emerging and becoming, the future is the dominant mode of time for them. People can be understood as they project themselves forward.

One intervention I have often used in group situations is to ask each person to imagine his or her life as he or she would like it to be. I have asked questions such as "What future do you want for yourself? What do you want to be able to say about yourself in relation to the significant people in your life? What would you like to have inscribed on your tombstone? What are you doing now, or what can you do now to make your vision a reality?" A look into the future can be a stimulus for people to see choices they have made and the ways in which they can create and shape their own future. In some real ways they can be the architects of their future life.

Directions: Write down a brief response to each of these questions. Then discuss your answers in class, either in small groups or in dyads.

1. What do you think your future will be like if you stay very much as you are now? Complete the following statement: If I make no major changes, then I expect _____
   _____
   _____

2. List some things, situations, or people that you see as preventing your change or as making your change difficult. _____
   _____

3. If you could make *one* significant change in your personality or behavior *now*, what would it be? _____
   _____

4. What do you see that you can do *now* to make that one change? _____
   _____

5. Write your own epitaph. _____
   _____

 # JERRY COREY COUNSELS STAN FROM AN EXISTENTIAL PERSPECTIVE

Session 4. Existential Therapy Applied to the Case of Stan

This session deals mainly with Stan exploring his anxiety around death, and he talks about the meaning of his life. The catalyst was Stan's father being hospitalized, which got Stan to wondering about the shortness of life. This situation led to anxiety on Stan's part over death and the purpose of his life.

Before viewing the session, read Chapter 6, pages 162–163 in the textbook and answer the questions under the heading "Follow-Up: You Continue as Stan's Existential Therapist." After reflecting on these questions, view the session. If you have been studying Stan up to this point, it is clear that he struggles with being his authentic self and building authentic relationships. What do you think are key factors that contribute to Stan's difficulties with authenticity? Which of the existential propositions (see the textbook) do you think are most pronounced in Stan's life? If you were his existential therapist, which of these themes would you target in therapy?

As you watch this counseling session, pay close attention to the relationship between Stan and the therapist. What do you notice? What do you see Jerry doing to develop a relationship with Stan? After viewing the session, discuss these questions:

1. What would you say to Stan when he brings up the matter of how he nearly lost his father and that Stan was concerned that his father would not live to see him become successful?

2. How can exploring Stan's fears about dying be a catalyst for Stan to make significant changes in his life?

3. In Stan's case, how are the themes of the reality of death and the meaning of life related?

4. What are you inclined to say to Stan when he says, "I'm 35 and I wonder what I have done with my life so far?"

5. To what extent do you agree with the notion that the reality of death jars us into taking the present moment seriously?

6. Stan tends to be hard on himself and is very critical of himself in most areas of his life. What thoughts do you have of how you might work with Stan on this?

7. Stan says that he would like to matter and wants to make a difference? What would you say to him at this point?

8. There are few techniques in existential therapy. How would this be for you in your work with Stan?

9. At this point, what do you imagine is the most challenging aspect of being Stan's therapist?

10. The therapist (Jerry) suggests that Stan write a letter to his father in his journal, but not mail this letter. If you were Stan's therapist, how would you follow up on this assignment?

A Suggested In-Class Activity

Form small groups and discuss your reactions to both the section in the text on existential therapy with Stan and the video counseling session with Stan. Again, your discussion could address your reactions to both Stan and to me as his therapist. What shifts did you notice in Stan's demeanor during this session? What ideas would you have wanted to encourage Stan to explore more fully if time permitted? In your small groups a good topic for discussion is how you could apply some of the key existential themes in this chapter to your counseling with Stan.

Also, consider exploring in your small groups these questions:

1. What did you find most interesting in this session? Why?

2. If you were counseling Stan from this particular theoretical framework, what is one additional technique you might use? What would you hope to accomplish with this intervention?

3. If you were the client, how would you be likely to respond to the therapist's (Jerry's) comments and interventions in this particular session?

This would be a good time to demonstrate ways of applying this approach by having one student role play Stan, another the counselor, and another be the process observer. After a few minutes of working in your group, spend some time talking with each other about what you learned from this exercise.

JERRY COREY'S WORK WITH RUTH FROM AN EXISTENTIAL PERSPECTIVE

Ruth states that her therapy is causing problems for her in her life. She even considered not coming to the session. She expresses her resistance about continuing with her therapy. I see it as important that she explore the meaning of her resistance. I am hopeful that she can share her doubts, and I encourage her to talk about her reservations and anxieties.

One of my aims is to show Ruth the connection between the choices she is making or failing to make and the anxiety she is experiencing. I do this by asking her to observe herself in various situations throughout the week. For instance, when does she put her own needs last and choose to be the giver to others? Through this self-observation process, Ruth gradually sees some specific ways in which her choices are directly contributing to her anxiety.

My goal in working with Ruth is not to eliminate her anxiety; rather, it is to help her understand what it means. Anxiety might well be a signal that she is ready for change. She is learning that how she deals with her anxiety will have a lot to do with the type of new identity she creates.

Perhaps the critical aspect of Ruth's therapy is her recognition that she has a choice to make. She can continue to cling to the known and the familiar, or she can recognize that in life there are no guarantees. Ruth can learn to accept the uncertainty and anxiety in her life and still act, making choices and then living with the consequences.

You Continue Working With Ruth From an Existential Perspective

1. Refer to *Case Approach to Counseling and Psychotherapy* (Chapter 4) for an illustration of how an existential therapist (Dr. Michael Russell) counsels Ruth. In this chapter I also demonstrate my style of counseling Ruth from an existential perspective.

2. See the *DVD for Integrative Counseling: The Case of Ruth and Lecturettes* (Session 7 on an emotive focus, and Session 5 on understanding and working with resistance session) for a demonstration of exploring existential themes in Ruth's life.

3. Part of the work of the existential counselor is to help clients make critical choices. How would you work with Ruth if she expresses to you that she has little confidence in her capacity to make wise choices?

4. How might you deal with Ruth when she informs you that she is thinking about quitting therapy because of her anxiety that those in her family will be threatened by her changes?

5. Ruth tells you that she is thinking of quitting therapy because of the negative reactions from her family. What are you inclined to say to her? How would you work with this possibility?

A CASE FROM AN EXISTENTIAL PERSPECTIVE

Mahvesh: "Caught Between Two Worlds"
By **David N. Elkins,** PhD, Professor Emeritus, Graduate School of Education and Psychology, Pepperdine University

Background Information

Mahvesh is a 22-year-old Iranian-American female who came to the United States with her parents when she was three. Mahvesh, who attended public schools and is now a senior in college, describes herself as "very American." Her parents, however, hold many of the cultural values with which they grew up in their small village in Iran. Mahvesh says she often feels "caught between two worlds" as she attempts to honor her parents' traditions while also trying to live her own life.

Recently, this struggle intensified and Mahvesh entered therapy. She told her therapist, "My parents want me to marry a man from their village in Iran, a man that I hardly know, but I am in love with a man I met in college. We have been dating for more than a year and I want to marry him. When I try to talk with my parents, my father becomes angry and says that I do not respect him. My mother is more understanding but basically agrees with my father. I try to tell them that arranged marriages are rare even in Iran today but my parents grew up in a rural area and hold a lot of conservative ideas. I love my parents but I want to make my own decisions, especially about the man I marry."

Dr. Dave Elkins' Way of Working With Mahvesh as an Existential Therapist

This case illustrates several of the concepts in Jerry's chapter on existential therapy. For example, it highlights the existential theme of taking responsibility for one's own life and, at the same time, shows how difficult this can be. Mahvesh *wants* to take responsibility for her life but she also loves her parents and does not want to alienate them. Mahvesh wants to be her authentic self—another existential theme—but the self is not created in isolation. It is created in the context of family, culture, and history. There are no "techniques" that the therapist can use to solve Mahvesh's problem. No therapist, regardless how competent, can tell her what she should do. Mahvesh must arrive at her own decisions and give her own answers to such existential questions as: "Who am I, really?" and "How shall I live my life?" Whatever decision she makes and whatever action she takes will affect her life for years to come.

As an existential therapist, I would begin simply by listening to Mahvesh—deeply and empathically, using what some existential therapists call the "phenomenological method." This method of listening requires the therapist to set aside his or her own ideas, as far as possible, and to enter into the subjective (or phenomenological) world of the client. This is a type of "deep empathy," with the aim of understanding how the client sees and experiences the world. Mahvesh is not just another case to be treated with a generic set of techniques. She is a complex human being with a unique inner world and before I can possibly be of help to her, I must understand who she is, how she views herself, others, and the world. So the first step in existential therapy—a step that lays the foundation for everything else—is to listen and try to understand. Empathic understanding of Mahvesh's subjective world will not only help me to work more effectively with her but it will also, in all probability, have a healing effect within itself. Research has confirmed again and again that empathy is one of the most powerful ingredients in therapeutic healing.

As an existential therapist, however, I would go further. I would encourage Mahvesh to explore the various aspects of her dilemma and, in time, to make a decision and take action. I would encourage her to clarify the steps she needs to take to address her dilemma. For example, does she know anyone in her extended family who has gone through a similar conflict and if so, would it be helpful for her to talk with that person? Is there a trusted religious leader, or some other respected person in the Iranian-American community, with whom she and her parents could discuss her situation? Would Mahvesh's parents be willing to come to therapy at some point to have a family session focused on these issues? What would happen if Mahvesh wrote a heartfelt letter to her parents, telling them how much she loves them and how much she values her heritage but how, at the same time, she needs to make her own decision about the man she will marry? What are Mahvesh's worst fears if she were to follow her parents' wishes and marry the man they have chosen for her? Conversely, what are her worst fears if she were to go against her parents' wishes to marry the man she loves? These are the types of questions and issues that I would encourage Mahvesh to explore in therapy. I would not *impose* topics on her and much of the therapy would consist of my following her lead and listening to what she wanted to talk about. At the same time, I would not hesitate to *suggest* topics to explore, allowing her to decide whether or not she wished to "go there." By exploring all aspects of her situation in therapy, by talking with others who might understand her situation, by enlisting the help of a respected leader in the Iranian-American community, and by involving her parents in the therapy if possible, Mahvesh is more likely to make the best decision possible and to be more fully aware of the consequences when she does so.

Follow-Up: You Continue as Mahvesh's Existential Therapist

1. Is it possible for a therapist to understand the subjective world of another person if the two come from very different family, cultural, and ethnic backgrounds? If your own background is different from Mahvesh's, do you think you could enter her subjective world and understand how she feels? How would you respond if Mahvesh said, "I don't see how you can really understand what I'm going through. You don't know much about the Iranian culture and I'm worried that you won't be able to understand my situation"?

2. The existential approach emphasizes the importance of making decisions, taking action, and creating one's own life. Do you think these concepts are viable in all cultures or do they reflect a Western bias? For example, would these ideas be viable in a collective culture where there is less emphasis on individuality and more emphasis on one's place in the larger community? Do you think these existential concepts are relevant to Mahvesh's situation? Why or why not?

3. Suppose Mahvesh ultimately decides to go against her parents' wishes and becomes engaged to the man she has been dating. What role, if any, might therapy play in her life after she makes such a decision?

 QUIZ ON EXISTENTIAL THERAPY

A Comprehension Check

Score _____%

Note: Refer to Appendix 1 for the scoring key.

True/false items: Decide if the following statements are "more true" or "more false" as they apply to existential therapy.

T F   1. The key concepts of the existential approach can be integrated into most therapeutic approaches.

T F   2. Existential therapists show wide latitude in the techniques they employ.

T F   3. According to Sartre, existential guilt is the consciousness of evading commitment to choose for ourselves.

T F   4. Existentialists maintain that our experience of aloneness is a result of our making inappropriate choices.

T F   5. Techniques are secondary in the therapeutic process, and a subjective understanding of the client is primary.

T F   6. To its credit, existential therapy is compatible with the trend toward evidence-based practice.

T F   7. Part of the human condition is that humans are both free and responsible.

T F   8. Anxiety is best considered as a neurotic manifestation; thus, the principal aim of therapy is to eliminate anxiety.

T F   9. Emmy van Deurzen has made significant contributions to the development of existential therapy in the United Kingdom through her writing and teaching.

T F 10. The existential approach is a reaction against *both* psychoanalysis and behaviorism.

Multiple-choice items: Select the *one best answer* of those alternatives given. Consider each question within the framework of existential therapy.

_____ 11. Who is the person who developed logotherapy?

a. Emmy van Deurzen

b. Rollo May

c. Irvin Yalom

d. James Bugental

e. Victor Frankl

_____ 12. Which is *not* a key concept of existential therapy?

a. It is based on a personal relationship between client and therapist.

b. It stresses personal freedom in deciding one's fate.

c. It places primary value on self-awareness.

d. It is based on a well-defined set of techniques and procedures.

_____ 13. One function of the existential therapist is to

a. develop a specific treatment plan that can be objectively appraised.

b. challenge the client's irrational beliefs.

c. understand the client's subjective world.

d. explore the client's past history in detail.

e. assist the client in working through transference.

_____ 14. According to the existential view, anxiety is a

a. result of repressed sexuality.

b. part of the human condition.

c. neurotic symptom that needs to be cured.

d. result of faulty learning.

_____ 15. Resistance is seen as part of _____: how a person understands his or her being and relationship to the world at large.

a. the existential vacuum

b. authenticity

c. the world-at-large concept

d. social interest

e. the self-and-world construct

_____ 16. What is the most crucial quality of a therapist in building an effective therapeutic relationship with a client?

a. the therapist's knowledge of theory

b. the therapist's skill in using techniques

c. the therapist's ability to diagnose accurately

d. the therapist's authenticity

e. the therapist's application of evidence-based practices

_____ 17. Who is the person who was the main American spokesperson of European existential thinking as it is applied to psychotherapy?

a. Rollo May

b. Erik Erikson

c. Rudolf Dreikurs

d. Carl Jung

_____ 18. Guilt and anxiety are viewed by existential therapists as

a. behaviors that are unrealistic.

b. the result of traumatic situations in childhood.

c. conditions that should be removed or cured.

d. all of the above.

e. none of the above.

_____ 19. The existential approach is based on

a. specific behaviors that can be assessed.

b. a scientific orientation.

c. a teaching–learning model that stresses the didactic aspects of therapy.

d. the philosophical concern with what it means to be fully human.

e. a manualized approach to treatment.

_____ 20. Existential therapy is basically

a. a behavioral approach.

b. a cognitive approach.

c. an experiential and relational approach.

d. an evidence-based approach.

e. a recent development of the psychoanalytic model.

_____ 21. Existential therapy places emphasis on

a. finding solutions to well-defined problems.

b. the quality of the client–therapist relationship.

c. teaching clients cognitive and behavioral coping skills.

d. uncovering early childhood traumatic events.

e. working through unconscious conflicts.

_____ 22. The central theme running through the works of Viktor Frankl is

a. that freedom is a myth.

b. the will to meaning.

c. overcoming our inferiority complex through striving for superiority.

d. the importance of understanding one's family of origin.

e. being thrown into the universe without purpose.

_____ 23. The existential therapist would probably agree that

a. aloneness is a sign of detachment.

b. aloneness is a condition that needs to be cured.

c. ultimately we are alone.

d. we are alone unless we have a religious faith.

e. we are alone if we are not loved by others.

_____ 24. The existential "givens of life" include all of the following except

a. death.

b. taxes.

c. freedom.

d. existential isolation.

e. meaninglessness.

_____ 25. Which of the following is a limitation of the existential approach in working with culturally diverse client populations?

a. the focus on understanding and accepting the client

b. the focus on finding meaning in one's life

c. the focus on death as a catalyst to living fully

d. the focus on one's own responsibility rather than on changing social conditions

e. the focus on the I/Thou relationship

Chapter 7

Person-Centered Therapy

PRECHAPTER SELF-INVENTORY

Directions: Refer to page 43 for general directions. Use the following codes:

5 = I *strongly agree* with this statement.

4 = I *agree*, in most respects, with this statement.

3 = I am *undecided* in my opinion about this statement.

2 = I *disagree*, in most respects, with this statement.

1 = I *strongly disagree* with this statement.

_____ 1. Therapists provide a supportive structure in which clients' self-healing capacities are activated, but clients are the primary agents of change.

_____ 2. People have the capacity for understanding their problems and the resources for resolving them.

_____ 3. The basic goal of therapy is to create a psychological climate of safety in which clients will not feel threatened and will be able to drop their pretenses and defenses.

_____ 4. The therapist's function is rooted not primarily in techniques but in his or her ways of being and attitudes.

_____ 5. Effective therapists use themselves as instruments of change.

_____ 6. The client uses the therapeutic relationship to build new ways of relating to others in the outside world.

_____ 7. The client can make progress in therapy without the therapist's interpretations, diagnoses, evaluations, and directives.

_____ 8. The relationship between the therapist and the client is the crux of progress in therapy.

_____ 9. The therapist's genuineness, accurate empathy, and unconditional positive regard are essential qualities of effective therapy.

_____ 10. It is the therapist's attitudes and belief in the inner resources of the client that create the therapeutic climate for growth.

_____ 11. Forming a diagnosis and developing a case history are not important prerequisites for therapy.

_____ 12. It is important that the therapist avoid being judgmental about a client's feelings.

_____ 13. The therapist's presence is far more powerful than techniques he or she uses to bring about change.

_____ 14. It is important that the therapist, while experiencing empathy with clients, retain his or her own separateness and not get lost in the client's world.

_____ 15. Therapist congruence, or genuineness, is one of the most important conditions for establishing a therapeutic relationship.

_____ 16. It is best that therapists avoid giving advice.

_____ 17. Skills can be taught, but an effective therapist must be grounded, centered, present, focused, patient, and accepting.

_____ 18. Communicating a deep sense of understanding should always precede problem-solving interventions.

_____ 19. The primary responsibility for the direction of therapy rests not with the therapist but with the client.

_____ 20. Exploring transference is neither essential nor significant in the therapeutic process.

OVERVIEW OF PERSON-CENTERED THERAPY

Key Figure and Major Focus

Founder: Carl Rogers. Key figure: Natalie Rogers. A branch of humanistic psychology that stresses a phenomenological approach, person-centered therapy was originally developed in the 1940s as a reaction against psychoanalytic therapy. Based on a subjective view of human experience, it emphasizes the client's resources for becoming self-aware and for resolving blocks to personal growth. It puts the client, not the therapist, at the center of therapy. Carl Rogers did not present his approach as being fixed and completed; rather, he expected the theory and practice to evolve over time. One way this theory has been expanded is through the work of Natalie Rogers, who has developed person-centered expressive arts therapy, in which the expressive arts are used in self-discovery, healing, and growth.

Philosophy and Basic Assumptions

The approach is grounded on a positive view of humanity that sees the person as innately striving toward becoming fully functioning. The basic assumption is that it is the therapist's attitudes and belief in the inner resources of the client that create the therapeutic climate for growth. By participating in the therapeutic relationship, clients' self-healing capacities are activated and they become empowered. Clients actualize their potential for growth, wholeness, spontaneity, and inner-directedness. It is not the therapist who primarily brings about change, but the client. The main source of successful psychotherapy is the client. The therapist's attention to the client's frame of reference fosters the client's utilization of inner and outer resources.

Key Concepts

A key concept is that clients have the resourcefulness for positive movement. The client has the capacity for resolving life's problems effectively without interpretation and direction from an expert therapist. This approach emphasizes fully experiencing the present moment, learning to accept oneself, and deciding on ways to change. More than the therapist or technique, it is the client who makes therapy work. What clients value most is being understood and accepted, which results in the creation of a safe place to explore feelings, thoughts, behaviors, and experiences. This approach views mental health as a congruence between what one wants to become and what one actually is.

Therapeutic Goals

A major goal is to provide a climate of safety and trust in the therapeutic setting so that the client, by using the therapeutic relationship for self-exploration, can become aware of blocks to growth. The client tends to move toward more openness, greater self-trust, more willingness to evolve as opposed to being a fixed product, and a tendency to live by internal standards as opposed to taking external cues for what he or she should become. The aim of therapy is not merely to solve problems but to assist in the growth process, which will enable the client to better cope with present and future problems. Person-centered therapists are in agreement on the matter of not setting goals for *what* clients need to change, yet they differ on the matter of *how* to best help clients achieve their own goals.

Therapeutic Relationship

Rogers emphasizes the attitudes and personal characteristics of the therapist and the quality of the client–therapist relationship as the prime determinants of the outcomes of therapy. The qualities of the therapist that determine the relationship include genuineness, nonpossessive warmth, accurate empathy, unconditional acceptance of and respect for the client, caring, and the communication of those attitudes to the client. These core characteristics are deemed both *necessary and sufficient* for therapeutic change to occur. Research has revealed that effective therapy is based on the relationship of the therapist and client in combination with the inner and external resources of the client. The client is able to translate his or her learning in therapy to outside relationships with others.

Techniques and Procedures

Like the existential approach, the person-centered approach stresses the client–therapist relationship, and techniques are secondary to the therapist's attitudes. The approach minimizes directive techniques, interpretation, questioning, probing, diagnosis, and collecting history. It maximizes active listening and hearing, empathic understanding, presence, reflection of feelings, and clarification. The full participation of the therapist as a person in the therapeutic relationship is currently being emphasized. The therapist strives to accurately understand the subjective world of the client; the focus of therapy is on clients' perceptions of reality.

Applications

The approach has wide applicability to many person-to-person situations. It is a useful model for individual therapy, group counseling, student-centered teaching and learning, parent–child relations, and human-relations-training labs. The approach has been effectively applied to a wide range of client problems including anxiety disorders, alcoholism, psychosomatic problems, agoraphobia, interpersonal difficulties, depression, cancer, and personality disorders. It is especially well suited for the initial phases of crisis intervention work. Its principles have been applied to administration and management and to working with systems and institutions.

Natalie Rogers has made a significant contribution to the application of the person-centered approach by incorporating the expressive arts as a medium to facilitate personal exploration, often in a group context. *Person-centered expressive arts therapy* uses various artistic forms—movement, drawing, painting, sculpting, music, writing, and improvisation—toward the end of growth, healing, and self-discovery. This is a multimodal approach integrating mind, body, emotions, and spiritual inner resources. This approach represents an alternative to traditional methods of counseling that rely on verbal means and often have particular applications for clients who rely heavily on cognitive ways of experiencing. Individuals who have difficulty expressing themselves verbally can find new possibilities for self-expression through the various nonverbal forms of expression available to them.

Group counseling from a person-centered perspective assumes that significant movement will occur within a group if the therapeutic core conditions are present. Regardless of a group counselor's theoretical orientation, establishing safety, acceptance, and trust are essential. This approach highlights the importance of the quality of therapeutic relationships among the members and between the facilitator and the members. When a healing climate is established, group members learn how to interact in honest and meaningful ways, and they move toward self-direction and empowerment.

Multicultural Perspectives

The emphasis on the core conditions makes the person-centered approach useful in understanding diverse worldviews. The underlying philosophy of person-centered therapy is grounded on the importance of hearing the deeper messages of an individual. Empathy, being present, and respecting the values of clients are essential attitudes and skills in counseling culturally diverse clients. The concepts of this approach have value in working within a multicultural context because the core therapeutic conditions are universal, regardless of an individual's cultural background. Person-centered counselors convey a deep respect for all forms of diversity; they value understanding the client's phenomenological world in an interested, accepting, and open way. This approach has been applied to bringing people from diverse cultures together.

Contributions

One of the first therapies to break from traditional psychoanalysis, person-centered therapy stresses the active role and responsibility of the client. It is a positive and optimistic view and calls attention to the need to account for a person's inner and subjective experiences. It makes the therapeutic process relationship-centered rather than technique-centered. It focuses on the crucial role of the therapist's attitudes. The model has generated a great deal of clinical research into both the process and the outcomes of therapy, which in turn has led to refining the tentative hypotheses.

Limitations

A possible danger is the therapist who, by merely reflecting content, brings little of his or her personhood into the therapeutic relationship. The core conditions are centered more in the therapist's attitudes and values than in the therapist's skills. Without a person-centered attitude or way of being, mere application of skills is not likely to be effective. The approach has limited use with nonverbal clients, and it tends to discount the significance of the past. Some of the main limitations are due not to the theory itself, but to some counselors' misunderstanding of the basic concepts and to their dogmatic practical applications. For those who value accountability within the framework of evidence-based practice, this approach is limited due to the lack of attention on using empirically proven techniques for specific problems.

 GLOSSARY OF KEY TERMS

Accurate empathic understanding   The act of perceiving accurately the internal frame of reference of another; the ability to grasp the person's subjective world without losing one's own identity.

Actualizing tendency   A growth force within us; a directional process of striving toward self-regulation, self-determination, realization, fulfillment, perfection, and inner freedom; the basis on which people can be trusted to identify and resolve their own problems in a therapeutic relationship.

Congruence   The state in which self-experiences are accurately symbolized in the self-concept. As applied to the therapist, congruence is matching one's inner experiencing with external expressions; congruence is a quality of realness or genuineness of the therapist.

Emotion-focused therapy   Rooted in a person-centered philosophy, EFT is integrative in that it synthesizes aspects of Gestalt therapy and existential therapy. Strategies used in EFT are aimed at strengthening the self, regulating affect, and creating new meaning.

Empathy   A deep and subjective understanding of the client *with* the client.

Expressive arts therapy   An approach that makes use of various arts—such as movement, drawing, painting, sculpting, music, and improvisation—in a supportive setting for the purpose of growth and healing.

Hierarchy of needs   We are able to strive toward self-actualization only after these four basic needs are met: physiological, safety, love, and esteem.

Humanistic psychology   A movement, often referred to as the "third force," that emphasizes freedom, choice, values, growth, self-actualization, becoming, spontaneity, creativity, play, humor, peak experiences, and psychological health.

Immediacy   Addressing what is going on between the client and therapist right now.

Motivational Interviewing (MI)   A humanistic, client-centered, psychosocial, directive counseling approach that was developed by William R. Miller and Stephen Rollnick in the early 1980s.

Positive psychology   A movement that has come into prominence, which shares many concepts on the healthy side of human existence with the humanistic approach.

Presence   The ability to "be with" someone fully in the present moment; being engaged and absorbed in the relationship with the client.

Self-actualization   The central theme of the work of Abraham Maslow. His theory of self-actualization is postulated on a hierarchy of needs as a source of motivation.

Stages of change   People are assumed to progress through a series of five identifiable stages of motivation and readiness to change in the counseling process. They include the precontemplation stage, the contemplation stage, the preparation stage, the action stage, and the maintenance stage.

The MI spirit   It is essential that therapists function within the spirit of MI, rather than simply applying the strategies of the approach. The attitudes and skills in MI are based on a person-centered philosophy.

Therapeutic core conditions   The necessary and sufficient characteristics of the therapeutic relationship for client change to occur. These core conditions include therapist congruence (or genuineness), unconditional positive regard (acceptance and respect), and accurate empathic understanding.

"Third force" in therapy   An alternative to psychoanalytic and behavioral approaches; under this heading are the experiential and relationship-oriented therapies (existential therapy, person-centered therapy, and Gestalt therapy).

Unconditional positive regard   The nonjudgmental expression of fundamental respect for the person as a human; acceptance of a person's right to his or her feelings.

QUESTIONS FOR REFLECTION AND DISCUSSION

1. Do you believe most clients have the capacity to understand and resolve their own problems without directive intervention by the therapist? Why or why not?

2. The person-centered view of human nature is grounded on the assumption that people have the tendency to develop in a positive and constructive manner *if* a climate of respect and trust is established. To what degree do you accept this premise?

3. A person-centered approach stresses listening to the deeper meanings of the client's behavior and allowing the client to provide the direction for the session. Are there any

circumstances under which you might want to interpret the meaning of your client's behavior? Can you think of any situations in which you might actively intervene by making suggestions or leading your client?

4. In counseling clients who have a different cultural background from yours, what potential advantages or disadvantages can you see in adopting a person-centered perspective?

5. Regardless of which approach guides your practice, the core therapeutic conditions and the type of relationship emphasized in the person-centered approach seem to serve as the foundation for counseling. What are the basic concepts of this theory that you might consider incorporating into your personal style of counseling?

6. What aspects of motivational interviewing seem similar to person-centered therapy? What are some ways that motivational interviewing is different from the traditional person-centered approach?

7. In making interventions with clients, it is essential to consider their readiness for change. What ideas can you take from the stages of change model in working with reluctance and ambivalence within clients?

8. What factors might interfere with your being genuine with a client? What about your need for the client's approval? Is there a danger that you might avoid a confrontation because you wanted to be liked?

9. What would make it difficult for you to convey accurate empathic understanding for a client? Do you have broad life experiences that will help you identify with your client's struggles?

10. What do you think it would be like for you to be a participant in a person-centered expressive arts group? How would it be different for you to express yourself through various art forms such as movement, drawing, painting, sculpting, and music rather than verbally? What advantages and disadvantages do you see in expressive arts therapy versus traditional talk therapies?

PRACTICAL APPLICATION: REFLECTING CLIENTS' FEELINGS

Directions: The person-centered approach to counseling emphasizes understanding clients from an internal frame of reference. To do that, the therapist must be able to discriminate clients' feelings, hear accurately what messages they are sending, and reflect the deeper meanings that they are attempting to communicate. A common mistake that counselors make is to give a superficial reflection by merely repeating almost the same words the client used. The following exercises are designed to help you learn to grasp the more subtle messages of clients and to reflect feelings as well as content. Of course, important nonverbal cues such as tone of voice and facial expressions are not captured in this exercise. Such nonverbal aspects would be most useful in understanding a client's message. First, write down a few key words or phrases that describe what the client is *experiencing*. Second, write down what your response would be if you were to *reflect* to the client what you heard.

Example: Woman, 42, tells you: "So often I feel that I'm alone, that nobody cares about me. My husband doesn't seem to notice me, my kids only demand from me, and I just dread getting up in the morning."

a. What is this person experiencing? *Ignored. Unappreciated. Taken advantage of. Unloved. A sense of futility.*

b. Respond by reflecting what you heard. *I sense a lot of loneliness and desperation, a feeling of "What's the use of going on this way?"*

1. Boy, 17, tells you: "I can't stand this school anymore. It doesn't mean anything. I'm bored and frustrated, and I hate school. I feel like dropping out today, but that's stupid because I'm graduating in 2 months."

   a. What is this person experiencing? _____
   _____

   b. Respond by reflecting what you heard. _____
   _____

2. Girl, 14, tells you: "I feel like running away from home. My stepfather always criticizes me, and he puts me on restriction for things he claims I do that I don't do. My mother doesn't ever listen to me and always sides with him. They don't trust me at all."

   a. What is this person experiencing? _____
   _____

   b. Respond by reflecting what you heard. _____
   _____

3. A fifth-grader tells you: "None of the other kids like me. They always pick on me and tease me. I try real hard to make friends, but everyone hates me."

   a. What is this person experiencing? _____
   _____

   b. Respond by reflecting what you heard. _____
   _____

4. Woman teacher, 33, tells you: "I have really noticed a tremendous difference since I've been coming here for counseling. I'm a lot more open with my kids, and they are really noticing a change in me and like it too! I am even able to talk to my principal without feeling like a scared little kid!"

   a. What is this person experiencing? _____
   _____

   b. Respond by reflecting what you heard. _____
   _____

5. Man, 45, tells you: "I'm so preoccupied since my wife left me that I can't think of anything but her. I keep going over in my head what I could and should have done so she would have stayed. It pisses me off that I can't get her out of my mind and go about my living!"

   a. What is this person experiencing? _____
   _____

   b. Respond by reflecting what you heard. _____
   _____

6. Man, 27, tells you: "Here I am, still in college and not a damn thing to show for my life. My wife is supporting me, and I know she resents me for not getting out and getting a job before this. But, you know, now I know what I want, and before I was just in school because my parents wanted me to be there."

   a. What is this person experiencing? _____
   _____

   b. Respond by reflecting what you heard. _____
   _____

JERRY COREY COUNSELS STAN FROM A PERSON-CENTERED PERSPECTIVE

Session 5. Person-Centered Therapy Applied to the Case of Stan

This session focuses on exploring the immediacy of our relationship and assisting Stan in finding his own way. The theme of this meeting is our work on our relationship. I have been counseling Stan for several sessions, and he worries about my judgment of him and what I really think of him. He has many doubts about his capacity to make good choices, and thus he hopes I will provide him with answers. In this demonstration I disclose my reactions to Stan on the assumption that this kind of here-and-now dialogue about our relationship is a core aspect of the therapeutic process.

Before viewing the session, read Chapter 7, pages 196–197 in the textbook and answer the questions listed under the heading "Follow-Up: You Continue as Stan's Person-Centered Therapist." Given what you have learned about Stan, how do you think he will respond to the person-centered approach? To what degree would you expect the necessary and sufficient conditions for change to fit for Stan's case? It is clear that Stan worries about what others think of him, and we could expect that this would apply to wondering about what his therapist thinks of him. If you were functioning as a person-centered therapist, how you would address Stan's concerns?

As you watch this counseling session, pay close attention to Jerry's therapeutic style. What specific interventions are most often made in this session? How does Stan seem to respond to this style? After viewing the session, discuss these questions:

1. At the beginning of the session Stan asks the therapist: "I have been wanting to contact my ex-wife, and I am wondering if this would be a good idea? What do you think?" As his therapist, how would you respond to him?

2. What do you think of Jerry's responses to what Stan is saying in this session?

3. How do you imagine it would be for you to stay within a person-centered framework in working with Stan?

4. Stan doubts his ability to make good decisions. He tells you, his therapist, that most of the decisions he has made have been poor ones and that he always "screws things up." Do you have any ideas of how you might work with him when he says these things?

5. If Stan were to ask you what you think of him, how would you be inclined to answer him?

6. Stan is concerned that his therapist might be saying things to make him feel better. Would you be inclined to say things to make Stan feel better? Why or why not?

7. In this session, Jerry strives to toward immediacy by sharing with Stan how he perceives him and what it is like to be his therapist. As his therapist, what possible advantages are there in disclosing your here-and-now reactions to Stan in this session? Are there any disadvantages in disclosing your here-and-now reactions to Stan in this session?

8. Would you want to give Stan answers to his problems? Why or why not? How do you think your answers might either help or hinder Stan in finding his own way?

9. What aspects of Stan's experience might you emphasize to deepen the therapeutic relationship with him?

10. What points most stood out for you in this particular session?

A Suggested In-Class Activity

Spend some time in small groups discussing what you saw in the video clip and what you read of the therapist's way of working with Stan in the text. There are not very many techniques associated with the particular approach as the emphasis is on the attitudes of the therapist. How would it be for you to counsel Stan using a person-centered approach? Would you find it freeing or problematic not to have techniques to keep the session moving? You might try practicing staying in a person-centered spirit to see what this would be like for you? If you do use the model of role-playing Stan and the counselor, be sure to talk about what it was like to be the client in this situation as well as the counselor. Here are three questions pertaining to this session to discuss in your small group:

1. What did you find most interesting in this session? Why?

2. If you were counseling Stan from this particular theoretical framework, what is one additional intervention you might use? What would you hope to accomplish with this intervention?

3. If you were the client, how would you be likely to respond to the therapist's (Jerry's) comments and interventions in this particular session?

JERRY COREY'S WORK WITH RUTH FROM A PERSON-CENTERED PERSPECTIVE

Ruth lets me know how difficult it is for her to talk personally to me, and she tells me that it's especially uncomfortable for her to talk with me because I'm a man. I feel encouraged because she is willing to talk to me about her reservations and bring some of her feelings toward me out in the open.

RUTH: I've become aware that I'm careful about what I say around you. It's important that I feel understood, and sometimes I wonder if you can really understand the struggles I'm having as a woman.

JERRY: Perhaps you could tell me more about your doubts about my ability to understand you as a woman.

RUTH: It's not anything you've said so far, but I'm fearful around you. I'm not sure how you might judge or react to me.

JERRY: I'd like the chance to relate to you as a person, so I hope you'll let me know when you feel judged or not understood by me.

RUTH: It's not easy for me to talk about myself to any man; all of this is so new to me.

Ruth continues by letting me know that she sometimes feels vulnerable when she talks about herself. She fears that if she shares some of her deepest struggles she will feel exposed. Furthermore, she wonders whether I will be able to really understand her and help her if she does share her feelings. Looking at herself and being the focus of attention is new for her, and she is still wondering about the process.

It is important that we pursue what might get in the way of Ruth's trust in me, for trust is the very foundation of the therapeutic relationship. As long as Ruth is willing to talk about what she is thinking and feeling while we are together in the sessions, we have a direction to follow. In this sample dialogue, my attempt is to use the immediacy of our relationship as the basis for further exploration. Staying with our relationship in the here and now will inevitably open up other channels of fruitful exploration.

You Continue Working With Ruth From a Person-Centered Perspective

1. Refer to *Case Approach to Counseling and Psychotherapy* (Chapter 5) for a demonstration of how a person-centered therapist (Dr. David Cain) assumes the role of helping Ruth learn how to learn. In this chapter I also demonstrate my style of applying person-centered concepts in counseling Ruth.

2. See the *DVD for Integrative Counseling: The Case of Ruth and Lecturettes* (Session 2 on the therapeutic relationship) for a demonstration of exploring person-centered themes in Ruth's life.

3. How would you respond to Ruth if she were to express her doubts about your capacity to understand her situation?

4. What steps can you think of taking to build and enhance a relationship with Ruth based on trust? What ideas do you have about how you could address Ruth's fears of feeling exposed and vulnerable?

5. How secure would you feel in counseling without relying on techniques, but dealing mainly with the immediacy between you and Ruth and following her leads for further exploration?

A CASE FROM A PERSON-CENTERED PERSPECTIVE

Judith: "I Have a Sexual Problem"
By **David N. Elkins,** PhD, Professor Emeritus, Graduate School of Education and Psychology, Pepperdine University

Background Information

Judith is a 25-year-old White female who works as a receptionist at a law firm. Six months ago she began dating Shawn, a 27-year-old man who lives in her apartment complex. Their relationship has deepened and they now see each other two or three times a week, despite their heavy work schedules. Recently, they began to talk about getting married.

Judith came to therapy because she is concerned about what she describes as her "sexual problem." Judith told her therapist, "When Shawn and I make love, I get turned on at first but then I just shut down. It's like my sexual feelings evaporate into thin air. Shawn is very understanding but I know it's difficult for him." Judith went on to say that she thought her strict religious upbringing was part of the problem. She said, "I grew up in a small Southern town and my family was almost fanatically religious. My parents thought sex was shameful and dirty and that premarital sex was a horrible sin. If they knew that Shawn and I were having sex, they would be appalled. I left the church when I was in college and I no longer believe many of the things my parents and church taught, but I think my upbringing has caused me to block out my sexual feelings."

Dr. Dave Elkins's Way of Working With Judith
From a Person-Centered Perspective

Person-centered theory posits that children, because they need the love of their parents, tend to "deny to awareness" experiences, including their own feelings, that do not fit their parents' value system. Judith's parents considered sex "shameful and dirty" and believed that premarital sex was a "horrible sin." Thus, it is understandable that Judith, as a child growing up in such an environment, might learn to block out or "deny to awareness" feelings related to sexuality. Although person-centered therapists do not focus on the past in therapy, they do understand that childhood experiences often explain why adults "block out" certain feelings or other aspects of themselves. Person-centered theory says that in order to reclaim previously denied aspects of their experiences, clients must be provided with a therapeutic environment characterized by empathy, congruence, and unconditional positive regard. To the degree the therapist is able to provide this environment and to the degree clients perceive it, they will begin to grow. Their growth will include a natural tendency to explore and gradually allow into awareness feelings that were previously denied.

Using this theoretical structure, it becomes obvious what I need to do in working with Judith from a person-centered perspective: I must provide her with a therapeutic relationship in which she feels deeply understood and accepted. As she begins to realize that I understand how she feels, that I accept and do not judge her, and that I, too, am trying to be open and honest in my relationship with her, Judith will increasingly feel free to be her real self in therapy and to explore and access parts of herself that she had previously blocked out or denied to awareness. As a person-centered therapist, I would not use techniques in my work with Judith nor would I push, cajole, or try to persuade her to do what I thought was best. Person-centered therapists believe that human beings grow naturally when they are provided with empathy, honesty, and acceptance—just as a flower grows naturally when it is provided with sunshine, water, and soil. Thus, based on my own clinical experience and a great deal of research that supports the effectiveness of a deeply human therapeutic relationship, I would predict that Judith, if she stays with the therapeutic process, will not only recover her sexual feelings but will also grow as a person, perhaps in ways that she has not even imagined.

Follow-Up: You Continue as Judith's Person-Centered Therapist

1. Suppose Judith is referred to you for continued person-centered therapy. Would you find it easy to give her empathy and not judge her? What if you are religious and agree with Judith's parents that premarital sex is wrong? Would you still be able to give Judith empathy and acceptance? At a more general level, do you think it's possible to accept and support someone even when you disagree with their values or actions? Explain your answer.

2. Person-centered therapists do not use therapeutic techniques. Instead, they try to create a therapeutic relationship characterized by empathy, acceptance, and genuineness. Would you feel comfortable working with clients in this way or would you want to use techniques in your work? Why or why not?

3. Suppose that after working with Judith for a few sessions you come to suspect, despite her physician's assurance to the contrary, that part of Judith's problem could be physiological in nature. How would you handle this? What specifically would you do?

 QUIZ ON PERSON-CENTERED THERAPY

A Comprehension Check

Score _____%

Note: Refer to Appendix 1 for the scoring key.

True/false items: Decide if the following statements are "more true" or "more false" as they apply to person-centered therapy.

T F 1. Person-centered therapy is best described as a completed and fixed "school," or model, of therapy.

T F 2. Diagnosis of clients is seen as an important beginning point for therapy.

T F 3. A major contribution of this approach has been the willingness of Rogers to state his formulations as testable hypotheses and submit them to research.

T F 4. The person-centered approach to group counseling is based on the assumption that the group members have the resourcefulness for positive movement without the facilitator of the group assuming an active and directive role.

T F 5. Directive procedures are called for when clients feel that they are "stuck" in therapy.

T F 6. Natalie Rogers expanded on her father's theory of creativity using the expressive arts to enhance personal growth for individuals and groups.

T F 7. Motivational interviewing rests on the therapeutic core conditions; however, it offers a range of strategies that enable clients to develop action plans leading to change.

T F 8. A limitation of this approach is that it is a long-term process.

T F 9. Methods of Natalie Rogers's expressive arts therapy are based on psychoanalytic concepts.

T F 10. Motivational interviewing is deliberately directive and is aimed at reducing client ambivalence about change and increasing intrinsic motivation.

Multiple-choice items: Select the *one best answer* of those alternatives given. Consider each question within the framework of person-centered therapy.

_____ 11. In person-centered group counseling, the role of the counselor is best described as a

a. coach.

b. teacher.

c. skilled group technician.

d. director.

e. facilitator.

_____ 12. Person-centered therapy is a form of

a. psychoanalysis.

b. humanistic therapy.

c. behavioral therapy.

d. cognitive-oriented therapy.

e. both (c) and (d).

_____ 13. Which of the following is considered important in person-centered therapy?

a. accurate diagnosis

b. accurate therapist interpretation

c. therapeutic experiments

d. all of the above

e. none of the above

_____ 14. Congruence refers to the therapist's

a. genuineness.

b. empathy for clients.

c. positive regard.

d. respect for clients.

e. judgmental attitude.

_____ 15. In person-centered therapy, transference is

a. a necessary, but not sufficient, condition of therapy.

b. a core part of the therapeutic process.

c. a neurotic distortion.

d. a result of ineptness on the therapist's part.

e. not an essential or significant factor in the therapy process.

_____ 16. Emotion-focused therapy

a. is rooted in a person-centered philosophy.

b. incorporates aspects of Gestalt therapy into the process.

c. incorporates aspects of existential therapy into the process.

d. both a and b.

e. all of the above.

_____ 17. Accurate empathic understanding refers to the therapist's ability to

a. accurately diagnose the client's central problem.

b. objectively understand the dynamics of a client.

c. like and care for the client.

d. sense the inner world of the client's subjective experience.

_____ 18. Which technique(s) is (are) most often used in the person-centered approach?

a. questioning and probing

b. analysis of resistance

c. free association

d. active listening and reflection

e. interpretation

_____ 19. Which statement is most true of person-centered theory?

a. Therapists should be judgmental at times.

b. Therapists should direct the session when clients are silent.

c. The skill a therapist possesses is more important than his or her attitude toward a client.

d. The techniques a therapist uses are less important than are his or her attitudes.

_____ 20. In what stage of change do individuals intend to take action immediately and report some small behavioral changes?

a. precontemplation

b. contemplation

c. preparation

d. action

e. maintenance

_____ 21. One strength of the person-centered approach is that

a. it offers a wide range of cognitive techniques to change behavior.

b. it teaches clients ways to explore the meaning of dreams.

c. it emphasizes reliving one's early childhood memories.

d. therapists have the latitude to develop their own counseling style.

e. clients are given a concrete plan to follow.

_____ 22. A limitation of the person-centered approach is a

a. lack of research conducted on key concepts.

b. tendency for practitioners to give support without challenging clients sufficiently.

c. lack of attention to the therapeutic relationship.

d. failure to allow clients to choose for themselves.

_____ 23. Rogers made a contribution to

a. developing the humanistic movement in psychotherapy.

b. pioneering research in the process and outcomes of therapy.

c. fostering world peace.

d. pioneering the encounter-group movement.

e. all of the above.

_____ 24. As a result of experiencing person-centered therapy, it is hypothesized that the client will move toward

a. self-trust.

b. an internal source of evaluation.

c. being more open to experience.

d. a willingness to continue growing.

e. all of the above.

_____ 25. Unconditional positive regard refers to

a. feeling a sense of liking for clients.

b. accepting clients as worthy persons.

c. approving of clients' behavior.

d. agreeing with clients' values.

e. accepting clients if they meet the therapist's expectations.

Chapter 8

Gestalt Therapy

PRECHAPTER SELF-INVENTORY

Directions: Refer to page 43 for general directions. Use the following code:

5 = I *strongly agree* with this statement.

4 = I *agree,* in most respects, with this statement.

3 = I am *undecided* in my opinion about this statement.

2 = I *disagree,* in most respects, with this statement.

1 = I *strongly disagree* with this statement.

_____ 1. Growth occurs out of genuine contact between therapist and client more than from the therapist's interpretations or methods.

_____ 2. Therapy aims at awareness, contact with the environment, and integration.

_____ 3. The here-and-now focus of therapy is more important than a focus on the past or on the future.

_____ 4. It is more fruitful for the therapist to ask "what" and "how" questions than to ask "why" questions.

_____ 5. Rather than merely talking about feelings and experiences in therapy, it is more productive for clients to relive and reexperience those feelings as though they were happening now.

_____ 6. One's past is important to the degree that it is related to significant themes in one's present functioning.

_____ 7. A major therapeutic function is to devise experiments designed to increase clients' self-awareness of *what* they are doing and *how* they are doing it.

_____ 8. A primary aim of therapy is to expand a person's capacity for self-awareness, which is seen as curative in itself.

_____ 9. Awareness includes insight, self-acceptance, knowledge of the environment, responsibility for choices, and the ability to make contact with others.

_____ 10. Unfinished business from the past usually manifests itself in present problems in functioning effectively.

_____ 11. Change best occurs when we become aware of *what we are* as opposed to trying to become *what we are not.*

_____ 12. Focusing on the past can be a way to avoid coming to terms with the present.

_____ 13. Effective contact means interacting with nature and with other people without losing one's sense of individuality.

_____ 14. Therapy best focuses on the client's feelings, present awareness, body messages, and blocks to awareness.

15. The therapist's main function is to assist the client in gaining awareness of the "what" and "how" of experiencing in the here and now.

16. The therapist should avoid diagnosing, interpreting, and explaining at length the client's behavior.

17. In therapy it is extremely important to pay attention to the client's body language and other nonverbal cues.

18. As therapy progresses, the client can be expected to assume increasing responsibility for his or her own thoughts, feelings, and behavior.

19. It is important that therapists actively share their own present perceptions and experiences as they encounter clients in the here and now.

20. The most effective experiments grow out of genuine interaction between client and therapist and generally help clients gain increased awareness of fragmented and disowned aspects of themselves.

OVERVIEW OF GESTALT THERAPY

Key Figures and Major Focus

Founders: Frederick ("Fritz") Perls and Laura Perls. Other key figures: the late Miriam Polster and Erving Polster. The approach is an experiential therapy that stresses here-and-now awareness and integration of the fragmented parts of the personality. It focuses on the "what" and "how" of behavior and on the role of unfinished business from the past in preventing effective functioning in the present.

Philosophy and Basic Assumptions

Gestalt therapy is an existential–phenomenological approach based on the premise that individuals must be understood in the context of their ongoing relationship with the environment. The approach is designed to help people experience the present moment more fully and gain awareness of what they are doing. The approach is *experiential* in that clients come to grips with what they are thinking, feeling, and doing as they interact with the therapist. Clients are assumed to have the capacity to do their own seeing, feeling, sensing, and interpreting. Growth occurs through the I/Thou relationship rather than through the therapist's techniques or interpretations. This therapeutic relationship is the context for designing experiments that grow out of the moment-to-moment experience.

Key Concepts

Key concepts are the here and now, direct (as opposed to talked-about) experiencing, awareness, and bringing unfinished business from the past into the present. Other concepts include energy and blocks to energy, contact and resistances to contact, attention to the body, and nonverbal cues. Five major channels of resistance are challenged in Gestalt therapy: introjection, projection, retroflection, confluence, and deflection. Some basic principles of Gestalt therapy are holism, field theory, the figure-formation process, and organismic self-regulation.

Therapeutic Goals

The goal is attaining awareness and expanding choices. Awareness, choice, and responsibility are cornerstones of practice. The initial goal is for clients to expand their *awareness* of what they are experiencing in the present moment. Awareness includes knowing the environment and knowing oneself, accepting oneself, and being able to make contact.

Clients are helped to note their own awareness process so that they can be responsible and can selectively and discriminatingly make choices. With awareness the client is able to recognize denied aspects of the self and proceed toward reintegration of all its parts.

Therapeutic Relationship

This approach stresses the I/Thou relationship. The focus is not on the techniques employed by the therapist but on who the therapist is as a person and what the therapist is doing. Contemporary Gestalt therapy (or relational Gestalt therapy) stresses factors such as presence, authentic dialogue, gentleness, more direct self-expression by the therapist, decreased use of techniques, and a greater trust in the client's experiencing. Clients are viewed as the experts on their own experience. The counselor assists clients in experiencing all feelings more fully and lets them make their own interpretations. The therapist does not interpret for clients but focuses on the "what" and "how" of their behavior. Clients identify their own unfinished business from the past that is interfering with their present functioning by reexperiencing past situations as though they were happening at the present moment.

Techniques and Procedures

Although the therapist functions as a guide and a catalyst, presents experiments, and shares observations, the basic work of therapy is done by the client, who is expected to be active. Technical expertise is important, but the therapeutic engagement is paramount. Therapists do not force change on clients; rather, they create experiments within a context of the I/Thou dialogue in a here-and-now framework. Gestalt therapists use active methods and personal engagement with clients to increase their awareness, freedom, and self-direction rather than directing them toward preset goals. Although the therapist suggests experiments, this is a collaborative process with full participation by the client. These experiments are the cornerstone of experiential learning. Gestalt experiments take many forms: setting up a dialogue between a client and a significant person in his or her life; reliving a painful event; or carrying on a dialogue between two conflicting aspects within an individual. Clients often engage in role playing. By playing out all the various parts and polarities alone, often through the empty-chair technique, clients gain greater awareness of the conflicts within themselves. For effective application of Gestalt procedures, it is essential that clients be prepared for such experiments.

Emotion-focused therapy (EFT) and process-experiential therapy are similar in some respects to Gestalt therapy. Emotion-focused therapy blends the relational aspects of the person-centered approach with the active phenomenological awareness experiments of Gestalt therapy. While EFT uses a similar methodology to that of Gestalt therapy, there is an emphasis on empirically supported treatments in EFT.

Applications

The approach is applicable to elementary and secondary classrooms, as well as having clinical applications. In deciding the appropriateness of employing Gestalt techniques, questions of "when," "with whom," and "in what situation" should be raised. The techniques are most effectively applied to overly socialized, restrained, and constricted individuals, and they can be useful in working with couples and families. These techniques are less applicable for more severely disturbed individuals. The methods are powerful catalysts for opening up feelings and getting clients into contact with their present-centered experience.

Although Gestalt therapy is well suited to *group counseling,* it can be used for individual counseling as well. In a group context there is emphasis on direct experiencing and action, rather than merely talking about problems or feelings. Experiments are the means for moving from *talking about* to action. Group members are expected to participate in experiments as a way for them to deepen their moment-by-moment experiencing. The focus of a Gestalt group is on awareness, contact, and experimentation.

Multicultural Perspectives

Gestalt therapy can be used creatively and sensitively with culturally diverse populations if interventions are used flexibly and in a timely manner. Competent Gestalt therapists consider the client's cultural framework and are able to adapt methods that are likely to be well received. They focus on the person and not on the use of techniques. Gestalt experiments work best when the therapist is respectful of the client's cultural background and is in good contact with the person. Experiments are done with the collaboration of the client and with the attempt to understand the background of the client's culture. Gestalt therapists are concerned about how and which aspects of this background become figural for their clients and what meaning clients place on what is central for them.

Contributions

By encouraging direct contact and the expression of feelings, the approach de-emphasizes abstract intellectualization of one's problems. Intense experiencing can occur quickly, so therapy can be relatively brief. The approach recognizes the value of working with the past as it is important to the here and now. Its focus is on recognition of one's own projections and emphasizes doing and experiencing as opposed to merely talking about problems in a detached way. Gestalt therapy gives attention to nonverbal and body messages. It provides a perspective on growth and enhancement, not merely a treatment of disorders. The method of working with dreams is a creative pathway to increased awareness of key existential messages in life.

Limitations

In the hands of an ineffective therapist, Gestalt procedures can become a series of mechanical exercises behind which the therapist as a person can remain hidden. The theoretical grounds of Gestalt therapy leave something to be desired. Moreover, there is a potential for the therapist to manipulate the client with these powerful methods. Training and supervision in Gestalt therapy are essential, as well as self-knowledge and introspection on the therapist's part. Competent practitioners need to have their own personal therapy, advanced clinical training, and supervised experience.

 GLOSSARY OF KEY TERMS

Awareness   The process of attending to and observing one's own sensing, thinking, feelings, and actions; paying attention to the flowing nature of one's present-centered experience.

Blocks to energy   Paying attention to where energy is located, how it is used, and how it can be blocked.

Confluence   A disturbance in which the sense of the boundary between self and environment is lost.

Confrontation   An invitation for the client to become aware of discrepancies between verbal and nonverbal expressions, between feelings and actions, or between thoughts and feelings.

Contact   The process of interacting with nature and with other people without losing one's sense of individuality. Contact is made by seeing, hearing, smelling, touching, and moving.

Continuum of awareness   Staying with the moment-to-moment flow of experiencing, which leads individuals to discover how they are functioning in the world.

Deflection   A way of avoiding contact and awareness by being vague and indirect.

Dichotomy   A split by which a person experiences or sees opposing forces; a polarity (weak/strong, dependent/independent).

Dream work   The Gestalt approach does not interpret and analyze dreams. Instead, the intent is to bring dreams back to life and relive them as though they were happening now.

Emotion-focused therapy   Emotion-focused therapy (EFT) entails the practice of therapy being informed by understanding the role of emotion in psychotherapeutic change.

Empty-chair technique   A role-playing intervention in which clients play conflicting parts. This typically consists of clients engaging in an imaginary dialogue between different sides of themselves.

Exercises   Ready-made techniques that are sometimes used to make something happen in a therapy session or to achieve a goal.

Experiments   Procedures aimed at encouraging spontaneity and inventiveness by bringing the possibilities for action directly into the therapy session. Experiments are designed to enhance here-and-now awareness. They are activities clients try out as a way of testing new ways of thinking, feeling, and behaving.

Field   A dynamic system of interrelationships.

Field theory   Paying attention to and exploring what is occurring at the boundary between the person and the environment.

Figure   Those aspects of the individual's experience that are most salient at any moment.

Figure-formation process   Describes how the individual organizes the environment from moment to moment and how the emerging focus of attention is on what is figural.

Ground   Those aspects of the individual's experience that tend to be out of awareness or in the background.

Holism   Attending to a client's thoughts, feelings, behaviors, body, and dreams.

Impasse   The stuck point in a situation in which individuals believe they are unable to support themselves and thus seek external support.

Introjection   The uncritical acceptance of others' beliefs and standards without assimilating them into one's own personality.

Organismic self-regulation   An individual's tendency to take actions and make contacts that will restore equilibrium or contribute to change.

Paradoxical theory of change   A theoretical position that authentic change occurs more from being who we are than from trying to be who we are not.

Phenomenological inquiry   Through a therapist asking "what" and "how" questions, clients are assisted in noticing what is occurring in the present moment.

Projection   The process by which we disown certain aspects of ourselves by ascribing them to the environment; the opposite of introjection.

Relational Gestalt therapy   A supportive, kind, and compassionate style that emphasizes dialogue in the therapeutic relationship, rather than the confrontational style of Fritz Perls.

Retroflection   The act of turning back onto ourselves something we would like to do (or have done) to someone else.

Techniques   Exercises or interventions that are often used to bring about action or interaction, sometimes with a prescribed outcome in mind.

Unfinished business   Unexpressed feelings (such as resentment, guilt, anger, grief) dating back to childhood that now interfere with effective psychological functioning; needless emotional debris that clutters present-centered awareness.

QUESTIONS FOR REFLECTION AND DISCUSSION

1. What are the values and limitations of the Gestalt focus on the here and now? Do you think this approach adequately deals with one's past and one's future? Explain.

2. Gestalt therapy discourages "why" questions and focuses instead on the "what" and "how" of experiencing. What are your reactions to this emphasis? Do you agree or disagree that "why" questions generally lead to heady ruminations?

3. Gestalt therapy tends to focus on what people are *feeling* moment to moment. Does this emphasis preclude thinking about one's experiencing? Explain.

4. Although challenging clients can be done in a gentle way with care, respect, and sensitivity, there are also some risks in challenging a client too soon. What could you do to assess a client's readiness to participate in some challenging experiments?

5. How comfortable do you think you would be using some of the experiments described in this chapter? Do you think it is important that *you* experience these experiments first *as a client* before you attempt to use them with others? How might you prepare your clients so that they would be more likely to benefit from Gestalt experiments?

6. In Gestalt therapy the past is dealt with by asking the client to bring it into the present and to confront significant people as though they were present. The emphasis is on having clients embody some conflict *now,* as opposed to merely talking about an issue. What are your reactions to such an approach?

7. How can unfinished business from the past affect current functioning? Can you think of any unfinished business in your life that has a significant influence on you today? How might Gestalt methods work for you in these areas?

8. Assume that you work with culturally diverse clients in a community agency. Given the challenges of meeting the needs of this diverse population, what promise do you see in employing certain Gestalt techniques? What are potential pitfalls when using Gestalt experiments with culturally diverse clients?

9. Gestalt therapy and person-centered therapy share some philosophical views regarding human nature. However, Gestalt therapy relies on active experimentation initiated by the therapist, whereas person-centered therapy de-emphasizes techniques and therapist direction. Do you see any basis for integrating Gestalt approaches with some person-centered concepts? Why or why not?

10. What are the implications of Gestalt therapy for your own personal growth? How can you use some of the techniques, experiments, and concepts as a way of furthering self-understanding and promoting personality change in yourself?

ISSUES AND QUESTIONS FOR PERSONAL APPLICATION

1. When a person talks about a problem in the past, he or she is asked to reenact the drama as though it were occurring *now* by "being there" in fantasy and reliving the experience psychologically. Following are two brief examples, one of a client talking about a problem with his father, and the other of the client talking directly (in fantasy) to his father.

   Example 1: When I was a kid, my father was never around. I wanted him to give me some approval and recognize that I existed. Instead, he was always doing other things. I know I was scared of him and hated him a bit for not being more of a father, but I just kept on feeling rejected by him. I guess that's why I have such a hell of a time showing affection to my own kids—I never really got any love from him. Do you suppose that's why I can't get *really* close to my own kids now?

   Assume that you are a Gestalt therapist. Instead of answering the client's last question, you ask him to *talk directly* to his father—that is, to be 16 years old again and to say in fantasy what he was not able to say then to his father. Ask him to relive his feelings of rejection as though they were happening now and to tell his father what he is experiencing.

   Example 2: You know, Dad, I hurt so much because all I really want is for you just to say that I mean something to you. I keep trying to please you, and no matter how hard I try, you never notice me. Damn it, I don't think there's anything I could ever do to make you care for me. I get so scared of you, because I'm afraid you'll beat me up if I let you know what I'm feeling. If I only knew what it would take to please you!

Do you see any qualitative difference between the two examples? Do you think the latter could lead the client to experience his feelings of rejection more fully than by merely talking about the rejection in an intellectual way? Now select a problem or concern that *you* have, and do two things: (1) deliberately talk about your problem, and (2) attempt, through fantasy, to put the problem into the here and now. What differences do you notice between the two approaches?

2. Unfinished business generally involves unexpressed feelings such as resentment, rage, hatred, pain, anxiety, grief, guilt, rejection, and so on. Because those feelings are not expressed, they are carried into the present in ways that interfere with effective contact with oneself and with others. Identify some aspect of unfinished business in your life now. How do you think it might affect you in your work as a counselor? Do you see any potential conflicts in working with your clients' unfinished business if you have the same problem?

3. According to Perls, it is imperative to express resentments, because unexpressed resentment is converted into guilt. Try this experiment: Make a spontaneous list of all your conscious guilt feelings. Then, change the word *guilt* to *resentment* and see if it is appropriate. For example, you might say, "I feel *guilty* because I don't make enough money to support my wife and kids in elegant style." Now, change the word *guilty* to *resentful*. Do this for every item on your list of things that you feel guilty about.

JERRY COREY COUNSELS STAN FROM A GESTALT THERAPY PERSPECTIVE

Session 6. Gestalt Therapy Applied to the Case of Stan

This session focuses on Stan reporting a dream in Gestalt fashion and his exploration of the personal meaning of his dream. One of the key components of Gestalt therapy is that it requires a lively imagination and creativity. The willingness to accept a therapist's invitation to enact experiments is a key component of building here-and-now awareness and of reowning parts of the self. Exploring dreams in the here and now is considered to be the royal road to integration. Given what you know of Stan, how do you imagine he will respond to this active, present-centered, creative approach to psychotherapy? Of all the Gestalt exercises listed in the chapter, which do you imagine might be most difficult for Stan, and why?

Before viewing the session, read Chapter 8, pages 234–236 in the textbook and answer the questions listed under the heading "Follow-Up: You Continue as Stan's Gestalt Therapist." After reflecting on these questions, view the session, and as you do so, pay careful attention to the use of dream work. Was this approach effective in the case of Stan? Why or why not? How does Stan seem to respond to this style? After you have seen this session, discuss these questions:

1. The therapist asks Stan to report his dream as though he were dreaming it in the present moment. What do you think are the differences between reporting a dream and reliving a dream as though it were occurring now?

2. What therapeutic value do you place on working with dreams in therapy?

3. If you were a client in Gestalt therapy, how willing would you be to work with your dreams by reliving them in a therapy session?

4. You ask Stan to try an experiment by becoming each part of his dream and giving voice to the different parts, but he refuses to cooperate with the experiment. What are you inclined to say or do next?

5. In Gestalt therapy, clients are asked to give their own interpretations of their dreams. What possible advantages can you see in Stan interpreting the meaning of his dream

versus the therapist interpreting Stan's dream? How does this compare to the use of working with dreams from a psychoanalytic perspective?

6. What most stood out for you as you listened to Stan reliving his dream?

7. What therapeutic benefit can be gained by asking Stan to put his father in another chair and talk to him? How might you introduce such an exercise to your clients?

8. What rationale can you give for asking Stan to "become his father" and talk to Stan?

9. In the dialogue enactment between Stan and his father, what were you most noticing?

10. What kind of unfinished business do you think Stan has with his father that is getting in his way now?

A Suggested In-Class Activity

Small groups would be a useful follow-up for discussing your reactions to both the section in the text on Gestalt therapy with Stan and the counseling session. Your discussion could address your reactions to both Stan and to me as his therapist. How willing did Stan seem to "become the various parts of his dream"? Did Stan seem to acquire any particular insights in this session? If you were counseling Stan from the Gestalt perspective, what are some techniques that you might have used? In your small groups a good topic for discussion is how you could apply some of your answers to the questions listed earlier in working with Stan. Also, these three questions can be explored in your groups:

1. What did you find most interesting in this session? Why?

2. If you were counseling Stan from this particular theoretical framework, what is one additional technique you might use? What would you hope to accomplish with this intervention?

3. If you were the client, how would you be likely to respond to the therapist's (Jerry's) comments and interventions in this particular session?

JERRY COREY'S WORK WITH RUTH FROM A GESTALT THERAPY PERSPECTIVE

In dealing with Ruth's past I ask her to reenact certain critical events that come to her awareness. In one of our sessions Ruth recalls an early experience with sexual experimentation during which her father discovered her. I ask her not merely to report what happened, but also to bring her father into the room now and talk to him about the feelings she is experiencing. She goes back to a past event and relives it—the time at 6 years old when she was reprimanded by her father in the bedroom. She begins by saying how scared she was then and how she did not know what to say to him after he had caught her in sexual play. I encourage her to stay with her scared feelings and to tell her father all the things that she was feeling then but did not say. Ruth says some of the following in the enactment: "I feel ashamed that I let you down. It's hard for me to look you in the eye. I feel guilty for what I did, and I don't know what to say to you. I am so afraid that you will never love me now for what I've done."

With the use of this Gestalt intervention, Ruth is reexperiencing some of the feelings she actually felt at the time her father found her with a neighbor boy. Ruth is no longer merely reporting an event; she symbolically talks to her father, and in doing so is bringing life to this situation. Some possibilities for Ruth's further work might involve the following:

■ Staying with whatever surfaces in her awareness and continuing her dialogue with her father

■ "Becoming her father," saying some of the things she suspects he thought and felt then

- Alternating in a dialogue, allowing herself to be the child and tell her father what it was like for her to be found out and then "becoming the father" and telling Ruth what he thinks of her
- Assuming the role of the ideal father and saying what she wished he would have said then
- Talking to her father in a role play and addressing the ways she is presently affected by his reaction to her sexual curiosity

You Continue Working With Ruth as Her Gestalt Therapist

1. Refer to *Case Approach to Counseling and Psychotherapy* (Chapter 6) for a Gestalt therapists' perspective (Dr. Jon Frew) on Ruth's case. In this chapter I also illustrate my Gestalt orientation in working with Ruth.

2. See the *DVD for Integrative Counseling: The Case of Ruth and Lecturettes* (Session 11 on exploring the past) for a demonstration of creating Gestalt experiments with Ruth.

3. From a Gestalt framework, what interventions would you make in helping Ruth deal with her feelings of shame and guilt?

4. What kind of role-playing possibilities would be useful in exploring the impact of this early event?

5. What value do you see in dealing with a past event by asking Ruth to bring her work into the here and now?

A CASE FROM A GESTALT PERSPECTIVE

David: "Following a Dream"

By **Jon Frew,** PhD, ABPP, Professor of Psychology, Pacific University School of Professional Psychology

Background Information

David is a 25-year-old second-generation Asian American. He is in his third year of medical school. He is seeking counseling (for the first time) because of "career" concerns. This is the second session.

Dr. Jon Frew's Way of Working with David From a Gestalt Perspective

Jon Frew demonstrates his way of working with David in the following dialogue and commentary.

JON: Hi David, good to see you again. I asked a lot of questions last week so I could get to know you and find out why you are coming to see me. Today, I would like you to decide where to start.

DAVID: (looking confused) I'm not sure where to start. You are the doctor. I assumed you would tell me what I need to talk about.

Commentary: Many clients coming to counseling for the first time do not know how it works, and may have expectations about how the therapist will proceed. Second meetings are pivotal. In a typical first session, the counselor is taking the lead gathering intake information. In the second meeting, I want to begin to develop the norm that the "best" place to begin each session is with a topic that has the most appeal, interest or energy for the client—in Gestalt terms, what is most "figural."

David's confusion about taking the lead in the second session is not uncommon. It is compounded by a cultural dynamic. For David, as an Asian American (and a medical student), I am the doctor, and thus the expert.

JON: Ok. Last week you talked about losing your motivation, having trouble studying, and being distracted by daydreams. Is that still something you are experiencing?

DAVID: Yes and it's getting worse. This past week I could not get myself to study for my anatomy final. I am sure I failed it.

Commentary: Gestalt therapists want to begin each session with what is most pressing for the client. They want to lay the foundation for a dialogic relationship, one characterized by collaboration and the absence of hierarchy. With David, however, I picked the topic to start the session and did not challenge the client's need to see me as the expert. In this case, cultural considerations trump theoretical ones. I did not impose on my client to play by my therapeutic orientation's rules. Notice also a key phrase of David's, "I could not get myself . . ." It is a signal of a potential internal conflict.

JON: What are you aware of as you are speaking to me?

DAVID: I am frustrated and mad at myself. I cannot afford to waste time. Medical school has been the plan since I was a teenager. Now that I am here and close to the end, I can't let up. I have to buckle down and get to work.

Again there is language to indicate that David is caught in an inner conflict between parts of himself ("mad at myself"). I am also curious about his phrase, "medical school has been the plan."

JON: You mentioned being distracted by daydreams. What do you dream about?

DAVID: Actually there is only one. I imagine myself playing my guitar with a small band. In my daydream we are playing my original songs in small clubs.

JON: I didn't realize you wrote and played.

DAVID: (becoming more animated and smiling for the first time) Oh yeah. I don't have the time anymore but I've been playing guitar since I was seven years old and I've written over 100 songs. A couple of my songs have been recorded by a band— (His affect shifts suddenly . . . he looks more serious). I'm sorry I did not mean to boast.

JON: Wow. Your demeanor shifted very abruptly. What just happened?

DAVID: My father taught me to never put forward individual accomplishments. I also got worried I was wasting our time with my *silly dream*.

JON: I noticed your excitement and energy as you talked about your music.

I am getting more of a line on the internal conflict David is dealing with. I am wondering about the "plan" to be a physician and that it may be more of a "should" (an introject) than something he wants for himself.

JON: Whose idea was medical school?

DAVID: (without hesitation) My father's. He killed himself working 70 hours a week in the family hardware store. He always said that as the only son, he wanted a better life for me. He wanted me to be a doctor.

JON: What did he think of your music?

DAVID: I never played around him. I felt like he only respected my academic endeavors, the ones that would get me into medical school. Then he died before he saw his dream come true. (A pause). Can I tell you something weird?

JON: Sure.

DAVID: Sometimes I allow myself to imagine what it would be like . . .

JON: What it would be like?

DAVID: I imagine dropping out of school and pursuing my music. (Another pause) I'm sorry.

JON: Sorry for what?

DAVID: I don't mean to waste your time. I know we are here to get me back on track for my medical studies.

Commentary: The two sides of David's internal conflict are becoming clearer. He also sees me like his father—his talk of music "wastes my time." An experiment to increase his awareness of these sides comes next.

DAVID: What do you think I should do Dr. Frew?

JON: Do about what?

DAVID: About medical school versus my music?

JON: I think you should buckle down and get back to your medical studies. You have invested time and money and you are very close to fulfilling your father's dream.

DAVID: (looking relieved) Thank you. I was afraid you would not be willing to advise me. I agree with you. I need to focus on my medical studies.

Commentary: I am sure you learned that counselors "should" never give advice. In this situation, however, my client sees me as the expert and is asking me what to do. He has an introjective style of contact with authority figures, so I take advantage of that. He is relieved because I just aligned with the part of himself that honors his father; this eliminates the conflict with his father, but not his internal conflict. Now for the second part of the experiment.

JON: I am not done with my advice. I think you should drop out of school and pursue your "silly dream."

DAVID: (looking confused) I don't understand. I though you told me to stay in school.

JON: I did. Tell me what you experienced when I offered my second piece of advice.

DAVID: A number of things . . . confusion, distrust like maybe you are playing "mind games."

JON: Anything else?

DAVID: I'm not sure.

JON: Let's try that one more time. David, I think you should quit school and pursue your music. What happens when I say that?

DAVID: I feel excited, like I have permission, like a weight has been lifted.

Commentary: The use of the *experiment* is central in Gestalt therapy. Usually, experiments are set up ahead of time and the client knows what's coming. In this situation, I moved into the experiment without telling David what I was doing. Now I will address his confusion and distrust.

JON: How are you doing with the advice I have given you?

DAVID: I'm not sure. You are telling me to do two things that are incompatible but, this is strange, I felt soothed and relieved by both pieces of advice.

JON: I was not "messing" with you by telling you two different things. There are two parts to you, David, sitting with me right now . . . the musician and the doctor-to-be. I wanted to honor both, which is difficult for you to do.

DAVID: You're right. I keep trying to get rid of the musician and that has not been working.

JON: I want to ask you a very simple question. What do you want to do?

DAVID: Well, as I said before, the plan is . . .

JON: No, David, not the plan . . . what do you want?

DAVID: I have no idea.

Commentary: When we introject we do what others tell us. Usually as we grow older and have more experience, "shoulds" are examined and either kept, modified, or discarded. David is in medical school because that is what his father wanted. At the age of 25, he does not know if he wants to be a physician. I do not have an agenda to "cure" David of his introjective style. In many cultures, unexamined introjects are a byproduct of respect for elders. I do, however, want to increase his awareness about how he takes in his environment, past and present, and how his current dilemma is related to shoulds and wants.

DAVID: I just remembered something. When I was 12, I told my father I wanted a new baseball glove. He said, "I am not interested in what you want. Family comes first. Work hard, excel in your studies, care for others. That is what you should want." It was one of the only times he got angry with me. I felt great shame.

JON: I understand why my "simple" question is not so simple.

DAVID: Now what?

JON: Perhaps you should ask your father.

DAVID: How can I do that?

JON: Close your eyes. Can you construct a picture, an image of him?

DAVID: (Smiling)

JON: What do you see?

DAVID: He is sitting in his favorite spot . . . on a bench in the garden. He is wearing that sweater I bought him. It was too big but he always wore it anyway.

JON: Ok. If there was one question you could ask him, what would it be?

DAVID: I would ask if he would like to hear me play a song I wrote about him just before he died.

JON: Approach him in the garden and ask that question. Do it in fantasy. I will stay here.

DAVID: (Tears begin to form and several minutes pass. He opens his eyes and looks at me.)

JON: How are you?

DAVID: He said he would be honored to hear my song.

Commentary: I finished with a final experiment. I suggest that David make contact with his father. It is crucial to be cautious when working across cultures with any experiments (e.g., talking to a parent who has died might violate a religious or cultural norm). The experiment unfolds in an unexpected way . . . the hallmark of experiments . . . David did not ask the question I thought he would but he was profoundly moved by the answer he got.

Follow-Up: You Continue as David's Gestalt Therapist

1. Overall, what are your general impressions of David? Does he evoke any reactions in you? Knowing what you know of yourself and of how David is described in this case, how do you think he will respond to you?

2. What are your reactions to the Gestalt experiments Dr. Frew suggested to David? If you were the client, how would it be for you to participate in such experiments?

3. David wanted advice from the therapist, and Dr. Frew complied, but with a twist. As his therapist, how would you respond to David's direct request for advice from you?

4. What aspects of David's culture would you be interested in further exploring with him?

5. Where would you go from here with David? What interventions might you make?

 ## QUIZ ON GESTALT THERAPY

A Comprehension Check

Score _____%

Note: Refer to Appendix 1 for the scoring key.

True/false items: Decide if the following statements are "more true" or "more false" as they apply to Gestalt therapy.

T   F   1. Resistance refers to defenses we develop that prevent us from experiencing the present in a full and real way.

T   F   2. Blocked energy can be considered a form of resistance.

T   F   3. The basic goal of Gestalt therapy is adjustment to society.

T   F   4. Recent trends in Gestalt practice include more emphasis on confrontation, more anonymity of the therapist, and increased reliance on techniques.

T   F   5. Dreams contain existential messages, and each piece of dream work leads to assimilation of disowned aspects of the self.

T   F   6. Gestalt therapy is well suited for group counseling, especially when there is a here-and-now emphasis within the group.

T   F   7. One of the functions of the therapist is to pay attention to the client's body language.

T   F   8. Gestalt techniques are primarily aimed at teaching clients to think rationally.

T   F   9. A major function of the therapist is to make interpretations of clients' behavior so that they can begin to think of their patterns.

T   F   10. The founder of Gestalt therapy contends that the most frequent source of unfinished business is resentment.

Multiple-choice items: Select the *one best answer* of those alternatives given. Consider each question within the framework of Gestalt therapy.

_____ 11. The main founder of Gestalt therapy is

a. Carl Rogers.
b. Fritz Perls.
c. Albert Ellis.
d. William Glasser.
e. none of the above.

_____ 12. Which is *not* true of Gestalt therapy?

a. The focus is on the "what" and "how" of behavior.
b. The focus is on the here and now.
c. The focus is on integrating fragmented parts of the personality.
d. The focus is on unfinished business from the past.
e. The focus is on the "why" of behavior.

_____ 13. Which of the following is *not* a key concept of Gestalt therapy?

a. acceptance of personal responsibility
b. intellectual understanding of one's problems
c. awareness of the present moment
d. unfinished business
e. dealing with the impasse

_____ 14. According to the Gestalt view, awareness

a. is by itself therapeutic.
b. is a necessary, but not sufficient, condition for change.

c. without specific behavioral change is useless.
d. consists of understanding the causes of one's problems.

_____ 15. The basic goal of Gestalt therapy is to help clients

a. move from environmental support to self-support.
b. recognize which ego state they are functioning in.
c. uncover unconscious motivations.
d. work through the transference relationship with the therapist.
e. challenge their philosophy of life.

_____ 16. The impasse is the point in therapy at which clients

a. do not have external support available to them.
b. experience a sense of "being stuck."
c. are challenged to get into contact with their frustrations and accept whatever is.
d. do all of the above.

_____ 17. Gestalt therapy can *best* be characterized as

a. an insight therapy.
b. an experiential therapy.

c. an action-oriented therapy.
d. an empirically validated treatment.
e. a cognitive approach.

_____ 18. Gestalt therapy encourages clients to

a. experience feelings intensely.
b. stay in the here and now.
c. work through the impasse.
d. pay attention to their own nonverbal messages.
e. do all of the above.

_____ 19. The focus of Gestalt therapy is on

a. the relationship between client and counselor.
b. free associating to the client's dreams.
c. recognizing one's own projections and refusing to accept helplessness.
d. understanding why we feel as we do.
e. all of the above.

_____ 20. A contribution of the Gestalt approach is that it

a. sheds light on transference.
b. is primarily a cognitive perspective.
c. stresses talking about problems.
d. deals with the past in a lively manner.

_____ 21. The process of distraction, which makes it difficult to maintain sustained contact, is

a. introjection.
b. projection.
c. retroflection.
d. confluence.
e. deflection.

_____ 22. The process of turning back to ourselves what we would like to do to someone else is

a. introjection.
b. projection.
c. retroflection.
d. confluence.
e. deflection.

_____ 23. The tendency to uncritically accept others' beliefs without assimilating or internalizing them is

a. introjection.
b. projection.
c. retroflection.
d. confluence.
e. deflection.

_____ 24. The process of blurring awareness of the boundary between self and environment is

a. introjection.
b. projection.
c. retroflection.
d. confluence.
e. deflection.

_____ 25. What is a limitation (or limitations) of Gestalt therapy as it is applied to working with culturally diverse populations?

a. Clients who have been culturally conditioned to be emotionally reserved may not see value in experiential techniques.
b. Clients may be "put off" by the emphasis on expressing feelings.
c. Clients may be looking for specific advice on solving practical problems.
d. Clients may believe showing one's vulnerability is being weak.
e. All of the above are limitations.

Chapter 9

Behavior Therapy

 PRECHAPTER SELF-INVENTORY

Directions: Refer to page 43 for general directions. Use the following code:

5 = I *strongly agree* with this statement.

4 = I *agree*, in most respects, with this statement.

3 = I am *undecided* in my opinion about this statement.

2 = I *disagree*, in most respects, with this statement.

1 = I *strongly disagree* with this statement.

_____ 1. Research methods are used to evaluate the effectiveness of both the assessment and treatment process.

_____ 2. People are not determined by environmental circumstances; they have the capacity for choosing how they will respond to external events.

_____ 3. In therapy the client controls *what* behavior is to be changed, and the therapist controls *how* behavior is changed.

_____ 4. A client's problems are influenced primarily by present conditions.

_____ 5. Understanding the origins of personal problems, or insight into underlying dynamics, is not essential for producing behavior change.

_____ 6. Clients tend to benefit the most when they have a variety of ways to cope with anxiety-arousing situations that they can continue to use once therapy has ended.

_____ 7. Past history should be the focus of therapy only to the degree to which such factors are actively and directly contributing to a client's current difficulties.

_____ 8. Therapy best focuses primarily on overt and specific behavior rather than on a client's feelings about a situation.

_____ 9. Any program of behavioral change should begin with a comprehensive assessment of the individual.

_____ 10. A good working relationship between the client and the therapist is a necessary but not sufficient condition for behavior change to occur.

_____ 11. Clients are both the producer and the product of their environment.

_____ 12. The client and therapist collaboratively specify treatment goals in concrete, measurable, and objective terms.

_____ 13. Some proper roles of the therapist include serving as teacher, consultant, facilitator, coach, model, director, and problem solver.

_____ 14. The skilled behavior therapist conceptualizes problems behaviorally and makes use of the client–therapist relationship in facilitating change.

_____ 15. It is important that clients be actively involved in the assessment, selecting of goals, planning, treatment, and evaluation of a therapy program.

_____ 16. Specific techniques of therapy or a behavior management program must be tailored to the requirements and needs of each individual client.

_____ 17. Therapeutic procedures and techniques should be aimed at behavior change.

_____ 18. Evidence-based treatments are an important means of accountability in behavior therapy.

_____ 19. Because real-life problems must be solved with new behaviors outside therapy, the process is not complete unless actions follow verbalizations.

_____ 20. It is essential that the outcomes of therapy be evaluated to assess the degree of success or failure of treatment.

OVERVIEW OF BEHAVIOR THERAPY

Key Figures and Major Focus

Key figures: B. F. Skinner, Joseph Wolpe, Arnold Lazarus, and Albert Bandura. Historically, the behavioral trend developed in the 1950s and early 1960s as a radical departure from the psychoanalytic perspective. Four major phases in the development of behavior therapy are (1) classical conditioning, (2) operant conditioning, (3) social learning theory, and (4) cognitive behavior therapy. The newest development is the "third wave" of behavior therapy, which includes dialectical behavior therapy, mindfulness-based stress reduction, mindfulness-based cognitive therapy, and acceptance and commitment therapy. These new approaches have expanded the cognitive behavioral tradition. Several key individuals have made significant contributions to the mindfulness and acceptance-based approaches. Marsha Linehan developed dialectical behavior therapy (DBT), which is a comprehensive cognitive behavioral treatment for people with borderline personality disorders. DBT has been demonstrated to be effective in reducing suicidal behaviors, psychiatric hospitalization, and in treating substance abuse, anger, interpersonal difficulties, and other dysfunctional behaviors. Linehan has translated aspects of both Zen and contemplative practices into behaviorally specific instructions for mindfulness practice that can be taught to therapy clients. Other key figures include Victoria Follette, who has used mindfulness and acceptance-based approaches in the treatment of trauma; and Steven Hayes, whose interests are in the area of the application of language and cognition to alleviating human suffering.

Philosophy and Basic Assumptions

Behavior is the product of learning. We are both the product and the producer of our environment. No set of unifying assumptions about behavior can incorporate all the existing procedures in the behavioral field. Due to the diversity of views and strategies, it is more accurate to think of _behavioral therapies_ rather than a unified approach. Contemporary behavior therapies encompass a variety of conceptualizations, research methods, and treatment procedures to explain and change behavior. These central characteristics unite the field of behavior therapy: a focus on observable behavior, current determinants of behavior, learning experiences to promote change, and rigorous assessment and evaluation.

Key Concepts

The behavior therapies emphasize current behavior as opposed to historical antecedents, precise treatment goals, diverse therapeutic strategies tailored to these goals, and objective evaluation of therapeutic outcomes. Therapy focuses on behavior change in the present and on action programs. Concepts and procedures are stated explicitly, tested empirically, and revised continually. Specific behaviors are measured before and after an intervention to determine whether behavior changed as a result of a procedure.

Therapeutic Goals

A hallmark of behavior therapy is the identification of specific goals at the outset of the therapeutic process. The general goals are to increase personal choice and to create new conditions for learning. An aim is to eliminate maladaptive behaviors and learn more effective behavior patterns. Generally, client and therapist collaboratively specify treatment goals in concrete, measurable, and objective terms.

Therapeutic Relationship

Clients make progress primarily because of the specific behavioral techniques used, but a good working relationship is an essential precondition for effective therapy. Most behavioral practitioners emphasize the importance of establishing a collaborative working relationship and use a flexible repertoire of relationship styles to enhance treatment outcomes. The skilled therapist can conceptualize problems behaviorally and make use of the therapeutic relationship in bringing about change. The therapist's role is primarily to explore alternative courses of action and their possible consequences. Part of the therapist's job is to teach concrete skills through the provision of instructions, modeling, and performance feedback. Therapists tend to be active and directive and to function as consultants and problem solvers. Clients must also be actively involved in the therapeutic process from beginning to end, and they are expected to cooperate in carrying out therapeutic activities, both in the sessions and outside of therapy.

Techniques and Procedures

Behavioral treatment interventions are individually tailored to specific problems experienced by different clients. Any technique that can be demonstrated to change behavior may be incorporated in a treatment plan. A strength of the approach lies in the many and varied techniques aimed at producing behavior change, a few of which are relaxation methods, systematic desensitization, exposure therapies, eye movement desensitization reprocessing, social skills training, self-modification programs, and multimodal therapy. Techniques such as role playing, behavior rehearsal, coaching, guided practice, modeling, feedback, learning by successive approximations, and homework assignments can be included in any therapist's repertoire, regardless of theoretical orientation. Some newer behavioral interventions include meditation, learning to be present in the moment, mindfulness, exploring spirituality, and acceptance.

Applications

The approach has wide applicability to a range of clients desiring specific behavioral changes. A few problem areas for which behavior therapy appears to be effective are phobic disorders, social fears, depression, anxiety disorders, sexual disorders, substance abuse, eating disorders, pain management, trauma, hypertension, children's disorders, and the prevention and treatment of cardiovascular disease. Going beyond the usual areas of clinical practice, behavioral approaches are deeply enmeshed in geriatrics, pediatrics, stress management, self-management, sports psychology, rehabilitation, behavioral medicine, business and management, gerontology, and education, to mention only a few.

Behavioral group counselors may develop techniques from diverse theoretical viewpoints. Behavioral practitioners make use of a brief, active, directive, structured, collaborative, psychoeducational model of therapy that relies on empirical validation of its concepts and techniques. This means that behavioral group therapy fits well within the context of evidence-based practice. The leader follows the progress of group members through the ongoing collection of data before, during, and after all interventions. Such an approach provides both the group leader and the members with continuous feedback about therapeutic progress. Behavioral group leaders adopt a teaching role and encourage members to learn and practice skills in the group that they can apply to everyday living. Group leaders are expected to assume an active, directive, and supportive role in the group and to apply their knowledge of behavioral principles and skills to the resolution of problems. Group leaders model active participation and collaboration by their involvement with members in creating an agenda, designing homework, and teaching skills and new behaviors.

Multicultural Perspectives

Behavior therapy has some clear advantages over many other theories with reference to counseling culturally diverse clients. Behavioral approaches can be appropriately integrated into counseling with culturally diverse client populations, particularly because of their emphasis on teaching clients about the therapeutic process and the structure that is provided by the model. Because the approach stresses changing specific behaviors and developing problem-solving skills, clients are likely to cooperate with the therapist because they can see that it offers them concrete methods for dealing with their practical problems. There is an attempt to develop culture-specific procedures and to obtain the client's adherence and cooperation. Some strengths pertaining to multicultural counseling include the behavioral emphasis on specificity, task orientation, objectivity, cognition and behavior, action orientation, dealing with the present more than the past, brief interventions, teaching coping strategies, and problem-solving orientation.

Contributions

Behavior therapy is a short-term approach that has wide applicability. It emphasizes research into and assessment of the techniques used, thus providing accountability. Behavioral approaches are in line with the movement toward evidence-based practice and manualized treatments, which fit well with managed care mental health programs. Specific problems are identified and explored, and clients are kept informed about the therapeutic process and about what gains are being made. Clients also provide the therapist with feedback on how they are experiencing the therapeutic process. The effectiveness of this approach has been researched with different populations and in many areas of human functioning. The concepts and procedures are easily grasped. The therapist is an explicit reinforcer, consultant, model, teacher, and expert in behavioral change. The approach has undergone significant development and expansion over the past two decades, and the literature continues to expand at a phenomenal rate. One example of this development involves the mindfulness and acceptance approaches, which offer avenues for the integration of spirituality in the therapeutic process.

Limitations

The success of the approach is in proportion to the ability to control environmental variables. In institutional settings (schools, psychiatric hospitals, mental health outpatient clinics) the danger exists of imposing conforming behavior. Therapists can manipulate clients toward ends they have not chosen. A basic criticism leveled at this approach is that it does not address broader human problems—such as meaning, the search for values, and identity issues—but focuses instead on very specific and narrow behavioral problems. Some of the more contemporary forms of behavior therapy (mindfulness and acceptance-based approaches) rest solidly on relationship factors and address these limitations.

Current behavior therapy stresses the therapeutic alliance and the importance of a collaborative relationship as ways to enhance the process and outcomes of therapy. These newer versions of behavior therapy address many of the limitations of the approach.

 GLOSSARY OF KEY TERMS

ABC model   This model of behavior posits that behavior (B) is influenced by some particular events that precede it, called antecedents (A), and by certain events that follow it called consequences (C).

Acceptance   A process involving receiving our present experience without judgment or preference, but with curiosity and gentleness, and striving for full awareness of the present moment.

Acceptance and commitment therapy (ACT) A mindfulness-based program that encourages clients to accept, rather than attempt to control or change, unpleasant sensations.

Anger management training   A social skills program designed for individuals who have trouble with aggressive behavior.

Antecedent events Ones that cue or elicit a certain behavior.

Applied behavior analysis   Another term for behavior modification; this approach seeks to understand the causes of behavior and address these causes by changing antecedents and consequences.

Assertion training   A set of techniques that involves behavioral rehearsal, coaching, and learning more effective social skills; specific skills training procedures used to teach people ways to express both positive and negative feelings openly and directly.

Assessment interview   Questioning that enables the therapist to identify the particular antecedent and consequent events that influence or are functionally related to an individual's behavior.

BASIC I.D.   The conceptual framework of multimodal therapy, based on the premise that human personality can be understood by assessing seven major areas of functioning: behavior, affective responses, sensations, images, cognitions, interpersonal relationships, and drugs/biological functions.

Behavior modification   A therapeutic approach that deals with analyzing and modifying human behavior.

Behavior rehearsal A technique consisting of trying out in therapy new behaviors (performing target behaviors) that are to be used in everyday situations.

Behavior therapy   This approach refers to the application of diverse techniques and procedures, which are supported by empirical evidence.

Behavioral analysis   Identifying the maintaining conditions by systematically gathering information about situational antecedents, the dimensions of the problem behavior, and the consequences of the problem.

Behavioral assessment   A set of procedures used to get information that will guide the development of a tailor-made treatment plan for each client and help measure the effectiveness of treatment.

Classical conditioning   Also known as Pavlovian conditioning and respondent conditioning. A form of learning in which a neutral stimulus is repeatedly paired with a stimulus that naturally elicits a particular response. The result is that eventually the neutral stimulus alone elicits the response.

Cognitive behavior therapy (CBT) An approach that blends both cognitive and behavioral methods to bring about change. (The term CBT has largely replaced the term "behavior therapy," due to the increasing emphasis on the interaction among affective, behavioral, and cognitive dimensions.)

Cognitive behavioral coping skills therapy Procedures aimed at teaching clients specific skills to deal effectively with problematic situations.

Cognitive processes   Internal events such as thoughts, beliefs, perceptions, and self-statements.

Consequences   Events that take place as a result of a specific behavior being performed.

Contingency contracting   Written agreement between a client and another person that specifies the relationship between performing target behaviors and their consequences.

Dialectical behavior therapy (DBT)   A blend of behavioral and psychoanalytic techniques aimed at treating borderline personality disorders; primarily developed by Marsha Linehan.

Evidence-based treatments Therapeutic interventions that have empirical evidence to support their use.

Exposure therapies Treatment for fears and other negative emotional responses by carefully exposing clients to situations or events contributing to such problems.

Extinction When a previously reinforced behavior is no longer followed by the reinforcing consequences, the result is a decrease in the frequency of the behavior in the future.

Eye movement desensitization and reprocessing (EMDR) An exposure-based therapy that involves imaginal flooding, cognitive restructuring, and the use of rhythmic eye movements and other bilateral stimulation to treat traumatic stress disorders and fearful memories of clients.

Flooding Prolonged and intensive in vivo or imaginal exposure to highly anxiety-evoking stimuli without the opportunity to avoid or escape from them.

Functional assessment The process of systematically generating information on the events preceding and following the behavior in an attempt to determine which antecedents and consequences are associated with the occurrence of the behavior.

In vivo desensitization Brief and graduated exposure to an actual fear situation or event.

In vivo exposure Involves client exposure to actual anxiety-evoking events rather than merely imagining these situations.

In vivo flooding Intense and prolonged exposure to the actual anxiety-producing stimuli.

Mindfulness A process that involves becoming increasingly observant and aware of external and internal stimuli in the present moment and adopting an open attitude toward accepting what is, rather than judging the current situation.

Mindfulness-based cognitive therapy (MBCT) A comprehensive integration of the principles and skills of mindfulness applied to the treatment of depression.

Mindfulness-based stress reduction (MBSR) This program applies mindfulness techniques to coping with stress and promoting physical and psychological health.

Modeling Learning through observation and imitation.

Multimodal therapy A model endorsing technical eclecticism; uses procedures drawn from various sources without necessarily subscribing to the theories behind these techniques; developed by Arnold Lazarus.

Negative punishment A reinforcing stimulus is removed following the behavior to decrease the frequency of a target behavior.

Negative reinforcement The termination or withdrawal of an unpleasant stimulus as a result of performing some desired behavior.

Operant conditioning A type of learning in which behaviors are influenced mainly by the consequences that follow them.

Positive punishment An aversive stimulus is added after the behavior to decrease the frequency of a behavior.

Positive reinforcement A form of conditioning whereby the individual receives something desirable as a consequence of his or her behavior; a reward that increases the probability of its recurrence.

Positive reinforcement An event whose presentation increases the probability of a response that it follows.

Progressive muscle relaxation A method of teaching people to cope with the stresses produced by daily living. It is aimed at achieving muscle and mental relaxation and is easily learned.

Punishment The process in which a behavior is followed by a consequence that results in a decrease in the future probability of a behavior.

Reinforcement A specified event that strengthens the tendency for a response to be repeated. It involves some kind of reward or the removal of an aversive stimulus following a response.

Self-directed behavior A basic assumption is that people are capable of self-directed behavior change and the person is the agent of change.

Self-efficacy An individual's belief or expectation that he or she can master a situation and bring about desired change.

Self-management Strategies in self-management programs include self-monitoring, self-reward, self-contracting, and stimulus control.

Self-modification A collection of cognitive behavioral strategies based on the idea that change can be brought about by teaching people to use coping skills in various problematic situations.

Self-monitoring The process of observing one's own behavior patterns as well as one's interactions in various social situations.

Social effectiveness training (SET)   A multi-faceted treatment program designed to reduce social anxiety, improve interpersonal skills, and increase the range of enjoyable social activities.

Social learning approach   A perspective holding that behavior is best understood by taking into consideration the social conditions under which learning occurs; developed primarily by Albert Bandura.

Social skills training   This training involves a broad category that deals with an individual's ability to interact effectively with others in various social situations. A treatment package used to teach clients skills that include modeling, behavior rehearsal, and reinforcement.

Systematic desensitization   A procedure based on the principles of classical conditioning in which the client is taught to relax while imagining a graded series of progressively anxiety-arousing situations. Eventually, the client reaches a point at which the anxiety-producing stimulus no longer brings about the anxious response.

QUESTIONS FOR REFLECTION AND DISCUSSION

1. What are the unique and defining characteristics common to all forms of behavior therapy? To what degree do you think you could function effectively within a behavioral framework?

2. An increasing emphasis in current behavior therapy is on teaching clients self-control procedures and self-management skills. The assumption is that learning coping skills can increase the range of self-directed behavior. What are the possibilities of behavior therapy, as you see them, for enhancing a client's choosing, planning, and self-direction?

3. Considering counseling from a diversity perspective, what are some of the merits of the behavioral approach? What specific aspects of behavior therapy, both concepts and techniques, would you want to apply in your work with culturally diverse clients?

4. Which behavioral techniques would you most be inclined to use in your counseling practice? Why? What problems and clients do you think are best suited for the techniques you have selected?

5. Recent developments of the behavioral tradition include dialectical behavior therapy, mindfulness-based stress reduction, mindfulness-based cognitive therapy, and acceptance and commitment therapy. A review of outcome research shows empirical support for these newer forms of integrative therapies. What are your thoughts about the value of these newer approaches?

6. What are some ways that you could incorporate mindfulness and acceptance-based skills into your personal life? To what extent would you be inclined to incorporate these techniques into your counseling practice?

7. There is a movement toward evidence-based practice (EBP), which is in keeping with the behavioral spirit. What advantages and disadvantages do you see in limiting your techniques to those that are empirically proven?

8. What is your view of the behavioral approach's stress on empirical research to validate therapy results? As a practitioner, what ideas do you have regarding assessing the process and the outcomes of therapy?

9. How can the concepts and techniques of the other therapy systems that you have studied be integrated with a behavioral framework? Can you think of ways to develop an integrative style as a counselor while staying within the behavioral spirit?

10. The text deals with five common criticisms and misconceptions regarding behavior therapy. What are your criticisms, if any, of behavior therapy?

ISSUES FOR PERSONAL APPLICATION

Designing a Self-Management Program

As you know from reading the textbook, there is an increased use of self-management strategies. These include self-monitoring, self-reward, self-contracting, and stimulus control. Select some behavior you might like to change (stopping excessive eating, drinking, or smoking; teaching yourself relaxation skills in the face of tense situations you must encounter; developing a regular program of physical exercising or meditating; and so forth). Show how you would specifically design, implement, and evaluate your self-change program. Ideally, you will consider actually trying out such a program for some behavior changes you want to make in your everyday life.

- What specific behavior(s) do you want to change?
- What specific actions will help you reach this goal?
- What self-monitoring devices can you use to keep a record of your progress?
- What reinforcements (self-rewards) can you use as a way of carrying out your plans?
- How well is your plan for change working? What revisions are necessary for your plan to work more effectively?

PRACTICAL APPLICATIONS

Translating Broad Goals Into Specific Goals

Directions: An area of major concern in behavior therapy is the formulation of *concrete* and *specific* goals for counseling. Clients often approach the first counseling session with vague, generalized, abstract goals. A task for the therapist is to help the client formulate clear, concrete goals. The following exercises are designed to give you practice in that task. For each general statement in items 4–7 write a concrete goal, as illustrated in the three examples:

1. Broad goal: *I would like to be happier. I suppose I want to become self-actualized.*

   Specific goal: *I want to learn to know what I want and to have the courage to get it. I want to feel that I am doing what I really want to be doing.*

2. Broad goal: *I'd like to work on improving my relationship with people.*

   Specific goal: *I want to be able to ask those I'm close to for what I want and need. So often I keep my desires unknown, and thus I feel cheated with those people.*

3. Broad goal: *I suppose I need to work on my communication with my wife.*

   Specific goal: *I need to learn how to tell my wife what I'm thinking and feeling and not bury all this and expect her to guess if I'm pleased or not.*

4. Broad goal: *I want to know why I play all these stupid games with myself in my head.*

   Specific goal: _____

5. Broad goal: *I need to get in touch with my values and my philosophy of life.*

   Specific goal: _____

6. Broad goal: *It's awfully hard for me to be an autonomous and assertive individual.*

   Specific goal: _____

7. Broad goal: *I have all sorts of fears and worries, and just about everything gets me uptight.*
_____

Specific goal: _____

Learning How to Be Concrete

One way to help clients become more specific in clarifying broad goals is to do it for yourself. Make a list of specific behaviors you would like to change in your own life. For example, your list might look like this:

1. I want to say no when I really mean no, instead of saying yes and feeling resentful.
2. I would like to spend less time studying and more time playing tennis and skiing.
3. I want to respond to my kids without shouting.
4. I want to lessen my fears about taking examinations.

List concrete goals in terms of specific *behavioral changes* you want for yourself:

1. _____
2. _____
3. _____
4. _____
5. _____
6. _____

SUGGESTED ACTIVITIES AND EXERCISES

Practicing Relaxation Training

Here is an exercise that you can do by yourself. For a period of at least a week, engage in relaxation training for approximately 20 to 30 minutes daily. The purpose of the exercise is to teach you to become more aware of the distinction between tension states and relaxation states. A further objective is to provide you with self-control procedures designed to reduce unnecessary anxiety and tension and to induce bodily relaxation.

Self-relaxation is best learned in a quiet setting and in a prone position. The strategy for achieving muscular relaxation is the repeated tensing and relaxing of various muscular groups. Begin by tensing a specific set of muscles for several seconds and then relaxing those muscles for several seconds. In using this procedure, you should cover all the major muscular groups by using about two tension/release cycles per muscular group. For the purpose of deepening your relaxation, auxiliary techniques such as concentrating on your breathing and imagining yourself in peaceful and personally relaxing situations can eventually be added to the self-relaxation procedure. You may want to make a tape of the sequence to listen to as you follow the instructions.

1. *Hands and arms.* Begin by sitting back or lying down in a relaxed position with your arms at your sides. Take several deep breaths to become relaxed, and hold each breath for at least 5 seconds. Keep your eyes closed during the exercise. Now hold out your dominant arm, and make a fist with the dominant hand. Clench your fist tightly, and feel the tension in the forearm and the hand. Now let go. Now feel the relaxation, and feel the difference from before. After 15 to 20 seconds repeat the procedure, this time concentrating on the differences between relaxation and tension. Repeat the process with the nondominant arm.

2. *Biceps.* Flex your dominant bicep, and notice the tension. Then, relax, tense, and relax again. Notice the warm feelings of relaxation.

3. *Fists.* Next, do the same for the dominant fist. Hold the fist tightly, relax, and study the differences. Then repeat the tension/relaxation procedure, making sure to take your time.

4. *Biceps.* Flex the nondominant bicep. Be aware of the tension, and then release. Repeat the tension/relaxation pattern. Take several deep breaths, hold them, and notice the relaxation in your arms.

5. *Fists.* Next, do the same for the nondominant fist. Hold the fist tightly, relax, and study the differences. Then repeat the tension/relaxation procedure, making sure to take your time.

6. *Upper face.* Tense up the muscles of your forehead by raising your eyebrows as high as possible. Hold this for 5 seconds and feel the tension building up. Relax and notice the difference. Then repeat this procedure.

7. *Eyes.* Now close your eyes tightly. Feel the tension around your eyes. Now relax those muscles, noting the difference between the tension and the relaxation. Repeat this process.

8. *Tongue and jaws.* Next clench your jaws by biting your teeth together. Pull the corners of your mouth back, and make an exaggerated smile. Release and let go, noticing the difference.

9. *Pressing the lips together.* Now press your lips together tightly, and notice the tension. Now relax the muscles around your mouth. Repeat.

10. *Breathing.* Take a few deep breaths and notice how relaxed your arms, head, and mouth feel. Enjoy these feelings of relaxation.

11. *Neck.* Try to touch your chin to your chest, and at the same time apply counterpressure to keep it from touching. Release, note the difference, and then repeat. Pull your head back, and try to touch your back, but push back the opposite way with the opposing muscles. Notice the tension, release, and relax. Then repeat this procedure.

12. *Chest and shoulders.* Next pull back your shoulders until the blades almost touch, and then relax. Repeat. Then try to touch your shoulders by pushing them forward as far as you can. Then release, and feel the difference. Repeat. Now shrug your shoulders, and try to touch them to your ears. Hold, release, and repeat.

13. *Breathing.* Take a deep breath, hold it for 7 seconds, and then exhale quickly. Do this again. Note the feelings of relaxation.

14. *Stomach muscles.* Tighten up your stomach muscles; make your stomach tight and hard like a knot. Relax those muscles. Repeat.

14. *Buttocks.* Now tighten your buttocks by pulling them together. Hold. Release. Repeat.

15. *Thighs.* Tense your thighs. Release the muscles quickly, and then repeat. Study the difference between the tension in the thighs and the relaxation you feel now.

17. *Toes.* Point your toes toward your head, and note the tension. Relax. Repeat. Then point your feet outward, and notice the tension. Release quickly and repeat. Point your feet inward and hold, and then relax. Repeat.

After each of the above muscle groups has been tensed and relaxed twice, the therapist typically concludes the relaxation training with a summary and review. This review consists of listing each muscle group and asking the client to let go of any tension. This is done for each of the above muscle groups, with the suggestion of becoming completely relaxed. The client is asked to notice the good feelings of relaxation, warmth, and calmness over the entire body.

Applying Systematic Desensitization to Yourself

Review the section in Chapter 9 of the textbook describing *systematic desensitization*. Select some anxiety-provoking experience for you, and then set up a systematic desensitization program to lessen your anxiety or fear. Follow your program privately as an out-of-class assignment. Class members may bring their results into class a week later to describe and share their experiences with the procedure. Following are a few guidelines for setting up a program for yourself:

1. Begin by using the relaxation procedure described in the previous exercise.

2. Decide what specific behavior or situations evoke anxiety reactions for you. For example, speaking in front of others may be anxiety producing for you.

3. Construct a hierarchy, which should be arranged from the worst situation you can imagine to a situation that evokes the least anxiety. For example, the greatest anxiety for you might result from the thought of delivering a lecture to hundreds of people in an auditorium. The least anxiety-provoking situation might be talking with a fellow student you know well.

4. Apply the relaxation procedures you have learned; keep your eyes closed, and begin by imagining yourself in the least anxiety-arousing situation on your hierarchy. Then, while imagining a peaceful and pleasant scene, allow yourself also to imagine yourself in the next most anxiety-arousing situation. At the moment you experience anxiety as you imagine the more threatening situation, switch off that scene, put yourself back into the pleasant scene, and relax again.

5. The idea is to move progressively up the hierarchy until you can imagine the scene that produces the greatest degree of anxiety and still be able to induce relaxation again. This procedure ends when you can remain in a relaxed state even while you are imagining a particular scene that formerly was the most disturbing to you.

Designing a Weight Control Program

Assume that your client expresses a desire to lose 20 pounds and then keep his weight down. Using learning principles and behavioral techniques, show the specific steps for *weight control* that you might take with your client. As guidelines you might consider the following questions:

1. Has the client consulted a physician about his weight problem? If he has not, would you undertake a therapy program without having him first visit a physician?

2. What is his motivation for losing weight? What specific reinforcements might help him stick with his weight reduction program?

3. What kind of self-observation and charting behavior would you suggest? Would you ask him to keep a record of when he eats, what he eats, and so on?

4. How would you deal with him if he went on eating binges and failed to follow through with his program? What might you say or do?

5. What are the specific learning concepts involved in the weight control program?

A Mindfulness Exercise: Being an Observer of Your Thoughts

This exercise can be done with a partner, and each of you can take a turn at observing your thoughts. As an alternative exercise, this can be done alone outside of the class setting.

All of us have thoughts. Most of the time when we have thoughts, we relate them directly to our feelings and behaviors or simply ignore them. A key component of mindfulness training is to learn how to observe your thoughts, without feeling an instant need to react to them. Mindfulness lets us choose which thoughts and feelings require action and which can simply be observed. For the next 5 minutes observe your thoughts: Notice them occurring, but do not judge them nor act upon them. Simply experience them as they happen. Notice any particularly interesting qualities your thoughts may contain. If they trigger feelings, notice what they are. Simply observe them as if they were a parade walking by instead of an incident requiring your immediate action. If you find yourself inclined to judge or respond to your thoughts, gently remind yourself, "These are just thoughts that I'm having. They require no response. Just observation." At the end of the exercise consider the following questions, and share your reactions with your partner.

- What is it like to simply observe your thoughts instead of reacting to them?
- What is it like to have feelings and thoughts in the moment, and to simply let them come and go, without analyzing them?
- What benefits, if any, did you experience from participating in this exercise?
- How might you apply mindfulness techniques in your work with clients?

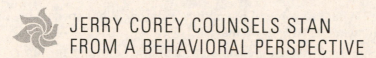 ## JERRY COREY COUNSELS STAN FROM A BEHAVIORAL PERSPECTIVE

Session 7. Behavior Therapy Applied to the Case of Stan

This session illustrates how homework and behavior rehearsals can be used to promote assertive behavior. Part of Stan's difficulty with self-esteem stems from his perception that perhaps he isn't good enough for others or that his needs and wants may not be valid. Behavior therapy uses assertion training to help individuals learn how to request what they need without experiencing shame and doubt. Can you recall a time when you were considering talking to a professor and shied away from doing so? As you reflect on your experience, what was your biggest difficulty in making the contact with your professor? What was particularly challenging about this interaction? What fears did you have? What would have helped you? What do you think Stan might be experiencing in his attempt to talk with a busy professor?

Before viewing the session, read Chapter 9, pages 276–277 and answer the questions listed under the heading "Follow-Up: You Continue as Stan's Behavior Therapist." After reflecting on these questions, view the session. As you observe me working with Stan on his fears and hesitations in approaching a professor, what do you notice about Stan? What was most effective and useful in our interaction? The questions below can be used to structure small discussion groups.

1. What kind of homework would you be inclined to use with Stan? How could you go about collaboratively designing meaningful homework with him? Do you think you would be consistent in checking with him regarding his experience in carrying out the homework?

2. Stan agreed to complete an out-of-the office assignment. At the next session he admits that he did not do the homework. How would you respond?

3. We dealt with present concerns and did not explore how Stan's past may be contributing to his lack of assertiveness today. To what extent do you think it is useful to talk about how Stan's past may have an influence on his current problems?

4. What value do you see in behavior rehearsals with Stan in preparation for him to talk to one of his professors during office time? To what other areas of his life could Stan apply these skills?

5. What kind of behavioral role plays can you think of to help Stan deal more effectively with his professors?

6. How comfortable would you be in conducting assertion training with Stan?

7. What is one other behavioral technique that you would want to use with Stan for the problem he is presenting about lacking confidence in his class?

8. What would you tell Stan about taking action outside of the therapy session?

9. If you were the client in this session, how do you imagine that would be for you?

10. Behavior therapists typically conduct a comprehensive assessment with a client prior to treatment. What are some advantages of doing a multimodal assessment with Stan? Can you think of ways that you could integrate assessment with treatment if you were working with Stan? How would it be for you to administer this assessment?

Assessing Stan From a Multimodal Perspective

Multimodal therapy begins with a comprehensive assessment of the various modalities of human functioning. For practice in thinking about assessment within this framework, consider the case of Stan, and attempt an initial assessment of him on the dimensions outlined here:

1. *Behavior.* How active is Stan? What are some of his main strengths? What specific behaviors keep him from getting what he says he wants?

2. *Affect.* How emotional does Stan seem? What are some problematic emotions for him?

3. *Sensation.* How aware of his senses is Stan? Does he appear to be making full use of all his senses?

4. *Imagery.* How would you describe Stan's self-image? How does he describe himself now? How does he see himself?

5. *Cognition.* What are some of the main "shoulds," "oughts," and "musts" that appear to be in Stan's life now? How do they get in the way of effective living for him? How do his thoughts affect the way he feels and acts?

6. *Interpersonal relationships.* How much of a social being is Stan? How capable does he appear to be of handling intimate relationships? What does he expect from others in his life?

7. *Drugs/biology.* What do you know about Stan's health? Does he have any concerns about his health? Does he use any drugs?

A Suggested In-Class Activity

As you view the counseling session using a behavioral approach with Stan, think of how this assessment can be used as a way to target specific problems to address in his counseling. Based on this initial assessment of Stan, what kind of treatment program would you outline for him as a behavior therapist? In small groups talk about how assessment and treatment could work together in Stan's case. To what degree do your classmates have similar views with respect to assessing Stan's main dynamics, behavior patterns, and problem areas? In what respects do you differ?

Consider these questions as topics for discussion in a small group:

1. What did you find most interesting in this session? Why?

2. If you were counseling Stan from this particular theoretical framework, what is one additional technique you might use? What would you hope to accomplish with this intervention?

3. If you were the client, how would you be likely to respond to the therapist's (Jerry's) comments and interventions in this particular session?

 # JERRY COREY'S WORK WITH RUTH FROM A BEHAVIORAL PERSPECTIVE

Functioning with a behavioral orientation, I pay considerable attention to assessment and establishing goals as a basis for the direction of therapy. After assessing Ruth's strengths and weaknesses, I clarify with her the behaviors she wants to increase or decrease in frequency.

I am interested in getting Ruth to be very specific and concrete in identifying her own goals. Before treatment we establish baseline data for those behaviors that she wants to change. The baseline period is a point of reference against which her changes can be compared during and after treatment. By establishing such baseline data, we will be able to determine therapeutic progress. There is continual assessment throughout therapy to determine the degree to which her goals are being effectively met.

Much of our therapy will involve correcting faulty cognitions, acquiring social and interpersonal skills, and learning techniques of self-management so that she can become her own therapist. Based on my initial assessment of Ruth and on another session in which we discuss the matter of setting concrete and objective goals, we establish the following goals to guide the therapeutic process:

- Ruth does not like her physical appearance and wants to lose weight.

- It is important for Ruth to learn to stick to an exercise program.

- Ruth has difficulty getting along with one of her daughters and wants to improve the relationship.

- Ruth would like to improve her relationship with her husband.

- Ruth would like to be more assertive when the situation calls for assertive behavior.

- Ruth wants to learn and practice methods of relaxation and ways to more effectively cope with stress.

I suggest that she begin writing in a journal to keep track of how she is doing in meeting her goals. It is essential that Ruth gives considerable thought to what she wants to explore in the counseling sessions. From a behavioral perspective, she is clearly the person who decides what she wants to explore and the areas she is most interested in changing.

Ruth will be able to make progress toward her self-defined goals because she is willing to become actively involved in challenging her assumptions and in carrying out behavioral exercises, both in the sessions and in her daily life. She sees the value of making specific plans aimed at translating what she is learning in the therapy sessions to various segments in her daily life. Although my job is to help Ruth learn how to change, she is the one who actually chooses to apply these skills, thus making change possible.

You Continue Working With Ruth as Her Behavior Therapist

1. Refer to *Case Approach to Counseling and Psychotherapy* (Chapter 7) for examples of two different behavior therapists' perspectives (Dr. Arnold Lazarus and Dr. Sherry Cormier) on Ruth's case. In this chapter, I also show my style of applying behavior therapy concepts in working with Ruth.

2. See the *DVD for Integrative Counseling: The Case of Ruth and Lecturettes* (Session 3 on establishing therapeutic goals, and Session 12 on working toward decisions and behavior change) for a demonstration of utilizing behavioral techniques in addressing concerns identified by Ruth. How would you assist Ruth in formulating specific, personal goals?

3. What are some ideas you have for working with Ruth on the specific target goals listed in this selection?

4. How would you help Ruth apply what she is learning in therapy sessions to the challenges she meets in daily life?

5. What techniques might you use from the other therapeutic approaches in helping Ruth reach the goals she has set for herself in therapy with you?

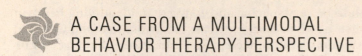

A CASE FROM A MULTIMODAL
BEHAVIOR THERAPY PERSPECTIVE

Lynn: "Struggles Over a Divorce"
By **Arnold A. Lazarus, PhD, ABPP**, Distinguished Professor Emeritus in the Graduate School of Applied and Professional Psychology at Rutgers University, and President of the Lazarus Institute in Skillman, New Jersey

Background of Client and Initial Assessment

As described in the textbook that accompanies this manual, multimodal therapists traverse the BASIC I. D., which provides a comprehensive framework to illuminate specific and interactive problems. In attempting to solve and resolve clients' problems, multimodal therapists may turn to resources outside their own orbits and think outside the proverbial box. This should become clear when I describe the means and methods that were employed in the case of "Lynn Peterson," a personable 55-year-old homemaker who suffered from a generalized anxiety disorder, depression, and several somatic afflictions. She had been seeing an internist and a psychopharmacologist without much improvement and was taking Xanax, Paxil, painkillers, anticholinergics, and a cache of over-the-counter medications.

Lynn was married to Peter, aged 54, for 29 years, and they had two adult sons. He had recently become a corporate CEO. There were no significant untoward events in Lynn's personal history. The first 10 years of the marriage were "very good" according to her, but when Peter became an upper-level manager "he turned into a workaholic." She states: "When our boys were about 8 and 6, I almost became a single parent. Peter went overseas on frequent business trips, and even when he was in town, he had to attend conferences and meetings and was often incommunicado."

After the initial interview, Lynn was handed the *Multimodal Life History Inventory* and asked to complete it at home. The following issues stood out in the completed questionnaire:

Behavior: Some minor compulsivity (e.g., too fastidious about housework). Avoids confrontations. Over apologetic. Has recently stopped playing the piano.

Affect: Anxiety. Depression. Disappointment. Feelings of inferiority and personal failure.

Sensation: Chronic pain (lower back, abdomen, neck and shoulders, head). Tension. Muscle spasms.

Imagery: Nightmares (usually centered on being lost, or pursued by hostile attackers). Unfavorable self-image. Romantic fantasies.

Cognition: Rather perfectionistic. Self-blame. "It is important to please other people." "It is wrong to complain. Grin and bear it."

Interpersonal: Often reticent. Seldom expresses anger. Too compliant. Often puts others' needs before her own. Unfulfilling marriage. Virtually no sex life. Has withdrawn from most of her friends.

Drugs/Biology: Under the care of an internist and psychopharmacologist who have prescribed various medications. Needs to improve her eating habits. Insufficient exercise.

Dr. Arnold Lazarus's Way of Working With Lynn From a Multimodal Perspective

When I initially suggested that it may be helpful if I could meet her husband, Peter, whose perspective may shed additional light on their relationship, Lynn emphatically declared that Peter was totally contemptuous of psychiatrists and psychologists and would never cooperate in any way with her therapy. Lynn had not informed Peter that she had seen a psychiatrist and was taking medication, and she had no intentions of telling him that she was seeing me, a clinical psychologist. She mentioned that she was paying for her therapy out of a private account that Peter did not know about.

We then spent time in her sessions working on specific areas she had identified. In multimodal terms, the modalities that had been the main focus of therapeutic attention were *Behavior, Sensation, Imagery, Cognition,* and *Interpersonal* dimensions. One of the goals identified was reducing Lynn's tension through a variety of behavioral methods. A few of these techniques included relaxation exercises, positive imagery projections, diaphragmatic breathing, and meditation. As she seemed able to conjure up vivid images, I encouraged her to practice positive coping images several times a day. I also addressed her unassertiveness, explored her rights and entitlements, encouraged her to challenge her self-abnegation, and persuaded her to spend more time with her friends, join a yoga class, and take up walking or some other form of exercise.

She had great difficulty in learning to stand up for herself. Assertion training is a form of social skills training that provides cognitive and behavioral methods for assisting clients like Lynn to recognize that she has rights and that she can assert herself. Together we explored Lynn's thoughts that were contributing to her lack of assertiveness.

About two months into the therapy there was clear evidence that Lynn was making progress. She reported feeling less depressed, she was less enervated, more enthusiastic, more self-accepting. Her headaches, bowel disturbances, and other physical afflictions had abated, and she was seeing her friends and practicing the piano again. (She had graduated from college with a major in music.)

Based on what I was hearing from Lynn about Peter in our sessions, I wondered if he had been sexually involved with other women during the course of their marriage, yet I kept this suspicion to myself. I asked her to share with me, as clearly as possible, the trajectory of her marriage from its inception to its present state of affairs (pun intended). It became more evident that the positive aspects had waned, especially over the past five years.

Lynn continued discussing her marriage over the next several therapy sessions. A couple of weeks later, Lynn stated that, in retrospect, she had long begun to feel that her marriage was doomed, but it was too scary for her to fully admit it. She also felt that her self-deception and denial and their attendant pressures lay behind many of her somatic problems. She indicated that if things did not change in her relationship, she was seriously considering a divorce as the best solution to her situation. I began to prepare Lynn to deal with the challenges of a possible divorce. I drew upon mental imagery techniques in the hope of enabling her to foresee a better quality of life without Peter. I introduced role-playing and behavior rehearsal techniques to ensure that she would not be browbeaten or intimidated by Peter. In some of these role-playing scenarios, I assumed Peter's role and Lynn tried on a variety of ways of dealing with what I was putting forth. My assumption is that by practicing new ways of behaving that she would not feel powerless in actually dealing with Peter at home.

I suggested that if I could meet with Peter I could try to facilitate a more amicable divorce process. Lynn assured me that I would get nowhere with Peter, but agreed to my phoning him at home to request a meeting. When I reached Peter by phone I said, "I have known your wife for a few months under somewhat artificial conditions, so there would undoubtedly be much helpful information you could provide after knowing her for almost three decades." Peter's comments went more or less as follows: "As far as I'm concerned all you shrinks are even crazier than the losers who waste their time and money on you. I'm a very busy man and I sure as hell won't waste my precious time talking to the likes of you." And he hung up. Lynn was served with divorce papers within two weeks of my brief phone call.

When Peter excoriated Lynn for secretly "crying on some stupid shrink's shoulder," she informed him that she was neither blind nor stupid. She told him that she was well aware of his extramarital exploits, that she firmly believed that his love of money meant more to him than his sons, and that in retrospect their marriage should have ended about 15 years ago. Lynn was able to deal with Peter in more assertive ways at home during conversations, because we had done considerable role-rehearsing in the office.

After several conversations with Peter during which she confronted him on his behavior, it became clear to her that they had very little future as a couple. She was disconcerted but not distraught. We agreed that the mainstay of the therapy would now focus primarily on getting Lynn through the divorce, which she said would undoubtedly be nasty.

In essence, Peter had control of virtually all their assets. He had retained two highly accomplished but unscrupulous attorneys to represent him. Peter, who was reputed to be worth millions, had offered Lynn a hundred thousand dollars as a divorce settlement, and Lynn's lawyer had advised her to accept his offer. With Lynn's permission, I called him to discuss the matter, pointing out that Lynn had been Peter's loyal and faithful wife for three decades, had raised their two sons, helped Peter climb the corporate ladder by running interference, entertaining clients, and taking care of all his creature comforts. It soon became apparent to me that her lawyer was afraid of going up against his lawyer. Her lawyer was clearly shortchanging her.

In multimodal therapy, we believe in the practice of going outside of the consulting office at times to most effectively work with a client. I reached out to a highly competent and respected attorney whom I knew and I managed to obtain *pro bono* services for Lynn. In essence, he crushed Peter's attorney and Lynn received a very generous financial settlement.

At the end of our therapy Lynn was notably more self-confident, less apologetic, less submissive, had stopped taking Paxil, and had cut back on most of the other medications. Her sons, who were obviously always much closer to her than to Peter, expressed their approval concerning the divorce. Two years later I received a wedding invitation from Lynn. She had inserted a note telling me she had been dating and was now marrying her college sweetheart.

Follow-Up: You Continue as Lynn's Multimodal Therapist

1. What specific additional interventions would you have made if Dr. Lazarus had referred Lynn and Peter to you for couple therapy?

2. When, if ever, would you be inclined to go outside of the therapy office and intervene of the behalf of a client? If you were the therapist, would you intervene as Lynn's advocate? Why or why not?

3. What advantages and disadvantages do you see in going outside of the office in working with a client?

4. This case illustrates linking assessment with treatment. If Lynn were your client, what areas would you deem as important to include in the assessment?

5. Given the data from this case, what other behavioral interventions might you have made if you were Lynn's therapist? How would you proceed in ways that are similar to or different from Dr. Lazarus's approach?

A CASE FROM A BEHAVIOR THERAPY PERSPECTIVE

"Nasty Nails No More: Helen's Triumph over Nail Biting"
By **Caroline Bailey, PhD.,** Assistant Professor of Social Work, California State University, Fullerton

Background Information

Helen, a nine-year-old Chinese American child lives with her mother Eleanor and her two younger brothers. She is a well-behaved and likeable fourth grader who is doing well academically. Helen has friends at school and also has several friends in her neighborhood. Most adults describe Helen as a "good kid." Her mother feels that Helen has always been a well-behaved child until recently.

About six months ago, Helen's father, an army captain, was deployed overseas. The night before he left Helen hid his car keys in an attempt to keep him from leaving. Her father was angry and disappointed with her behavior but understood her feelings. Soon after this occurred, Helen began biting her fingernails. At first, the problem was mild, causing uneven nails and torn cuticles and Eleanor thought Helen had simply picked up a type of "nervous habit" that she would eventually "grow out of." Yet, over time, Helen's nail biting became increasingly pronounced, resulting in nails gnawed down to the nail beds and infected cuticles. On several occasions, Helen's infected nails have required treatment from her pediatrician who has referred Helen for counseling to address the nail biting behavior.

Eleanor is ambivalent about seeking counseling because culturally, she would prefer to help her child privately, at home with the support of her family. However, she has tried several remedies at home, including putting a spicy hot sauce on Helen's fingertips, without success. Eleanor is willing to try counseling to see if it can help her daughter.

Dr. Carolyn Bailey's Way of Working With Helen and Eleanor From a Behavior Therapy Perspective:

Input and support of loved ones is often useful in behavior therapy because they can provide excellent sources of reinforcement and motivation for behavior change. Also, loved ones can provide important information about the way the client's behaviors affect the client's life. When working with school-aged children, primary care givers play an integral role in supporting their children's therapy outside of the therapy session by prompting their children to use a specific behavioral strategy when needed and helping their children to complete their therapy homework assignments.

My first session is spent working collaboratively with Helen and her mother to develop clear treatment goals. Both Eleanor and Helen were initially apprehensive about meeting with a counselor. This is understandable not only because counseling is a new experience for the family, but also because young children often associate going to the "doctor's office" with having medical procedures done. In light of this, I began my session by giving an age appropriate description of what the counseling process entails and made sure to tell Helen that unlike other times she had been to see a doctor, that today she would *not* be getting a shot. I also allowed Helen ample opportunities to ask questions about the counseling process and about me as her therapist until she felt comfortable starting our work together.

Helen and Eleanor both clearly stated their shared goal of helping reduce Helen's nail biting. Eleanor was concerned for Helen's health and while Helen mentioned that biting her nails "hurts a lot," she was most concerned about the teasing she receives from the children at school who call her names like "nasty nails." Helen said the teasing makes her feel sad and bad about herself and that she wishes all the kids at school would just "knock it off." With both Eleanor and Helen on board with shared treatment goals, psychotherapy could begin.

Behavior therapists work collaboratively with clients and empower them to change maladaptive behaviors into more helpful actions through teaching behavior modification strategies. The first step of this process is providing clients with *psychoeducation* about how behavior therapy works and how clients can learn to make choices about how they behave. When working with children, use of age appropriate examples and developmentally appropriate terminology is very helpful in explaining how behavioral principles work.

In our first session I explained to Helen that while some behaviors are reflexes (like coughing when you eat too much pepper), most of our behaviors are learned and that this means that we can learn to change them. I also explained to her that most people's behaviors, even the behaviors that we wish we didn't have, are often executed because of the consequences the behaviors yield. One example I used to illustrate this concept is that although most children do not like being upset and throwing tantrums, if they have learned these tantrums will get them out of doing chores, they are much more likely to throw them. Next, I had Helen generate some examples from her life of how her behaviors are maintained by contingencies and highly praised her for her participation in this exercise. By teaching Helen that behaviors are governed by reinforcement contingencies that can be modified and that most behaviors are triggered by their antecedents and consequences, she is learning the basic principles necessary to use a behavior therapy technique called *self-monitoring*.

Self-monitoring requires clients to be mindful of the "what," "where," "when," and "why" of the behavior they have targeted for change and to keep a careful and detailed record of their thoughts, feelings, actions and their environment at the moment that behavior occurred. Clients are also asked to keep track of the antecedents and consequences of their behaviors. In order to help Helen learn this technique, I asked Helen if she could think of the last time she noticed herself biting her nails. When she was able to picture that moment in her mind, I asked her to tell me what she was doing, feeling and thinking at the moment she noticed the nail biting. She stated that she was in class and being asked to read out loud by her teacher and felt nervous. Helen was hoping she would not make a mistake when reading because she didn't want kids to start teasing her. Next, I provided Helen with a small, blank journal and worked with her and her mother to develop a recording system that Helen could use during the day to monitor this behavior. For homework, I asked Helen to self-monitor her nail biting over the next week. Her mother agreed to help Helen keep her journal and agreed to ask Helen's teacher to allow Helen to keep her journal during class.

In our next session, reviewing Helen's homework revealed Helen tends to bite her nails at times when she feels self conscious or nervous about her performance and when she fears that others will evaluate her negatively. She also bites her nails when she is worried that adults in her life might abandon her or leave her behind. Helen bites her nails about twenty-five times during a school day but very infrequently at home. Helen mentioned that she thinks the nail biting "takes her mind off of" the anxious feelings she is having.

While Helen's underlying anxiety is important, Helen's nail biting is causing her injury and must be worked on immediately. Knowing some of the contingencies that reinforced her nail biting enabled Helen and I to create a *behavioral substitution plan*, where she executes a more adaptive behavior in place of the nail biting. Together, Helen and I agreed that when she begins to feel her anxious feelings she will make careful efforts to replace her nail biting with a new, less harmful behavior of rubbing her thumb across her fingertips. Eleanor agreed to help Helen monitor her progress on the behavioral substitution program, and will provide Helen with a double scoop, chocolate ice-cream cone if Helen can go an entire school day without biting her nails.

Three weeks later, Helen proudly stated that she was able to reduce her nail biting from an average of 25 times a day to only 2 times a day. She felt that for the most part the behavior substitution program is working. Her nails were healing nicely and children at school were teasing her less.

Follow Up: You Continue as Helen's Therapist

Even though Helen has been able to successfully reduce her nail biting behavior she still has more work to do in counseling. Helen would like to learn how to cope with her underlying anxieties that trigger the nail biting, and eventually extinguish the substitute of running her thumb against her fingers. Relaxation training and systematic desensitization are behavior therapy techniques that will likely be useful in working with Helen to meet her goals. As you continue working with Helen, consider the following questions:

1. Do you believe the structured therapy techniques used with Helen are particularly well suited to counseling children? Why or why not?

2. What are your thoughts about including Eleanor in portions of Helen's therapy? Was Eleanor's support a powerful reinforcer for Helen's behavior change?

3. Helen tends to bite her nails more frequently at school than at home. Is it important for you to do a school observation to see her in this environment?

 ## QUIZ ON BEHAVIOR THERAPY

A Comprehension Check

Score _____%

Note: Refer to Appendix 1 for the scoring key.

True/false items: Decide if the following statements are "more true" or "more false" as they apply to behavior therapy.

T   F   1. Operant conditioning was mainly developed by B. F. Skinner.

T   F   2. Behavior therapists look to current environmental events that maintain problem behaviors and help clients produce behavior change by changing environmental contingencies.

T   F   3. The emphasis of contemporary behavior therapy is on evidence-based treatments.

T   F   4. Acceptance and commitment therapy (ACT) is based on helping clients control or change unpleasant sensations and thoughts.

T   F   5. Behavioral techniques can be effectively incorporated into a group counseling format.

T   F   6. Typically, the goals of the therapeutic process are determined by the therapist.

T   F   7. Behavior therapists tend to be active and directive, and they function as consultants and problem solvers.

T   F   8. Multimodal therapy consists of a series of techniques that are used with all clients in much the same way.

T   F   9. Relaxation training has benefits in areas such as preparing patients for surgery, teaching clients how to cope with chronic pain, and reducing the frequency of migraine attacks.

T   F   10. A program of behavioral change should begin with a comprehensive assessment of the client.

Multiple-choice items: Select the *one best answer* of those alternatives given. Consider each question within the framework of behavior therapy.

_____ 11. Behavior therapy is grounded on

a. the psychodynamic aspects of a person.
b. the principles of learning.
c. a philosophical view of the human condition.
d. the events of the first 5 years of life.

_____ 12. Mindfulness and acceptance-based approaches

a. have received empirical support as an effective form of therapy.
b. have no legitimate place in behavior therapy.
c. have no research evidence to support the value of the techniques used.
d. are a part of traditional behavior therapy.

e. have not yet been accepted into the behavioral tradition.

_____ 13. In behavior therapy it is generally agreed that

a. the therapist should decide the treatment goals.
b. the client should decide the treatment goals.
c. goals of therapy are the same for all clients.
d. goals are not necessary.

_____ 14. Which is *not* true as it is applied to behavior therapy?

a. Insight is necessary for behavior change to occur.
b. Therapy should focus on behavior change and not attitude change.

c. Therapy is not complete unless actions follow verbalizations.

d. A good working relationship between client and therapist is necessary for behavior change to occur.

_____ 15. According to most behavior therapists, a good working relationship between client and therapist is

a. a necessary and sufficient condition for behavior change to occur.

b. a necessary, but not sufficient, condition for behavior change to occur.

c. neither a necessary nor a sufficient condition for behavior change to occur.

_____ 16. Applied behavior analysis makes use of

a. classical conditioning techniques.

b. operant conditioning techniques.

c. cognitive behavioral techniques.

d. all of the above.

e. none of the above.

_____ 17. Mindfulness practices rely on

a. positive reinforcement.

b. negative reinforcement.

c. didactic instruction.

d. high intellectual abilities.

e. experiential learning and client discovery.

_____ 18. Dialectical behavior therapy

a. has no empirical support for its validity.

b. is a promising blend of behavioral and psychoanalytic techniques.

c. is a long-term therapy for treating depression.

d. is a form of operant conditioning.

e. is a form of classical conditioning.

_____ 19. Which is *not* true of dialectical behavior therapy (DBT)?

a. DBT was formulated for treating borderline personality disorders.

b. DBT emphasizes the importance of the client–therapist relationship.

c. DBT incorporates mindfulness training and Zen practices.

d. DBT is a blend of Adlerian concepts and behavioral techniques.

e. DBT relies on empirical data to support its effectiveness.

_____ 20. An exposure-based procedure that involves imaginal flooding, cognitive restructuring, and the induction of rapid, rhythmic eye movements aimed at treatment of traumatic experiences is called

a. flooding.

b. in vivo desensitization.

c. systematic desensitization.

d. relaxation training.

e. eye movement desensitization and reprocessing.

_____ 21. Prolonged/intense exposure—either in real life or in imagination—to highly anxiety-evoking stimuli is called

a. self-management training.

b. in vivo desensitization.

c. systematic desensitization.

d. flooding.

e. eye movement desensitization and reprocessing.

_____ 22. A limitation of traditional behavior therapy is its

a. lack of research to evaluate the effectiveness of techniques.

b. de-emphasis on the role of feelings in therapy.

c. lack of clear concepts on which to base practice.

d. disregard for the client–therapist relationship.

e. overemphasis on early childhood experiences.

_____ 23. Contemporary behavior therapy places emphasis on

a. the interplay between the individual and the environment.

b. helping clients acquire insight into the causes of their problems.

c. a phenomenological approach to understanding the person.

d. encouraging clients to reexperience unfinished business with significant others by role-playing with them in the present.

e. working through the transference relationship with the therapist.

_____ 24. Which is *not* true as it applies to multimodal therapy?

a. Therapeutic flexibility and versatility are valued highly.
b. Therapists adjust their procedures to effectively achieve the client's goals in therapy.
c. Great care is taken to fit the client to a predetermined type of treatment.
d. The approach encourages technical eclecticism.
e. The therapist makes a comprehensive assessment of the client's level of functioning at the outset of therapy.

_____ 25. Which of the following is *not* considered one of the basic characteristics of contemporary behavior therapy?

a. Experimentally derived principles of learning are systemati-cally applied to help people change their maladaptive behaviors.
b. Emphasis is on using evidence-based treatment interventions.
c. The focus is on assessing overt and covert behavior directly, identifying the problem, and evaluating change.
d. The therapy is an experiential and insight-oriented approach.
e. There is an attempt to develop culture-specific procedures and obtain clients' adherence and cooperation in a treatment program.

Chapter 10

Cognitive Behavior Therapy

PRECHAPTER SELF-INVENTORY

Directions: Refer to page 43 for general directions. Use the following code:

    5 = I *strongly agree* with this statement.

    4 = I *agree*, in most respects, with this statement.

    3 = I am *undecided* in my opinion about this statement.

    2 = I *disagree*, in most respects, with this statement.

    1 = I *strongly disagree* with this statement.

Note: Items 1–7 refer to Ellis's rational emotive behavior therapy.

_____ 1. We contribute to our own psychological problems by the way we interpret events and situations.

_____ 2. We originally learn irrational beliefs from others during childhood, yet we tend to unthinkingly keep reindoctrinating ourselves.

_____ 3. Therapy is largely an educational process.

_____ 4. The main goal of therapy should be to reduce clients' self-defeating outlook and help them acquire a more rational philosophy of life.

_____ 5. Central functions of the therapist include challenging clients' illogical ideas and teaching them how to think and evaluate in a rational way.

_____ 6. It is appropriate for a therapist to persuade, to be highly directive, and to confront faulty thinking.

_____ 7. A warm or deeply personal relationship between client and therapist is neither a necessary nor a sufficient condition for psychotherapy.

Note: Items 8–14 refer to Beck's cognitive therapy.

_____ 8. The therapist's role is to help clients look for evidence that either supports or refutes their hypotheses and views.

_____ 9. To understand the nature of emotional disturbances, it is essential to focus on the cognitive content of an individual's reactions to the upsetting event.

_____ 10. Therapy is best structured as a present-centered, problem focused, brief, psychoeducational approach.

_____ 11. Thinking plays a major role in depression.

_____ 12. The most direct route to changing dysfunctional emotions and behaviors is to modify inaccurate and faulty thinking.

_____ 13. The therapist functions as a catalyst and a guide who helps clients understand how their beliefs and attitudes influence the way they feel and act.

_____ 14. Therapy should consist of a process of co-investigation, or collaborative empiricism, as a way to uncover and examine faulty interpretations.

Note: Items 15–20 refer to Meichenbaum's cognitive behavior modification.

_____ 15. As a basic prerequisite to behavior change, clients need to notice how they think, feel, and behave and the impact they have on others.

_____ 16. Therapy involves helping clients become aware of their self-talk and the stories they tell about themselves.

_____ 17. Much of the therapy process consists of teaching clients more effective coping skills in the sessions.

_____ 18. In stress management training it is essential to teach clients how they contribute to their stress and also specific coping strategies for effectively dealing with stress.

_____ 19. If clients hope to change, it is imperative that they practice new self-statements and apply their new skills in real-life situations.

_____ 20. It is important to provide a simple conceptual framework to clients outlining how they can interpret and react to stress differently.

OVERVIEW: RATIONAL EMOTIVE BEHAVIOR THERAPY AND COGNITIVE THERAPY

Key Figures and Major Focus

Founders: Albert Ellis is the founder of rational emotive behavior therapy (REBT) and is the grandfather of the other cognitive behavioral approaches. Aaron Beck is the founder of, and key spokesperson for, cognitive therapy (CT). Another key figure in the development of cognitive therapy and teaching this approach is Judith Beck. Donald Meichenbaum is a pioneer in cognitive behavior modification and his cognitive behavioral approach combines some of the best elements of behavior therapy and cognitive therapy.

A highly didactic, cognitive behavior-oriented approach, REBT stresses the role of action and practice in combating irrational, self-indoctrinated ideas. It focuses on the role of thinking and belief systems as the roots of personal problems. Beck's CT shares with REBT the active, directive, time-limited, present-centered, structured approach used to treat various disorders such as depression, anxiety, and phobias. It is an insight-focused therapy that emphasizes recognizing and changing negative thoughts and maladaptive beliefs. Meichenbaum's cognitive behavioral approach suggests that it may be easier and more effective to _behave_ our way into a new way of thinking, than to _think_ our way into a new way of behaving.

Originally called _behavior therapy_, the more contemporary term _cognitive behavior therapy_ (CBT) was introduced in the mid-1970s as therapists began emphasizing the interaction among behavioral, cognitive, and affective dimensions. Contemporary CBT is a blend of cognitive and behavioral concepts and techniques.

Philosophy and Basic Assumptions

REBT assumes that thinking, evaluating, analyzing, questioning, doing, practicing, and redeciding are at the base of behavior change. REBT is a didactic and directive model. Therapy is a process of reeducation. The cognitive behavioral approaches are based on the assumption that a reorganization of one's self-statements will result in a corresponding reorganization of one's behavior.

Like REBT, cognitive therapy rests on the premise that cognitions are the major determinants of how we feel and act. CT assumes that the internal dialogue of clients plays a major role in their behavior and feelings. Changing thoughts is the path to changing behaviors and feelings. The ways in which individuals monitor and instruct themselves and interpret events shed light on the dynamics of disorders such as depression and anxiety.

Donald Meichenbaum's cognitive behavior approach to training—(*self-instructional training* and *stress inoculation training*—focuses more on helping clients become aware of their self-talk and the stories they tell about themselves. Meichenbaum's cognitive behavioral modification process consists of helping clients interrupt the downward spiral of thinking, feeling, and behaving, and teaching them more adaptive ways of coping using the resources they bring to therapy. His stress inoculation training is a complex, multifaceted cognitive-behavioral intervention that is both a preventive and treatment approach.

Key Concepts

Ellis makes it clear that REBT holds that although emotional disturbance is rooted in childhood, people keep telling themselves irrational and illogical sentences. The approach is based on the A-B-C theory of personality: A = actual event; B = belief system; C = consequence. Emotional problems are the result of one's beliefs, which need to be challenged by a variety of different methods. Cognitive restructuring involves detecting and debating faulty thinking and substituting negative self-talk with constructive beliefs and thoughts. Eventually, clients acquire an effective philosophy and also create a new set of feelings.

According to Beck's cognitive therapy, psychological problems stem from commonplace processes such as faulty thinking, making incorrect inferences on the basis of inadequate or incorrect information, and failing to distinguish between fantasy and reality. Cognitive therapy consists of changing dysfunctional emotions and behaviors by modifying inaccurate and dysfunctional thinking. The techniques are designed to identify and test the client's misconceptions and faulty assumptions.

A basic premise of Meichenbaum's cognitive behavior modification (CBM) is that clients, as a prerequisite to behavior change, must notice and become aware of how they think, feel, and behave, and the impact they have on others. For change to occur, clients need to interrupt the scripted nature of their behavior so that they can evaluate their behavior in various situations.

Therapeutic Goals

The goal of REBT is to eliminate a self-defeating outlook on life and acquire a more rational and tolerant philosophy. Clients are taught that the events of life themselves do not disturb us; rather, our interpretation of events is what is critical. Clients are taught how to identify and uproot their "shoulds," "musts," and "oughts." Further, they are taught how to substitute preferences for demands.

The goal of cognitive therapy is to change the way clients think by using their automatic thoughts to reach the core schemata and begin to introduce the idea of schema restructuring. Changes in beliefs and thought processes tend to result in changes in the way people feel and how they behave. Through a Socratic dialogue with the therapist, clients in CT are encouraged to gather and weigh the evidence in support of their beliefs. CT employs collaborative empiricism as a way of helping clients test the beliefs they live by. Clients learn to discriminate between their own thoughts and the events that occur in reality.

Meichenbaum's stress inoculation training involves collaborative goal setting that nurtures hope, direct-action skills, and acceptance-based coping skills. These coping skills are designed to be applied to both present problems and future difficulties.

Therapeutic Relationship

In REBT, a warm relationship between the client and the therapist is not essential. However, the client needs to feel unconditional positive regard from the therapist. The therapist does not blame or condemn clients; rather, he or she teaches them how to avoid rating and condemning themselves. The therapist functions as a teacher; the client functions as a student. As clients begin to understand how they continue to contribute to their problems, they need to actively practice changing their self-defeating behavior and converting it into rational behavior.

Cognitive therapy emphasizes a collaborative effort. Together, the therapist and client frame the client's conclusions in the form of a testable hypothesis. Cognitive therapists are continuously active and deliberately interactive with the client; they also strive to engage the client's active participation and collaboration throughout all phases of therapy. CT is based on the premise that the quality of the therapeutic alliance is related to therapy outcomes.

Techniques and Procedures

Rational emotive behavior therapists are eclectic in that they use a variety of cognitive, affective, and behavioral techniques, tailoring them to individual clients. The approach borrows many methods from behavioral therapy. Cognitive techniques include disputing irrational beliefs, cognitive homework, changing one's language, cognitive role playing, and the use of humor. Emotive techniques include rational emotive imagery, role playing, and shame-attacking exercises. Behavioral techniques include operant conditioning, self-management strategies, and modeling. Techniques are designed to induce clients to critically examine their present beliefs and behavior.

With respect to techniques and therapeutic style, there are some differences between REBT and cognitive therapy. REBT is highly directive, persuasive, and confrontational. Cognitive therapy (CT) emphasizes a Socratic dialogue and helping clients discover their misconceptions for themselves. Through a process of guided discovery, the CT practitioner functions as a catalyst and guide who helps clients understand the connection between their thinking and the ways they feel and act.

Meichenbaum has designed a three-stage model for stress inoculation training: (1) the conceptual-educational phase, (2) the skills acquisition and skills consolidation phase, and (3) the application and follow-through phase. Some of the techniques that are used during the various phases of the training are: establishing a therapeutic alliance, providing clients with a conceptual framework in simple terms designed to educate them about ways of responding to a variety of stressful situations, learning a new set of coping self-statements, practicing relaxation methods, and practicing new self-statements and applying new skills.

Applications

Applications of REBT include individual therapy, ongoing group therapy, marathon encounter groups, brief therapy, marriage and family therapy, sex therapy, and classroom situations. REBT is applicable to clients with moderate anxiety, neurotic disorders, character disorders, psychosomatic problems, eating disorders, poor interpersonal skills, marital problems, poor parenting skills, addictions, and sexual dysfunctions. It is most effective with those who can reason well and who are not seriously disturbed.

Cognitive therapy is a structured therapy that is present-centered and problem-oriented; CT can be effective in treating depression and anxiety in a relatively short time. CT has been applied successfully in treating a broad range of problems with children, adolescents, and adults. It has applications for managing stress and parent training. Cognitive methods have also been very useful in treating posttraumatic stress disorder, schizophrenia, bipolar disorders, and various personality problems.

Meichenbaum's stress inoculation training (SIT) has useful applications for a wide variety of problems and clients and for both remediation and prevention. Some of these applications include anger control, anxiety management, assertion training, improving creative thinking, treating depression, and dealing with health problems. Stress inoculation training has been employed with medical patients and with psychiatric patients. SIT has been particularly successful in treating people with posttraumatic stress disorder (PTSD) and with veterans and combat-related PTSD.

Because the cognitive behavioral therapies are structured approaches, they are well suited as *brief therapies*. Clients acquire new knowledge and skills that they apply to understanding and resolving specific problems. The change process is effective because of the emphasis given to practicing new ways of thinking and acting outside of the therapy sessions through collaboratively designed homework assignments.

Cognitive behavioral therapy (CBT) has many applications to a variety of *counseling groups* in many different settings. Cognitive behavioral group therapy is effective for treating a wide range of emotional and behavioral problems. CBT in groups has been demonstrated to have beneficial results for specific problems such as anxiety, depression, phobia, obesity, eating disorders, dual diagnoses, and dissociative disorders.

Multicultural Perspectives

CBT tends to be culturally sensitive because it uses the individual's belief system, or worldview, as part of the method of self-exploration. The collaborative nature of CBT offers clients the structure many clients want, yet the therapist still strives to enlist their active participation in the therapeutic process. Because of the way CBT is practiced, it is ideally suited to working with clients from diverse backgrounds. Some factors that make CBT diversity effective include tailoring treatment to each individual, addressing the role of the external environment, the active and directive role of the therapist, the emphasis on education, relying on empirical evidence, the focus on present behavior, and the brevity of the approach. Cognitive behavioral practitioners function as teachers; clients acquire a wide range of skills they can use in dealing with the problems of living. This educational focus appeals to many clients who are interested in learning practical and effective methods of bringing about change.

Contributions

REBT is a comprehensive, integrative approach to therapy that uses cognitive, emotive, and behavioral methods to try to change disturbances in thinking, feeling, and behaving. REBT has shed much light on how people can change their emotions by changing the content of their thinking. It is in many ways the forerunner of other increasingly popular cognitive behavioral approaches.

With respect to cognitive therapy, Beck has made pioneering efforts in the treatment of anxiety, phobias, and depression, and this approach has received a great deal of attention by clinical researchers. He developed specific cognitive procedures that are useful in challenging a depressive client's assumptions and beliefs and in teaching clients how to change their thinking.

Cognitive behavior therapy has wide applicability. A strength of CBT consists of integrating assessment throughout therapy, which is an action that communicates respect for clients' viewpoints regarding their progress. Counseling is brief and places value on active practice in experimenting with new behavior so that insight is carried into doing. It discourages dependence on the therapist and stresses the client's capacity to control his or her own destiny.

Meichenbaum's stress inoculation training places special emphasis on practicing new skills both in the training itself and in daily life, and homework is a key part of the training process. A key strength of this approach involves clients learning how to generalize coping skills to various problem situations and acquiring relapse prevention strategies to ensure that their gains are consolidated.

A major contribution made by Ellis, the Becks, and Meichenbaum is the demystification of the therapy process. The cognitive behavioral approaches are based on an educational model that stresses a working alliance between therapist and client. CBT practitioners are able to obtain continuous feedback from clients on how well treatment strategies are working. Clients are active, informed, and responsible for the direction of therapy because they are partners in the enterprise.

Limitations

REBT does not provide a rationale for or clear explanation of why one tends to reindoctrinate oneself with irrational beliefs or why one clings to those beliefs. It does not apply to persons with limited intelligence. Possible dangers are the imposition of the therapist's own philosophy on the client and the psychological harm done to the client by the therapist who is overly confrontive or persuasive. Some cognitive behavioral approaches have the limitation of not emphasizing the expression and exploration of emotional issues. Increasingly, contemporary CBT practitioners are emphasizing the interplay of thoughts, feelings, and behaviors. In CBT the focus is on the present, which can result in failing to recognize the role of the past in a client's development. Cognitive behavioral assessments involve the investigation of a client's *personal* history. If therapists are unaware of a client's *cultural* beliefs that are rooted in the past, they may have difficulty in interpreting a client's personal experiences accurately.

 GLOSSARY OF KEY TERMS

A-B-C model of personality   Temporal sequence of antecedents, behavior, and consequences. The theory that people's problems do not stem from activating events but, rather, from their beliefs about such events. Thus, the best route to changing problematic emotions is to change one's beliefs about situations.

Arbitrary inferences   A form of cognitive distortion that refers to making conclusions without supporting and relevant evidence.

Automatic thoughts   Maladaptive thoughts that appear to arise reflexively, without conscious deliberation.

Cognitive behavior modification (CBM)   A therapeutic approach that focuses on changing the client's self-verbalizations.

Cognitive behavior therapy (CBT)   A treatment approach that aims at changing cognitions that are leading to psychological problems.

Cognitive distortions   In cognitive therapy, the client's misconceptions and faulty assumptions. Examples include arbitrary inference, selective abstraction, overgeneralization, magnification and minimizations, labeling and mislabeling, dichotomous thinking, and personalization.

Cognitive restructuring   A process of actively altering maladaptive thought patterns and replacing them with constructive and adaptive thoughts and beliefs.

Cognitive structure   The organizing aspect of thinking, which monitors and directs the choice of thoughts; implies an "executive processor," one that determines when to continue, interrupt, or change thinking patterns.

Cognitive therapy (CT)   An approach and set of procedures that attempts to change feelings and behavior by modifying faulty thinking and believing.

Cognitive triad   A pattern that triggers depression.

Collaborative empiricism   A strategy of viewing the client as a scientist who is able to make objective interpretations. The process in which therapist and client work together to phrase the client's faulty beliefs as hypotheses and design homework so that the client can test these hypotheses.

Constructivist approach   A recent development in cognitive therapy that emphasizes the subjective framework and interpretations of the client rather than looking to the objective bases of faulty beliefs.

Constructivist narrative perspective   An approach that focuses on the stories that people tell about them themselves and others regarding significant events in their lives.

Coping skills program   A behavioral procedure for helping clients deal effectively with stressful situations by learning to modify their thinking patterns.

Dichotomous thinking A cognitive error that involves categorizing experiences in either-or extremes.

Distortion of reality Erroneous thinking that disrupts one's life; can be contradicted by the client's objective appraisal of the situation.

Homework Carefully designed and agreed upon assignments aimed at getting clients to carry out positive actions that induce emotional and attitudinal change. These assignments are checked in later sessions, and clients learn effective ways to dispute self-defeating thinking.

Internal dialogue The sentences that people tell themselves and the debate that often goes on "inside their head"; a form of self-talk, or inner speech.

Irrational belief An unreasonable conviction that leads to emotional and behavioral problems.

Musturbation A term coined by Ellis to refer to behavior that is absolutist and rigid. We tell ourselves that we *must, should,* or *ought to* do or be something.

Overgeneralization A process of holding extreme beliefs on the basis of a single incident and applying them inappropriately to dissimilar events or settings.

Personalization A tendency for people to relate external events to themselves, even when there is no basis for making this connection.

Rational emotive behavior therapy (REBT) A theory that is based on the assumption that cognitions, emotions, and behaviors interact significantly and have a reciprocal cause-and-effect relationship.

Rational emotive imagery A form of intense mental practice for learning new emotional and physical habits. Clients imagine themselves thinking, feeling, and behaving in exactly the way they would like to in everyday situations.

Rationality The quality of thinking, feeling, and acting in ways that will help us attain our goals. Irrationality consists of thinking, feeling, and acting in ways that are self-defeating and that thwart our goals.

Relapse prevention Procedure for promoting long-term maintenance that involves identifying situations in which clients are likely to regress to old patterns and to develop coping skills in such situations.

Schema Core beliefs that are centrally related to dysfunctional behaviors. The process of cognitive therapy involves restructuring distorted core beliefs (or schema).

Selective abstraction A cognitive distortion that involves forming conclusions based on an isolated detail of an event.

Self-instructional therapy An approach to therapy based on the assumption that what people say to themselves directly influences the things they do. Training consists of learning new self-talk aimed at coping with problems.

Self-talk What people "say" to themselves when they are thinking. The internal dialogue that goes on within an individual in stressful situations.

Shame-attacking exercises A strategy used in REBT therapy that encourages people to do things despite a fear of feeling foolish or embarrassed. The aim of the exercise is to teach people that they can function effectively even if they might be perceived as doing foolish acts.

Socratic dialogue A process that cognitive therapists use in helping clients empirically test their core beliefs. Clients form hypotheses about their behavior through observation and monitoring.

Stress inoculation Individuals are given opportunities to deal with relatively mild stress stimuli in successful ways, so that they gradually develop a tolerance for stronger stimuli.

Stress inoculation training (SIT) A form of cognitive behavior modification developed by Donald Meichenbaum that is a combination of information giving, Socratic discussion, cognitive restructuring, problem solving, relaxation training, behavioral rehearsals, self-monitoring, self-instruction, self-reinforcement, and modifying environmental situations.

Therapeutic collaboration A process whereby the therapist strives to engage the client's active participation in all phases of therapy.

 QUESTIONS FOR REFLECTION AND DISCUSSION

1. Do you agree with the assumption of REBT that the basis for emotional disturbance lies in irrational beliefs and thinking? To what degree do you accept the notion that

events themselves do not cause emotional and behavioral problems; rather, that it is our cognitive evaluation and beliefs about life events that lead to our problems?

2. According to Ellis, effective psychotherapy can take place without personal warmth from the therapist. He contends that too much warmth and understanding can be counterproductive by fostering dependence on the therapist for approval. Beck emphasizes the collaborative nature of the therapeutic relationship, viewing it as essential for effective therapy to take place. Which of these views comes closer to your thinking about the role of the client–therapist relationship?

3. REBT tends to be highly directive, persuasive, and confrontive and involves a teaching role for the therapist. In contrast, cognitive therapy places more stress on Socratic dialogue, a process of posing open-ended questions to clients and letting them arrive at their own conclusions. If you were a client, which style do you think would be more effective with you? As a counselor, which role might you favor? Why?

4. In Beck's cognitive therapy the assumption is that a client's internal dialogue plays a major role in behavior. For him, how individuals monitor themselves, how they give themselves praise or criticism, how they interpret events, and how they make predictions of future behavior are directly related to emotional disorders. How could you apply his ideas to counseling a depressed client? How might you teach such a client to challenge his or her own thinking and develop new thinking?

5. Beck maintains that systematic errors in reasoning lead to faulty assumptions and misconceptions, which he terms "cognitive distortions." After reviewing his list of cognitive distortions, which, if any, apply to you? Which CT procedures might be of value to you in examining your faulty assumptions?

6. In Meichenbaum's cognitive behavior modification, cognitive restructuring is vital in teaching people how to deal effectively with stress. Part of his program involves teaching clients cognitive and behavioral strategies to cope with stressful situations. If you had a client who wanted to learn self-management techniques to reduce stress, what are some specific steps you would teach the client?

7. What do you consider to be some of the major contributions of the cognitive behavioral approaches? How do you think cognitive factors influence one's emotions and behaviors?

8. Think of situations in which you might encounter clients with culturally diverse backgrounds. What aspects of cognitive behavioral therapy do you think might work well in multicultural counseling? How might you have to modify some of your techniques so that they would be appropriate for the client's cultural background?

9. Homework is a part of all of the cognitive behavioral approaches. What are some ways in which you might attempt to incorporate homework in your counseling practice? Can you think of ways to increase the chances of your client cooperating and carrying out the homework?

10. What are some ways to incorporate exploration of feelings in the cognitive behavioral approaches? Of the theories you've studied so far, what approaches might you want to blend with cognitive behavioral therapy? What are a few experiential techniques that you might want to add to the cognitive and behavioral techniques?

 ## ISSUES AND QUESTIONS FOR PERSONAL APPLICATION

The following questions and some of the underlying issues can be applied personally to help you get a better grasp of cognitive behavior therapy. Bring the questions to class for discussion.

1. Are you aware of reindoctrinating yourself with certain beliefs and values that you originally accepted from your parents or from society? Make a list of some of your beliefs and values. Do you want to keep them? Do you want to modify them?

2. Are you able to accept yourself in spite of your limitations and imperfections? Do you blame yourself or others for your limitations?

3. Review Ellis's list of irrational ideas. How many can you identify with? How do you think your life is affected by your irrational beliefs? How do you determine *for yourself* whether your beliefs are rational or irrational?

To help focus your thinking on the above issues, put a check mark (√) before each of the following irrational beliefs that apply to you:

_____ a. "I must be thoroughly competent in everything I do."

_____ b. "Others must treat me fairly and in ways that I want them to."

_____ c. "I must have universal approval, and if I don't get this approval from everyone, it's horrible and I feel depressed."

_____ d. "Life must be the way I want it to be, and if it isn't, I can't tolerate it."

_____ e. "If I fail at something, the results will be catastrophic."

_____ f. "I should feel eternally guilty and rotten and continue to blame myself for all of my past mistakes."

_____ g. "Because all of my miseries are caused by others, I have no control over my life, and I can't change things unless *they* change."

List a few other statements you tend to make that might pinpoint your core irrational ideas:

_____

_____

_____

4. Select one of your beliefs that causes you trouble. Then review the A-B-C model of personality and attempt to apply that method to changing your irrational belief. What is the experience like for you? Do you think the method holds promise for helping you lead a less troubled life?

5. How can you challenge your own irrational beliefs and attitudes? Once you are aware of some basic problems or difficulties, what do you see that you can do *for yourself* to change toward a more rational system?

6. REBT practitioners are highly active and directive, and they often give their own views without hesitation. Does that style fit you personally? Could you adopt it and feel comfortable? Why or why not?

7. The REBT practitioner acts as a model. What implications do you see for self-development of the client? Can the client grow to become his or her own person, or does he or she become a copy of the therapist?

8. In being a model for clients, it is important that therapists not be highly emotionally disturbed, that they live rationally, that they not be worried about losing their clients' love and approval, and that they have the courage to confront clients directly. Would you have any difficulty in being that type of model? Explain.

9. Consider the applications of REBT to school counseling or to counseling in community mental health clinics. Assume that a practitioner who employs the principles and methods of REBT does not have a doctorate, has not had any supervised internship, and has not had extensive training in REBT. What cautions do you think need to be applied? What are the potential misuses of the approach? How can the approach have more potentially harmful results than, for example, the person-centered approach?

10. If you were to be a client in counseling, which approach might you favor for yourself—Ellis's REBT or Beck's cognitive therapy? What specific features of REBT might be

useful in helping you cope with your problems? And what aspects of cognitive therapy could you use?

11. According to Meichenbaum's cognitive theory of behavior change, there are three relevant phases. Clients are asked to (1) observe and monitor their own behavior, identifying negative thoughts and feelings; (2) begin to create a new internal dialogue by substituting positive and constructive self-statements for negative ones; and (3) acquire more effective coping skills that they can practice both in the therapy session and in real-life situations. For at least one week, identify some behavior you would like to change and apply this three-phase process. Can you think of ways to use this strategy with your clients? In what counseling situations might you use Meichenbaum's cognitive restructuring techniques?

12. Assume that you are working with a small group of college students who have problems with test anxiety and fears relating to failure. If you were to employ *cognitive methods* to change their mental set and expectations, what are some things you might say to these students? In what ways might thoughts, self-talk, self-fulfilling prophecies, and attitudes of failure (all examples of cognitive processes) influence these students' *behavior* in test-taking situations?

    a. How would you set up your program?

    b. What cognitive techniques would you use? What other behavioral techniques would you employ to change these students' cognitive structures and their behavior?

    c. What are some ways by which you might evaluate the effectiveness of your program?

13. Complete the REBT Self-Help Form on page 151 by making it a homework assignment for a week. After you complete the form, look for patterns in your thinking. What connections do you see between your beliefs and the way you feel? Focus especially on creating *disputing* statements.

PRACTICAL APPLICATIONS

REBT is based on the assumption that people create their own emotional disturbances. It places the individual squarely in the center of the universe and gives individuals almost full responsibility for choosing to make or not to make themselves seriously disturbed. It follows logically that if people have the capacity to make themselves disturbed by foolishly and devoutly believing in irrational assumptions about themselves and others, they can generally make themselves undisturbed again. REBT assumes that change can best be accomplished through rational emotive procedures and that to effect behavioral change, hard work and active practice are essential.

The homework assignment method is one good way of assisting clients in putting new behavior into practice. The method encourages clients to actively attack the irrational beliefs at the roots of their problems. In this exercise, suggest what you consider might be an appropriate homework assignment for each situation described.

1. The client, a college sophomore, wants to overcome his shyness around women. He does not date and even does his best to keep away from women because he is afraid they will reject him. But he does want to change that pattern. What homework might you suggest? _____

    _____

    _____

    _____

2. The client says that because she feels depressed much of the time she tries to avoid facing life's difficulties or anything about her that might make her feel more depressed. She

would like to feel happy, but she is afraid of doing much. What homework might you suggest? _____

_____

_____

3. The client feels that he must win everyone's approval. He has become a "super nice guy" who goes out of his way to please everyone. Rarely does he assert himself, for fear that he might displease someone who then would not like him. He says he would like to be less of a nice guy and more assertive. What homework might you suggest?

_____

_____

_____

_____

4. The client would like to take a course in creative writing, but she fears that she has no talent. She is afraid of failing, afraid of being told that she is dumb, and afraid to follow through with taking the course. What homework might you suggest? _____

_____

_____

_____

_____

5. The client continually accepts blame by telling himself how terrible he is because he does not give his wife enough attention. He feels totally to blame for the marital problems between him and his wife, and he says he cannot let go of his guilt. What homework might you suggest? _____

_____

_____

_____

6. Each week the client comes to his sessions with a new excuse for why he has not succeeded in following through with his homework assignments. Either he forgets, gets too busy, gets scared, or puts it off—anything but actually *doing* something to change what he *says* he wants to change. Instead of really doing much of anything, he whines each week about how rotten he feels and how he so much would like to change but just doesn't know how. What homework might you suggest? _____

_____

_____

_____

JERRY COREY COUNSELS STAN FROM A COGNITIVE BEHAVIORAL PERSPECTIVE

Session 8. Cognitive Behavior Therapy Applied to the Case of Stan

As you have come to know Stan, you have learned that he has many maladaptive thoughts in relation to his capabilities and performance. Cognitive behavior therapy aims to identify faulty thinking and to reframe beliefs into more constructive thoughts. This demonstration of CBT focuses on exploring some of Stan's faulty beliefs through the use of role reversal and cognitive restructuring techniques.

Rational Emotive Behavior Therapy
Self-Help Form

A   (Activating Event)

(blank box)

- Briefly summarize the situation you are disturbed about (what would a camera see?).
- An A can be internal or external, real or imagined.
- An A can be an event in the past, present, or future.

C   (Consequences)

Major unhealthy negative **emotions**:
Major self-defeating **behaviors**:

(blank box)

Unhealthy negative emotions include:

• Anxiety	• Depression	• Low Frustration Tolerance
• Shame/ Embarrassment	• Hurt	
• Rage	• Guilt	• Jealousy

IBS (IRRATIONAL BELIEFS)	D (DISPUTING IBS)	RBS (RATIONAL BELIEFS)	E (NEW EFFECT)
• _____ • _____ • _____ • _____	• _____ • _____ • _____ • _____	• _____ • _____ • _____ • _____	New healthy **negative behaviors:** New constructive **behaviors:**

To identify IBs, look for:

- **Dogmatic Demands** (musts, absolutes, shoulds)
- **Awfulizing** (It's awful, terrible, horrible)
- **Low Frustration Tolerance** (I can't stand it)
- **Self/Other Rating** (I'm/he/she is bad, worthless.)

To dispute, ask yourself:

- Where is holding this belief getting me? Is it *helpful* or *self-defeating*?
- Where is the evidence to support the existence of my irrational belief? Is it consistent with reality?
- Is my belief *logical*? Does it follow from my preferences?
- Is it really *awful* (as bad as it could be)?
- Can I really not stand it?

To think more rationally, strive for:

- **Non-Dogmatic Preferences** (wishes, wants, desires)
- **Evaluating Badness** (It's bad, unfortunate.)
- **High Frustration Tolerance** (I don't like it, but I can stand it.)
- **Not Globally Rating Self or Others** (I—and others—are fallible human beings.)

Healthy negative emotions include:

- Disappointment
- Concern
- Annoyance
- Sadness
- Regret
- Frustration

Source: Dryden, W. (1995a). *Brief Rational Emotive Behaviour Therapy.* London: Wiley. Reprinted by Permission of Albert Ellis.

Before viewing the session, read Chapter 10, pages 318–319 in the textbook and answer the questions listed under the heading "Follow-Up: You Continue as Stan's Cognitive Behavior Therapist." What are a few of Stan's problematic beliefs that you would encourage him to explore? As you watch this counseling clip, note what appear to be Stan's thoughts? What is his self-talk like? See if you can identify the specific type of cognitive distortion in each thought he shares. How does the counselor reframe these thoughts in the session? How would this approach work for you if you were the client? After you have viewed the video, reflect upon and discuss these questions:

1. Can you identify with any of Stan's faulty beliefs? Is so, which ones?

2. How effective do you think Jerry's interventions with Stan were?

3. CBT is based on the premise that our beliefs influence what we do and how we feel. To what degree do you agree with that assumption?

4. In what ways might you have worked differently with Stan from what you saw in this demonstration?

5. Jerry disputes Stan's belief by a role-reversal technique. Can you see yourself using this technique with Stan? Why or why not?

6. What possible therapeutic advantages can you see in asking Stan, "Where is the evidence for this belief?" What would you say if he provided "good" evidence?

7. What specific aspects of cognitive behavior therapy would you want to incorporate into your own therapeutic style?

8. What is one of Stan's beliefs that you would ask him to challenge?

9. How does the technique of active disputation lead to cognitive restructuring?

10. What kind of homework might you suggest to Stan toward the end of this session?

A Suggested In-Class Activity

Small groups would be a useful follow-up for discussing your reactions to both the section in the text on CBT with Stan and the CBT demonstration that you viewed. As you were observing the session, what shifts, if any, did you notice in Stan's thinking? In your small groups apply the principles of cognitive restructuring to one of your own beliefs. Consider these questions as topics for discussion:

1. What did you find most interesting in this session? Why?

2. If you were counseling Stan from this particular theoretical framework, what is one additional technique you might use? What would you hope to accomplish with this intervention?

3. If you were the client, how would you be likely to respond to the therapist's (Jerry's) comments and interventions in this particular session?

If time allows, one student can role play Stan, another the counselor, and another the process observer. Try you hand at applying cognitive behavioral techniques in small groups.

JERRY COREY'S WORK WITH RUTH FROM A COGNITIVE BEHAVIORAL PERSPECTIVE

In working with Ruth as a cognitive behavior therapist, I employ a directive, structured, and action-oriented approach. In many ways the client–therapist relationship is like the student–teacher relationship. I view therapy as a learning process that will afford Ruth the opportunity to explore ways of changing her thinking, feeling, and behaving. I assist her in identifying a number of her core beliefs, many of which she acquired from her parents. Once we have identified some of her major beliefs, I will ask her to begin thinking about the decisions she made about herself, others, and the world. I will also ask her to reflect on the direction her early decisions are taking her.

To achieve the goal of assisting Ruth in achieving a constructive set of beliefs and acquiring a self-enhancing internal dialogue, I perform several tasks as her therapist. First, I assist Ruth in critically evaluating the self-defeating beliefs she originally accepted without questioning. Throughout the therapeutic process, I attempt to actively teach Ruth that being overly self-critical is the basis of many of her emotional and behavioral problems. Basically, Ruth tells herself that she must be perfect at everything. She berates herself when she does not measure up to expectations that others have set for her. She is beginning to realize that she is performance-oriented and rarely allows herself to enjoy the process.

I suggest a cognitive role-play situation in which I take on the role of Ruth's critical self and Ruth assumes the role of the side that would like to relax and let up on her demands.

RUTH: [*playing her more accepting side*] You don't need to drive yourself so hard. Be kinder to yourself, and give yourself room to make mistakes.

JERRY: [*playing Ruth's self-critical side*] But it's up to me to take care of everything! If I don't, things will fall apart at home.

RUTH: Well, others in my family can take more responsibility. I'm tired of being the only one who is responsible for everything in the family.

JERRY: But if I let down, my family will suffer. So I must do everything!

After engaging in a process of argumentation where Ruth tries to convince me that she has a right to lighten up, she becomes emotional. She realizes how exhausting it is to demand perfection of herself at all times. Listening to me as I played her critical side, she becomes aware of the price she pays. She is now in a position to actively challenge her self-talk and work toward replacing some faulty beliefs that influence what she does.

My major focus with Ruth is on her thinking. Only through learning to apply rigorous self-challenging methods will she succeed in freeing herself from the defeatist thinking that led to her problems. I am concerned that Ruth not only recognize her self-defeating thought patterns and the resultant feelings but also take steps to dispute and change them. Ruth's real work consists of doing homework in everyday situations and bringing the results of these assignments to our sessions for analysis and evaluation.

You Continue Working With Ruth as Her Cognitive Behavior Therapist

1. Refer to *Case Approach to Counseling and Psychotherapy* (Chapter 8) for examples of two different cognitive-oriented approaches to working with Ruth: Dr. Albert Ellis's rational emotive behavior therapy and Dr. Frank Dattilio's cognitive behavioral approach in family therapy. In this chapter, I also show my style of applying cognitive behavioral techniques in working with Ruth.

2. See the *DVD for Integrative Counseling: The Case of Ruth and Lecturettes* (Session 6 on a cognitive focus) for a demonstration of how to utilize cognitive behavioral techniques in addressing Ruth's faulty thinking. Do you identify with any of Ruth's faulty beliefs? How might cognitive therapy help you?

3. What are some of Ruth's faulty beliefs that you would want to target for intervention? How would you proceed in assisting her to challenge her thinking?

4. From what you know of Ruth, what kinds of homework would you suggest that could result in her examining her self-talk and core beliefs?

5. What are some cognitive and behavioral techniques that you are most likely to employ?

A CASE FROM A COGNITIVE BEHAVIORAL PERSPECTIVE

Brittany: "Addressing Acting-Out Behavior in an Adolescent Girl"
By **Caroline Bailey, PhD.,** Assistant Professor of Social Work, California State University, Fullerton

Background Information

Brittany is a sixteen-year-old girl of mixed Caucasian and African American decent. Her family has recently moved from a large, diverse, metropolitan area to a small midwestern town. According to her mother and father, Brittany did not respond well to the move.

Prior to the move, Brittany's parents reported that she was a very well-behaved child who did well in school and participated in extracurricular sports. She was an active member of the student council and worked after school at a coffee shop in the local mall to save money for college. Brittany dreamed of becoming a veterinarian. However, all of this changed when she arrived at her new school. She has only been in school three months and is already failing chemistry and shows no interest in after school activities. She was kicked off the track team after only two practices for arguing with the coach. She has been suspended once for fighting with another student and sent to detention 14 times for speaking disrespectfully to her teachers and disrupting class. Of great concern to Brittany's mother is that Brittany has recently dyed her hair pink and pierced her lip. Brittany's father is concerned because she is generally disagreeable at home, refuses to do her chores, and has not completed a homework assignment in three weeks. Brittany's parents brought her to counseling because they are at a loss for how to control her behavior. They hope that therapy can help Brittany change back to her "old self."

Dr. Caroline Bailey's Way of Working With Brittany From a Cognitive Behavioral Perspective

When I greeted Brittany in the waiting room, she was sitting on the couch with her back turned toward her parents. Her parents were eager to speak with me alone. However, I was clear that while I valued their input and would make time to speak with them at a later time, this particular session belonged to Brittany. In hearing this, Brittany smirked at her parents and quickly walked into my office. When I asked Brittany how she felt about coming to counseling, she replied, "Well—at least it is better than having to talk to *them*!" as she rolled her eyes in the direction of the waiting room.

In talking with Brittany, several themes of her life became clear. One of these themes involved her contention that her parents had already changed her life quite drastically by moving her across the country to a new school. In this setting none of the other students resembled her in terms of ethnicity, interests, or sophistication. She had no intention of "changing back" to her "old self" just to please *them*. The next issue Brittany mentioned was that she found her new school "too easy," and her teachers to be "close-minded," and therefore not worth listening to or respecting. Third, Brittany mentioned that she deeply missed her friends from home and felt that her new peers were unable to accept her because she was so different from them in her upbringing, culture, and beliefs. She finally noted that she was the only bi-racial student in her grade and that she felt alone and isolated. When I asked her about her behavioral outbursts at school, Brittany articulately explained that she feels she is responding appropriately to an impossible situation. She was clear that she did not care if her peers, teachers and parents felt she was acting out because none of them would even accept her. However, she agreed to participate in therapy because she "didn't like feeling sad and bitter all the time" and wanted to work on getting in less trouble at school. Although Brittany was tired of detention, she was adamant that she had no desire to work on her behavior at home because she felt her parents deserved what they got for moving her in the first place.

Ideally, I believed it would be helpful for Brittany to work on creating a more positive relationship with her parents from a developmental psychopathology perspective. At the same time, I realized that Brittany was a teenage girl working on the important task of individuation and was appropriately focused on asserting her own identity within her family context. Hence, some familiar discord at this point in time was to be expected. As such, Brittany and I agreed that we would focus on her school-related goals during our time together. Brittany was very clear that we would discuss her parents only if it pertained to school and as she felt it was necessary to vent about how they "complicated her life" and "misunderstood her." I agreed to her boundary, but also let her know that I was open to talking about her relationship with her parents if that was something she would like to explore, but that this was not an expectation of therapy. It was her choice.

Some of Brittany's ideas, feelings, and actions are considered age-appropriate tasks of adolescent identity development, such as experimentation with social roles and personal appearance. It was also clear that Brittany's attitude and behavior in her new environment were clearly disrupting her functioning in key developmental areas, namely, her school performance and social interactions. As a CBT therapist, I was acutely aware of Brittany's use of "absolute" terms in her language as she described her circumstances. Her account of her life was filled with many overt and covert "musts" and "shoulds" as well as a good deal of "all or nothing" thinking. Brittany held several fixed, maladaptive beliefs, or *cognitive distortions* about her new environment. These distortions caused angry and sad feelings that in turn, directly affected her behavior. As her cognitive behavioral therapist, I was very interested in working with Brittany in changing her maladaptive thoughts, feelings, and behaviors into more constructive beliefs, sentiments, and actions.

The first cognitive behavioral technique Brittany and I used together was learning to *identify and label her cognitive distortions*. For example, after two counseling sessions Brittany was able to tell me that her belief that "none of her peers would ever accept her" contained two types of cognitive distortions: *all-or-nothing thinking* and *jumping to conclusions*. In her next session, Brittany learned that she could *dispute her self-defeating thoughts* through examining the evidence that supports them. For example, although Brittany feared social rejection, she was able to realize that she really did not have any factual evidence to support her unrealistic fear that every student in the school would reject her both currently and in the future. Brittany playfully admitted that she didn't have a crystal ball and could not foresee the future and that perhaps, some day, some other student might actually want to be her friend.

Once Brittany learned to identify and accurately label her cognitive distortions, we began to *reframe* her inaccurate beliefs and responses into more helpful, adaptive thoughts and actions. For example, Brittany was able to take her existing, maladaptive belief that all of the teachers at her school were "closed-minded" and "not worth listening to" and modify these convictions in ways that were more in line with her goal of not getting in trouble. Brittany now listens to her teachers and evaluates whether or not they are closed-minded before she decides whether or not to speak disrespectfully to them. Over time spent in therapy, Brittany found that she actually felt better about herself when her thoughts, actions, and feelings were geared toward helping her be successful rather than geared toward maladaptive behaviors that led to undesirable outcomes like detention and being grounded. Over the last two months, Brittany has only served three detentions.

Follow Up: You Continue as Brittany's Therapist

Brittany has made progress in identifying and reframing her cognitive distortions. However, she still remains angry with her parents for moving her family across the country and is still behaving poorly at home. Likewise, she continues to have trouble making friends with her peers. She continues to feel that she is very different from other students in terms of her beliefs, culture, and interests. As you continue working with Brittany consider the following questions:

1. What cognitive behavioral techniques might be appropriate to use with Brittany as she explores her angry feelings toward her parents who want her to be her "old self," an identity that Brittany clearly rejects?

2. Adolescence is a time of social experimentation and identity development. How would a cognitive behavioral therapist determine what portion of Brittany's feelings of "not fitting in" are consistent with her developmental stage and what portion are indicative of social skills difficulties?

3. How would you use cognitive behavioral therapy techniques in a culturally sensitive manner to address Brittany's feelings about being the only biracial student in her class?

QUIZ ON COGNITIVE BEHAVIOR THERAPY

A Comprehension Check

Score _____ %

Note: Refer to Appendix 1 for the scoring key.

True/false items: Decide if the following statements are "more true" or "more false" as they apply to REBT or other cognitive behavioral approaches.

T F   1. REBT makes use of both cognitive and behavioral techniques, but it does not use emotive techniques.

T F   2. REBT stresses the importance of the therapist demonstrating unconditional positive regard for the client.

T F   3. Cognitive therapy for depression was developed by Meichenbaum.

T F   4. A major contribution made by Ellis, the Becks, and Meichenbaum is the demystification of the therapy process.

T F   5. Ellis shares Rogers's view of the client–therapist relationship as a condition for change to occur within clients.

T F   6. Beck developed a procedure known as stress-inoculation training.

T F   7. To feel worthwhile, human beings need love and acceptance from *significant* others.

T F   8. Ellis maintains that events themselves do not cause emotional disturbances; rather, it is our evaluation of and beliefs about these events that cause our problems.

T F   9. A difference between Beck's cognitive therapy and Ellis's REBT is that Beck places more emphasis on helping clients discover their misconceptions for themselves than does Ellis.

T F   10. According to Beck, people become disturbed when they label and evaluate themselves by a set of rules that are unrealistic.

Multiple-choice items: Select the *one best answer* of those alternatives given. Consider each question within the framework of cognitive behavior therapy.

_____ 11. Which of the following is **not** a part of stress inoculation training?

a. Socratic discovery-oriented inquiry

b. relaxation training

c. behavioral rehearsals

d. self-reinforcement

e. exception questions

_____ 12. REBT is based on the philosophical assumption that human beings are

a. innately striving for self-actualization.
b. determined by strong unconscious sexual and aggressive forces.
c. potentially able to think rationally but have a tendency toward irrational thinking.
d. trying to develop a lifestyle to overcome feelings of basic inferiority.
e. determined strictly by environmental conditioning.

_____ 13. REBT stresses that human beings

a. think, emote, and behave simultaneously.
b. think without emoting.
c. emote without thinking.
d. behave without emoting or thinking.

_____ 14. REBT views neurosis as the result of

a. inadequate mothering during infancy.
b. failure to fulfill our existential needs.
c. excessive feelings.
d. irrational thinking and behaving.

_____ 15. In cognitive behavioral group therapy

a. there is some research that shows that this approach is effective for treating a wide range of emotional and behavioral problems.
b. the group leader assumes a blank screen demeanor so as to enhance transference feelings of the members.
c. the assumption is that a therapeutic atmosphere is both necessary and sufficient for change to occur.
d. the group leader believes that using techniques interferes with the group process.
e. the emphasis is on having members identify and express feelings.

_____ 16. REBT contends that people

a. have a need to be loved and accepted by everyone.
b. need to be accepted by most people.

c. will become emotionally sick if they are rejected.
d. do not need to be accepted and loved.
e. need to be accepted and will become sick if they are rejected.

_____ 17. According to REBT, we develop emotional disturbances because of

a. a traumatic event.
b. our beliefs about certain events.
c. abandonment by those we depend on for support.
d. withdrawal of love and acceptance.

_____ 18. Meichenbaum's _____ focuses on helping clients become aware of their self-talk and the stories they tell about themselves.

a. self-instructional training
b. narrative therapy
c. self-awareness conditioning
d. self-talk analysis
e. cognitive behavioral training

_____ 19. In cognitive therapy the assumption is that psychological problems stem from processes such as

a. faulty thinking.
b. making incorrect inferences on the basis of inadequate or incorrect information.
c. failing to distinguish between fantasy and reality.
d. negative automatic thoughts.
e. all of the above.

_____ 20. Cognitive therapy is based on the assumption that

a. our feelings determine our thoughts.
b. our feelings determine our actions.
c. cognitions are the major determinants of how we feel and act.
d. the best way to change thinking is to reexperience past emotional traumas in the here and now.
e. insight is essential for any type of change to occur.

_____ 21. In cognitive therapy techniques are designed to

a. assist clients in substituting rational beliefs for irrational beliefs.
b. help clients experience their feelings more intensely.

c. identify and test clients' misconceptions and faulty assumptions.

d. enable clients to deal with their existential loneliness.

e. teach clients how to think only positive thoughts.

_____ 22. The type of cognitive error that involves thinking and interpreting in all-or-nothing terms or categorizing experiences in either-or extremes is known as

a. magnification and exaggeration.

b. polarized thinking.

c. arbitrary inference.

d. overgeneralization.

e. none of the above.

_____ 23. Beck's cognitive therapy differs from Ellis's REBT in that Beck emphasizes

a. a Socratic dialogue.

b. helping clients discover their misconceptions by themselves.

c. working with the client in collaborative ways.

d. more structure in the therapeutic process.

e. all of the above.

_____ 24. Beck's cognitive therapy has been most widely applied to the treatment of

a. stress symptoms.

b. psychosomatic reactions.

c. phobias.

d. depression.

e. cardiovascular disorders.

_____ 25. In self-instructional training, which of the following is given primary importance?

a. detecting and debating irrational thoughts

b. the role of inner speech

c. learning the A-B-C model of emotional disturbances

d. identifying cognitive errors

e. exploring feelings that are attached to early decisions

Reality Therapy

PRECHAPTER SELF-INVENTORY

Directions: Refer to page 43 for general directions. Use the following code:

5 = I *strongly agree* with this statement.

4 = I *agree*, in most respects, with this statement.

3 = I am *undecided* in my opinion about this statement.

2 = I *disagree*, in most respects, with this statement.

1 = I *strongly disagree* with this statement.

_____ 1. The underlying problem of most clients is the same: they are either involved in a present unsatisfying relationship or lack a significant relationship.

_____ 2. Therapy is literally teaching clients how to make better choices in dealing with the people they need in their lives.

_____ 3. Responsibility implies meeting one's own needs in such a way that others are not deprived of fulfilling their needs.

_____ 4. Our behavior, which is internally motivated and chosen, is always our best attempt to get what we want to satisfy our needs.

_____ 5. Insight is *not* essential to producing change.

_____ 6. There can be no basic personal change unless the client makes an evaluation of his or her behavior and then decides that a change is important.

_____ 7. It is a client's responsibility, not the therapist's, to evaluate his or her current behavior.

_____ 8. The way we *perceive* the world has more significance in therapy than the real world.

_____ 9. The notion of transference can keep the therapist hidden, and it does not have much relevance for therapy.

_____ 10. It is not productive for therapists to listen very long to a client complaining, blaming, and criticizing.

_____ 11. Essentially we choose all we do, which means we are responsible for what we choose.

_____ 12. Since the past is over, revisiting it is not a productive use of therapy time; therapy should focus on *present behavior*.

_____ 13. Although the past has propelled us to the present, it does not have to determine our future.

_____ 14. There is little value in talking about what clients cannot control; the only person a client can control is him- or herself.

_____ 15. Unless the therapist creates an involvement with the client, no motivation for therapy exists.

_____ 16. Early in counseling it is essential to discuss with clients the overall direction of their lives, including where they are going and where their behavior is taking them.

_____ 17. For therapy to be effective, clients must decide on a plan for action and make a commitment to implement this plan in daily life.

_____ 18. Therapy can be considered a mentoring process in which the therapist is the teacher and the client is the student.

_____ 19. Much of the significant work of the counseling process focuses on helping clients identify specific ways to fulfill their wants and needs.

_____ 20. Because reality therapy is based on universal principles, this theory has applicability to diverse client populations.

OVERVIEW OF REALITY THERAPY/CHOICE THEORY

Key Figures and Major Focus

Key figures: William Glasser and Robert Wubbolding. *Reality therapy* was developed by William Glasser in the 1950s and 1960s. Then Glasser began teaching *control theory*, which states that all people have choices about what they are doing. By 1996 Glasser had revised this theory and renamed it *choice theory*, which provides a framework of why and how people behave. Choice theory is concerned with the phenomenological world of the client and stresses the subjective way in which clients perceive and react to their world from an internal locus of evaluation. Behavior is viewed as our best attempt to get what we want. Behavior is purposeful; it is designed to close the gap between what we want and what we perceive we are getting. Specific behaviors are always generated from this discrepancy. Our behaviors come from the inside, and thus we choose our own destiny.

Philosophy and Basic Assumptions

Reality therapy is grounded on the basic premises of choice theory, which asserts that we are self-determining beings. Because we choose our total behavior, we are responsible for how we are acting, thinking, feeling, and for our physiological states. Choice theory posits that we are not born blank slates waiting to be externally motivated by forces in the external world. A major premise of choice theory is that all behavior is aimed at satisfying the needs for survival, love and belonging, power, freedom, and fun. Acting and thinking are chosen behaviors, which should be the focus of therapy. When we change our acting and thinking, we also indirectly influence how we are feeling as well as our physiological state. Choice theory explains how we attempt to control the world around us and teaches us ways to satisfy our wants and needs more effectively.

Key Concepts

The main idea is that behavior is our attempt to control our perceptions of the external world so they fit our internal and need-satisfying world. *Total behavior* includes four inseparable but distinct components of acting, thinking, feeling, and the physiology that accompanies all our actions. Although we all possess the same five human needs, each of us fulfills them differently. We develop an inner "mental picture album" (or quality world) of wants, which contains precise images of how we would best like to fulfill our needs. A core principle of reality therapy/choice theory is that no matter how dire the circumstances, people always have a choice. The emphasis of reality therapy is on assuming personal responsibility and on dealing with the present. Reality therapy rejects the medical model of psychoanalytic therapy and also rejects key concepts such the focus on the past, the exploration of dreams, dwelling on feelings or insight, transference, and the unconscious.

Therapeutic Goals

The overall goal of this approach is to help people find better ways to meet their needs for survival, love and belonging, power, freedom, and fun. Reality therapists assist clients in making more effective and responsible choices related to their wants and needs. Changes in behavior should result in the satisfaction of basic needs. Other goals besides behavioral change include personal growth, improvement, enhanced lifestyle, and better decision making. Therapists help clients gain the psychological strength to accept personal responsibility for their lives and assist them in learning ways to regain control of their lives and to live more effectively. Clients are challenged to examine what they are doing, thinking, and feeling to figure out if there is a better way for them to function. Clients are assisted in evaluating their own behavioral direction, specific actions, wants, perceptions, level of commitment, possibilities for new directions, and action plans. The therapist does not determine what behaviors clients should change. Rather, clients make this decision and then formulate a plan to facilitate desired changes.

Therapeutic Relationship

The therapist initiates the therapeutic process by becoming involved with the client and creating a warm, supportive, and challenging relationship. Clients need to know that the therapist cares enough about them to accept them and to help them fulfill their needs in the real world. Both *involvement with* and *concern for* the client are demonstrated throughout the entire process. Once this involvement has been established, the counselor confronts clients with the reality and consequences of their actions. Throughout therapy the counselor avoids criticism, refuses to accept clients' excuses for not following through with agreed-on plans, and does not easily give up on clients. Instead, therapists assist clients in the continual process of evaluating the effectiveness and appropriateness of their current behavior.

Techniques and Procedures

The practice of reality therapy can best be conceptualized as the cycle of counseling, which consists of two major components: (1) the counseling environment and (2) specific procedures that lead to change in behavior. These procedures are based on the assumption that human beings are motivated to change (1) when they determine that their current behavior is not getting them what they want and (2) when they believe they can choose other behaviors that will get them closer to what they want. Some of the specific procedures in the practice of reality therapy are summarized in the "WDEP" model, which refers to the following clusters of strategies:

W = wants: exploring wants, needs, and perceptions.

D = direction and doing: focusing on what clients are doing and the direction that this is taking them.

E = evaluation: challenging clients to make an evaluation of their total behavior.

P = planning and commitment: assisting clients in formulating realistic plans and making a commitment to carry them out.

(For a more detailed summary of the procedures that lead to change, see the two-page chart "Cycle of Managing, Supervising, Counseling, and Coaching" on pages 000–000.)

Applications

Originally designed for working with youthful offenders in detention facilities, choice theory and reality therapy are applicable to people with a variety of behavioral problems and for relationship enhancement. Choice theory can be applied to counseling, marital and family therapy, social work, and education. Used on both the elementary and secondary school levels, the approach has been applied to teaching and administration. The approach is also applicable to crisis intervention, institutional management, and community development. It has found wide application in military clinics that treat alcohol and drug abusers.

Applied to *group counseling*, reality therapy provides a context for group members to explore their wants, needs, and perceptions to determine if what they are doing is helping them satisfy their needs. Once group members get a clearer picture of what they have in their life now and what they want to be different, they are able to use the group in exploring alternative ways of behaving. It is the members, not the leader, who evaluate their own behavior and decide whether or not they want to change. Considerable time in a group is devoted to developing and implementing action plans. Reality therapy focuses on making changes in the present and is an effective, short-term approach to group work.

Multicultural Perspectives

Reality therapy is based on universal principles, which means that it is highly relevant in the area of multicultural counseling. However, reality therapy principles and procedures need to be applied differently in various cultures and must be adapted to the psychological and developmental levels presented by individuals. Reality therapists demonstrate their respect for the cultural values of their clients by helping them explore how satisfying their current behavior is both to themselves and to others. After clients make this assessment for themselves, they identify those problems that present difficulty for them. They are then in a position to formulate realistic plans that are consistent with their cultural values. This type of specificity and the direction that is provided by an effective plan are beneficial in working with diverse client groups.

Contributions

As a short-term approach, reality therapy can be applied to a wide range of clients. It provides a structure for both clients and therapists to evaluate the degree and nature of changes. It consists of simple and clear concepts that are easily understood by many in the human services field, and the principles can be used by parents, teachers, ministers, educators, managers, consultants, supervisors, social workers, and counselors. As a positive and action-oriented approach, it appeals to a variety of clients who are typically viewed as "difficult to treat." The existential underpinnings of choice theory are a major strength of this approach, which accentuates taking responsibility for what we are doing. The heart of reality therapy consists of accepting personal responsibility and gaining more effective control. People take charge of their lives rather than being the victims of circumstances beyond their control. This approach teaches clients to focus on what they are able and willing to do in the present to change their behavior.

Limitations

Reality therapy does not give enough emphasis to feelings, the unconscious, the therapeutic value of dreams, the place of transference in therapy, the effect of early childhood trauma, and the power of the past to influence one's present personality. There is a tendency for this approach to play down the crucial role of one's social and cultural environment in influencing behavior. It may foster a treatment that is based on solving problems and discourage an exploration of deeper emotional issues.

GLOSSARY OF KEY TERMS

Choice theory   The view that humans are internally motivated and behave to control the world around them according to some purpose within them. We are basically self-determining and create our own destiny.

Commitment   The act of sticking to a realistic plan aimed at change.

Cycle of counseling   Specific ways of creating a positive climate in which counseling can occur. The proper environment is based on personal involvement and specific procedures aimed at change.

Involvement   Therapist interest in and caring for the client.

Paining behaviors   Choosing misery by developing symptoms (such as headaching, depressing, and anxietying) because these seem like the best behaviors available at the time.

Perceived world   The reality that we experience and interpret subjectively.

Picture album   An image of our specific wants as well as precise ways to satisfy these wants.

Psychological needs   The needs for belonging, power, freedom, and fun; these are the forces that drive humans and explain behavior.

Quality world   The perceptions and images we have of how we can fulfill our basic psychological needs; another phrase for *picture album*.

Reality therapy   Based on choice theory, this approach provides a way of implementing therapeutic procedures for helping individuals take more effective control of their lives.

Responsibility   Satisfying one's needs in ways that do not interfere with others' fulfilling their needs.

SAMIC³   An acronym pertaining to the essence of a good action plan: simple, attainable, measurable, immediate, involved, controlled by the planner, committed to, and continuously done.

Self-evaluation   Clients' assessment of current behavior to decide whether it is working and if what they are doing is meeting their needs. It is the cornerstone of reality therapy procedures.

Total behavior   The integrated components of doing, thinking, feeling, and physiology. Choice theory assumes that all elements of behavior are interrelated.

WDEP system   The key procedures applied to the practice of reality therapy groups. The strategies help clients identify their wants, determine the direction their behavior is taking them, make self-evaluations, and design plans for change.

QUESTIONS FOR REFLECTION AND DISCUSSION

1. Choice theory is based on the premise that although outside events influence us, we are not determined by them. To what degree do you agree with the assumption that our actions, thoughts, and emotions are the product of our choices? What are the implications for counseling practice of the way you answer this question?

2. Choice theory rests on the assumption that everything we do, think, and feel is generated by what happens inside us. What are the implications of this perspective for counseling practice? How would this view influence the interventions you may make?

3. What is the importance of defining and clarifying wants or "pictures"? What are the implications of counselors' helping clients express realistic wants?

4. If you were working with a man who was depressing and he insisted he couldn't help the way he felt, how would you deal with him by teaching him choice theory? Assume that he told you he was coming to you because he was not capable of getting out of his pit of depression. How would you proceed?

CYCLE OF COUNSELING, COACHING, MANAGING, AND SUPERVISING

PROCEDURES

ENVIRONMENT

W D E P

D

Explore Total Behavior: Direction "Doing" ("Acting") Aspect, Self-Talk, and Core Beliefs.
Explore Two-Fold Purpose of Behavior: to impact the outer world and to communicate a message to it.

E — EVALUATION (8 Types)

P — Make "SAMIC³" Plans P (2 Types)

PERCEPTION OF CURRENT REALITY

TRUST HOPE
F F F F

TOXIC RELATIONSHIPS

A. Argue, Attack, Accuse
B. Boss Manage, Blame, Belittle
C. Criticize, Coerce, Condemn

D. Demean, Demand
E. Encourage Excuses
F. Instill Fear, Find Fault
G. Give Up Easily, Take for Granted
H. Hold Grudges

TONIC RELATIONSHIPS

Follow Up, Consultation, Continuing Education

W — BUILD RELATIONSHIPS

A. Use "attending behaviors"
B. AB-CDE
C. Suspend Judgment
D. Do the Unexpected; Paradoxical Techniques
E. Use Humor
F. Establish Boundaries & Policies
G. Share Self & Adapt to Own Personality
H. Listen for Metaphors and Use Stories
I. Listen for Themes
J. Summarize & Focus
K. Allow or Impose Consequences
L. Allow Silence
M. Show Empathy
N. Be Ethical
O. Create Anticipation
P. Practice Lead Management
Q. Discuss Quality
R. Increase Choices
S. Discuss problems in the past tense and solutions in present and future tenses.
T. Withdraw from Volatile Situations if helpful
U. Talk about non-problem areas
V. Connect with the person's thinking & feeling
W. Invite solutions
X. Use broken record technique
Y. Use affirming language

4 A C T

ESPECIALLY FOR PARENTS

C. Get a Commitment (5 levels)
B. Share wants and perceptions
A. Explore wants, needs, & perceptions

ENVIRONMENT

Developed by **Robert E. Wubbolding, EdD**
from the works of William Glasser, MD

Copyright **1986 Robert E. Wubbolding, EdD**
17th Revision 2010. Reprinted by permission

SUMMARY DESCRIPTION OF THE
"CYCLE OF COUNSELING, COACHING, MANAGING, AND SUPERVISING"

The Cycle is explained in detail in books by Robert E. Wubbolding:
Employee Motivation, 1996: *Reality Therapy for the 21st Century, 2000*
A Set of Directions for Putting and Keeping Yourself Together, 2001
Reality Therapy In APA's *Theories of Psychotherapy Series, 2010*

Introduction:

The Cycle consists of two general concepts: Environment conducive to change and Procedures more explicitly designed to facilitate change. This chart is intended to be a **brief** summary. The ideas are designed to be used with employees, students, clients as well as in other human relationships.

Relationship between Environment & Procedures:

1. As indicated in the chart, the Environment is the foundation upon which the effective use of Procedures is based.

2. Though it is **usually** necessary to establish a safe, friendly Environment before change can occur, the "Cycle" can be entered at any point. Thus, the use of the cycle does **not** occur in lock step fashion.

3. Building a relationship implies establishing and maintaining a professional relationship. Methods for accomplishing this comprise some efforts on the part of the helper that are Environmental and others that are Procedural.

ENVIRONMENT:

Relationship Tonics: a close relationship is built on TRUST and HOPE through friendliness, firmness and fairness.

A. Using Attending Behaviors: Eye contact, posture, effective listening skills.
B. AB = "Always **B**e . . ." **C**onsistent, **C**ourteous & **C**alm, **D**etermined that there is hope for improvement, **E**nthusiastic (Think Positively).
C. Suspend Judgment: View behaviors from a low level of perception, i.e., acceptance is crucial.
D. Do the Unexpected: Use paradoxical techniques as appropriate; Reframing and Prescribing.
E. Use Humor: Help them fulfill need for fun within reasonable boundaries.
F. Establish boundaries: the relationship is professional.

(oval diagram: 4 A C T)

- Affirm feelings
- Accept
- Show affection
- Action consequences
- Conversation (WDEP)
- Time together

G. Share Self: Self-disclosure within limits is helpful; adapt to own personal style.
H. Listen for Metaphors: Use their figures of speech and provide other ones. Use stories.
I. Listen to Themes: Listen for behaviors that have helped, value judgements, etc.
J. Summarize & Focus: Tie together what they say and focus on them rather than on "Real World."
K. Allow or Impose Consequences: Within reason, they should be responsible for their own behavior.
L. Allow Silence: This allows them to think, as well as to take responsibility.
M. Show Empathy: Perceive as does the person being helped.
N. Be Ethical: Study Codes of Ethics and their applications, e.g., how to handle suicide threats or violent tendencies.
O. Create anticipation and communication hope. People should be taught that something good will happen if they are willing to work.
P. **Practice lead management, e.g., democracy in determining rules**.
Q. **Discuss quality.**
R. **Increases choices.**
S. Discuss problems in the past tense, solutions in present and future tenses.
T. Withdraw from volatile situations if helpful.
U. Talk about non-problem areas.
V. Connect with the person's thinking and feeling.
W. Invite solutions.
X. Use broken record technique.
Y. Use affirming language.

Relationship Toxins:

Argue, **Boss Manage,** or Blame, Criticize or Coerce, Demean, Encourage Excuses, Instill Fear, or Give up easily, Hold Grudges.

Rather, stress what they **can** control, accept them as they are, and keep the confidence that they can develop more effective behaviors. Also, continue to us "WDEP" system without giving up.

Follow Up, Consult, and Continue Education:

Determine a way for them to report back, talk to another professional person when necessary, and maintain ongoing program of professional growth.

PROCEDURES:

Build Relationships:

A. Explore **W**ants, Needs & Perceptions: Discuss picture album or quality world, i.e., set goals, fulfilled & unfulfilled pictures, needs, viewpoints and "locus of control."
B. Share Wants & Perceptions: Tell what you want from them and how you view their situations, behaviors, wants, etc. This procedure is secondary to A above.
C. Get a Commitment: Help them solidify their desire to find more effective behaviors.

Explore Total Behavior:

Help them examine the **D**irection of their lives, as well as specifics of how they spend their time. Discuss core beliefs and ineffective & effective self talk. Explore two-fold purpose of behavior: to impact the outer world and to communicate a message to it.

Evaluation – The Cornerstone of Procedures:

Help them evaluate their behavioral direction, specific behaviors as well as wants, perceptions and commitments. Evaluate own behavior through follow-up, consultation and continued education.

Make **P**lans: Help them change direction of their lives.

Effective plans are **S**imple, **A**ttainable, **M**easurable, **I**mmediate, **C**onsistent, **C**ontrolled by the planner, and **C**ommitted to. The helper is **P**ersistent. Plans can be linear or paradoxical.

Note: The "Cycle" describes specific guidelines & skills. Effective implementation requires the artful integration of the guidelines & skills contained under Environment & Procedures in a spontaneous & natural manner geared to the personality of the helper. This requires training, practices & supervision. Also, the word "client" is used for anyone receiving help: student, employee, family member, etc.

For more information contact:

Robert E. Wubbolding, EdD, Director

Center for Reality Therapy
7672 Montgomery Road, #383
Cincinnati, Ohio 45236

(513) 561-1911 • FAX (513) 561-3568
E-mail: wubsrt@fuse.net • www.realitytherapywub.com

5. In what specific areas or situations might you have trouble allowing your clients to make self-evaluations? Might you be inclined to impose your values or perceptions on your clients? Would you be inclined to make evaluations for certain clients?

6. How would you proceed with a client who consistently refused to make any plans to change? How would you intervene with a client who made plans, but then did not carry them out?

7. What are your reactions to reality therapy's focus on current behavior and its lack of interest in exploring the past? Compare and contrast this view of the role of the past with the psychoanalytic view.

8. Although reality therapists do not ignore feelings, they do not encourage clients to focus on feelings as if they were separate from actions and thoughts. What is your reaction to this approach?

9. If you were working with a culturally diverse population, how well do you think the concepts of choice theory and the practices of reality therapy might work? Assume that your clients want to focus on factors such as institutional racism, environmental barriers, and social injustices that they are dealing with daily. How would it be for you (and for your clients) if you worked exclusively with reality therapy?

10. Assume that you are working with involuntary clients, mostly youths associated with gangs. Also assume that your clients are not particularly motivated to change their behavior but are motivated only to keep out of the courtroom. In what ways might you apply the principles of reality therapy?

PRACTICAL APPLICATIONS OF REALITY THERAPY AND CHOICE THEORY

This set of exercises is based on a modification of the WDEP model as developed by Dr. Robert Wubbolding. One of the best ways to learn how to work with clients from a reality therapy perspective is for you to apply the procedures to your own life. Take time to engage in this self-reflection and self-evaluation. Doing so could help you make some significant changes in your life as well as enhance your skills in applying the WDEP model in your work with clients.

W = What Is It That You Want?

Explore your wants, needs, and perceptions. If you had what you wanted now, how would your life be different?

Reflect on what you most want from yourself, friends, spouse or partner, religion or spirituality, work, and the world around you. Select *one* area as a target for further exploration. Apply this specific target example to the following questions.

1. What are you doing now to get what you say you want? How much effort are you devoting to get what you want?

2. How do you perceive yourself and significant others in your life?

3. How are you meeting your basic needs?

Reflect on the ways in which your needs are being met, as well as how you see them influencing your daily behavior. Rank the five basic needs in the order of their priority for you. As you reflect on your needs, ask yourself in what areas you would like to make changes.

Survival. To what degree are you maintaining vitality and good health, rather than merely surviving?

Belonging. What do you do to meet your needs for meaningful relationships? In what ways do you feel a sense of belonging?

Power or achievement. When do you feel a sense of power? In what areas of your life are you making significant achievements? When do you feel recognized?

Freedom or independence. To what degree do you feel that you are in charge of your life and are moving in the direction that you want?

Fun or enjoyment. What are those activities that you do for fun? Do you have as much fun as you would like?

Choose one specific need that you would like to change. For example, if you are not having as much fun in your life as you would like, what specifically would you like to be doing by way of fun that you are not? Reflect on what you are willing to do to change this aspect of your life.

D = What Are You Doing?

Explore the *direction* in which your *total behavior* is moving you. What are you currently doing, and to what degree is it working for you?

1. Where is the overall direction of your life leading you? Where is your overall journey taking you? Is your destination taking you in a place you want to be? If you continue in the direction you are going now, where will you be in one year? In five years?

2. Is the general direction of your life in your own best interest? Are you getting closer to your core goals? Is your overall direction moving you closer to the people with whom you want to be involved?

3. Is your behavior congruent with what you say you want? To what degree are your present actions in line with your core values?

4. How satisfied are you with most of your actions? Are there some ways you'd like to be acting that you are not? How would your life be different if you were acting the way you want?

5. More specifically, is your present behavior helping you get what you want? To what degree are your current actions helping or hurting you and your significant others?

6. Are your wants realistic and attainable? If you had in your life what you wanted at this point, what would that be like?

E = How Willing Are You to Make a Searching Self-Evaluation?

Total behavior is composed of action, thinking, feelings, and physiology in an attempt to meet your needs and fulfill wants. You have most control over your actions, so let's focus on the acting dimension. Engage in a comprehensive self-evaluation to determine whether you are getting what you want. As you review your behavior on a given day, think about what you would most want to change about yourself. Make a global self-assessment first.

1. What would you most want to accomplish in your life in the next few years in these areas: Physically? Emotionally? Socially? Spiritually? Intellectually? Professionally? Family relationships? Contributing to humanity? Financial security?

2. What specific actions or thoughts would you like to change because they are not working for you?

3. To what degree do you think you are getting what you want?

4. Select one area in which you are willing to invest time and effort to bring about change. Reflect on the specific kinds of changes you most want to make in this particular area. To what degree are your current actions, cognitions, and feelings helping you?

5. What are you willing to do to make the changes you want?

6. Are you committed to taking action to change?

P = Are You Ready to Make Plans to More Effectively Meet Your Needs?

Make plans designed to change the direction of your life. Take a particular target area that you have decided is important enough to you that you are willing to actually make a plan that will result in change. Think about a particular behavior you want to change and are willing to change. One of the best ways to understand the process of formulating personal plans is to develop such a plan yourself. In making your plan, consider SAMIC^3—your plan should be simple, attainable, measurable, immediate, involved, controlled by the planner, committed to, and continuously done.

■ Design a long-range plan with specific short-range steps you can take to attain your overall goals.

■ Work out the details of your plan.

■ Be ready to make a commitment to sticking to a plan that is important to you and one you have decided you want to implement.

Apply these questions to developing your plan.

1. What kind of specific plan would you be interested in developing as a way to enhance your life?

2. How can you design a specific plan for change?

3. What will help you follow through with your plan and make a commitment to change?

4. If you follow through on your plan, how might your life be different?

Using WDEP as an Approach to Self-Improvement

Select a number of specific aspects of your life that you are interested in changing and apply the WDEP model to your self-improvement program. For example, if you are not satisfied with your current level of exercise or the way you feel physically, consider what kinds of action plans you would be willing to incorporate in your daily life. It is important to be specific and begin with those areas you are willing to expend effort in exploring. Once you have made some concrete changes in the direction that is satisfying to you, it will be easier to tackle other areas of thinking, feeling, and acting that you want to modify. If you can do this kind of personal change, the chances are far greater that you will be able to inspire and motivate your clients to identify what they want, to assess the overall direction of their lives, to make a searching self-inventory of their total behavior, and to make workable plans aimed at change.

JERRY COREY COUNSELS STAN FROM A REALITY THERAPY PERSPECTIVE

Session 9. Reality Therapy Applied to the Case of Stan

Reality therapy stresses the importance of choices and acting on them; the WDEP model is an important element of this approach. This session deals with assisting Stan in forming an action plan.

Before viewing the demonstration, read Chapter 11, pages 352–353 in the textbook and answer the questions under the heading "Follow-Up: You Continue as Stan's Reality Therapist." Then, as you watch this session, try to identify the elements in the planning phase of the WDEP model. Write down your observations and discuss these with a classmate. Did you identify the same elements? What were the similarities and differences between your observations and those of your classmates? Answer these questions after viewing the video:

1. What possible advantage do you see in focusing on Stan's behavior rather than on his feelings or his thoughts?

2. What difference do you see between a client saying "I'm depressed" and "I'm depressing?"

3. If you were a client in counseling, what would help you to focus on a specific behavior you would most want to change?

4. As a client, what would help you to develop a realistic and effective plan of action?

5. What kind of support system do you think would be useful for Stan?

6. How might you use this approach at the beginning of Stan's therapy? How might your approach be different from the way you would use it toward the end of Stan's therapy?

7. There is some laughter in this session. What impact does this laughter have on Stan's therapy? What therapeutic value do you see in using humor?

8. What can you think of as Stan's therapist to help him carry out a plan that he worked out with you?

9. What would you say to Stan if he seemed very reluctant to formulate an action plan?

10. How important is making a plan and developing a commitment to carrying it out as a requisite for bringing about changes the client wants? Explain.

A Suggested In-Class Activity

In small groups have each person identify one behavior that he or she would like to change. Spend some time talking about ways you could apply the WDEP model to self-improvement. What are some ways each of you can create a specific plan of action to bring about change you want? In your group, also explore what you saw in the video in assisting Stan in forming a plan. How important do you think it is to develop a systematic plan aimed at change? Here are three other questions for discussion in your small group:

1. What did you find most interesting in this session? Why?

2. If you were counseling Stan from this particular theoretical framework, what is one additional technique you might use? What would you hope to accomplish with this intervention?

3. If you were the client, how would you be likely to respond to the therapist's (Jerry's) comments and interventions in this particular session?

 ## JERRY COREY'S WORK WITH RUTH FROM A REALITY THERAPY PERSPECTIVE

As a reality therapist, I do not tell Ruth what she should change, but I encourage her to examine what she wants and determine whether what she is doing is meeting her needs. It is up to Ruth to decide how well her current behavior is working for her. Once she makes her own evaluation about what she is actually doing, she can take some significant steps toward making changes for herself. She has a tendency to complain of feeling victimized and controlled, and my intention is to help her see how her behavior actually contributes to this perceived helplessness. Rather than focusing on her feelings of depression and anxiety, I choose to focus on what she actually *does* from the time she wakes up to the time she goes to bed. Through a self-observational process, Ruth gradually assumes more responsibility for her actions.

In applying reality therapy with Ruth, much of what we do consists of developing realistic and specific plans and then talking about how she might carry them out in everyday life. After she becomes clearer about certain patterns of her behavior, I encourage her to develop a specific plan of action that can lead to the changes she desires. When she does not stick with a subgoal or carry out a plan for the week, I am not likely to listen to any excuses. Eventually, she gets better at setting smaller goals and making more realistic plans. She stops and says, "Now I wonder if I really want to do this, or am I hearing someone else tell me that I should want it?"

You Continue Working With Ruth as Her Reality Therapist

1. Refer to *Case Approach to Counseling and Psychotherapy* (Chapter 9) for examples of two different reality therapists' perspectives (Drs. William Glasser and Robert Wubbolding) on Ruth's case. In this chapter, I also show my style of applying reality therapy concepts in working with Ruth.

2. See the *DVD for Integrative Counseling: The Case of Ruth and Lecturettes* (Session 8 on a behavioral focus) for a demonstration of developing plans with Ruth that she can carry out in everyday life.

3. If Ruth were your client, how would you assist her in establishing specific action plans?

4. What might you say to Ruth if she did not follow through with some of her commitments in implementing her plan?

5. I expect Ruth to engage in self-evaluation. It is not my place as her counselor to evaluate her behavior; rather, it is my job to provide a structure that will enable her to make evaluations of what she is doing. How might you work with Ruth to ensure that she would make her own assessment of what she is currently doing and how well it is working for her?

A CASE FROM A REALITY THERAPY PERSPECTIVE

Sunmei: "I'm Only Here Because the Judge Ordered It"

By Robert E. Wubbolding, EdD, Professor Emeritus of Counseling at Xavier University and Director of the Center for Reality Therapy in Cincinnati

Dr. Robert Wubbolding's Way of Working With Sunmei From a Reality Therapy Perspective

The client, Sunmei, is a Korean woman, age 25. She was a court referral to counseling because of being arrested for selling small amounts of marijuana and for prostitution. Sunmei is on probation and the judge ordered her to receive mental health counseling.

After providing a thorough explanation of informed consent issues, I ask Sunmei if she has ever received counseling in the past. She replies that she has not. I explain reality therapy to her in simple and clear terms. I ask her if she feels comfortable talking about her current situation. We explore together her comfort or discomfort in talking to a counselor who is different from her in age, gender and race.

She indicates that she has had very little contact with white men who are older than she is and so she is doubtful as to whether I could help her. Consequently, I believe that my initial task is twofold: to help her feel comfortable talking to someone that she perceives as different and also to deal effectively with these differences so that they do not impede the counseling process. From the point of view of reality therapy, establishing an appropriate counseling environment is an indispensible precondition for the effective use of the WDEP system. My chart, *Cycle of Counseling, Coaching, Managing, and Supervising,* is included in this chapter (on pages 164–165). This chart indicates how the counseling environment is foundational to the procedures used in reality therapy. The effective use of the WDEP system enhances and maintains the therapeutic alliance that fuels behavioral change.

In order to become part of Sunmei's quality world so that she can perceive me as someone who can help her I emphasize to her that the barriers are definitely a factor and that they impose limitations on the assistance that I can provide. At the same time I help her come to the conclusion that there are issues that fall within my knowledge and ability to deal with. The very admission of these barriers lessens the force of their negative influence. I say to her, "Yes, we are very different in some ways. But I believe I can help you fulfill the expectations of the judge who requires you to avoid drugs, look for a job, find new friends and treat your children better." I add, "I can't help you be more street wise, sell drugs or prostitute, but I can help you find alternatives to these choices. I can also help you establish relationships, find groups of people who will support you, and assist you in achieving a different lifestyle. I can help you in staying out of trouble and getting along with other human beings." I am convinced that by using reality therapy I can assist my clients in searching for better alternatives. I acknowledge that cultural differences are real, but not insurmountable.

The above interaction contains a subtle, but definite, teaching element. Explicit in my comments is the word "choice." I am indirectly teaching a component of choice theory/reality therapy: we choose our behavior. This concept empowers clients, especially those who feel oppressed and rejected by society. They often see themselves as powerless and as having no choices. Through the use of reality therapy, they learn that regardless of their current plight, no matter how desperate they are, and in spite of the trouble they have experienced, they *at least* have more choices available to them than previously known. I believe that when counselors incorporate deep within themselves the conviction that all human beings are capable of making choices, counseling interventions become more than mere techniques.

I say to Sunmei: "Your situation offers you much misery and you have suffered greatly. And yet, somehow you are managing your life. I'm sure that much of what you do does not get you in trouble. There are many people who would not have managed as well as you have. I will help you add to your successes." Then I help her explore and describe whether she has met anyone who has been able to put destructive experiences behind them. If she knows of no one, I would ask her to think about whether she would like to meet such people. If she says she knows even one such person I would ask her to describe what that individual does that is different from what she does. I would help her describe in detail how the other individual uses her time, and what she does that is internally satisfying to her. Most especially, I would help her identify feelings of happiness that the other person possesses that have resulted from her relationships with others. I would say to her, "What you're telling me is that your friend is happy when she feels connected with her family, neighbors, or associates."

There are two components to the above counseling interventions: First, I ask her to describe her friend's behavior that is *different*, not better than hers. This is an illustration of my attempt to avoid criticizing her. Second, I describe the other person as her *friend*, and therefore, a possible ally or mentor. Implicit is the hint that self-recrimination about past behavior negatively impacts her and that better human relationships constitute the cornerstone of better mental health and a more satisfying life.

With my guidance she then describes what she wants from the counseling process, from the court, from her family and from her friend. At a later time she would present what she wants from her support group, her church, her community and from all the relationships in her life. Most importantly, after she has stated that she wants to achieve something different in her overall lifestyle, I help her refine her thoughts and state clearly her level of commitment, namely, how hard she wants to work to achieve the goals that she has formulated, such as getting off probation.

Helping Sunmei to Evaluate Her Behavior and to Make Plans for Change

As she reviews her current actions and her wants, I help her examine by means of both questions and exploratory statements the realistic attainability of her wants, the appropriateness of her wants, the effectiveness of her actions that are aimed at fulfilling her wants, the utility of her self-talk and the efficacy of her plans. These efforts make concrete the "E" of the WDEP system, which means helping clients conduct a searching and fearless self-evaluation of what they want as well as the efficacy of their behavior. The following questions and exploratory statements illustrate self-evaluation (E), the cornerstone in the practice of reality therapy:

- Is what you want attainable?
- Tell me how this specific want fits or does not fit the wants imposed on you by the court.
- Did your actions last night help you or delay you from getting off probation?
- Describe how any specific action or the overall direction of your choices is satisfying to you, unsatisfying to you, meets or does not meet the criteria laid down by the court.
- Tell me how your current level of commitment will help you achieve—or will hinder you from the attainment of—your goals.
- How does your plan meet the criteria for formulating an effective plan?

The final question is based on both the counselor's and the client's awareness that an effective plan has several characteristics. To achieve its purpose a plan must be simple–not complicated, attainable–realistically doable, measurable–exact and precise, immediate–carried out soon, controlled by the planner–not dependent on other people.

The above interventions render the application of reality therapy as a WDEP system relevant and precise for Sunmei, a specific client. The further use of the WDEP system applied to Sunmei consists of helping her to revisit her wants and to describe her current behaviors. Following upon the gentle but persistent application of the WDE is the formulation of plans (P), aimed at the appropriate and legal satisfaction of her inner needs: belonging, power or inner control, fun or enjoyment, and freedom or independence.

Follow-Up: You Continue as Sunmei's Reality Therapist

1. What specific additional interventions would you make to lower the perceived barriers between you the counselor and the client?

2. How would you help Sunmei evaluate her quality world, wants, actions, self-talk, and level of commitment?

3. What role do you believe your relationship with her plays in counseling her?

4. Assume that she informed you that the only reason she was seeing you is because the court ordered her to do so. What actions would you take if Sunmei informed you that she did not think she had a problem and was not interested in making any changes in her life?

5. What plans do you think would help Sunmei satisfy each of her needs: belonging, power or achievement or inner control, fun or enjoyment, and freedom or independence?

 QUIZ ON REALITY THERAPY

A Comprehension Check

Score _____%

Note: Refer to Appendix 1 for the scoring key.

True/false items: Decide if the following statements are "more true" or "more false" as they apply to reality therapy.

T   F   1. What is important is not the way the real world exists but the way we perceive the world to exist.

T   F   2. Choice theory is the framework for the practice of reality therapy.

T   F   3. A good way to change behavior is for us to be self-critical.

T   F   4. It is important to explore the past as a way to change current behavior.

T   F   5. One of the therapist's functions is to make judgments about clients' present behavior.

T   F   6. The focus of reality therapy is on attitudes and feelings.

T   F   7. The use of contracts is often part of reality therapy.

T   F   8. Reality therapy is grounded on some existential concepts.

T   F   9. It is the client's responsibility to decide on the goals of therapy.

T   F   10. Appropriate punishment is an effective way to change behavior.

Multiple-choice items: Select the *one best answer* of those alternatives given. Consider each question within the framework of reality therapy.

_____ 11. The founder of reality therapy is

   a. Albert Ellis.
   b. Albert Bandura.
   c. Joseph Wolpe.
   d. Robert Wubbolding.
   e. William Glasser.

_____ 12. According to this approach, insight

   a. is necessary before behavior change can occur.
   b. is not necessary for producing behavior change.
   c. will come only with changed attitudes.
   d. can be given to the client by the teachings of the therapist.
   e. will be discovered by the client alone.

_____ 13. The view of human nature underlying reality therapy is

   a. that we have a need for identity.
   b. that we have the need to feel loved and to love others.
   c. that we need to feel worthwhile to ourselves and others.
   d. all of the above.
   e. none of the above.

_____ 14. Which is **not** a key concept of reality therapy?

   a. focus on the present
   b. unconscious motivation
   c. self-evaluations
   d. involvement as part of the therapy process
   e. responsibility

_____ 15. Which of the following is **not** true of reality therapy?

   a. It is based on the premise that acting and thinking are chosen behaviors.
   b. Clients must make commitments.

   c. Therapists do not accept excuses or blaming.
   d. Therapy is a didactic process.
   e. Working through the transference relationship is essential for therapy to occur.

_____ 16. Regarding the goals of reality therapy,

   a. it is the therapist's responsibility to decide specific goals for clients.
   b. it is the client's responsibility to decide goals.
   c. the goals of therapy should be universal to all clients.
   d. society must determine the proper goals for all clients.
   e. both (c) and (d) are true.

_____ 17. In reality therapy, our quality world is likened to

   a. a picture album.
   b. a reality TV show.
   c. an expensive sports car.
   d. a celebrity's life.
   e. none of the above.

_____ 18. Which statement is **not** true of reality therapy?

   a. It is based on a personal relationship.
   b. It focuses on attitude change as a prerequisite for behavior change.
   c. Planning is essential.
   d. The focus is on the client's strengths.

_____ 19. Reality therapy was designed originally for working with

   a. elementary school children.
   b. youthful offenders in detention facilities.
   c. alcoholics.
   d. drug addicts.
   e. people with marital conflicts.

_____ 20. Which of the following would **not** be used by a reality therapist?

   a. analysis of the transference relationship
   b. hypnosis
   c. the analysis of dreams
   d. the search for causes of current problems
   e. all of the above

_____ 21. Which of the following statements is true as it applies to choice theory?

   a. Behavior is the result of external forces.
   b. We are controlled by the events that occur in our lives.
   c. We can control the behavior of others by learning to actively listen to them.
   d. We are motivated completely by internal forces, and our behavior is our best attempt to get what we want.
   e. We can control our feelings more easily than our actions.

_____ 22. According to Glasser, all of the following are basic psychological needs except for

   a. competition.
   b. belonging.
   c. power.
   d. freedom.
   e. fun.

_____ 23. An axiom of choice theory is that

   a. the past is the problem.
   b. although the past may have contributed to a current problem the past is never the problem.
   c. all serious problems are rooted in unconscious drives that dictate behavior.
   d. mental illness is the cause of bad choices people make.

_____ 24. Sometimes it seems as though people actually choose to be miserable (depressed). Glasser explains the dynamics of *depressing* as being based on

   a. keeping anger under control.
   b. getting others to help us.
   c. excusing our unwillingness to do something more effective.
   d. all of the above.
   e. none of the above.

_____ 25. All of the following are procedures in reality therapy that are said to lead to change except for

   a. exploring wants, needs, and perceptions.
   b. focusing on current behavior.
   c. the therapist's evaluating of the client's behavior.
   d. the client's evaluating of his or her own behavior.
   e. the client's committing to a plan of action.

Chapter 12

Feminist
Therapy

PRECHAPTER SELF-INVENTORY

Directions: Refer to page 43 for general directions. Use the following code:

5 = I *strongly agree* with this statement.

4 = I *agree*, in most respects, with this statement.

3 = I am *undecided* in my opinion about this statement.

2 = I *disagree*, in most respects, with this statement.

1 = I *strongly disagree* with this statement.

_____ 1. Feminist therapy has applications to both women and men.

_____ 2. Therapy practice needs to shift from its reliance on an intrapersonal psychopathology perspective to a focus on understanding the pathological forces in the culture that damage and constrain women.

_____ 3. The appropriate aims of therapy are social transformation and individual change.

_____ 4. The socialization of women inevitably affects their identity development, self-concept, goals and aspirations, and emotional well-being.

_____ 5. Feminist therapists are committed to monitoring their own biases and distortions, especially the social and cultural dimensions of women's experiences.

_____ 6. Although the therapeutic relationship is important, the relationship, in and of itself, is not sufficient to produce change.

_____ 7. Appropriate self-disclosure by the counselor can be therapeutic.

_____ 8. Individuals are not to blame for personal problems that are largely caused by dysfunctional social environments, yet they are responsible for working toward change.

_____ 9. It is important that clients tell their stories and give voice to what they are experiencing in the present.

_____ 10. The therapist works to demystify therapy and to include the client as an active partner in the assessment and treatment process.

_____ 11. Including the client in the therapeutic process increases the chances that interventions will be culturally appropriate.

_____ 12. Social action is an essential part of the therapy process.

_____ 13. The therapist should be viewed as one source of information rather than as the best or "expert" source.

_____ 14. The environment is a major source of pathology in the lives of women and men.

_____ 15. Gender and power are essential considerations in effective therapy practice.

_____ 16. It is appropriate for therapists to help clients come to an understanding of how they are influenced by gender-role expectations and socialization.

_____ 17. An appropriate aim of therapy is to confront institutional policies that discriminate on any grounds.

_____ 18. Therapists would do well to empower clients to live according to their own values and to rely on an internal locus of control in determining what is right for them.

_____ 19. Therapist and client should take active and equal roles, working together to determine goals and procedures of therapy.

_____ 20. The therapist should strive to develop a collaborative relationship in which the client can become an expert on her- or himself.

 # OVERVIEW OF FEMINIST THERAPY

Key Figures and Major Focus

Feminist therapy does not have a founder or a single individual who developed the approach. Some of the women who have made significant contributions are Jean Baker Miller, Carol Gilligan, Carolyn Enns, Laura Brown, Lillian Comas-Diaz, and Olivia Espin. Feminist therapy has developed in a grassroots manner, responding to the emerging needs of women. Gender and power are at the heart of this approach. A central concept in this perspective is the concern for the psychological oppression of women and the socialization of women that affects their identity development.

Philosophy and Basic Assumptions

Practitioners interpret the basic tenets of therapy in different ways depending on the feminist philosophy they espouse. Currently, there are at least eight basic philosophies underlying feminist practice: liberal, cultural, radical, socialist, postmodern, women of color, lesbian, and global/international. These various philosophies have differing views on the sources of oppression and what is needed to bring about substantial social transformation. All of these theoretical perspectives focus on issues of diversity, the complexity of sexism, and the centrality of social context in understanding gender issues. Feminist therapists have challenged the male-oriented assumptions regarding what constitutes a mentally healthy individual. The underlying philosophy of feminist theory can be described as being gender neutral, flexible, interactional, and life-span-oriented. Feminist therapists emphasize that gender-role expectations profoundly influence our identity from birth onward. Thus, therapy has the task of bringing to one's awareness how gender-role socialization is deeply ingrained in adult personality.

Key Concepts

Feminist therapy is based on six interrelated principles:

- The personal is political.
- Commitment to social change.
- Women's and girl's voices and ways of knowing are valued and their experiences are honored.
- The counseling relationship is egalitarian.
- A focus on strengths and a reformulated definition of psychological distress.
- All types of oppression are recognized.

A key concept of feminist therapy is the notion that societal gender-role messages influence how individuals view themselves and behave. Through therapy the impact of these socialization patterns are identified so that clients can critically evaluate and modify early messages pertaining to appropriate gender-role behavior. Most feminist therapists believe gender is always an important factor, but they realize that ethnicity, sexual orientation, and class may be more important factors in given situations and across situations for many women. The practice of contemporary feminist therapy is based on the assumption that gender cannot be considered apart from other identity areas such as race, ethnicity, class, and sexual orientation. A key concept pertaining to understanding symptoms is that problematic symptoms can be viewed as coping or survival strategies rather than as evidence of pathology. Although individuals are not to blame for personal problems largely caused by dysfunctional social environments, they are responsible for working toward change.

Therapeutic Goals

Six goals for feminist therapy have been proposed: equality, balancing independence and interdependence, self-nurturance, empowerment, social change, and valuing and affirming diversity. Feminist therapists believe gender is central to therapeutic practice and that understanding a client's problems requires adopting a sociocultural perspective. A goal of feminist therapy is to empower all people to create a world of equality that is reflected at individual, interpersonal, institutional, national, and global levels. Both individual transformation and societal changes are crucial goals of therapy. At the individual level, therapists work to help women and men recognize, claim, and embrace their personal power. As a consciously political enterprise, another goal is social transformation. The aim is to replace the current patriarchy with a feminist consciousness, thus creating a society that values equality in relationships, that stresses interdependence rather than dependence, and that encourages people to define themselves rather than being defined by societal demands.

Therapeutic Relationship

The therapeutic relationship is based on empowerment, deliberately equalizing the power base between client and therapist. Empowerment and egalitarianism are guiding principles. The structure of the client–therapist relationship models how to identify and use power responsibly. Emphasis is given to mutuality, or a condition of authentic connection between client and therapist. The therapist works to demystify therapy and to include the client as an active partner in the assessment and treatment process. The process of feminist therapy begins with the informed consent process, which establishes a framework that is egalitarian. Collaboration with the client in all aspects of therapy leads to a genuine partnership with clients. Therapists teach clients to recognize that how they define themselves and how they relate to others are inevitably influenced by gender-role expectations.

Techniques and Procedures

Feminist therapy is a technically integrative approach that stresses tailoring interventions to meet clients with their strengths. Feminist practitioners also draw upon strategies from many other therapy models, such as the use of therapeutic contracts, homework, bibliotherapy, therapist self-disclosure, empowerment, role playing, cognitive restructuring, reframing, relabeling, and assertiveness training. In addition, feminist procedures include gender-role analysis and intervention, power analysis and intervention, and social action. Feminist therapists have challenged assessment and diagnostic procedures on the grounds that they are often influenced by subtle forms of sexism, racism, ethnocentrism, heterosexism, ageism, or classism. In the feminist therapy process, diagnosis of distress becomes secondary to identification and assessment of strengths, skills, and resources.

Many of the strategies of multicultural feminist therapy fall under the general umbrella of empowerment, which enables people to see themselves as active agents on behalf of themselves and others. Feminist therapists work in an egalitarian manner and use empowerment strategies that are tailored to each client.

Applications

Feminist therapy can be applied to individual therapy for both women and men and for couples therapy, family therapy, group counseling, and community intervention. Feminist principles can also be applied to supervision, teaching, consultation, ethics, research, theory building, and to addressing social injustices. Key concepts of this approach can be applied to most of the other theories of counseling.

   Group work fits well with the spirit of feminist therapy. Consciousness-raising groups initially provided a forum for women to share their experiences with oppression and powerlessness. Self-help groups offered many women encouragement to challenge social patterns of the time. Groups provide a context in which women can examine the messages they have internalized about their self-worth, their gender-role identity, and their place in society. Although these groups are as diverse as the women who comprise them, they share a common goal of offering support for the experience of women. By participating in a group, women may become aware that their individual experiences are often rooted in problems within the system. Ideally, a group experience can motivate the members to get involved in some type of social action to bring about both individual and system change.

Multicultural Perspectives

Feminist therapy and multicultural/social justice perspectives have a great deal in common. The feminist perspective on power in relationships has application for understanding power inequities due to racial and cultural factors. The "personal is political" principle can be applied both to counseling women and counseling culturally diverse client groups. Neither feminist therapy nor multicultural perspectives focus exclusively on individual change. Instead, both approaches emphasize direct action for social change as a part of the role of therapists. Many of the social action and political strategies that call attention to oppressed groups have equal relevance for women and for other marginalized groups. Both feminist therapists and multicultural therapists have worked to establish policies that lessen the opportunities for discrimination of all types—gender, race, culture, sexual orientation, ability, religion, and age.

Contributions

A key contribution of feminist therapy is the potential for integration of feminist therapy principles and concepts with other therapeutic systems. Feminist theorists have contributed to increasing awareness of one's attitudes and biases pertaining to gender and culture, regardless of one's theoretical orientation. Theories can be evaluated against the criteria of being gender free, flexible, interactionist, and life-span-oriented. Therapists of any orientation can infuse feminist practices in their work if they conduct therapy with a positive, egalitarian attitude toward both women and men and are willing to confront patriarchal systems. The feminist approach emphasizes the importance of considering the context of women's lives rather than focusing narrowly on symptoms and behaviors. Feminism has done a great deal to sensitize therapists to the gendered uses of power in relationships, which can be applied to counseling with women and men. In addition, feminist therapy groups actively worked to establish shelters for battered women, rape crisis centers, and women's health and reproductive health centers. Building community, providing authentic mutual empathic relationships, creating a sense of social awareness, and the emphasis on social change are all significant strengths of this approach.

Limitations

Feminist therapists do not take a neutral stance; they advocate for change in social structures. A potential limitation pertains to therapists who may impose their values on clients regarding the need to challenge the status quo. However, culturally competent feminist therapists look for ways to work within the clients' culture by exploring consequences and alternatives without making decisions for clients. There is an appreciation of the complexities involved in changing within one's culture. Another criticism is that feminist therapy was developed by White, middle-class, heterosexual women and that its underlying assumptions are biased due to this narrow viewpoint.

 ## GLOSSARY OF KEY TERMS

Androcentric   Using male-oriented constructs to draw conclusions about human, including female, nature.

Cultural feminists   These feminists believe oppression stems from society's devaluation of women's strength, values, and roles. They believe the solution to oppression lies in feminization of the culture so that society becomes more nurturing, intuitive, subjective, cooperative, and relational.

Deterministic   Assumes that personality patterns and behavior are fixed at an early stage of development.

Egalitarian relationship   Power should be balanced in a relationship. In feminist therapy the voices of the oppressed are acknowledged as authoritative and valuable sources of knowledge.

Ethnocentrism   The idea that one's own cultural group is superior to others and that other groups should be judged based on one's own standards.

Flexible–multicultural perspective   Uses concepts and strategies that apply equally to individuals and groups regardless of age, race, culture, gender, ability, class, or sexual orientation.

Gendercentric   Believing that there are two separate paths of development for women and men.

Gender-fair approaches   Explain differences in the behavior of women and men in terms of socialization processes rather than on the basis of our "innate" natures, thus avoiding stereotypes in social roles and interpersonal behavior.

Gender-neutral theory   Explains differences in the behavior of women and men in terms of socialization processes rather than viewing gender differences as fixed in nature.

Gender-role analysis   Used to help clients understand the impact of gender-role expectations in their lives. Some feminist therapists prefer to use the term "social identity analysis" rather than gender-role analysis, to reflect the importance of assessing all relevant aspects of a client's identity.

Gender-role intervention   Provides clients with insight into the ways social issues affect their problems.

Gender schema   An organized set of mental associations people use to interpret their perceptions about gender.

Global/international feminism   This approach takes a worldwide perspective and seeks to understand the ways in which racism, sexism, economics, and classism affect women in different countries.

Heterosexist   Views a heterosexual orientation as normative and desirable and devalues same-sex relationships.

Interactionist   Concepts specific to the thinking, feeling, and behaving dimensions of human experience that account for contextual and environmental factors.

Intrapsychic orientation   Attributing behavior to internal causes, which often results in blaming the victim and ignoring sociocultural and political factors.

Lesbian feminists   This group of feminists views women's oppression as related to heterosexism and sexualized images of women.

Liberal feminists   These feminists focus on helping individual women overcome the limits and constraints of traditional gender-role socialization patterns; they argue for a transformation from accepting traditional gender roles to creating equal opportunities for both women and men.

Life-span perspective   Assumes that human development is a lifelong process and that personality patterns and behavioral changes can occur at any time.

Personal is political Individuals' personal problems have social and political causes. Therapy is aimed at helping clients change their own behavior and become active participants in transforming society.

Postmodern feminists This group of feminists provides a model for critiquing other traditional and feminist approaches, addressing the issue of what constitutes reality and proposing multiple truths as opposed to a single truth.

Power analysis Emphasis is on the power difference between men and women in society. Clients are helped to recognize different kinds of power they possess and how they and others exercise power.

Radical feminists This group of feminists focuses on the oppression of women that is embedded in patriarchy and seek to change society through activism and equalizing power.

Reframing A technique whereby the counselor changes the frame of reference for looking at an individual's behavior. There is a shift from an intrapersonal (or "blaming the victim") stance to a consideration of social factors in the environment that contribute to a client's problem.

Relabeling An intervention that changes the label or evaluation applied to the client's behavioral characteristics. Generally, the focus is shifted from a negative to a positive evaluation.

Relational-cultural theory A perspective suggesting that a woman's sense of identity and self-concept develop in the context of relationships.

Self-in-relation The idea that a woman's sense of self depends largely on how she connects with others.

Social action Participating in some activity outside of the therapy office (such as some kind of volunteer work in the community) that is likely to empower clients by helping them see the link between their personal experiences and the social context in which they live.

Socialist feminists These feminists aim to transform social relationships and institutions. They focus on multiple oppressions and believe solutions to society's problems must include considerations of class, race, sexual orientation, economics, nationality, and history.

White privilege An invisible package of unearned assets White people enjoy that are not extended to people of color.

Women of color feminists This group of feminists believes it is essential that feminist theory be broadened and made more inclusive by addressing multiple oppressions, taking into consideration privilege and power, and emphasizing activism.

 QUESTIONS FOR REFLECTION AND DISCUSSION

1. Feminist therapists teach their clients that uncritical acceptance of traditional roles can greatly restrict their range of freedom to define the kind of person they want to be. What are your thoughts about this?

2. The principle "the personal is political" holds that clients' problems have social and political causes. This implies that therapy should focus not only on individual change but on social change as well. If you accept this principle, how would this affect your way of working with clients?

3. Feminist therapists do not restrict their practice to women; they also work with men, couples, families, and children. What are some ways feminist therapy concepts can be applied to counseling men?

4. What common concepts are shared by both feminist therapy and multicultural counseling? What basic ideas from both of these approaches would you want to incorporate into your own counseling perspective?

5. In feminist therapy the therapeutic relationship is based on empowerment and egalitarianism. If you were to practice from this perspective, how could you work to actively break down the hierarchy of power in the therapy relationship? What interventions would you make to increase the empowerment of clients?

6. What are some ways you could demystify the therapeutic process at the initial session? What kinds of information would you most want to give to your clients? How would you go about promoting a collaborative partnership?

7. Feminist therapists do not use diagnostic labels, or they use them reluctantly. They are critical of traditional assessment and diagnosis because of the belief that these procedures are often based on sexist assumptions. What are your thoughts concerning the feminist critique of diagnosis?

8. How could you apply what you have learned in your study of the previous other traditional theories to the practice of feminist therapy? Do you see any basis for integrating some of the concepts and techniques of the traditional models of counseling with feminist therapy? What concepts of traditional therapy are in conflict with a feminist orientation?

9. In what ways might the therapist's goals of including sociopolitical change interfere or conflict with a client's personal goals for therapy? If a conflict did occur, how do you think it could be negotiated?

10. What do you consider to be the major contributions of the feminist approach to the counseling profession? What are some criticisms or shortcomings of this approach?

JERRY COREY COUNSELS STAN FROM A FEMINIST PERSPECTIVE

Session 10. Feminist Therapy Applied to the Case of Stan

This session deals with Stan's exploration of his gender-role identity and messages he has incorporated about being a man. Before viewing the session, read Chapter 12, pages 382–384 in the textbook, and answer the questions under the heading "Follow-Up: You Continue as Stan's Feminist Therapist." After reflecting on these questions, view the video.

As you observe Stan exploring several messages he internalized from his parents and society, what shifts in his thinking do you notice, if any? Do you think you would be able to challenge Stan's views about "what a man should be" if you have not examined your own gender-role socialization? To what degree have you thought about societal messages that you have heard regarding appropriate behavior for your gender? After viewing this session, address these questions:

1. What usefulness do you see in suggesting reading as a way to encourage Stan to challenge his views on gender roles?

2. How might you help Stan challenge some of the messages he received from society about what a man is supposed to be?

3. Stan says that his father often said to him, "Suck it up and be a man." What kind of intervention might you make at this point?

4. Feminist therapy emphasizes an egalitarian and collaborative relationship. If you were Stan's counselor, what are some specific things you would say and do to establish this equality? What are some aspects of his therapy that you would most want to collaborate on with him?

5. Feminist therapy deals with the need for social action to bring about change. What kind of social action program might you encourage Stan to consider?

6. In this session Jerry asks Stan if he wants to be the way his father is (like a rock). What are your thoughts about this question?

7. In what ways might you incorporate cognitive behavioral techniques in this session to assist Stan in critically examining his beliefs about being a man?

8. For Stan, being competent is a big part of his adequacy as a man. What might you do with this notion of Stan's?

9. Would you encourage Stan to join a men's group on campus? Why or why not?

10. Do you think there is a place for feminist therapy in a situation with a male therapist and a male client? Explain.

A Suggested In-Class Activity

Spend some time in small groups discussing what you saw in the video clip and what you read of the therapist's way of working with Stan in the text. How would it be for you to counsel Stan from a feminist perspective? Explore these three questions in your small group:

1. What did you find most interesting in this session? Why?

2. If you were counseling Stan from this particular theoretical framework, what is one additional technique you might use? What would you hope to accomplish with this intervention?

3. If you were the client, how would you be likely to respond to the therapist's (Jerry's) comments and interventions in this particular session?

Talk in your group about the differences in feminist therapy from most of the other approaches you have studied thus far. I also suggest that you practice applying feminist techniques to Stan. If you do use the model of role-playing Stan and the counselor, be sure to talk about what it was like to be the client in this situation as well as the counselor.

JERRY COREY'S WORK WITH RUTH FROM A FEMINIST PERSPECTIVE

I use contracts as a way to make the goals and processes of therapy overt rather than covert and mysterious. This is in keeping with the feminist perspective of striving to make the client a therapeutic partner. When I first mention to Ruth that our work will be defined by a therapeutic contract, she seems put off. She thinks it sounds legalistic, and she wonders why it is necessary.

JERRY: A contract sets the focus for therapy. As the client, you decide what specific beliefs, emotions, and behaviors you plan to change to reach your stated goals.

RUTH: But I'm not quite sure what I want to change. I was counting on you to point out to me what I should work on. There's so much to change, and I'm at a loss where to begin.

JERRY: Part of our work here will entail determining where in your life you want to take on more responsibility.

At this point Ruth and I discuss this issue in some detail. I let her know that my approach to therapy is based on the expectation that clients focus on their goals and make a commitment. It emphasizes the division of responsibility and provides a point of departure for working.

RUTH [*after some exploration*]: I want to be me. I want to be happy. I'm tired of taking care of everyone else. I want to take care of me, not just others.

JERRY: That's a start, but can you narrow this down? What would make you happy? What do you mean by taking care of yourself? How will you do this? And in what ways are you not being you?

I work with Ruth until she eventually comes up with clear statements of what she wants from therapy, what steps she will take to get what she wants, and how she will determine when her contract is fulfilled. After much discussion and a series of negotiations, Ruth comes up with a list of changes she is willing to make.

RUTH: For one, I'm willing to approach my husband and tell him how I feel about our relationship. I know you say I can't change him and that I can only change myself, so I'll tell him what I intend to do differently. And later, I would like to deal directly with my four children. They all take advantage of me, and I intend to change that. I can begin by telling them what I'm willing to do and what I'm no longer willing to do.

Although this list is more specific than her original goals, there is still a need for greater specificity. I ask Ruth exactly what she does want to change about each area she has mentioned, including what she intends to do differently. One part of Ruth's contract involves asking her husband to attend at least one of the sessions so that she can tell him the specific things she most wants to change in their relationship.

For most of her life Ruth has believed she should be what others expect her to be, that she should not voice what she wants, and that she should go along with the program others have for her. I will employ some assertiveness training strategies at this point, and we will spend considerable time exploring where Ruth acquired her views about the "proper role of women." As Ruth begins to restructure some of her beliefs, she recognizes she has a right to be different. Once Ruth begins to think differently, she is more amenable to learning specific skills for being assertive.

You Continue Working With Ruth as Her Feminist Therapist

1. Refer to *Case Approach to Counseling and Psychotherapy* (Chapter 10) for a comprehensive illustration of three feminist therapists (Kathy Evans, Susan Seem, and Elizabeth Kincade) who collaboratively work with Ruth. What interventions did Drs. Evans, Seem, and Kincade use with Ruth that you would want to incorporate in your way of working with her?

2. See the *DVD for Integrative Counseling: The Case of Ruth and Lecturettes* (first three sessions) and analyze my attempt to incorporate feminist principles and concepts in my beginning work with Ruth. How would you work with Ruth in these early sessions?

3. What would you want to tell Ruth about the therapy process from the beginning? How would you obtain her informed consent?

4. If you were to continue counseling Ruth, what direction would you likely follow?

5. If Ruth and John were to attend a session with you, what would be your interventions with them as a couple?

A CASE FROM A FEMINIST THERAPY PERSPECTIVE

Brooklin

By **Kathy M. Evans, PhD,** Associate Professor at the University of Southern Carolina and the Coordinator of the Counselor Education Program. This piece was done in collaboration with: **Elizabeth A. Kincade, PhD,** Chair of the Counseling Center at Indiana University of Pennsylvania; and **Susan Rachael Seem, PhD,** Professor in the Department of Counselor Education at The College of Brockport, State University of New York.

Background Data on Brooklin

Brooklin, a 21-year-old, African American woman from a major northeastern city attends college at a small state university. She is a Dean's List student, a marketing major. When Brooklin first enters my office, I (Kathy Evans) want her to feel that she is welcomed and respected. I am also an African American and hope that this will help establish our relationship but I don't take this for granted. I have experienced clients who look like me but were angry that they were assigned to a Black counselor. Some assumed that Black clients were assigned to me regardless of my abilities. To the contrary, Brooklin appears relaxed and accepting. I begin by presenting my therapeutic style and discuss the values, philosophy and techniques of feminist therapy. She learns that in my model many problems are rooted in oppression. I help clients understand the consequences of oppression and socialization and help them take action to change societal and individual beliefs that are harmful and change the systems that support these beliefs. Brooklin is conceptualized as a respected partner in the counseling relationship and after we discuss my style of counseling, she receives the option of continuing to work with me or transferring to a counselor that would better fit her needs. She states that she could identify with the concept of societal expectations and would like to explore this further. If she had wanted to transfer we would have worked together to find her another counselor.

Brooklyn complains of sadness and loneliness. As we talk, Brooklin reveals that she has had limited contact with her family over the past year. About a year ago, she began dating Richard, another marketing major. They are in the same clubs and activities on campus. Richard is White. Brooklin's family expressed misgivings about this interracial relationship. They told her that Richard will use her while in college but not maintain a relationship with her afterwards. Brooklin divulged that she is frequently unhappy in the relationship as Richard does not take her home to his family and still sees his high school girlfriend, who is White. She said she is hurt and confused when Richard compares her to this woman. When asked why she stays with Richard she cites their many professional interests in common and that when they are alone he is sweet and loving.

Working With Brooklin From a Feminist Therapy Perspective

Brooklin and I work on establishing a relationship that is respectful of both of our areas of expertise; that is, *an egalitarian relationship*. I phrase it this way since for some African American clients, it is important that professional helpers, especially those who are also African American, are treated with respect for their status and accomplishments rather than as equals or friends. I discuss our relationship to see how comfortable Brooklin is with us relating to each other in an egalitarian manner.

In feminist counseling and therapy, diagnosis does not focus on *individual psychopathology* but rather on societal pathology. I listen to Brooklin's narrative and take note of societal and political influences in her life. We explore the influences of her family as well as her culture and larger society. We discuss racism from both her personal experiences and her cultural perceptions. We examine racist institutional practices that mitigate her personal, social and political power. Later, we do similar explorations of Brooklin's gendered experiences in a patriarchal society. As an African American woman, these experiences are intertwined for Brooklin, so we talk about them together.

From her *racial/ethnic background,* Brooklin learned that African American women are strong and independent. She admires these qualities in the women in her family but has doubts about her own ability to be strong and independent. She enjoys that Richard makes many of the decisions in their relationship. She interprets his concern for her whereabouts and how she presents herself to others as care. Her parents and siblings are strong in their disapproval of these behaviors. Her dependence on Richard is seen as betrayal of her family and cultural values. Brooklin, on the other hand, believes that her relationship with Richard does not mean she has forgotten or abandoned her identity as an African-American woman. Her family doubts this and because of this Brooklin has become estranged from her family.

We discuss Brooklin's rebellion against cultural expectations through her dependence on Richard and what it has done to her perceived and actual power. She realizes that her family and culture value strong, independent women but she is envious of many White women's cultural privilege to be taken care of and provided for by men. She comes to understand that she wants that privilege, as well.

Brooklin is African American, thus we perform *gender role and cultural analyses* simultaneously. Brooklin shared her primary gender role message: successful women are married and support their husbands. While not socialized to be dependent on her husband, Brooklin learned that she must take care of a husband and relinquish power to him. As head of the family, a husband's decision is the final decision. As we explore messages about gender, power and culture, Brooklin realizes that these contradictory messages confuse her. She has sought to be strong and independent through her academics and career plans. However, she was also taught to put her needs second in a relationship and has done so. We explore these contradictions. Brooklin realizes that gradations of dependence and independence exist. A strong woman has more input into decision-making in relationships than she has. Due to this, she lost contact with her family, formerly a great source of strength and support. She also recognizes that racial/cultural gender expectations highlight the importance of marriage and heterosexual relationships. Thus, she has endured more from Richard (verbal and emotional abuse) than a strong and respected woman should. The gender role/cultural analysis results in Brooklin's rejecting cultural messages that emphasize having a man over her own self-worth. She also realizes that relinquishing power is equally devastating.

During the *power analysis*, Brooklin realizes that Richard uses power in a number of different ways—threats, rewards, and withholding information. Abuse of his inherent power is evident in that he continues to see his high school girlfriend, who is White, when he is with his family. He then compares Brooklin to this woman and enumerates Brooklin's faults. Brooklin responds by placating him and attempting to change herself to fit his needs. However, she understands that there are some attributes she cannot acquire or change due to racial and cultural differences. She feels powerless. In addition, her commitment to Richard is responsible for her estrangement from her family. Richard has not lost contact with his family because he does not tell them that this is a serious relationship. Brooklin knows that she also uses her power over Richard to shape his behavior. She takes advantage of his guilt over their relationship, coupled with his need to control and take care of her, by manipulating him with direct and indirect requests for gifts and favors. Brooklin realizes that exertion of this kind of power is personally unhealthy but understands that it is one of the few power bases available to women in male-controlled relationships.

The difference in racial backgrounds is also an issue of power. Richard is a member of the most powerful group in U. S. society. As a White male, he embodies the oppression of Brooklin's racial group. Her family expects him to abuse his power and the fact that he does angers Brooklin's family even more. Brooklin is ashamed because Richard keeps the serious nature of their relationship from his family, whereas, involvement in this relationship caused estrangement from her family. She believes that if she breaks up with Richard, it will prove to her family and herself that White people are not trustworthy. She also fears that this distrust might generalize to her White women friends, her professors, other classmates and so on. She states that she is deeply invested in the relationship and does not want to end it.

After the power analysis, Brooklin decides that she no longer wants to endure Richard's verbal and emotional abuse and that she wants to confront him on it. She elucidates the healthy elements of the relationship and states that she has the right to have a voice in the relationship. We work on ways to reduce the abuse of power—the coercion in their relationship. We discuss the possibility of feminist couples work that would engage both Brooklin and Richard in exploration of deeply held gender and cultural beliefs.

Finally, we focus on her estrangement from her family. We explored ways that Brooklin can share with them her emerging strength in the relationship with Richard. We talked about Brooklin hearing and honoring her family's pride in her academic accomplishments and her changing her internalized beliefs about relationships and self-esteem. Brooklin made decisions to address her needs in her relationship with Richard and began to consider ways that she could reconnect with her family without giving up a part of herself.

Follow-Up: You Continue as Brooklin's Feminist Therapist

1. How do you help Brooklin integrate her emerging sense of self-worth and self-esteem with her personal needs and cultural mandate to be in a male/female relationship? What interventions would you use?

2. One possibility for Brooklin and her partner Richard is feminist couples therapy focusing on societal power and gender roles. Assume that Richard accompanies Brooklin to one session and is hesitant to commit to couples therapy. What might you say to him to introduce him to feminist couples work (or individual feminist therapy for himself) and how it might be helpful for his relationship with Brooklin?

3. You do not think that this is a healthy relationship. However, Brooklin is committed to staying in the relationship. How do you proceed with counseling? To what degree do you introduce your own opinions into your counseling with Brooklin?

4. Brooklin tells you that after thinking about it, she would prefer to transfer to another counselor. She is not a feminist and believes that you will influence her to leave Richard because feminists do not like men. How do you respond?

ANOTHER CASE FROM A FEMINIST THERAPY PERSPECTIVE

Marina: "Searching for Identity"

By **Mary M. Read, PhD,** Director of Clinical Training in the Counseling Department at California State University, Fullerton.

Background Information

Marina is a 38-year-old single woman who came into therapy to better understand her emerging racial and sexual identities, as well as cope with some issues surfacing from her traumatic childhood. She is having trouble keeping her job at present, due to excessive tardiness. She links this to her "head feeling scattered" from new information she just received about her ethnic background, and a budding attraction to women, where she had previously expressed herself as heterosexual. She admits to feeling "extremely down" at times, and struggling to deal with incorporating conflicting views of herself on her own.

Dr. Mary Read's Way of Working With Marina From a Feminist Perspective

Marina was referred to me by a co-worker, specifically because of my feminist orientation to therapy. "I don't want anyone to tell me what to do or how to be—I just want to get a handle on who I am so I can get on with my life," she tells me in our first meeting. I assure her that we will explore her issues together, focusing on her strengths, and that she will be responsible for making the choices for her own life. She will be the expert on who she is and wants to become, while I will work to provide hope, encouragement and support as she moves through this process. We discuss what feminism means in the context of therapy, and I leave plenty of time for Marina to ask me questions about my background, training and therapy process, leveling the power differential between us somewhat.

Significantly, Marina was unaware that her father is African American until just recently, since he left the family before she was three. Her mother's family, of northern European descent, never shared with Marina why she did not have blonde hair and blue eyes like the rest of her family. She assumed, since her brown hair, eyes and café au lait skin tone matched others in her primarily Latino neighborhood, that he was Hispanic.

She has now met him once, and finds that "a piece of the puzzle of who I am just fell into place," yet some of the information he imparted is also very upsetting. Her father confirmed some of the memories Marina has about being verbally and physically abused by her mother and maternal aunt when she was very young, which progressed to sexual abuse when she reached puberty. Being sexually victimized by female relatives has made it very hard for Marina to explore her own sexuality, especially her developing realization of bisexual attractions.

Since Marina's job is on the line, we focus first on what it would take to please her boss (a woman) enough to successfully complete the remediation plan at work to salvage her job, then earn a better employee evaluation for the next period. This brings up Marina's lack of sleep from frequent nightmares, resulting in missing her alarm once she finally returns to sleep. As well, Marina's mood at work has been "grumpy and distracted" by her own admission. I ask if Marina has shared with her boss any of the extenuating circumstances that have caused a drop in her work performance, and she hasn't. This brings up a choice point, where Marina could go along one path or another, disclosing personal information to her boss or not. Marina and I explore different avenues (mainly by role play and visualization) before she makes her selection, as part of informed consent. Understanding the risk-to-benefit ratio of her choices is part of what gives Marina the empowerment to make changes in her life.

I also encourage Marina to get a good physical from a medical doctor, since she has been ignoring her health for some time. There are several female physicians to whom I routinely refer, and Marina agrees to make an appointment with one. The whole person is a focus of feminist therapy, and self-care is a vital tool of empowerment. We also discuss the possibility of seeing a psychiatrist if her depression worsens, or if her post-traumatic symptoms continue to interrupt her sleep. She is hesitant to follow through with this referral, since "I don't want to be called crazy for what I remember." I assure Marina that I do not see her as crazy, and that it is very common for children in abusive situations to develop coping skills that, in the moment, help them survive, yet in the long run also cause some problems.

Apparently, this has happened for Marina, who admits at our third meeting that she had seen a psychologist previously for a few sessions. "He gave me some tests, then said I was 'Borderline' which sounded pretty hopeless, so I didn't go back." I explained to Marina that sometimes children who experience very early trust wounds, usually with their primary caregivers, later have difficulty figuring out who they are relative to others, and go back and forth on whether others are trustworthy or not. Given Marina's complicated history with multiple losses and traumas, this pattern of development made sense. I encourage her to read books on the subject of surviving trauma in childhood, including John Briere's (1992) *Child Abuse and Trauma*, which talks about psychological symptoms as coping strategies that fit within the context of abuse. This feminist view of the diagnostic process allows for the development of better coping skills over time, emphasizing choice and empowerment vs. abnormality and deficit. A strengths-based perspective, essential in feminist therapy, is thus preserved in the context of diagnosis.

Rather than see Marina through the lens of her diagnosis, she and I discuss how she is feeling about our relationship in each session. We make room for her to feel positively and negatively toward me, the therapy process, and the therapeutic relationship, not taking the feelings of the moment as the last word, but simply another layer of information to guide our work together. When she is angry with me, we explore what she might have wanted to be different, and whether that can be arranged, within the boundaries of therapy. For example, when I looked at the clock near the end of one session to be sure we ended on time, Marina came in the following session accusing me of being uncaring and wanting to be rid of her. Now, if I wonder about the time, I ask her where she thinks we are in the session, and we look at the clock together to gauge how to process where she is and where she'd like to be by session's end. We both approach the end of the session differently now, and are learning from that shift.

To explore her emerging identities, I encourage Marina to participate in cultural events that provide a systemic context for her unique ways of being. She is becoming active in an African American singing and drumming group, wearing traditional African garb for performances. The rich cultural inheritance she now embraces helps her move from feeling "different" to "special," which is increasing her self-esteem. I also encourage her to participate in events like Pride Festivals for the LGBT (Lesbian, Gay, Bisexual and Transgender) communities, where many participants experience and express a sense of sexuality alternative to society's hetero-normative views.

Embracing two identities that have been heavily stigmatized and oppressed over the years is a challenge for Marina, because of society's injustice, not a deficit in Marina. She now realizes that her differences can be causes for celebration rather than discrimination, that social justice demands equality for all races and sexualities, and that finding her way in these alternative identities will take some navigating over time and in different contexts. Marina continues to use the support of feminist counseling to help her embrace her emerging identities, and to explore ways to work for a more inclusive, tolerant society.

Follow-Up: You Continue as Marina's Therapist

1. Marina decides to talk to her boss about why she has had issues being tardy (interrupted sleep) but only discloses learning of her father's ethnicity, not her child abuse history or shifting sense of sexuality. Marina reports that her boss responded by making a derogatory comment about African Americans. How would you process this with Marina? What are your responsibilities as a feminist counselor?

2. Given that therapy is an intimate context, Marina begins to indicate she is experiencing feelings of attraction to you. How do you process this from a feminist perspective? How do you balance power-sharing with keeping appropriate therapeutic boundaries?

3. Marina eventually loses her job, and with it the insurance coverage that paid for her therapy with you. As a feminist, how do you negotiate a new arrangement with Marina, ensuring she continues to receive needed support?

 QUIZ ON FEMINIST THERAPY

A Comprehension Check

Score _____%

Note: Please refer to Appendix 1 for the scoring key.

True/false items: Decide if the following statements are "more true" or "more false" as they apply to feminist therapy.

T   F   1. Although feminist therapy addresses social and political issues pertaining to gender-role stereotyping, this approach does not address most other forms of oppression.

T   F   2. One of the goals of feminist therapy is to help women understand how sexist and oppressive societal beliefs and practices influence them in negative ways.

T   F   3. A criticism of feminist therapy is that it was developed by White, middle-class, heterosexual women.

T   F   4. Therapist self-disclosure is rarely used in feminist therapy.

T   F   5. Gender-role analysis involves a cooperative exploration by client and therapist of the impact of gender on the client's distress.

T   F   6. In feminist therapy, clients are viewed as active participants in redefining themselves in the context of the therapeutic relationship, rather than the therapist being viewed as the best or "expert" source.

T   F   7. Feminist therapy is an approach that is applicable to women but not to men.

T   F   8. Instead of being diverse, feminist practice is a single and unified approach to therapy.

T   F   9. Women now are assuming positions of leadership in government and business, and this can be interpreted to mean that women no longer have difficulty making life choices.

T   F   10. It is probably accurate to say that in today's society barriers no longer stand in the way of gender equity.

Multiple-choice items: Select the *one best answer* of those alternatives given. Consider each question within the framework of feminist therapy.

_____ 11. Which branch of feminist therapy provides a model for critiquing the value of other traditional and feminist approaches?

   a. postmodern feminism
   b. women of color feminism
   c. lesbian feminism
   d. global/international feminism
   e. none of the above

_____ 12. All of the following are considered aspects of the "third wave" of feminist perspectives except for

   a. postmodern feminism.
   b. women of color feminism.
   c. lesbian feminism.
   d. cultural feminism.
   e. global/international feminism.

_____ 13. All of the following are ways feminist therapy differs from traditional therapy except for

   a. viewing problems in a sociopolitical and cultural context.
   b. demystifying the therapeutic process.
   c. accepting the premise that diagnosis is a basic prerequisite for effective treatment.
   d. creating a therapeutic relationship that is egalitarian.
   e. recognizing that clients know what is best for their life and are experts in their own life.

_____ 14. Which of the following interventions is least likely to be used by a feminist therapist?

   a. analysis and interpretation of transference
   b. sex-role analysis and intervention
   c. power analysis and intervention
   d. encouraging clients to take social action
   e. assertiveness training

_____ 15. Which of the following is considered to be a major contribution feminists have made to the field of counseling?

   a. pioneering research in the therapy process
   b. creating a brief, solution-focused therapy approach
   c. integrating a diagnostic perspective in counseling practice
   d. paving the way for gender-sensitive practice

_____ 16. A goal of feminist therapy is to empower all people to create a world of equality that is reflected at which of the following levels?

   a. individual and interpersonal
   b. institutional
   c. national
   d. global
   e. all of the above

_____ 17. Feminist therapists refer to

   a. women's problems as a reflection of hormonal imbalances.
   b. distress rather than psychopathology.
   c. feelings of emptiness and invisibility as deficits in one's psychic structure.
   d. women's anger as a reflection of the aggressive drive.

_____ 18. The feminist philosophy that emphasizes the differences between women and men and views the goal of therapy as being the infusion of cooperative values in society is

   a. liberal feminism.
   b. cultural feminism.

c. postmodern feminism.

d. social feminism.

_____ 19. The feminist philosophy that emphasizes helping individual women overcome the limits and constraints of their socialization problems is

a. liberal feminism.

b. cultural feminism.

c. global/international feminism.

d. social feminism.

_____ 20. This approach to feminism focuses on multiple oppressions and has the goal of transforming social relationships and institutions.

a. liberal feminism

b. cultural feminism

c. radical feminism

d. social feminism

_____ 21. Feminist therapists use self-disclosure to

a. equalize the client–therapist relationship.

b. normalize women's collective experiences.

c. empower clients.

d. establish informed consent.

e. all of the above

_____ 22. Part of the feminist critique of assessment and diagnosis is that these procedures

a. are often based on sexist assumptions.

b. minimize the effect of environmental factors that influence behavior.

c. provide different treatments to women and men who display similar symptoms.

d. tend to reinforce gender-role stereotypes and encourage adjustment to the status quo.

e. do all of the above.

_____ 23. Which of the following is **not** considered to be a basic principle of feminist therapy?

a. All types of oppression are recognized.

b. Commitment to social change.

c. Definitions of psychological distress and mental illness are based on the *DSM-IV-TR*.

d. Counseling is based on a relationship that is egalitarian.

e. The personal is political.

_____ 24. What perspective calls for feminist theory to include an analysis of multiple identities and their relationship to oppression?

a. postmodern feminism

b. lesbian feminism

c. radical feminism

d. cultural feminism

e. liberal feminism

_____ 25. Which of the following statements about feminist therapy is **not** true?

a. Therapy is relatively short term.

b. The model underlying practice tends to be static.

c. A goal is to replace the current patriarchal system with feminist consciousness.

d. Women are encouraged to define themselves rather than being defined by societal demands.

e. Feminist therapy differs from traditional therapy in a number of ways.

Chapter 13

Postmodern Approaches

PRECHAPTER SELF-INVENTORY

Directions: Refer to page 43 for general directions. Use the following code:

5 = I *strongly agree* with this statement.

4 = I *agree,* in most respects, with this statement.

3 = I am *undecided* in my opinion about this statement.

2 = I *disagree,* in most respects, with this statement.

1 = I *strongly disagree* with this statement.

_____ 1. Assessments and provisional diagnoses are best arrived at in a collaborative conversation with clients.

_____ 2. Changing the direction in therapy from a problem-focus to a solution-focus can dramatically change clients' beliefs about their life situation.

_____ 3. An appropriate aim of therapy is to create conversations with clients that allow for developing new meanings for problematic thoughts, feelings, and behaviors.

_____ 4. A *not-knowing position* allows therapists to follow, affirm, and be guided by the stories of their clients.

_____ 5. People live their lives according to the stories people tell about them and the stories they tell themselves.

_____ 6. The client can be considered as the expert on his or her own life.

_____ 7. Clients are often stuck in a pattern of living a problem-saturated story that is not working for them.

_____ 8. Clients are able to build more satisfying lives in a relatively short period of time in the context of an effective therapeutic relationship.

_____ 9. It is important that clients tell their stories and give voice to their experiencing.

_____ 10. A problem-focused approach to therapy is likely to cement unhelpful modes of behavior.

_____ 11. Including the client in the therapeutic process increases the chances that interventions will be culturally appropriate.

_____ 12. Rather than dwelling on what is wrong with people, it is more useful to view the client as resourceful and competent.

_____ 13. The therapist should be viewed as one source of information rather than as the best or "expert" source.

_____ 14. Collaboration, compassion, respect, reflection, and discovery are characteristic of effective therapeutic relationships.

_____ 15. The therapist's role of being respectfully curious encourages clients to explore the impact of the problem on them.

_____ 16. As clients become free of problem-saturated stories, they become more able to envision and plan for a less problematic future.

_____ 17. An appropriate aim of therapy is assist clients in creating a more satisfying alternative story.

_____ 18. A useful strategy is to attempt to separate a problem from a person's identity.

_____ 19. For therapy techniques to effectively be implemented, it is essential that a quality relationship exists between client and therapist.

_____ 20. Empathy and the collaborative partnership in the therapeutic process are more important than assessment or technique.

OVERVIEW OF POSTMODERN APPROACHES

Key Figures and Major Focus

Founders and Key Figures: Two co-founders of solution-focused brief therapy are Insoo Kim Berg and Steve de Shazer. Two co-founders of narrative therapy are Michael White and David Epston. Many of the postmodern approaches do not have a single founder, and instead, they represent a collective effort by many. Some of the major postmodern approaches include social constructionism, solution-focused brief therapy, and narrative therapy. In these approaches the therapist disavows the role of expert, preferring a more collaborative and consultative stance. Solution-focused brief therapy (SFBT) is a future-focused, goal-oriented therapeutic approach to brief therapy that shifts the focus from problem solving to an emphasis on solutions. SFBT emphasizes people's strengths and resiliencies by focusing on exceptions to their problems and their conceptualized solutions. In narrative therapy the focus is on searching for times when clients were strong or resourceful and on helping clients separate from the dominant cultural narratives they have internalized so as to open space for the creation of alternative life stories.

Philosophy and Basic Assumptions

From the viewpoint of social constructionism, the stories that people tell are about the creation of meaning. There may be as many stories of meaning as there are people who tell stories, and each of these stories is true for the individual who is telling the story. Postmodernists assume that realities are socially constructed. There is no absolute reality, and therapists should not impose their vision of reality or their values on an individual. Both solution-focused brief therapy and narrative therapy are based on the optimistic assumption that people are healthy, competent, resourceful, and possess the ability to construct solutions and alternative stories that can enhance their lives. Complex problems do not necessarily require complex solutions. The expertise of the therapist involves helping clients recognize the competencies they possess. Attention is given to what clients are doing that is working and helping them to build on their potential, strengths, and resources. Narrative therapists strive to avoid making assumptions about people out of respect for each client's unique story and cultural heritage. Change begins by deconstructing the power of cultural narratives and then proceeds to the co-construction of a new life of meaning.

Key Concepts

Key concepts of _solution-focused brief therapy_ include a movement from problem-talk to solution-talk and a focus on keeping therapy simple and brief. There are exceptions to every problem, and by talking about these exceptions, clients are able to conquer what seem to be gigantic problems. Solution-focused therapists make the assumption that clients are competent and that the therapist's role is to help clients recognize the competencies they already possess and apply them toward solutions. Thus, attention is paid to what is working, and clients are encouraged to do more of this. Change is constant and inevitable, and a small change leads to other changes until the "solution momentum" outweighs the problem momentum. Little attention is paid to pathology or to giving clients a diagnostic label. A therapist's not-knowing stance creates an opportunity for the client to construct a solution.

Some key concepts of *narrative therapy* include a discussion of how a problem has been disrupting, dominating, or discouraging the person. The therapist attempts to separate clients from their problems so that they do not adopt a fixed view of their identities. Clients are invited to view their stories from different perspectives and eventually to co-create an alternative life story. Clients are asked to find evidence to support a new view of themselves as being competent enough to escape the dominance of a problem and are encouraged to consider what kind of future could be expected from the competent person that is emerging.

Therapeutic Goals

The *solution-focused model* emphasizes the role of clients establishing their own goals and preferences. This is done when a climate of mutual respect, dialogue, inquiry, and affirmation are a part of the therapeutic process. Working together in a collaborative relationship, both the therapist and client develop useful treatment goals. Through the use of the miracle question, solution-focused therapists help clients identify goals and potential solutions. The heart of the therapeutic process from the postmodern perspectives involves identifying how societal standards and expectations are internalized by people in ways that oftentimes constrain and narrow the kind of life they are capable of living. The general theme of *narrative therapy* is to invite clients to describe their experience in fresh language, which tends to open up new vistas of what is possible.

Therapeutic Relationship

From the social constructionist viewpoint, therapy is a collaborative venture; the therapist strives to carry out therapy *with* an individual, rather than doing therapy *on* an individual. Instead of aiming to *make* change happen, the therapist attempts to create an atmosphere of understanding and acceptance that allows individuals to tap their resources for making constructive changes. Both solution-focused and narrative therapists adopt a "not-knowing" position to put clients in the position of being the experts about their own lives. The therapist-as-expert is replaced by the client-as-expert. Therapists do not assume that they know more about the lives of clients than they do. Clients are the primary interpreters of their own experiences. Therapists attempt to create collaborative relationships based on the assumption that collaboration opens up a range of possibilities for present and future change. One way of creating a working therapeutic partnership is for the therapist to show clients how they can use the strengths and resources they already possess to construct solutions. In the narrative approach, the therapist seeks to understand clients' lived experience and avoid efforts to predict, interpret, or pathologize. Narrative therapists collaborate with clients in assisting them to experience a heightened sense of agency or ability to act in the world.

Techniques and Procedures

Social constructionists use a range of techniques, depending on the therapist's orientation. Some therapists ask the client to externalize the problem and focus on strengths or unused resources. Others challenge clients to discover solutions that might work. Their techniques focus on the future and how best to solve problems rather than on understanding the cause of problems.

The *solution-focused approach* represents a different perspective from most of the traditional therapy models with respect to thinking about and doing brief therapy. A number of solution-focused brief therapy techniques are frequently used, including pretherapy change, exception questions, the miracle question, scaling questions, homework, and summary feedback.

- *Pretherapy change* involves asking clients at the first session, "What have you done since you called for an appointment that has made a difference in your problem?" Asking this question tends to encourage clients to rely less on the therapist and more on their own resources to reach their goals.

- *Exception questions* direct clients to those times in their lives when their problems did not exist. The therapist asks clients what has to happen for these exceptions to occur more often. Exploring exceptions offers clients opportunities for evoking resources, engaging strengths, and creating possible solutions. Illustrations of questions looking for exceptions are: "When was the last time that things were better? Talk about times when things were going well for you? What were you doing then? What are some things that you have done that helps with your problem? How will you know when you are handling your problem well?"

- *The miracle question* allows clients to describe life without the problem. This question involves a future focus that encourages clients to consider a different kind of life than one dominated by a particular problem. The miracle question focuses clients on searching for solutions. Examples are: "How will you know when things are better? What will be some of the things you will notice when life is better?"

- *Scaling questions* require clients to specify, on a scale of zero to 10, improvement on a particular dimension. This technique enables clients to see progress being made in specific steps and degrees.

- *Homework* often consists of asking clients to observe events that they would like to see occur more frequently in the future.

- *Summary feedback* involves the therapist pointing out particular strengths that clients have demonstrated.

Narrative therapy emphasizes the quality of the therapeutic relationship and the creative use of techniques within this relationship. In narrative therapy the therapy process provides the sociocultural context in which clients are assisted in separating themselves from their problems and are afforded the opportunity of authoring new stories. Some specific narrative techniques include externalizing, mapping the effects, deconstruction, co-authoring alternative stories, and building an audience as a witness to the emerging preferred story. Narrative therapy's most distinctive feature is captured by the statement, "The person is not the problem, but the problem is the problem." Externalizing conversations are aimed at separating the problem from the person rather than insisting that the person own the problem. Externalization is based on the notion that when clients view themselves as "being" the problem they are greatly limited in the ways they can effectively deal with the problem. The assumption is that clients can develop alternative and empowering stories once they have distanced themselves from the problems and cultural notions they have internalized. In narrative therapy it is through a systematic process of careful listening, coupled with curious, persistent, and respectful questioning that the therapist works with clients to explore the impact of the problem on them and what they are doing to reduce the effects of the problem. It is through this process that the client and therapist co-construct enlivening alternative stories.

Applications

Solution-focused brief therapy can be applied to individual therapy in a wide array of settings, including inpatient treatment centers, schools, and medical settings. The approach has been used to address diverse clinical problems, including substance abuse, depression, sexual abuse, child abuse, and spousal abuse.

Narrative therapy has been applied to a broad range of human problems, including relationship problems, depression, eating disorders, and problems in childhood and adolescence. Narrative ideas are applied in various areas, some of which are school counseling, marital and family therapy, couples therapy, mediation, substance abuse counseling, and clinical supervision.

Solution-focused brief therapy (SFBT) has many applications for different kinds of *counseling groups* in various settings. Because SFBT is designed to be brief, the counselor has the task of keeping group members on a solution track rather than a problem track. Members are assisted in developing small, realistic, and achievable goals as soon as possible. Group leaders ask questions from a position of respect, genuine curiosity, sincere interest, and openness. They use questions that presuppose change and are both goal-directed and future-oriented. SFBT holds a good deal of promise for counselors who want a practical and time-effective approach in both school settings and community agencies.

The narrative approach to group counseling also lends itself well to working with children and adolescents in the school setting. The narrative emphasis on creating an appreciative audience for new developments in an individual's life lends itself to group counseling.

Multicultural Perspectives

Social constructionism is congruent with the philosophy of multiculturalism. With the emphasis on multiple realities and the assumption that what is perceived to be a truth is the product of social construction, the postmodern approaches are a good fit with diverse worldviews. *Solution-focused therapists* learn from their clients about their experiential world, rather than approaching clients with a preconceived notion about their experience. Narrative therapy, which is grounded in a sociocultural context, makes this therapy especially relevant for working with culturally diverse clients. *Narrative therapists* operate on the premise that problems are identified within social, cultural, political, and relational contexts rather than existing within individuals. They incorporate in their practice factors such as gender, ethnicity, race, disability, sexual orientation, social class, and spirituality and religion. Therapy becomes a place to reauthor the social constructions and identity narratives that clients are finding problematic.

Contributions

A key contribution of all the postmodern approaches is the optimistic orientation that views people as being competent and able to create better solutions and more life-affirming stories. The nonpathologizing stance taken by postmodern practitioners moves away from dwelling on what is wrong with a person to emphasizing creative possibilities. Problems are not viewed as pathological manifestations but as ordinary difficulties and challenges of life. As therapists listen to a client's story, they pay attention to details that give evidence of a client's competence in taking a stand against an oppressive problem. A strength of both solution-focused and narrative therapies is the use of questioning, which can assist clients in developing their stories and discovering better ways to deal with their present concerns and to think about how they might solve potential problems in the future. Effective questioning can help individuals in examining their stories and finding new ways to present their stories.

Limitations

Many of the limitations of both solution-focused and narrative therapies pertain to lack of skill on the part of the therapist when implementing techniques. Some inexperienced or untrained therapists may be enamored by any number of techniques: the miracle question, scaling questions, the exception question, and externalizing questions. Although a number of techniques are available to both solution-focused and narrative therapists, the attitude of the therapist is critical to the success of outcomes. To effectively practice solution-focused brief therapy, it is essential that therapists are skilled in brief interventions. This means that in a relative short time practitioners are able to make quick assessments, assist clients in formulating specific goals, and effectively use appropriate interventions. In the practice of narrative therapy, there is no recipe, no set agenda, and no formula that the therapist can follow to assure desired outcomes. These are not necessarily limitations, but unless the therapist is personally and professional mature, the techniques used will have little therapeutic value.

GLOSSARY OF KEY TERMS

Alternative story   The story that develops in counseling in contradiction to the dominant story that is embedded in a client's problem.

Co-authoring   The process by which both therapist and client share responsibility for the development of alternative stories.

Deconstruction   The exploration of meaning by taking apart, or unpacking, the taken-for-granted categories and assumptions underlying social practices that pose as truth.

Dominant story   A way of understanding a situation that has been so widely accepted within a culture that it appears to represent "reality." Growing out of conversations in a social and cultural context, dominant stories shape reality in that they construct and constitute what people see, feel, and do.

Exception questions   Solution-focused therapists inquire about those times in clients' lives when the problems they identify have not been problematic. Exploring these exceptions reminds clients that problems are not all-powerful and have not existed forever.

Exceptions   Past experiences in a client's life when it would be reasonable to have expected the problem to occur, but somehow it did not.

Externalizing conversation   A way of speaking in which the problem may be spoken of as if it is a distinct entity that is separate from the person.

Formula first session task   A form of homework a therapist might give clients to complete between their first and second therapy sessions. Clients are asked to simply observe what is happening in their lives that they want to continue happening.

Mapping-the-influence questions   A series of questions asked about a problem that a client has internalized as a means of understanding the relationship between the person and the problem.

Miracle question   A solution-focused technique that asks clients to imagine how their life would be different if they woke up tomorrow and they no longer had their problem.

Narrative   A social constructionist conceptualization of how people create "storied" meaning in their lives.

Narrative therapy   A postmodern approach to therapy that is based on the therapist's personal characteristics that allow for creating a climate that encourages clients to see their stories from different perspectives. Grounded in a philosophical framework, narrative practices assist clients in finding new meanings and new possibilities in their lives.

Not-knowing position   A therapist's stance that invites clients to become the experts who are informing the therapist about the significant narratives of their lives.

Positive psychology   An approach that concentrates on what is right and what is working for people rather than dwelling on deficits, weaknesses, and problems.

Postmodernism   A philosophical movement across a variety of disciples that has aimed at critically examining many of the assumptions that are part of the established truths of society. The postmodern worldview acknowledges the complexity, relativity, and intersubjectivity of all human experience.

Postmodernist A believer in subjective realities that cannot exist independently of the observational processes used. Problems exist when people agree that there is a problem that needs to be addressed.

Pretherapy change At the first therapy session, solution-focused therapists often inquire about presession improvements, or anything clients have done since scheduling the appointment that has made a difference in their problems.

Problem-saturated story People often come to therapy feeling overwhelmed by their problems to which they are fused. Narrative therapists assist clients in understanding that they do not have to be reduced by these totalizing descriptions of their identity.

Re-authoring A process in narrative therapy in which client and therapist jointly create an alternative life story.

Scaling questions A solution-focused technique that asks clients to observe changes in

feelings, moods, thoughts, and behaviors. On a scale of zero to 10, clients are asked to rate some change in their experiences.

Social constructionism A therapeutic perspective within a postmodern worldview that stresses the client's reality without disputing the accuracy or validity of this reality. Social constructionism emphasizes the ways in which people make meaning in social relationships.

Solution-focused brief therapy A postmodern approach to therapy that provides a context whereby individuals focus on recovering and creating solutions rather than talking about their problems.

Totalizing descriptions A categorical description of people that constricts them to a single dimension that purports to capture their identity.

Unique outcome Aspects of lived experience that lie outside the realm of dominant stories or in contradiction to the problem-saturated story.

QUESTIONS FOR REFLECTION AND DISCUSSION

1. What do you imagine it would be like for you to be a client with a solution-focused therapist? A narrative therapist? What would you particularly like about the experience, if anything? What would have difficulty with, if anything?

2. Both narrative therapists and solution-focused therapists are very concerned with establishing truly collaborative relationships with their clients. Clients are co-creators of solutions and are co-authors in the process of reauthoring their life stories. As a therapist, what kind of collaborative partnership would you want to form with your clients?

3. The postmodern therapies are based on the assumption that the therapist takes a not-knowing position and clients are viewed as the experts on their own lives. To what degree do you think you could assume this stance as a therapist? What role would you assume if you were not the expert?

4. Solution-focused brief therapy eschews the past in favor of both the present and the future. What implications does this time perspective have for the practice of therapy? What are your thoughts about getting clients to work toward present and future solutions?

5. Solution-focused brief therapists strive to get their clients away from talking about their problems and instead emphasize talking about solutions. How does solution-oriented therapy differ from problem-oriented therapy? As a counselor, how comfortable would you be in focusing on constructing solutions with clients rather than resolving problems?

6. What thoughts do you have about the value of asking clients to talk about the exceptions to their problems and to adopt a positive perspective on what they are doing that is working in their lives? If you build your therapy practice on the notion of helping clients recognize their strengths and resources, what implication does this have for the way you would work with clients?

7. Solution-focused therapists often ask clients the miracle question. What value do you see in asking clients to imagine their problems would vanish one night when they were asleep? How does the miracle question enable clients to focus on ways of creating solutions?

8. In narrative therapy, the emphasis is on being able to listen to the problem-saturated story of the client without getting stuck. What are your thoughts about the narrative approach of separating the person from the problem as you listen and respond to your client? To what extent do you think you might be able to engage your clients in externalizing conversations in which they are able to experience their problems as something distinct from their identities?

9. In practicing narrative therapy, the attitudes of the therapist are at least as important as the therapist's techniques. What are some therapist attitudes that you see as being most important in encouraging clients to share their stories and discover ways to create alternative stories?

10. What are some specific ways the postmodern approaches can be applied to working with culturally diverse client populations? How would you compare the postmodern approaches with the traditional approaches you have studied with respect to working from a multicultural perspective?

ISSUES AND QUESTIONS FOR PERSONAL APPLICATION

Imagine yourself being a client in therapy and address the following issues and questions as a way for you to get a sense of your experience of both solution-focused brief therapy and narrative therapy.

1. Assume your therapist asks you what you most want to accomplish from your therapy (or to state your major therapeutic goal). In concrete terms, what would be one important goal you want to accomplish? _____

_____

_____

_____

2. How might you react if your therapist said: "Although I have expertise, I am not the expert on your life. You are the expert on your life." _____

_____

_____

_____

3. To what degree would you appreciate the shift from problem-talk to solution-talk? ___

_____

_____

_____

4. How ready would you be for a collaborative relationship with your therapist? What kind of resources do you have that you could draw from in making the changes you most desire? _____

_____

_____

_____

5. If your therapist told you that she was opposed to formal diagnosis because of her belief that diagnosis leads to pathologizing and labeling clients, how would you react?

_____

_____

_____

6. If your therapist informed you that he eschewed the past in favor of both the present and the future and had little interest in gaining an understanding of the problem, what might you say? _____

_____

_____

_____

7. Assume your therapist asks you: "If a miracle happened and the problem you have was solved overnight, how would you know it was solved, and what would be different?" How might you reply? _____

_____

_____

_____

8. If you were asked to externalize a problem you have, by considering the problem as something that is separate from who you are, what would this be like for you? _____

_____

_____

_____

9. What do you think the process would be like for you to reauthor a new story? _____

_____

_____

_____

10. Finding an appreciative audience to support you in the changes you are making is a critical aspect of narrative therapy. Who would you most want to include in this audience that would appreciate your new story? _____

_____

_____

_____

11. As clients become free of problem-saturated stories of the past, they are then able to envision and plan for a less problematic future. If your therapist asked you what you would most want in your future, what would you say? _____

_____

_____

_____

12. Questions are often used in both solution-focused and narrative therapy. What are a few questions that you think would be timely and useful for you to consider as a client?

_____

_____

_____

13. Imagine a problem that you might want to address. If your therapist said, "Tell me about a time when your problem did not exist," what would you say? _____

_____

_____

_____

14. Again, imagine a problem that you would bring to your therapy. Your therapist asks you: "Was there ever a time in which [your problem] wanted to take you over and you resisted? What was that like for you? How did you do it?" Your reply: _____

_____

_____

_____

15. With these approaches your therapist would encourage you to decide when to terminate therapy. What specific criteria would you use to determine when it was timely and appropriate for you to end your therapy? _____

_____

_____

_____

A Suggested In-Class Activity

A way to maximize learning based on the questions for personal application is to discuss (in small groups) the one question that you found most challenging to answer. Talk with your classmates about what you think it would be like for you to be a client in either solution-focused brief therapy or narrative therapy.

JERRY COREY COUNSELS STAN FROM A SOLUTION-FOCUSED BRIEF THERAPY PERSPECTIVE

Session 11. Solution-Focused Brief Therapy Applied to the Case of Stan

Session 11 illustrates techniques of solution-focused brief therapy such as identifying exceptions, the miracle question, and scaling. Before viewing the session, read Chapter 13, pages 421–423 in the textbook, and answer the questions under the heading "Follow-Up: You Continue as Stan's Postmodern Therapist." After reflecting on these questions, view the session. If you have been studying Stan up to this point, you will see that this approach is somewhat different from most other theories in that SFBT is more concerned about generating solutions than talking about problems. What advantages do you see, if any, with this focus on the client's strengths and resources?

As you watch this counseling session, notice how Stan reacts to the SFBT techniques. How effective do you see these interventions as being? After you complete the viewing, discuss these questions:

1. Stan says, "I am always down on myself and feeling hopeless." The therapist asks if there are any exceptions to feeling hopeless. What do you think of this technique?

2. If you were a client, how would it be for you to think of exceptions to one of your presenting problems?

3. Select one of your problems. Imagine that you wake up and this problem is gone. What difference would this make in your life?

4. What value do you see in the miracle question? In what situations, if any, would you want to use this technique with a client?

5. What do you think of the therapist's question to Stan about what he could do to bring about small miracles?

6. How can the smallest of steps lead to significant change?

7. What are your thoughts about the scaling technique that involved Stan being asked to rate a change in a particular behavior on a scale from zero to 10?

8. From solution-focused brief therapy, what technique do you find most useful?

9. What specific aspects of solution-focused brief therapy would you most like to incorporate into your style of counseling?

10. Would you like to be a client in this approach to counseling? Why or why not?

A Suggested In-Class Activity

To get a better experiential sense of applying solution-focused techniques, consider doing the following exercise in class. Consider a recent problem in your life that you have mild concerns about. Do not select a serious problem, but a problem that has posed some challenge for you. Pair up with a classmate and act as each other's solution-focused therapist. *Without ever having your partner specify the details of his or her problem,* interview this person using either the *miracle question* or the *exception question*. After a few minutes, switch roles so that each of you has a chance to be both the "client" and the "counselor." After you have both assumed the role of a client and found some solution to your problem, briefly describe your problem with your partner. Discuss the following questions:

■ From the counselor's perspective, would your knowing the problem have changed the solution your client reached?

■ What was it like as a "counselor" to make interventions without knowing the specific nature of the problem?

■ From the client's perspective, what was it like for you to engage in a therapeutic dialogue without disclosing the specifics of your problem?

■ How effective do you think this method was in helping you identify a solution to your problem?

■ How effective do you imagine this approach would be in solving significant life problems?

Having done this brief exercise, what do you see as potential strengths and limitations of the solution-focused approach?

 ## JERRY COREY COUNSELS STAN FROM A NARRATIVE PERSPECTIVE

Session 12. Narrative Therapy Applied to the Case of Stan

Session 12 focuses on Stan's creating a new story of his life. Before viewing the session, read Chapter 13, pages 421–423 in the textbook, and answer the questions under the heading "Follow-Up: You Continue as Stan's Postmodern Therapist." As you view this session, pay attention to the interchange between the client and the counselor when Stan did not cooperate with the technique of revising a book as a metaphor for writing a new life story? What similarities do you notice between solution-focused brief therapy and narrative therapy? What differences do you note? Does Stan react any differently to each of these postmodern approaches? How do these postmodern approaches differ from the other therapies that you have studied so far?

After viewing the session, discuss these questions:

1. The therapist suggests to Stan a technique of thinking of revising a book and applying this to changes he would like to make in his life. Stan was not responsive to this exercise. What are you likely to say to Stan if he did not respond favorably to an exercise you introduced?

2. What did you most notice when Stan talked about changes he would make in his life by thinking of the process of remodeling a house?

3. What is your opinion of the value of asking Stan to find an audience (some person who would support his changes) as a way to sustain changes he is making?

4. What do you think of the technique of asking Stan to detach himself from his problem? How might you help Stan to construct a new story as opposed to a problem-saturated story?

5. How might you encourage Stan to create a new vision for himself?

6. If Stan were being seen at a counseling center with a brief therapy model (6–8 sessions), do you think narrative therapy would be appropriate? Explain.

7. How is narrative therapy related to existential therapy?

8. How comfortable would you be in implementing narrative therapy in practice?

9. What specific changes, if any, do you notice in Stan's demeanor in this session from earlier sessions?

10. How would you describe the relationship between Stan and Jerry at this juncture?

A Suggested In-Class Activity

The theme of this narrative therapy session is to assist Stan in revising his life story. In small groups, discuss how you could apply at least one narrative therapy technique to help Stan create an alternative narrative. In your group I suggest that you talk about what changes you have noticed in Stan's behavior and manner from the initial meeting to this session. If you were Stan's counselor, what kind of feedback could you give him about specific changes you have noticed during the course of his counseling? What ideas do you have about reinforcing his positive changes? These three questions can be explored in your group:

1. What did you find most interesting in this session? Why?

2. If you were counseling Stan from this particular theoretical framework, what is one additional technique you might use? What would you hope to accomplish with this intervention?

3. If you were the client, how would you be likely to respond to the therapist's (Jerry's) comments and interventions in this particular session?

JERRY COREY'S WORK WITH RUTH FROM A NARRATIVE PERSPECTIVE

Narrative therapy emphasizes the value of devoting time to listening to clients' stories and to looking for events that can open up new stories. Ruth's life story influences what she notices and remembers, and in this sense her story influences how she will face the future. Although I am somewhat interested in Ruth's past, we will not dwell on her past problems. Instead, our focus will be on what Ruth is currently doing and on her strivings for her future. One of my tasks is to help Ruth rewrite the story of her life.

Working within a narrative approach, I am influenced by the notion that our collaboration will be aimed at freeing Ruth from the influence of oppressive elements in her social environment and empowering her to become an active agent who is directing her own life. Part of our work together will be to look for personal resources Ruth has that will enable her to create a new story for herself.

A method of supporting Ruth with the challenges she faces is to get her to think of her problems as external to the core of her selfhood. A key concept of narrative therapy is that the problem does not reside in the person. Even during the early sessions, I encourage Ruth to separate her being from her problems by posing questions that externalize her problem. I view Ruth's problems as something separate from her, even though her problems are influencing her thoughts, feelings, and behaviors. She presents many problems that are of concern to her, yet we cannot deal with all of them at once. When I ask her what one problem most concerns her right now, she replies, "Anxiety. I feel anxious so often over so many things. No matter what I do, I worry a great deal."

My intention is to help Ruth come to view her problem of anxiety as being separate from who she is as a person. I ask Ruth how her anxiety occurs and ask her to give examples of situations in which she experiences anxiety. I am interested in charting the influence of the problem of anxiety. I also ask questions that externalize the problem, such as the following: "How does anxiety get you, and what are you doing to let it become so powerful?" "How has anxiety dominated and disrupted your life?" "In what ways does anxiety and self-doubt attempt to trip you up?"

In this narrative approach, I follow up on these externalizing questions with further questions aimed at finding exceptions: "Has there ever been a time when anxiety could have taken control of you, but didn't? What was it like for you? How did you do it?" "How is this different from what you would have done before?" "What does it say about you that you were able to do that?" "How do you imagine your life would be different if you didn't have anxiety and you did not doubt your every decision?"

My questioning is aimed at discovering moments when Ruth hasn't been dominated or discouraged by the problem of anxiety. When we identify times when Ruth's life was not disrupted by anxiety, we have a basis for considering how life would be different if anxiety were not in control. As our therapy proceeds, I expect that Ruth will gradually come to see that she has more control over her problem of anxiety than she believed. As she distances herself from defining herself in terms of problematic themes (such as anxiety and self-doubt), she will be less burdened by her problem-saturated story and will discover a range of options. She will likely focus more on the resources within herself to construct the kind of life she wants.

You Continue Working With Ruth as Her Postmodern Therapist

1. Refer to *Case Approach to Counseling and Psychotherapy* (Chapter 11) for a comprehensive illustration of three postmodern therapists (Drs. John Murphy, Gerald Monk, and John Winslade) who each demonstrate their own approaches in working with Ruth.

2. See the *DVD for Integrative Counseling: The Case of Ruth and Lecturettes* (Session 9 on an integrative perspective, and Session 12 on working toward decisions and behavior change). What concepts and techniques from both solution-focused brief therapy and narrative therapy are you likely to draw upon in counseling Ruth?

3. If they do make use of diagnosis, narrative therapists make this a joint process with the client. How would you work with Ruth to collaboratively establish a diagnosis?

4. What are some of the advantages to the approach of externalizing the problem from the client? How would you get Ruth to see anxiety as something separate from herself as a person?

5. Asking clients to think of exceptions to their problems often gets them to think about a time when a particular problem did not have such power. What are some advantages you see in asking Ruth to talk about a time when she did not have a given problem? How might you build on times of exceptions?

A CASE FROM A SOLUTION-FOCUSED BRIEF THERAPY APPROACH

Keisha

By John J. Murphy, PhD, Professor of Psychology and Counseling at the University of Central Arkansas

Background Information

Keisha, a 16-year-old Caucasian, is referred for counseling by several teachers who are concerned about her "disrespectful" behavior and sporadic assignment completion. She lives with her natural mother (Diane), who was recently granted full custody of Keisha after a two-year estrangement during which Keisha lived with an uncle while Diane received treatment for substance abuse problems. Keisha has rarely seen her father since her parents divorced 10 years ago. She has received formal counseling on two separate occasions, the most recent of which was about one year ago.

Keisha repeated 2nd grade and has attended four different schools since then. Most of these school moves were prompted by custody issues that have hopefully been resolved now that her mother is drug free and determined to fulfill her role as a parent. Her teachers report that "she can be sweet at times" and that she is capable of passing her classes if she would only apply herself and complete more assignments. Keisha is currently failing two classes, science and history, both of which are required for high school graduation. The fact that she repeated a grade and is older than most 10th graders, coupled with the possibility of failing one or more classes this semester, seriously jeopardizes Keisha's chances of graduating on time.

The school has tried various incentive programs, such as allowing Keisha to earn special tokens that can be cashed in for items at the school supply store contingent on better behavior and more work completion. The school counselor has talked with Keisha twice during the past month, and several teachers have met with her to "find out what's going on" and "motivate her" to take school more seriously. When asked how Keisha responded, the counselor and teachers said she shrugs her shoulders and offers no explanations or plans related to school problems or solutions. Keisha was referred to me because none of these interventions have produced noticeable or lasting changes in her school performance.

Dr. John Murphy Works With Keisha From a Solution-Focused Brief Therapy Perspective

My main goals in working with Keisha are to (a) enlist her active involvement, (b) develop concrete goals that matter to her, and (c) encourage her to recognize and apply her unique strengths and resources toward solutions. These goals and the techniques that flow from them are based on research-identified elements of effective counseling such as eliciting client feedback and resources, building a strong therapeutic alliance, and instilling hope. Although I will also work with her mother and teachers, this discussion focuses on my work with Keisha.

Keisha's perceptions are always more important than mine or anyone else's when it comes to developing customized interventions that fit her personal style and preferences. In that spirit, I offer the following orientation statement to open our first session: "Keisha, my goal is to be useful to you. I need you to teach me what you want from counseling, so I'll be asking you how our meetings are going and what I can do to make things work better for you. Can you help me with that?" This statement conveys a spirit of collaboration and cultural respect by putting Keisha at center stage and making it clear that I work for her and not the other way around.

I tell Keisha that the best way for me to evaluate and improve my services is to obtain her feedback on a couple of short forms that assess her perceptions of (a) changes in key areas of concern (done at the beginning of each session) and (b) the client-counselor alliance (done at the end of each session). Obtaining systematic client feedback helps me to provide more culturally responsive, client-driven services than would be possible if I were to guess or make assumptions about how things are going for Keisha.

Language is key in SFBT, and phrases such as "I need you to teach me" and "Can you help me" grab Keisha's attention by putting her in the unexpected role of teacher/helper— a role that she and most young clients seldom experience. I ask Keisha what was most and least helpful in her previous counseling experiences so that I can build on what worked and avoid what didn't.

I begin to explore Keisha's goals later in the first session. Instead of opening the goal-related conversation by focusing on school, a topic that Keisha is probably tired of hearing about, I begin with something she may not expect: "Keisha, I want to ask you a question that might be the most important question of all. What do you want your life to stand for?" This question invites Keisha to step outside the school arena and reflect on her deepest values. She looks puzzled at first, but eventually tells me that she wants to be a songwriter, performer, or producer of rap music. She has already written a couple of songs and is working on another one. When I ask how she learned to write songs and where she gets her inspiration, Keisha seems more engaged and alive than she has been throughout the entire session.

Having discovered an area of life that excites and energizes Keisha, we start to explore any connections between her musical aspirations and school performance: "I'm wondering if or how school has any bearing on your music goals. What do you think?" Linking the conversation to an area of personal interest for Keisha increases the chance of maintaining her attention and involvement as compared to restricting our discussion to school issues. I invite Keisha to give this question more thought and discuss it with anyone she wishes before our next session. She mentions the possibility of discussing it with her mother and with two musicians from her church.

As the session concludes, I compliment Keisha on the courage and resilience required to cope with the many changes and challenges in her life instead of giving up altogether. I also offer what is referred to as the "formula first session task" in SFBT: "Between now and our next meeting, make a list of all the things in your life that you want to continue happening." The compliment acknowledges Keisha's grit and perseverance while the task invites her to consider exceptions to the problem and other resources that might be helpful in constructing school solutions.

From this point forward, our subsequent conversations and sessions are anchored in small, short-term goals that are directly related to Keisha's long-term musical aspirations. This reinforces the client-driven notion that she is always working toward something more personal and significant than completing a particular assignment, pleasing her teachers, or passing a class. Working toward a goal that matters to Keisha increases the likelihood that she will persist in efforts at school and elsewhere to move closer and closer, one small step at a time, toward her ultimate goal of a career in music. I will continue to scale and monitor Keisha's perceptions of progress and alliance and to adjust my approach based on her feedback.

Follow-Up: You Continue as Keisha's Solution-Focused Therapist

1. Imagine Keisha saying, "How can you possibly help me when you're a totally different age and race and you haven't been through anything like I've been through?" How do you think you would respond to her?

2. Practitioners of SFBT use various techniques to discover and increase exceptions to the problem. One such technique is asking Keisha to list aspects of her life that are not problematic. If Keisha responds by telling you that she gets along well with her math teacher and has fewer discipline problems in that class, what specific steps can you take to build on this exception at school?

3. Most child/adolescent referrals are initiated by teachers or parents, as was the case with Keisha. What are the therapeutic implications of this in working with young people and their caregivers?

4. Upon being asked how things went after one of your sessions, Keisha tells you that it was really boring and that she has trouble talking with you about things. How would you feel? What would you do?

5. Every client embodies a unique culture that differs from yours in ways that include age, gender, race, and so forth. While many such differences are unchangeable and beyond our control, there are things we can do to enhance our success with a diverse range of clients. Drawing from the ideas of SFBT, describe at least one technique that will help you work with Keisha in ways that honor her cultural experiences and perspectives.

A CASE FROM A NARRATIVE THERAPY APPROACH

Natasha

By John Winslade, PhD, Professor of Counseling at California State University at San Bernardino and Associate Dean of the College of Education

Background Information

Natasha is a fifteen-year-old African-American high school student. She was suspended for continuous fighting at her high school and has been referred to a continuation school. If she succeeds in improving her grades and her behavior, she will earn the right to return to her previous high school, which she wants to do. She is required at her new school to come to counseling once a week.

Dr. John Winslade's Work With Natasha as a Narrative Therapist

JOHN: So how are things going for you?

NATASHA: It is OK here but I really want to go back to my old school.

JOHN: Help me understand what is important to you about going back.

NATASHA: Well, all my friends are there. And besides I know I won't get into trouble again if I go back there.

JOHN: How do you know that?

NATASHA: I just know that I won't. I am not the same as I was before.

Commentary: Double listening alerts me here to the possible presence of two different identity stories for Natasha. One story relates to the fights that led to the suspension. The counter story relates to the intention not to get into trouble again and to return to her old school. I will be concerned to separate these two stories, create an externalizing conversation around the problem story, and work to build the story that Natasha would prefer. First, however, I need to map out the problem story.

JOHN: I'd like to understand how fighting kept on drawing you in?

NATASHA: Everybody just saw me as the tough girl. So they always wanted me to fight battles on their behalf.

JOHN: OK, that's what everybody else wanted. I'm still interested in how fighting won you over to do what they wanted.

NATASHA: I guess I wanted people to see me as the boss. And that I wasn't afraid of anyone. It seems stupid now though. Because they're all still back there and I'm the one who got suspended.

JOHN: So have you changed how you think about what happened a little bit?

NATASHA: Yes, I was shocked when I was suspended. I wasn't really expecting that.

JOHN: So what did that shock get you thinking?

NATASHA: Maybe that I had been acting stupid.

JOHN: So what effect would you say 'acting stupid' was having?

NATASHA: It was getting me some friends but it was also making other people afraid of me and getting me into trouble every week, and it had teachers watching my every move.

JOHN: What effect was all that having inside you?

NATASHA: I felt like I was powerful and strong in one way but in another way it felt like it was all out of control.

JOHN: Did you like that feeling?

NATASHA: No I didn't after a while. At first it was OK, but then I kind of knew I couldn't keep going like this and I started to feel stink.

JOHN: What about at home? Did your family know how much fighting and acting stupid were taking over?

NATASHA: My Mom started to yell at me when she kept hearing from the school. She said I was ruining my education and that was the best chance I had in life.

JOHN: Did you believe her?

NATASHA: Nah. I just switched off when she went on. But now I think I should have listened more.

JOHN: When did you start to think maybe what she was saying was important?

NATASHA: When I started at this school.

JOHN: How did that change happen? Was it something that came over you suddenly or what?

NATASHA: Yeah I started to think about where all this was heading. Before that I was just going with it without thinking.

Commentary: Natasha is starting to speak about a counter story that has her doing some different thinking. My task as counselor is to hear these moments of difference. Then, these isolated moments need to be connected up with actions, thoughts, and feelings within the client.

JOHN: So when you started thinking, what did you think about?

NATASHA: How I had messed up and kept getting into trouble when I didn't really want to.

JOHN: What helped you change this thinking?

NATASHA: At first it was just the shock of being suspended. And then my Mom started to cry one day when she was talking to me. She told me she wanted me to be more of an example to my younger brother. He's only seven.

JOHN: So how is your younger brother important to you?

NATASHA: Well I have looked after him since he was a baby, especially when my Mom was working.

JOHN: Sounds like you love him a lot. And your eyes soften up when you think of him. What's his name?

NATASHA: Yeah he's special to me. His name is Leroy.

JOHN: So how did thinking about Leroy make a difference to you at school?

NATASHA: I don't really know. But I just started to change and think about my life.

JOHN: Did you notice yourself doing anything different as a result?

NATASHA: Yeah I started to really work hard in my classes. Especially in math. I used to not really care about math. But I started to want to understand it more.

JOHN: Did anyone notice?

NATASHA: Yes, my math teacher here seems to really like me. He's very strict but I like how he explains things. He helps me a lot.

JOHN: Has anything else helped you make this change?

NATASHA: Well last weekend I talked with the youth leader at my church.

JOHN: What difference did that make?

NATASHA: She talked to me about being a leader of this group of younger kids and told me I was a natural leader.

JOHN: Does 'being a natural leader' fit with you?

NATASHA: Yes it feels good.

JOHN: How does that connect with your school situation?

NATASHA: It kind of does. Because I am changing my attitude to lots of things.

JOHN: What would you call the new attitude you are developing?

NATASHA: Maybe Natasha 2.0.

JOHN: So how does Natasha 2.0 act differently at school?

NATASHA: I don't get worked up about things that are unfair so much. Like yesterday my English teacher gave me a detention for laughing when someone said something smart to her. It wasn't really fair but I thought, "It's not worth getting upset about. Just do it and get back to learning. That's more important."

JOHN: Would Natasha 1.7 have thought that?

NATASHA: No way. She would have pouted and acted up and made lots of noise. And got into more trouble.

Commentary: Natasha is now articulating a story of difference and it has acquired a name. I shall continue to help her grow this story by finding more unique outcomes and linking them to the growing counter story. Natasha will be invited to attach significance and meaning to this growing story.

It is also important for this story to not just exist inside Natasha. To be viable, it must connect with her relational world. This is a world of personal connections and also one in which power relations and injustices exist. She may, for example, still experience her English teacher's actions as unfair and perhaps develop a consciousness of how racism works, often unintentionally, to single out African American students for negative attention. My aim will be for her figure out how to protest against such injustice in ways that do not bring trouble down on her own head.

I shall also aim to embed the counter story in her cultural world. The more detail it has and the more other people participate in it, the more likely it will thrive. Narrative practice focuses especially on relationship work – that is relationships in families, schools or communities. As a counselor in a school, I would invite teachers to notice the Natasha 2.0 story and to talk with her about it. Natasha's math teacher, her mom, and the youth group leader might each be included at some point in the community of care that is built up around the counter story. Each can be invited to share what they have noticed as different about Natasha and to comment on what these observations mean to them personally.

Differences that can be identified between the story of Natasha as a fighter and the Natasha 2.0 story will be documented and sent to Natasha along with further questions. She may receive an email or a letter containing many of her own words and contrasting the problem story with the counter story. School documents, files and recording systems will also be used for this purpose. Eventually, perhaps, Natasha might be invited to become a 'consultant' and support another student who is also trying to extract herself from the influence of fighting. She might be asked to share with this student her own hard-won knowledge of how to go about this.

Follow-Up: You Continue as Natasha's Narrative Therapist

1. Double listening is an important key to narrative counseling practice. Find examples of statements made by Natasha that allude to two competing stories. There are a number of them throughout the case study.

2. Where are the examples of the use of externalizing conversation in this dialogue?

3. In what ways does the counselor seek to develop more detail in the counter story?

4. Look at each of the questions asked by the counselor. What kind of work does each question do?

5. What do you imagine to be the logic behind questions that attend to the audience who might notice changes that Natasha makes?

QUIZ ON POSTMODERN APPROACHES

A Comprehension Check

Score _____%

Note: Please refer to Appendix 1 for the scoring key.

True/false items: Decide if the following statements are "more true" or "more false" as they apply to social constructionism, solution-focused brief therapy, and narrative therapy.

T   F   1. Narrative therapists believe new stories take hold only when there is an audience to appreciate and support such stories.

T   F   2. One of the functions of a narrative therapist is to ask questions of the client and, based on the answers, generate further questions.

T   F   3. Narrative therapy is a relational and anti-individualistic practice.

T   F   4. Narrative practitioners encourage clients to avoid being reduced by totalizing descriptions of their identity.

T   F   5. Narrative therapists pay more attention to a client's past than they do to the client's present and future.

T   F   6. In solution-focused therapy, gathering extensive information about a problem is a necessary step in helping clients find a solution to the problem.

T   F   7. Solution-focused therapists assist clients in paying attention to the exceptions to their problem patterns.

T   F   8. Solution-focused therapists use questions that presuppose change, posit multiple answers, and remain goal-directed and future-oriented.

T   F   9. In solution-focused therapy, the role of the client is to create solutions based on his or her internal resources.

T   F   10. Because solution-focused therapy is designed to be brief, it is essential that therapists teach clients specific strategies for understanding their problems.

Multiple-choice items: Select the *one best answer* of those alternatives given. Consider each question within the framework of the postmodern therapies.

_____ 11. Which of the following is true of narrative therapy and solution-focused therapy?

a. The client is an expert on his or her own life.

b. The therapeutic relationship should be hierarchical.

c. The therapist is the expert on a client's life.

d. Clients should adjust to social and cultural norms.

e. For change to occur, clients must first acquire insight into their problems.

_____ 12. A major goal of narrative therapy is to

a. shift from problem-talk to solution-talk.

b. assist clients in designing creative solutions to their problems.

c. invite clients to describe their experience in new and fresh language, and in doing this open up a new vision of what is possible.

d. uncover a client's self-defeating cognitions.

e. enable clients to gain clarity about the ways their family of origin still affect them today.

_____ 13. All of the following are true of narrative therapy except for

a. viewing problems in a sociopolitical and cultural context.

b. assisting clients in developing an alternative life story.

c. accepting the premise that diagnosis is a basic prerequisite for effective treatment.

d. creating a therapeutic relationship that is collaborative.

e. recognizing that clients know what is best for their life and are experts in their own life.

_____ 14. Which of the following interventions is least likely to be used by a narrative therapist?
a. externalizing conversations
b. mapping the influence of a problem
c. power analysis and intervention
d. the search for unique outcomes
e. documenting the evidence

_____ 15. Which of these techniques is *not* used in solution-focused therapy?
a. a lifestyle assessment
b. scaling questions
c. the miracle question
d. formula first session task
e. exception questions

_____ 16. A major strength of both solution-focused and narrative therapies is the
a. empirical evidence that has been collected on both approaches.
b. attention given to how one's early history sheds light on understanding current problems.
c. history-taking procedure used during the intake interview.
d. use of questioning.

_____ 17. Two of the major founders of solution-focused brief therapy are
a. Michael White and David Epston.
b. Insoo Kim Berg and Steve de Shazer.
c. Harlene Anderson and Harold Goolishian.
d. Tom Andersen and Bill O'Hanlon.
e. John Walter and Jane Peller.

_____ 18. Two of the major founders of narrative therapy are
a. Michael White and David Epston.
b. Insoo Kim Berg and Steve de Shazer.
c. Marlene Anderson and Harold Goolishian.
d. Tom Andersen and Bill O'Hanlon.
e. John Walter and Jane Peller.

_____ 19. The therapeutic process in solution-focused brief therapy involves all of the following except for the notion
a. of creating collaborative therapeutic relationships.
b. of asking clients about those times when their problems were not present or when the problems were less severe.
c. that clients are the experts on their own lives.
d. that solutions evolve out of therapeutic conversations and dialogues.
e. that therapists are experts in assessment and diagnosis.

_____ 20. Which of the following is *not* a basic assumption guiding the practice of solution-focused brief therapy?
a. Individuals who come to therapy have the ability to effectively cope with their problems.
b. There are advantages to a positive focus on solutions and on the future.
c. Clients want to change, have the capacity to change, and are doing their best to make change happen.
d. Using techniques in therapy is a way of discounting a client's capacity to find his or her own way.

_____ 21. In solution-focused therapy, which kind of relationship is characterized by the client and therapist jointly identifying a problem and a solution to work toward?
a. customer-type relationship
b. the complainant
c. a visitor
d. a compliant client

_____ 22. Pretherapy change is a solution-focused therapy technique that
a. is arrived at by asking clients about exceptions to their problems.
b. asks clients to address changes that have taken place from the time they made an appointment to the first therapy session.
c. is based on a series of tests that the client takes prior to beginning therapy to get baseline data.

d. involves the therapist offering clients ways they can change their perspective on the problems that brought them to therapy.

_____ 23. Which of these solution-focused therapy techniques involves asking clients to describe life without the problem?
a. pretherapy change
b. the miracle question
c. exception questions
d. scaling
e. formula first session task

_____ 24. In narrative therapy, the process of finding evidence to bolster a new view of the person as competent enough to have stood up to or defeated the dominance or oppression of the problem refers to
a. the initial assessment.
b. exploring problem-saturated stories.

c. objectifying the problem.
d. the search for unique outcomes.

_____ 25. Which of the following statements about creating alternative stories is *not* true?
a. Constructing new stories goes hand in hand with deconstructing problem-saturated narratives.
b. The narrative therapist analyzes and interprets the meaning of a client's story.
c. The therapist works with clients collaboratively by helping them construct more coherent and comprehensive stories that they live by.
d. The development of alternative stories is an enactment of ultimate hope.
e. The narrative therapist listens for openings to new stories.

Chapter **14**

Family Systems
Therapy

 PRECHAPTER SELF-INVENTORY

Directions: Refer to page 43 for general directions. Use the following code:

5 = I *strongly agree* with this statement.

4 = I *agree,* in most respects, with this statement.

3 = I am *undecided* in my opinion about this statement.

2 = I *disagree,* in most respects, with this statement.

1 = I *strongly disagree* with this statement.

_____ 1. Individuals are best understood through assessing the interactions between and among family members.

_____ 2. Symptoms of an individual's problems are best understood within the context of a dysfunctional system.

_____ 3. Because an individual is connected to a living system, change in one part of that system will result in change in other parts.

_____ 4. To focus primarily on studying the internal dynamics of an individual without adequately considering family dynamics yields an incomplete picture of the person.

_____ 5. Significant changes within an individual are not likely to be made or maintained unless the client's network of intimate relationships is taken into account.

_____ 6. Family therapy needs to include an examination of how one's culture has influenced each member.

_____ 7. Actions by any individual family member will influence all the others in the family, and their reactions will have a reciprocal effect on the individual.

_____ 8. It is not possible to accurately assess an individual's concerns without observing the interaction of the other family members.

_____ 9. Differentiating oneself from one's family of origin is best viewed as a lifelong developmental process.

_____ 10. Rather than losing sight of the individual, family therapists understand the person as specifically embedded in larger systems.

_____ 11. Family therapy serves a valuable function in challenging patriarchy and other forms of dominant culture privilege, bias, or discrimination.

_____ 12. Family therapists can no longer ignore their personal influence as part of their therapy.

_____ 13. Because the larger social structure affects the organization of a family, it is essential that the influence of the community on the family be considered.

_____ 14. Effective family therapy tends to be brief, focuses on solutions, and deals with the here-and-now interactions within a family.

_____ 15. It is the family therapist's responsibility to plan a strategy for resolving clients' problems.

_____ 16. A family therapist needs to be active and sometimes directive in working with a family.

_____ 17. Families are multilayer systems that both affect and are affected by the larger systems in which they are embedded.

_____ 18. Families can be described in terms of their individual members and the various roles they play, the relationships between the members, and the sequential patterns of the interactions and the purposes these sequences serve.

_____ 19. An appropriate goal of family therapy is the growth of individuals and the family rather than merely stabilizing the family.

_____ 20. Family therapists begin to form a relationship with clients from the moment of first contact.

OVERVIEW OF FAMILY SYSTEMS THERAPY

Key Figures and Major Focus

Key figures of Adlerian family therapy are Alfred Adler and Rudolf Dreikurs.

The key figure of the multigenerational approach to family therapy is Murray Bowen. He stresses exploring patterns from one's family of origin.

The key figure of the human validation process model is Virginia Satir. This form of therapy focuses on the interpersonal relationship between the therapist and the family members.

The key figure associated with experiential family therapy is Carl Whitaker. His approach assumes that it is experience that changes families, not education.

The key figures associated with structural-strategic family therapy are Salvador Minuchin, whose structural model focuses on the family as a system and its subsystems, boundaries, and hierarchies; and Cloé Madanes and Jay Haley, whose strategic model stresses parental hierarchies and cross-generational coalitions.

Philosophy and Basic Assumptions

If we hope to work therapeutically with people, family therapists believe it is critical to consider clients within their family system. An individual's dysfunctional behavior grows out of the interactional unit of the family as well as the larger community and societal systems. Almost all of these theories view the family from an interactive and systemic perspective, which sees an individual's dysfunctional behavior as a manifestation of dysfunctional behavior within the system or as affecting the system negatively.

Family therapy is a diverse field, comprising various theories of how change occurs within the family and an equally diverse set of intervention strategies. The theories of family therapy share a common philosophy of the importance of dealing with all parts of a system if change is to take place and be maintained. The family systems therapy models are grounded on the assumptions that a client's problematic behavior may (1) serve a function or purpose for the family, (2) be a function of the family's inability to operate productively, especially during developmental transitions, or (3) be a symptom of dysfunctional patterns handed down across generations. All these assumptions challenge the more traditional intrapsychic frameworks for conceptualizing human problems and their formation.

The multilayered process of family therapy represents different perspectives in working with any family. The goal is to provide the therapist with multiple perspectives for tailoring therapy to the needs and situations of a family.

Key Concepts

Because there are so many separate schools of family therapy, it is difficult to identify general concepts that cut across all of these orientations. Each school of therapy has its own key concepts:

- *Adlerian family therapists* focus on a *relationship* based on mutual respect, investigation of birth order and mistaken goals, and reeducation.
- *Bowenians* focus on *extended-family patterns*. This multigenerational approach is based on a number of key ideas, two of which are differentiation of the self and triangulation.
- *Satir's human validation process model* utilizes a *communication process* to assist a family in moving from status quo through chaos to new possibilities and new integrations.
- The *experiential family therapists* take a *developmental perspective* in explaining individual growth in a systemic context.
- *Structuralists* emphasize the *family as a system*, subsystems, boundaries, and hierarchies. The therapist joins the family in a leadership role and changes these structures.
- *Strategic therapists* base their interventions on a *communications model*, which focuses on stuck interactional sequences in a family. Change occurs through action-oriented directives and paradoxical interventions.
- A multilayered process of family therapy provides a context for developing an *integrative approach* in working with families.

Therapeutic Goals

Most family therapists share some general goals, but specific goals are determined by the practitioner's theoretical orientation or by a collaborative process between the therapist and the family. Global goals include intervening in ways that enable individuals and the family to relieve their distress. Although many family therapists agree on the goals, their interventions differ.

Here is a summary of the therapeutic goals associated with some of the various theories of family therapy:

- *Adlerians* emphasize unlocking mistaken goals and interactional patterns in the family and promotion of effective parenting.
- *Bowenian* (multigenerational) therapy seeks to (1) decrease anxiety and bring about relief from distressing symptoms and (2) bring about the maximum self-differentiation for each family member within his or her family and cultural context.
- The goals *of the human validation process model* parallel Satir's view of the process of change. Specific goals include generating self-esteem and hope, identifying and strengthening coping skills, and facilitating movement toward health and actualization.
- The goals for *experiential family therapy* include increasing awareness of one's present experiencing, facilitating individual growth and more effective interactional patterns, and promoting authenticity.
- *Structural family therapy* aims at both treating symptoms and changing dysfunctional transactional patterns within the family. Rules are identified that govern interactions among family members, with the purpose of helping them develop clear boundaries and appropriate hierarchies.
- In *strategic family therapy* insight is considered unimportant. The central goal of this approach is to resolve a family's presenting problem (or symptoms) by focusing on changing its current behavioral sequences.

Therapeutic Relationship

In the strategic and structural approaches to family therapy, the therapeutic relationship is not emphasized. However, the experiential and human validation models are based on the quality of that relationship. Many family therapists are primarily concerned with teaching members how to modify dysfunctional interactional patterns and change stereotypical patterns. Some family therapists are more concerned with implementation of techniques designed to solve presenting problems than with the quality of the therapeutic relationship. Others realize that their relationship with family members is temporary, and thus they focus more on the quality of relationships within a family.

Role and Function of Family Therapists

Here are some central roles associated with the major approaches to family therapy.

- *Adlerian family therapists* assume the roles of educators, motivational investigators, and collaborators.

- In *Bowen's multigenerational therapy*, therapists function as guides and objective researchers. Therapists monitor their own reactions and take an active role in facilitating change in a family. Once individuals have gathered information about their family of origin, the therapist coaches each person in developing strategies for dealing with significant others outside of the therapy sessions.

- In the *human validation process model* of family therapy, the fundamental function of the therapist is to guide the individual family members through the process of change. The therapist provides the family with new experiences and teaches members how to communicate openly. In this model the therapist is an active facilitator who models congruence and serves as a resource person.

- The *experiential family therapist* functions as a family coach, challenger, and model for change through play. Therapists have various functions at different points in therapy, including being a stress activator, a growth activator, and a creativity stimulator.

- *Structural family therapists* function as stage directors. They join the system and attempt to manipulate family structure for the purpose of modifying dysfunctional patterns. The therapist's central task is to deal with the family as a unit, in the present, with the goal of initiating a restructuring process.

- In the *strategic model* therapists function in active and directive ways. Working as consultants and experts, they are manipulative and authoritarian in dealing with resistive behaviors. The therapist is the agent responsible for changing the organization of a family and resolving the family's presenting problems.

- In the *integrative approach* to family therapy, therapists look at a family from multiple perspectives and collaboratively work out with a family specific processes and practices that will lead to change.

Techniques and Procedures

The techniques and procedures family therapists employ are best considered in conjunction with their personal characteristics. Although techniques are tools for achieving therapeutic goals, these intervention strategies do not make a family therapist. Personal characteristics such as respect for clients, compassion, empathy, and sensitivity are qualities that influence the degree to which techniques are effective. Faced with meeting the multiple demands of clinical practice, family therapists need to be flexible in selecting intervention strategies.

An integrative approach to the practice of family therapy includes guiding principles that help the therapist organize goals, interactions, observations, and ways to promote change. Certain family systems therapy models focus on perceptual and cognitive change, others deal mainly with changing feelings, and still other theories emphasize behavioral change. For any theoretical orientation that a family therapist operates from, change needs to happen relationally, not just intrapsychically. Regardless of the theoretical orientation therapists assume, it is critical for them to be aware of their values and monitor how these values influence their practice with families.

There is a diversity of techniques, depending on the therapist's theoretical orientation, and a considerable degree of flexibility in applying them, even among practitioners within a school. Family therapists tend to be active, directive, oriented toward the solution of problems, and open to using techniques borrowed from various approaches. Here are some of the primary intervention strategies associated with the various schools of family therapy.

- *Adlerian family therapists* employ techniques such as family constellation, reporting of a typical day, goal disclosure, and logical consequences.
- *Multigenerational family therapy* focuses on asking questions, tracking interactional sequences, assigning homework, and educating.
- Throughout Satir's use of the *human validation process model*, various techniques are used to facilitate enhanced interpersonal communication within the family, a few of which are drama, reframing, humor, touch, family reconstruction, role playing, family life-fact chronology, and family sculpture.
- *Experiential family therapists* utilize themselves as their best therapeutic technique, creating interventions that grow out of the phenomenological context in working with a family.
- *Structural family therapists* engage in tracking transactional sequences, reframing, issuing directives, joining and accommodating a family, restructuring, and enactment.
- *Strategic therapists* utilize reframing, directives, and paradoxical interventions, and they also track interactional sequences.

Applications

Family therapy is not limited to working exclusively with families. There are many ways to apply concepts of family systems therapy to both individual and group counseling. To focus primarily on the internal dynamics of an individual without adequately considering family dynamics yields an incomplete picture of the person. Thus, it is useful to bring a client's family background into the context of individual and group counseling when appropriate. For individual counseling, during the assessment process, the therapist can raise questions about a client's family of origin and how certain experiences in the family have current influences. With respect to group counseling, there are ample opportunities for group members to explore concerns they have with parents and siblings. In many therapeutic groups, considerable time is devoted to a discussion of painful events associated with growing up in a family. Even though family members are not part of a counseling group, the members can still do considerable work with them through role playing and other techniques aimed at helping members explore how they are still being affected by family experiences.

Multicultural Perspectives

A key strength of the systemic perspective in working from a multicultural framework is that many ethnic and cultural groups value the extended family. Understanding cultures allow therapists and families to appreciate diversity and to contextualize family experiences in relation to the larger cultures. Therapists, regardless of their model of therapy, must find ways to enter the family's world and honor the traditions that support the family. Contemporary family therapists explore the individual culture of the family, the larger cultures to which the family members belong, and the host culture that dominates the family's life. They look for ways in which culture can both inform and modify their work with a family. A therapist's interventions are adapted to these cultural systems.

Contributions

The main contribution of a family systems approach is the inclusion of all parts of the system rather than being limited to the "identified patient." A major strength of most systemic approaches is that neither the individual nor the family is blamed for a particular dysfunction. Instead of a blaming stance, the entire family has an opportunity to (a) examine the multiple perspectives and interactional patterns that characterize the unit and (b) participate in finding solutions. Because an individual's problems are relational, it makes sense to focus on all of the interactions and external factors that impinge on the person. A systems perspective recognizes that individuals and families are affected by external forces and systems such as illness, shifting gender patterns, culture, and socioeconomic considerations. If change is to occur in families or with individuals, therapists must be aware of as many systems of influence as possible. Given the larger systems in which families are embedded, a multilayered approach to family therapy is essential.

Limitations

A major limitation of systemic approaches is the potential to lose sight of the individual by focusing on the broader system. If a family comes in for therapy, there are some real advantages to working with the entire unit. However, the language and focus of systems have often placed a primary emphasis on the family whole at the expense of individuals. Postmodern thinking and the natural development of the profession are beginning to integrate the person back into the system.

GLOSSARY OF KEY TERMS

Adlerian family therapy An approach that is based on the premise that parents and children often become locked in repetitive, negative interactions based on mistaken goals that motivate all parties involved.

Boundary In structural family therapy, an emotional barrier that protects individuals within a system.

Coaching Bowen's and Whitaker's view of the role of the therapist in assisting clients in the process of differentiating the self.

Coalition An alliance between two people against a third.

Conjoint family therapy An early human validation process model developed by Virginia Satir that emphasizes communication and emotional experiencing.

Differentiation of self Bowen's concept of psychological separation of intellect and emotions and of independence of the self from others. The greater one's differentiation, the better one's ability to keep from being drawn into dysfunctional patterns with other family members.

Disengagement Minuchin's term for a family organization characterized by psychological isolation that results from rigid boundaries.

Enactment In structural family therapy, an intervention consisting of a family playing out its relationship patterns during a therapy session so that the therapist can observe and then change transactions that make up the family structure.

Enmeshment Minuchin's term referring to a family structure in which there is a blurring of psychological boundaries, making autonomy very difficult to achieve.

Experiential therapy A therapeutic approach that emphasizes the value of the therapist's realness in interacting with a family.

Family dysfunction The inability of a family to attain harmonious relationships and to achieve interdependence.

Family life cycle The series of events that marks an individual's life within a family, from separation from one's parents to marriage to growing old and dying.

Family life-fact chronology Satir's experiential technique in which clients retrace their family history for the purpose of gaining insight into current family functioning.

Family of origin The original nuclear family into which one was born or adopted.

Family rules The implicit agreements that prescribe the rights, duties, and range of appropriate behaviors within the family.

Family sculpting A nonverbal experiential technique that consists of physically arranging members of a family in space, which reveals significant aspects of their perceptions and feelings about one another.

Family structure   The functional organization of a family, which determines interactional patterns among members.

Functional family   A family in which the needs of the individual members are met and there is a balance of interdependence and autonomy among members.

Genogram   A schematic diagram of the family system, usually including at least three generations; employed by many family therapists to identify recurring behavior patterns within the family.

Hierarchical structure   Family functioning based on generational boundaries that involve parental control and authority.

Human validation process model   An experiential and humanistic approach developed by Virginia Satir, which viewed techniques as being secondary to the relationship a therapist develops with the family.

Identified patient   A family member who carries the symptom for a family and who is identified by the family as the person with the problem. In genograms this person is the index person.

Joining   In structural family therapy, accommodating to a family's system to help the members change dysfunctional patterns.

Multigenerational family therapy   An approach that operates on the premise that a predictable pattern of interpersonal relationships connects the functioning of family members across generations.

Multigenerational transmission process   The way in which dysfunctional patterns are passed from one generation to the next.

Multilayered process of family therapy   This perspective serves as a basic structure for assessment both of the family members and the system.

Paradoxical directive   A technique in strategic family therapy whereby the therapist directs family members to continue their symptomatic behavior. Change occurs through defying the directive.

Postmodern approaches to family therapy   These models seek to reduce or eliminate the power and impact of the family therapist. They include solution-focused and solution-oriented therapies as well as narrative therapy.

Reframing   Relabeling a family's description of behavior by putting it into a new and more positive perspective.

Strategic therapy   A therapeutic approach whereby the therapist develops a specific plan and designs interventions geared toward solving a family's presenting problems.

Structural therapy   A therapeutic approach directed at changing or realigning the organization of a family to modify dysfunctional patterns and clarify boundaries.

Structural-strategic approaches   By the late 1970s, these complimentary approaches were the most used models in family systems therapy. Interventions generated in these models became synonymous with a systems approach; they included joining, boundary setting, unbalancing, reframing, ordeals, paradoxical interventions, and enactments.

Triangle   A three-person system; the smallest stable emotional unit of human relations.

Triangulation   A pattern of interaction consisting of detouring conflict between two people by involving a third person.

QUESTIONS FOR REFLECTION AND DISCUSSION

1. What are some of the main differences between family systems approaches and individual counseling approaches?

2. A basic assumption of Bowen's multigenerational family therapy is that unresolved emotional issues, such as an individual's failure to differentiate from the family, will be passed on from generation to generation. As you study your own family, are you aware of any patterns you have "inherited"?

3. Whitaker typically makes use of the co-therapy model in doing family therapy. What are the advantages of such an approach? Are there any disadvantages?

4. The core of Satir's human validation process model is the therapist's use of self as a facilitator of change whereby the family moves from being psychologically stuck to a

place of wellness. To what extent do you agree (or disagree) with the notion that the use of the therapist's self is more important than any technique? How does this model differ from strategic therapy in this respect?

5. Minuchin's structural family therapy model emphasizes the therapist's role in joining and accommodating the family. As you picture yourself as a family therapist, what difficulties, if any, do you imagine you might have in these two areas with certain families?

6. In strategic family therapy the therapist is expected to be in charge of the session, which often includes issuing directives and planning a strategy to solve the client's problems. How comfortable would you be in carrying out this role? With what specific clients do you think strategic approaches would be best suited?

7. What are some ways in which you could apply what you learned in your study of the previous theories to the practice of family therapy? To what degree do you see a basis for integrating some of the concepts and techniques of the individual counseling models with family systems therapy models?

8. How useful do you find the multilayered process of family therapy?

9. To practice with families in an ethical and effective manner, what kind of education, training, and supervision would you need? Do you have any ideas about how you might seek competence in working with families?

10. What do you consider to be the main contribution of the family therapy perspective? What are the main limitations of family therapy?

SUGGESTED ACTIVITIES AND EXERCISES FOR PERSONAL APPLICATION

How Your Past Influences Your Present

When you counsel an individual, a couple, or a family, you are not always perceiving them with a fresh and unbiased perspective. When a new person whom you encounter represents some unresolved relationship with someone from your past, you can unconsciously attempt to deal with old relationships through your current relationships. The more you are aware of your patterns with your own family members, the greater is the benefit to your clients. It is crucial that you know to whom you are responding: to the individual in front of you or to a person from your past.

Try this exercise Satir used to demonstrate that we are constantly revisiting significant people and family members in our lives:

> Stand in front of someone (Person A) in your current life who interests you or with whom you are having some difficulty. This individual might be a client, an associate, a family member, or a friend. If the person is not present, you can imagine him or her. Take a good look at this person, and form a picture on the screen of your mind. Now, let a picture of someone in your past come forward (Person B). Who comes to mind? How old are you and how old is Person B? What relationship do you, or did you, have with this individual you are remembering? What feelings are linked with this relationship? What did you think about Person B?
>
> Now, examine again your current emotional reactions to Person A. Do you see any connection between what Person A is evoking in you and the past feelings that Person B has evoked?

You can apply this exercise by yourself through the use of imagery when you have intense emotional reactions to other people, especially if you do not know them well. This exercise can help you begin to recognize how your past relationships may sometimes affect the here-and-now reactions you are having toward people that you initially encounter.

Perhaps what is most important is simply to be aware of ways in which you are carrying your past into present interactions.

Understanding Your Family Structure

Family structure also includes factors such as birth order and the individual's perception of self in the family context. A facet of family structure is a particular pattern such as nuclear, extended, single-parent, divorced, or blended. As you reflect on these questions, identify what is unique in the structure of your family.

- In what type of family structure did you grow up? It might be that the structure of your family changed over time. If so, what were these changes? What do you most remember about growing up in your family? What were some of the most important values? What most stands out for you about your family life? In what ways do you think these experiences have a continuing influence on the person you are today?

- What is your current family structure? Are you still primarily involved in your family of origin? If your current family is different, what roles do you play that you also enacted in your original family? Have you carried certain patterns from your original family to your current family? How do you see yourself as being different in the two families?

- Draw a genogram of your family of origin. Include all the members of your family, and identify significant alliances among the various members. Identify the relationship you had as a child with each person and your relationship with each member now.

- Make a list of the siblings from oldest to youngest. Give a brief description of each (including yourself). What most stands out for each sibling? Which sibling(s) is (are) most different from you, and how? Which is most like you, and how?

- Review some key dimensions of your experiences as a child growing up in your family. How would you describe yourself as a child? What were some of your major fears? Hopes? Ambitions? What was school like for you? What was your role in your peer group? Were there any significant events in your physical, sexual, and social development during childhood?

- Identify one of your personal problems. How do you think your relationship with your family has contributed to the development and perpetuation of this problem? Besides blaming your family for this problem, what options are open to you for making substantial changes in yourself? What are a few ways you can be different in your family?

A Balance of Being Separate and of Belonging to a Family

- In what significant ways, if any, do you see yourself as having a distinct identity and being psychologically separate from your family of origin? And in what ways, if any, are you still psychologically fused with your family of origin? Are there any aspects of this that you want to change?

- In some cultures autonomy is not a cherished value. Instead, children are viewed as having an obligation not to emerge too distinctly from the rest of the family. A collective sense is given more value than individual independence. What cultural values influenced the degree to which you have striven toward autonomy? Are there any values that stem from your culture that you want to retain? Any that you want to challenge or to modify?

- The concept of *boundaries* as used in family therapy refers to emotional barriers that protect and enhance the integrity of members of a system. It also refers to a delineation between members that is governed by implicit or explicit rules pertaining to who can participate and in what manner. Apply the notion of boundaries to your development.

In growing up in your family, what boundaries existed between you and your parents? Between your parents and the siblings? Among the siblings? Between your parents? What did you learn about boundaries? Do you have any problems with boundaries today?

Understanding the Rules of Your Family

Rules or messages that were delivered by our parents and parent substitutes are often couched in terms of "Do this or that." Consider the following "do" messages: "Be obedient." "Be practical at all times." "Be the very best you can be." "Be appropriate." "Be perfect." "Be a credit to your family." At this point, reflect on the rules that seemed apparent in your family. What were some of the major rules that governed your family? What were some unspoken rules between the adults? What rules did you learn about appropriate gender-role behavior? What did you learn about femininity? About masculinity? To what degree did you abide by all these rules? Were there any that you challenged? How did unspoken rules affect you? Were there rules surrounding what could not be mentioned? If there were secrets in your family, how did this affect the family atmosphere?

Consider some of the major "do's" and "don'ts" that you heard growing up in your family, and your reactions to them.

- What are a few messages or rules that you did accept?

- What were some rules that you fought against?

- Which of your early decisions do you deem to be most significant in your life today? What was the family context in which you made these decisions? If you grew up in your family thinking "I am never enough," how has this conclusion about yourself played out in your current relationships in various aspects of your life?

- Do you ever hear yourself giving the same messages to others that you heard from your parents?

- Consider for a moment the overall impact of the messages that you have been exposed to, both from your parents and from society. How have these messages influenced your self-worth? Your view of yourself as a woman or as a man? Your trust in yourself? Your ability to be creative and spontaneous? Your ability to receive love and give love? Your willingness to make yourself vulnerable? Your sense of security? Your potential to succeed?

Significant Developments in Your Family

You might find it useful to describe your family of origin's life cycle. Chart significant turning points that characterize its development. One way is to look at family albums and see what the photos are revealing. Let these pictures stimulate your memories, and see what you can learn. As you view photos of your parents, grandparents, siblings, and other relatives, look for patterns that can offer clues to family dynamics. In charting transitions in the development of your family, reflect on these questions:

- What were the crisis points for your family?

- Can you recall any unexpected events that affected your family?

- Were there any periods of separation due to employment, military service, or imprisonment?

- Who tended to have problems within the family? How were these problems manifested? How did others in the family react to the person with problems?

- In what ways did births affect the family?

- Were there any serious illnesses, accidents, divorces, or deaths in your family of origin? If so, how did they affect individual members in the family and the family as a whole?

JERRY COREY'S WORK WITH RUTH
FROM A FAMILY SYSTEMS PERSPECTIVE

In Ruth's individual sessions it becomes evident that many of her current issues pertain to relationships in her family. She has concerns about several of her children, and she is greatly troubled about her present relationship with her husband, John. I recommend that Ruth bring her entire family into the therapeutic process. Because changes that occur in any one part of the system will change other parts, changes in Ruth have affected the equilibrium of this family. It is important to have the whole family enter treatment so that the changes that occur are productive for Ruth's family as well as for her.

After an initial session with Ruth's family, several tentative conclusions are formed. (See Drs. Mary Moline and James Bitter's piece in Chapter 12 of *Case Approach to Counseling and Psychotherapy* for a detailed discussion of several family sessions.) In this family there is an enmeshment among members. They lack a clear sense of their individuality and roles in the family. Families such as this one are prone to conflict and confusion, and the behavior of one member or unit, in this case both Ruth and John, immediately affects the other members of the family.

Ruth and John are learning new behaviors. She is learning not to maintain her role as peacemaker, and he is gradually learning to be more supportive of her. As a result, the other family members are being forced to learn to deal with one another. The children have been increasing the conflict among themselves and with Ruth to bring her back into her previous role as mediator. In family therapy terms this involves prompting a return of the family (Ruth) to the former status.

You Continue Working With Ruth as Her Family Systems Therapist

1. Refer to *Case Approach to Counseling and Psychotherapy* (Chapter 12) for a comprehensive illustration of how two family therapists (Drs. Mary Moline and James Bitter) work with Ruth from a systemic perspective. What are some positive outcomes for Ruth from family therapy?

2. See the *DVD for Integrative Counseling: The Case of Ruth and Lecturettes* (Session 7 on emotive focus) and analyze my attempt to incorporate family systems ideas in Ruth's counseling.

3. To what extent do you see it as essential to deal with Ruth's concerns from a systemic perspective? What value, if any, do you see in dealing with the environmental factors (especially family influences) related to Ruth's struggles?

4. How would you deal with Ruth if she were resistant to the idea of including any of her family members in her therapy?

5. How might you proceed in dealing with Ruth's parents and the role she feels they have played in her life? Do you think this can be done symbolically (through role playing), or is it necessary for Ruth to deal directly with her parents? In what ways might you want to work with Ruth's family of origin?

A CASE FROM A FAMILY SYSTEMS APPROACH

Laura

By Melanie Horn Mallers, PhD, Assistant Professor of Human Services at California State University, Fullerton

Background Information

This session summarizes work with Laura, a 27-year-old Caucasian woman. Laura's father is 67 years old and has early-onset Alzheimer's disease. Laura also has a 56-year-old mother, who is in excellent physical health, and a 31-year-old sister. Laura reports her father's health is rapidly declining. He has limited cognitive ability and memory, including loss of recall for faces and names.

Laura is seeking therapy currently because she is experiencing depression and having trouble functioning. During her intake, she also reports having a great deal of anger towards her mom and openly shares her intense feelings of loss due to her father's declining health; she reports deeply missing the emotional bond they once shared. She also reports having a solid relationship with her sister, though she wishes they were emotionally closer. Laura is not married but expressed interest in finding a partner.

Dr. Melanie Horn Mallers's Way of Working With Laura From a Family Systems Approach

Before describing to Laura the basic tenets of family systems, I first commend her for seeking out help. I also assure her that her feelings are real and that she is going through a tremendously stressful period in her life. I want her to know that she has my full emotional support and that I am encouraged to work with her. I also share with her some local and international resources for individuals and families caring for loved ones suffering from Alzheimer's. I encourage her to consider participating in a support group. I want Laura to know that she is not alone.

I then explain to Laura the basic approach to family systems theory and how it can assist her with understanding both her depression and her anger towards her mom. Systems theory focuses on how dysfunctional or maladaptive behavior results from and/or contributes to the overall structure of one's family; that symptoms can only be understood via examination of the habits and patterns within a family. Like a car, if one part of the car, such as the brakes, no longer works properly, the overall functioning of the car becomes minimized or compromised. Laura's depression and anger are merely symptoms or reflections of her family dynamics and its current inability to operate productively.

To assess then her family structure, I have Laura describe in greater detail the physical and emotional roles of each family member. Specifically, I have her relay a "typical day" in her family both during childhood and currently. I have her discuss the "ebbs and flows" and common routines embedded in her family system. In so doing, I also have her discuss how conflict is resolved in her family. It becomes apparent that Laura, as well as her mother and sister, highly rely on the father for balance, consistency, a sense of emotional safety, and for strong, close relationships. In other words, the father's role was to create a routine that enabled the family to meet their everyday emotional needs. With his memory loss and confusion, as well as his inability to connect and relate to those he loves, Laura is mourning the loss of a critical relationship with her father. According to a family systems perspective, when one individual role in the routine breaks down, the whole system must adjust. Unfortunately, many systems stay broken because they are unwilling to change and develop.

From Laura's discussion of her family, it further becomes apparent to me that Laura's mom is a highly competent and sensible woman whose strength lies in meeting the functional needs of the family. Unlike Laura's father, who provided unconditional acceptance and reward, Laura's mother made all of the major decisions in the family (such as finances, education, religion) and ensured family life was consistent and reliable (such regular mealtimes, expectations to complete homework, doing chores). She thus served as the instrumental gatekeeper for the family. Laura's anger towards her mom is in part due to the fact that her mom did not serve as her emotional support system and now, with her father's illness, Laura is replacing this loss with anger. I share with Laura what is known as the process lens of family systems theory, such that families need to stay balanced to function. I suggest that her mom and dad maintained different, but complementary roles, in order to have equilibrium. Had that balance not been present, family life could have been quite chaotic and with little direction for achieving goals. At this point, Laura reports that she understands logically what is going on. She shares how her mom created an environment where she and her sister learned routine and the reality of consequences for bad behavior. She explains that this taught her to be reliable and dependable. Her father, in contrast, insisted on few rules and never disciplined nor got angry. Laura begins to see that her mom's and dad's role served to create a holistic and balanced family system.

To help the family recreate some balance, I tell Laura I have an idea and ask if she would be open to it. I explain that the next step is to facilitate change in her family and that I am interested in bringing her mom and sister to the next therapy session. She thinks this is a good idea and agrees to invite them to her next session. Though the sister is unavailable to attend, the mom is able to attend.

At this family session, I briefly summarize the family systems perspective. I encourage Laura to share her feelings with her mom. I validate her perspective by reiterating that the emotional foundation of their family has changed. At this point, I ask the mom to share her feelings about the role and strengths of her husband and then her own. She confirms she too is mourning the loss of her husband and that she is just not as good at being "touchy-feely." She also reports that she feels like she cannot always talk to Laura, because she feels Laura is often impatient with her. Laura is quite surprised to hear this, as she views herself as someone who is open-minded and a good listener. I then ask Laura and her mom to describe both their meaning of and goals for each member of the family. Their responses are quite similar—they both want someone to listen to them, nurture and validate their feelings. I ask them if with some instruction and practice in compassionate communication, they could begin to absorb their father's role into their own. At this point, I am trying to get both Laura and her mom to reframe their roles and reconfigure their family system. To begin this reframing process, I have them do some role-playing, whereby each woman takes a turn "being" the father/husband, while practicing a typical conversation with him. I also have them "play themselves" engaged in conversation, while attempting to incorporate responses their father/husband would say. This activity provided a good foundation for Laura's family to promote both insight and self-esteem, as well as restructure their family organization.

Finally, in additional other sessions with Laura, we continue to talk about her depression, as well as other ways she can continue to use herself as a change agent. We also begin to talk about the type of intimate partner she is attracted to and steps necessary to bring balance into such future relationships.

Follow-Up: You Continue as Laura's Family Therapist

1. How might your family systems approach change if Laura was of another ethnicity? That is, how would you incorporate the multicultural lens of family systems theory?

2. Similarly, if Laura were much older or younger, how would you change your technique? How could the developmental lens of family systems theory be incorporated?

3. Do you think the outcomes would be different had Laura's sister participated in the therapy session? Explain.

4. How would you work with Laura had her family been unwilling to change?

5. How might your own relationships with your family members enhance or hinder your work with Laura?

QUIZ ON FAMILY SYSTEMS THERAPY

A Comprehension Check

Score _____%

Note: Refer to Appendix 1 for the scoring key.

True/false items: Decide if the following statements are "more true" or "more false" as they apply to the perspective of family systems therapy.

T   F   1. The trend today is toward reliance on a single theory of family therapy rather than using an integrative approach.

T   F   2. The emergence of feminist and postmodern perspectives has moved the field of family therapy toward more egalitarian, collaborative, and co-constructing relationships.

T   F   3. Experiential family therapy relies on the expert use of directives aimed at changing dysfunctional patterns.

T   F   4. A multilayered process of family therapy is best supported by a collaborative therapist–client relationship in which mutual respect, caring, empathy, and a genuine interest in others is primary.

T   F   5. Conducting an assessment is one of the phases of the mutilayered perspective in family therapy.

T   F   6. Understanding family process is almost always facilitated by "how" questions.

T   F   7. In terms of assessment, it is useful to inquire about family perspectives on issues inherent in each of the lenses.

T   F   8. The family therapist's skill in communicating understanding and empathy through active listening lays the foundation for an effective working relationship.

T   F   9. All change in human systems starts with understanding and accepting things as they are.

T   F   10. Reframing is the art of putting what is known in a new, more useful perspective.

Multiple-choice items: Select the *one best answer* of those alternatives given. Consider each question within the framework of approaches to family systems therapy.

_____ 11. Which of the following family therapy models makes the most use of genograms, dealing with family-of-origin issues, and detriangulating relationships?

a. Adlerian family therapy
b. Bowenian multigenerational family therapy
c. structural family therapy
d. strategic therapy
e. experiential family therapy

_____ 12. Which of the following approaches most often employs a co-therapist model, makes use of self-disclosure, uses the therapist's self as change agent, and frequently uses confrontation?

a. Bowenian family therapy
b. Adlerian family therapy

c. structural family therapy
d. strategic therapy
e. experiential family therapy

_____ 13. Which of the following is **not** a key general movement of the multilayered approach to family systems therapy?

a. forming a relationship
b. conducting an assessment
c. hypothesizing and sharing meaning
d. conducting empirical research to evaluate outcomes
e. facilitating change

_____ 14. Differentiation of the self is the cornerstone of which theory?

a. Bowenian family therapy
b. Adlerian family therapy

c. social constructionism

d. strategic therapy

e. experiential family therapy

_____ 15. Virginia Satir outlined four communication stances that people tend to adopt under stress. They include all of the following stances except for

a. blaming.

b. placating.

c. super reasonable.

d. irrelevant.

e. sabotaging.

_____ 16. The antidote to stress communications, according to Satir, is _____, in which family members are emotionally honest, speak for themselves, stay grounded (or centered), and are able to share their feelings and ask for what is needed.

a. congruence

b. unconditional positive regard

c. detriangulation

d. emotional decompression

e. differentiation of self

_____ 17. In assessing families, what question(s) might a structural-strategic therapist ask?

a. "What were the routines that made up your early life, and what rules governed these routines?"

b. "Who was aligned with whom— and what did they use that alignment to achieve?"

c. "What rules and boundaries were set around each sub-system?"

d. "What were common interactional sequences in your family?"

e. All of the above.

_____ 18. _____ views the counselor and therapist as an observer who is outside of the system, can assess what is going on, and can promote change—all without ever becoming part of the system.

a. First-order cybernetics

b. Second-order cybernetics

c. Third-order cybernetics

d. Fourth-order cybernetics

e. None of the above.

_____ 19. What best defines the focus of family therapy?

a. Most of the family therapies tend to be brief.

b. Family therapy tends to be solution-focused.

c. The focus is on here-and-now interactions in the family system.

d. Family therapy is generally action-oriented.

e. all of the above

_____ 20. Within the field of family therapy, _____ has been the most influential leader in the development of both gender and cultural perspectives and frameworks in family practice.

a. Monica McGoldrick

b. Jay Haley

c. Michele Weiner-Davis

d. John Gottman

e. Carl Whitaker

_____ 21. Which of the following roles and functions would be most atypical for a structural family therapist?

a. joining the family in a position of leadership

b. giving voice to the therapist's own impulses and fantasies

c. mapping the underlying structure of a family

d. intervening in ways designed to transform an ineffective structure of a family

e. being a stage director

_____ 22. A family therapist poses the following question: "Who seems to be most upset when mom comes home late from work?" She is asking _____ question.

a. an intrusive

b. a thought-provoking

c. a circular or relational

d. an exception

e. a scaling

_____ 23. Directives and paradoxical procedures are most likely to be used in which approach to family therapy?

a. strategic family therapy

b. Adlerian family therapy

c. multigenerational family therapy

d. experiential family therapy

e. structural family therapy

———— 24. Which approach to family therapy stresses the importance of returning to one's family of origin to extricate oneself from triangular relationships?

    a. Bowenian family therapy
    b. Adlerian family therapy
    c. structural family therapy
    d. strategic family therapy
    e. experiential family therapy

———— 25. Which approach to family therapy stresses unlocking mistaken goals, investigating birth order and family constellation, and reeducation?

    a. Bowenian family therapy
    b. structural family therapy
    c. Adlerian family therapy
    d. strategic family therapy
    e. experiential family therapy

PART 3

Integration and Application

An Integrative Perspective

In this chapter most of the exercises are designed to help you make some comparisons among the various therapy approaches, to help you see a basis for the integration of several approaches, to encourage you to think of the aspects you particularly like about each therapy, and to give you some practice in applying specific therapies to various client populations.

GLOSSARY OF KEY TERMS

Assimilative integration Selectively incorporating a variety of interventions from other therapeutic approaches, but grounded in a single coherent theoretical system.

Common factors approach A search for common elements across different theoretical systems.

Evidence-based practice The shift toward adopting therapeutic practices that are grounded in empirical evidence reflects a commitment to "what works, not on what theory applies."

Psychotherapy integration Looks beyond and across the confines of single-school approaches to see what can be learned from other perspectives.

Spiritual/religious values These play a major part in the lives and struggles of many people. Exploring spiritual/religious values, when deemed important by the client, can enhance the therapy process.

Syncretism A practitioner, lacking in knowledge and skill in selecting interventions, grabs for anything that seems to work, often making no attempt to determine whether the therapeutic procedures are indeed effective.

Technical integration (technical eclecticism) A focus on selecting the best treatment techniques for the individual and the problem. It tends to focus on differences, chooses from many approaches, and is a collection of techniques.

Theoretical integration A conceptual or theoretical creation beyond a mere blending of techniques with the goal of producing a synthesis of the best aspects of two or more theoretical approaches; assumes that the combined creation will be richer than either theory alone.

APPLICATIONS OF THEORETICAL APPROACHES TO SPECIFIC CLIENT POPULATIONS OR SPECIFIC PROBLEMS

As a basis for review and to help you compare and integrate the approaches, I am presenting a list of specific clients, problems, or situations. Decide which of the approaches or techniques you would be likely to use in each case. There is no one "right technique" for these cases, and in some cases you might want to employ several techniques. Keep in mind that the purpose of these exercises is to stimulate your thinking in *applying the theories and techniques you have studied to specific cases.*

1. Monica is a 27-year-old Latina from Mexico. She recently married a U.S. citizen and has moved to the United States. She comes for counseling because she wants help changing her accent. She states that she becomes very self-conscious whenever she speaks because she worries that others are judging her because of her accent and is concerned that they will think she "just swam across the river." She comes from a privileged family in Mexico.

   a. What is your first priority with this client? _____
   _____
   _____

   b. What technique would you select as being appropriate, and why? _____
   _____
   _____

2. Majed is a 23-year-old Persian man who has sought political asylum in the United States after being a victim of torture by his government in his home country. Majed's presenting problem is severe anxiety that includes suicidal ideation. This occurred after he was arrested for driving under the influence of alcohol. He is very concerned that he will have to go to jail for a period of time and worries that he will not survive in an American jail. His court date is in two weeks, but Majed's anxiety is so intense that he cannot keep food down, is having nightmares, and has stopped attending work.

   a. What is your first priority with this client? _____
   _____
   _____

   b. What technique would you select as being appropriate, and why? _____
   _____
   _____

3. Mark is a 38-year-old Caucasian man who has recently returned to college after spending several years in prison for a violent offense. He expresses concern that he is having difficulty trusting people in his new environment. He describes everybody as being "too nice" and has difficulty understanding what their "ulterior motives" might be. Mark also states that he wants to put his past behind him and find a way to "deserve to be in college." He is reluctant to discuss his experiences in prison.

   a. What is your first priority with this client? _____
   _____

   b. What technique would you select as being appropriate, and why? _____
   _____
   _____

4. Jeff is a 19-year-old bi-racial (Caucasian/Asian) male who is a college student. He states that he has never had close friends and was often the target of bullying and ridicule in high school. He tells you that this is the reason he moved across the country to attend college. He also tells you that he is very attracted to a young woman in one of his classes, with whom he has never spoken. He then shows you an expensive-looking ring that he recently purchased and states that he wants advice regarding how he can ask the young woman to marry him.

   a. What is your first priority with this client? _____
   _____
   _____

b. What technique would you select as being appropriate, and why? _____
_____
_____

5. Chelsea is a 21-year-old Asian-American female. She is in distress because her father committed suicide one month ago. She reports that she thought she was handling things well until she found her father's journal and learned how depressed he had been for many years. She expresses strong feelings of guilt and tells you that she "should have known how bad things were." She tearfully states that she can never forgive herself for "letting him die."

   a. What is your first priority with this client? _____
   _____
   _____

   b. What technique would you select as being appropriate, and why? _____
   _____
   _____

6. Todd is a 22-year-old married Caucasian male who is in the National Guard. He recently learned that he will be deployed to a combat zone and states that he has been experiencing significant anxiety. He expresses concern that his wife will not be faithful to him while he is deployed. He also expresses worry that he will come back from his deployment with PTSD and that combat will change who he is as a person. He states that he intends to follow his orders and seek assistance managing his anxiety before he is ordered to serve overseas.

   a. What is your first priority with this client? _____
   _____
   _____

   b. What technique would you select as being appropriate, and why? _____
   _____
   _____

7. Jenny is a 32-year-old, Black, lesbian female who describes significant depressive symptoms that she says have been present for several years. She reports stressful interpersonal relationships wherein she often feels her friends do not understand her. She states: "Once people get to know me, they disappear." She describes several instances in which people treated her as if she was "not a real person" and in which she became fearful of being harmed. She states that her family rejected her when one of her "friends" outed her to them. Jenny states she would like to feel less depressed and "get along better" with others.

   a. What is your first priority with this client? _____
   _____
   _____

   b. What technique would you select as being appropriate, and why? _____
   _____
   _____

8. John is a 33-year-old married Asian-American male. He comes for counseling at the urging of his wife who told him that he needs to "get a handle on anger." He expresses confusion about this and has difficulty providing instances wherein he has argued with his wife and times when he had angry outbursts in her presence. He admits that there are many things his wife does that cause him annoyance and upset, but reiterates his tendency to not express his anger toward her. He discloses that his father was a very angry man who used to beat him in front of his siblings.

a. What is your first priority with this client? _____

_____

b. What technique would you select as being appropriate, and why? _____

_____

9. Matt is a 22-year-old Caucasian male. He is a senior in college and states that he wants to drop out. He expresses feelings of anger and shame that he has spent so many years pursuing a degree that he does not want. He tells you that he has felt pressure to succeed academically after his older sister died 6 years ago. Recently, a close friend back home died and Matt has wanted to drop out of school ever since. He reports that he does not know what to do because his parents have invested so much in his education. He has stopped attending classes and started using alcohol and marijuana to escape feelings of grief and shame.

a. What is your first priority with this client? _____

_____

_____

b. What technique would you select as being appropriate, and why? _____

_____

_____

10. Charlene is a 47-year-old, single, bi-racial female (Caucasian/Latina). She reports a long history of anxiety with panic attacks. She states that she was recently caught shoplifting and is mandated to come to counseling to address her problems. She reports that she has used shoplifting as a means of managing her anxiety for years. She worries that if she does not successfully find a more adaptive way of managing anxiety that she will lose her job and eventually be incarcerated.

a. What is your first priority with this client? _____

_____

_____

b. What technique would you select as being appropriate, and why? _____

_____

_____

11. Roger, at age 33, is extremely inhibited. He finally seeks out therapy because he is in so much pain over his fears of talking to others or being in public. Roger is very nonverbal and gives only skimpy details; he obviously wants direction and help in conquering his severe inhibitions. During the initial interview he appears extremely uncomfortable and strained whenever he is expected to talk.

a. What is your first priority with this client? _____

_____

_____

b. What technique would you select as being appropriate, and why? _____

_____

_____

12. Cheath is a 40-year-old engineer who says he has gone to many encounter groups and has had a good deal of therapy. He says: "In spite of all these groups, I still don't seem to be able to get past the insight level. I see a lot of things I didn't see before, and I understand more why I'm the way I am, but I still don't seem to be able to use

what I know to make changes in my life. I'm still troubled by the same old problems, and so far I haven't been able to do much about resolving them."

a. What is your first priority with this client? _____

_____

_____

b. What technique would you select as being appropriate, and why? _____

_____

_____

13. An adolescent girl is having extreme difficulty coping with stress and the demands of school. Rosanna has many fears of failing, of not being liked by other students, and of being seen as "different," and she suffers from headaches and physical tenseness. She says she would like to lead a "normal life" and be able to go to school and function adequately. She is afraid that unless she can deal with these stresses, she will "go crazy."

a. What is your first priority with this client? _____

_____

_____

b. What technique would you select as being appropriate, and why? _____

_____

_____

14. A married couple, Meghan and Scott, present themselves for marriage counseling. Scott did not particularly want to come in, but he is willing to give things a try. He basically feels that life is fine, the marriage is all right, and there are no major problems with their children. In short, he likes his life, except he wishes that *she* could be more at peace, and that she would stop bugging him! Meghan feels pretty discouraged about life. Her kids do not appreciate her, and surely her husband does not recognize or appreciate her. She feels that she has to be both the mother and the father at home, that she has to make all the decisions, and that Scott will not listen to her. She wants to feel heard by him.

a. What is your first priority with this client? _____

_____

_____

b. What technique would you select as being appropriate, and why? _____

_____

_____

15. Kara is returning to college now that her children are in high school. She says: "I feel as if I don't know who I am anymore. At one time I knew what my purpose was, and now I just feel confused (and scared) most of the time. I like going to college and doing something for myself, and at the same time I feel guilty. I ask myself what I'm trying to prove. The most recurring feeling I have is that it's wrong for me to be enjoying college and doing this just for me."

a. What is your first priority with this client? _____

_____

_____

b. What technique would you select as being appropriate, and why? _____

_____

_____

16. The client, Yvonne, specifically wants to work on her dreams. She says that they are frequent and powerful and that she wants to learn what they are telling her about what is going on in her life.

   a. What is your first priority with this client? _____

   _____

   _____

   b. What technique would you select as being appropriate, and why? _____

   _____

   _____

17. Leticia comes in for crisis counseling. This young woman complains of chronic depression and is frightened by the frequency of her suicidal thoughts and impulses. She attempted suicide several years ago and was committed to a state mental hospital for a time. She fears being "sent up" again, because she does not know how to cope with her bouts of depression.

   a. What is your first priority with this client? _____

   _____

   _____

   b. What technique would you select as being appropriate, and why? _____

   _____

   _____

18. The clients are a group of elderly people on a ward of a state mental hospital. Most of them suffer from severe dementia and have little capacity to relate to one another. They are typically people who feel lost, abandoned, and depressed, and they have lost much of the meaning in their lives. The program director would like some form of therapy aimed at enabling these patients to learn to make contact with one another and to encourage them to talk about their feelings and their experiences.

   a. What is your first priority with this client? _____

   _____

   _____

   b. What technique would you select as being appropriate, and why? _____

   _____

   _____

19. Mark comes to therapy to help work through his feelings about his divorce. He feels that the divorce was his fault and that if he had been different his wife would not have left. He keeps talking about the fact that she left him. He feels devastated to the extent that he can hardly function. He is preoccupied with getting her back.

   a. What is your first priority with this client? _____

   _____

   _____

   b. What technique would you select as being appropriate, and why? _____

   _____

   _____

20. Jake, who is middle-aged, is seeking therapy because he wants to learn how to deal with his anger. For as long as he can remember, he has felt anger toward someone: his mother, his wife, his children, his boss, and his few friends. He says that he is frightened of his anger and of what he might do, so he keeps it all bottled up. He reports that

as a child he was always given the message that anger is a bad emotion and that you should surely never show angry feelings. Jake also realizes that he fears getting close to people, and he would like to explore his fear of intimacy as well as his fear of his anger.

a. What is your first priority with this client? _____

_____

_____

b. What technique would you select as being appropriate, and why? _____

_____

_____

A Suggested In-Class Activity

These exercises make good discussion material for small groups in class. In addition to comparing and discussing their selections, my own students have found it valuable in these small groups to get some practice in role playing. One of the students might assume the identity of a given client while another student functions as a counselor by using a particular technique that is a part of one of the theories. This activity may last about 10 minutes; then others in the group give the "counselor" their reactions, and another student may work with the client using a different approach. This combination of practice and discussion typically works well. As an alternative structure, these exercises can be done in triads, with one student being the "client," another the "counselor," and another the process observer.

 # ADDITIONAL CASES FOR PRACTICE

Show how you would work, *using an integrative approach*, with the situations presented in the following six brief cases. These cases are designed to give you some additional practice in applying concepts and techniques from the various approaches to specific situations. I suggest that you use the material I have provided merely as a point of departure. You can flesh out each case yourself by creating additional data. Apply the following questions to each of the vignettes.

1. What ethical and clinical issues does each case represent? What is your assessment of each of these key issues? What value issues arise in each case? How might your values affect the way in which you intervene?

2. Which theoretical approaches would be most helpful to you in counseling the clients involved in each case? What specific concepts would be useful? What techniques and procedures are you likely to employ?

3. What is your assessment of the core of the problem involved in each scenario? Show how you would proceed, and give your rationale for the interventions you would expect to make.

4. In each vignette, what are some special considerations relative to factors such as differences in ethnicity, cultural values, socioeconomic status, religious values, sexual orientation, lifestyle characteristics, and gender-role expectations?

A Husband Betrayed by His Wife

The Reverend Joshua Hunter, an African American Baptist minister in his late 30s, lives with his wife and children in a small town. About a month ago his wife told him that she had been having an affair for more than a year and intended to ask for a divorce. At first Joshua was totally shocked and went into denial. He thought to himself that he must be having a horrible dream. As reality hit him, he experienced a range of emotions. He is seeking counseling because he says that he cannot cope with his feelings and is just not able to function and get through a day. In counseling he tells you:

> I feel so humiliated and shamed in front of all those who respect me. It's hard to face anyone. With all this going on, I just don't know how I can continue in the ministry in my town. It's hard to understand why this happened to me; I've always tried to be the best husband and father that I could be. I know I was gone a lot, with all the work that needed to be done in the parish, but it's so hard to understand why she is doing this to me. As hard as I try to put this crazy thing out of my mind, it's just impossible to do so.

A Lesbian Confronting Her Parents

Gail is seeking counseling because she feels a strong need to tell her parents about her true identity as a person and her sexual orientation. Her parents are devoutly religious people who are highly intolerant of homosexuality. For most of her life Gail struggled with hiding the feelings she had for other women. She tells you that she has been living a lie so as not to be disowned by her mother and father. She says, however, that from her adolescence she has known deep down that she is a lesbian but was not able to actually admit it to herself until her junior year at college. She then went on to graduate school and got a master's degree in clinical social work. She is involved in a long-term relationship, and the two women have been considering taking steps to adopt a child. If this happens, there will be no way that she can continue hiding her sexual orientation. Although she counsels others, she is coming to you for counseling because she wants to clarify her priorities and make some key decisions about taking the risk of confronting her parents. She wants their acceptance of the person who she is, yet she finds herself resenting them when she thinks of how they are likely to react to her decisions.

A Man With a Disability Searching for Meaning and Spiritual Identity

Herb suffered a spinal-cord injury when a tree he was cutting fell on him. For a time after the accident, he continually asked himself, "Why did this have to happen to me?" He tells you that for the first 2 years after he became a paraplegic, he fantasized about suicide a great deal. He had been very active, and to be confined to a wheelchair for the rest of his life was more than he thought he could bear. It has been 5 years since his injury, and he says he has a better outlook on life than he had then, but he still goes into periods of depression and wonders what the meaning of his life is, especially when he considers all the physical activities that he loved so much that he can no longer do. A close friend urged Herb to get into counseling to work on his dissatisfaction and help him find a new direction in his life. He tells you that he would really like to discover a way to feel worthwhile again, and he seems somewhat inspired when he thinks of the accomplishments of some of his physically disabled friends. He says: "If they can overcome odds, even in sports, maybe I could too. It's just that I get discouraged, and then it seems like such hard work to get myself into gear. I'm so much hoping that I can find this motivation in counseling."

A Woman Struggling With Her Cultural Background

Dr. Deborah Wong is from a second-generation Chinese family. She tells you that even though she has lived in the United States all of her life, her Chinese roots are deep, and she has many conflicts over whether she is Chinese or American. Sometimes she feels like neither. Deborah has distinguished herself in her profession, and she holds a highly responsible position as a pediatrician. She feels married to her work, which she says is the thing she can do best in life. She has not made the time to cultivate intimate relationships with either sex, and she tells you that she very much feels as if she is "missing out" on life. She has always felt tremendous pressure to excel and never to let her family down. She feels as if she is in a competitive race with her older brothers, with whom her parents have always compared her. No matter how hard she works or what she accomplishes, she always feels a sense of inadequacy and experiences "not being enough." With some mixed feelings she is seeking counseling because she wants to feel "sufficient as a person." Although she enjoys her profession, she'd like to learn to take some time for herself. She also wants to develop a close relationship with a man. Yet whenever she is not working, she experiences guilt.

A Man Grieving Over the Loss of His Wife

At age 74 Erving says he has been totally lost ever since his wife, Amanda, "left" him after her long battle with lung cancer. A hospice worker strongly encouraged him to participate in counseling to work through his grief reactions. During her illness the hospice group was of tremendous help to both Amanda and Erving. After her death, however, he felt strange when he'd go to a hospice group meeting. He tells you:

> More than 90 percent of the group members are widows, and I keep thinking that I wish it had been me who died instead of Amanda. Even though it has been over a year since her death, I still feel lost and struggle to get through each day. I'm so lonely and miss her so much. They say it takes time, but I don't seem to be getting any better. Nothing seems very worthwhile anymore, and without her in my life I can't find anything I really like doing. Amanda was really my only friend, and now that she's gone, it doesn't seem that there is any way to fill this huge gap in my life.

He would like to get over feeling regret at what he didn't say to her as well as what he didn't do with her when she was alive. He'd like to resolve feeling so guilty that he is alive while she is gone.

A Woman Who Wants Her Marriage and Her Affair

Loretta and Bart come to you for marriage counseling. In the first session you see them as a couple. Loretta says that she can't keep going on the way they have been for the past several years. She tells you that she would very much like to work out a new relationship with him. He says that he does not want a divorce and is willing to give counseling his "best shot." Loretta comes to the following session alone because Bart had to work overtime. She tells you that she has been having an affair for 2 years and hasn't yet mustered up the courage to leave Bart for this other man, who is single and is pressuring her to make a decision. She relates that she feels very discouraged about the possibility of anything changing for the better in her marriage. She would, however, like to come in for some sessions with Bart because she doesn't want to hurt him.

JERRY COREY'S WORK WITH RUTH FROM AN INTEGRATIVE PERSPECTIVE

In this section I provide a concise presentation of the 13 sessions with Ruth that I demonstrate in the *DVD for Integrative Counseling: The Case of Ruth and Lecturettes*. For each session with Ruth, I include a brief description of my thinking regarding integrating concepts and techniques from the various theoretical orientations. Then I raise questions for you to think about regarding how you might pursue work with Ruth from an integrative perspective in each session.

Session 1. Beginning of Counseling

When we begin, I am mainly interested in structuring the therapeutic relationship. My hope is that Ruth will have enough information after our first session to decide if she wants to continue with me and that she will be able to make informed decisions about her therapy. I listen to Ruth's story and try to get a sense of what is bringing her to counseling at this time. We explore her expectations pertaining to the therapeutic venture. As much as possible, I want to demystify the therapeutic process, which I do by teaching her how to get the most from her work with me. It is important that Ruth reflect on what she wants to talk about in our sessions and that she learns how to be an active participant in her counseling. The informed consent process and teaching about how counseling works is not something that is finished after the first session; rather, these issues are revisited throughout the duration of our work together.

During our initial session, several theories may influence the direction I take. I think the person-centered approach is an excellent foundation for initiating the counseling process. I need to understand Ruth as fully as possible and create a climate whereby she will feel free to talk about those matters that are of deepest concern to her.

1. How would you begin your work with Ruth? What would you most want to accomplish by the end of the first session?
2. Feminist therapists stress the role of educating clients about the therapy process. What kind of information would you want to convey during the early phases of therapy? How would you go about making Ruth a collaborative partner?

Session 2. The Therapeutic Relationship

Regardless of the theoretical orientation, the client–therapist relationship is of paramount importance to therapeutic outcomes. I attempt to establish a collaborative relationship whereby therapy becomes a partnership. I ask Ruth to reflect out loud about her reactions to our last session. She admits that counseling is all new to her; she is not used to being the focus of attention nor is she used to looking at herself. She is somewhat concerned about sharing herself in personal ways and worries that she will feel exposed if she reveals "too much." As Ruth talks about her vulnerability, it is essential that I be nonjudgmental and that I listen to her fears. Trust will be the foundation of our working relationship.

In deciding how you would establish a working relationship with Ruth, consider these questions:

1. What value do you place on the quality of your relationship with Ruth? How important is the client–therapist relationship for you as a determinant of therapeutic outcomes?
2. What life experiences have you had that would most help you in working with Ruth? What personal characteristics might hinder your work with her?

Session 3. Establishing Therapeutic Goals

Ruth makes a list of goals that she would like to explore in her therapy sessions. These are the themes we identified as the target of our remaining sessions:

1. "I don't trust myself to find my own answers to life."
2. "I'm afraid to change for fear of breaking up my marriage."
3. "It's hard for me to ask others for what I want."
4. "It's hard for me to have fun. I'm so responsible."
5. "I'm afraid to make mistakes."
6. "I've lived by the expectations of others for so long that I don't know what I want anymore."

7. "I'm afraid to tell my husband what I really want with him, because I'm afraid he will leave me."

8. "There's not enough time for me to be doing all the things I know I should be doing."

9. "I'm afraid of my feelings toward other men."

10. "When my children leave, I'll have nothing to live for."

Examine this list of Ruth's statements. Collaboratively, how would Ruth and you decide what themes to focus on? How would you help Ruth clarify her goals for therapy? How would you help her make her goals concrete? How would you assess the degree to which she was meeting her goals?

Session 4. Understanding and Addressing Diversity

Early in our work Ruth brings up the matter of our differences. One of the areas she is concerned about is our differences in religion. She is wondering if I will be able to understand her. I must be finely attuned to any differences between us that may pose a problem for her, and together we explore the meaning of differences in religion, gender, and life experiences. I do not want to make the assumption that there will necessarily be a gap in understanding because she is a female client and I am a male therapist. I let Ruth determine which of our many differences are salient in our relationship, which we then will discuss fully.

1. As you become aware of differences between you and your client, would you bring up such differences for discussion? How might you handle the matter of Ruth wondering if you will be able to understand her because of whatever differences exist?

2. What kinds of differences—gender, sexual orientation, religious—between you and your client might be problematic for you?

Session 5. Understanding and Working With Resistance

After four sessions, Ruth wonders if therapy is creating more problems in her life than it is solving. Indeed, she hesitated in keeping her appointment. She is afraid that if she changes too much this will cause real problems with her husband and children. From my perspective, it is essential that we explore resistance, not fix it or simply get around it. Gently challenging resistance can open up new vistas for the client. I do not want to judge Ruth's behavior, but I do want to point out what I see her doing and ask her to reflect and comment on certain of her behaviors. When she wonders if she should continue or quit therapy, I do not want to respond defensively. Instead, my hope is that she will make her own decision. Even though she may be frightened of the prospects of remaining in therapy because of transformations in herself, Ruth can challenge her fears and move forward. She could also decide to terminate therapy.

1. How do you think you would respond to Ruth telling you that she is thinking of quitting therapy because of her fear of what will happen if she continues changing?

2. How do you view resistance? And how might resistance in your clients affect you?

Session 6. Cognitive Focus in Counseling

In this session Ruth discloses her belief that she must be perfect at everything she does. Ruth is a performance-oriented person, and the demands she puts on herself in living up to external standards are leading her toward exhaustion. I find value in getting Ruth to reflect on her beliefs and how these beliefs affect how she feels and what she is doing. I introduce a cognitive role-play situation, which leads to a realization of how tired she is because of all the ways she burdens herself. Working within the framework of cognitive behavioral therapy, Ruth and I explore specific messages she continues to tell herself. We look at alternative beliefs, ones that will allow her to be freer and less bound by perfectionistic goals.

Although I value dealing with how clients think about life, I do not narrowly stay with identifying and challenging self-talk and core beliefs. Thinking, feeling, and behaving are interactive aspects, and these three dimensions can be blended in the work of a single session. I may begin by suggesting a cognitive role play with Ruth in which we might deal mainly with some of her faulty beliefs or self-talk that tend to get her into trouble. As we engage on the cognitive level, Ruth is likely to experience feelings about her awareness of what she tells herself. Thus, we can shift to doing some experiential work or to a role play dealing with emotional issues. We may end the session by discussing how beliefs and feelings often influence the way we behave.

1. Would you be more inclined to focus on Ruth's feelings? Her thought processes and other cognitive factors? Her ability to take action as measured by her behaviors?

2. What specific concepts from the cognitive behavioral therapies would you draw on in working with Ruth's perfectionism and her other faulty beliefs?

Session 7. Emotive Focus in Counseling

Ruth mentions that she would like to talk about her relationship with her husband, John. She feels depressed when she thinks about their relationship. I ask Ruth to pay attention to what she is experiencing in the here and now as she is talking about what is missing in her marriage. She feels unappreciated and unloved. I suggest a role play that entails Ruth talking to me as John. As she talks to me (as her husband) in the present tense, she becomes aware of her feelings of sadness and cries. I think it is important to allow clients to experience whatever they are feeling and to allow those feelings to deepen. A Gestalt therapy perspective is extremely useful in facilitating Ruth's exploration of a range of feelings. At this point it is not useful to make interpretations, to give advice, or to suggest solutions. Instead, it is therapeutic to simply move with the moment-by-moment awareness of the client. From the existential perspective, I am attempting to enter her world and see reality as she does.

1. What therapeutic approaches are useful for you in dealing with the emotional dimension of counseling?

2. What value do you see in asking Ruth to stay with her present awareness and express what she is feeling moment by moment?

3. Given the fact that you are limited to brief therapy with Ruth (about 13 sessions), how inclined are you to encourage her to identify, express, and explore a range of feelings? Do you see ways of dealing with the emotive dimension and still work both cognitively and behaviorally?

Session 8. Behavioral Focus in Counseling

The prior session was an emotional one, so I ask Ruth at the beginning of this session if she reflected on last week or had any afterthoughts. Ruth admits that she feels a bit embarrassed over making herself that vulnerable. She wrote in her journal about the sadness she feels about her relationship with John and her children. Then she initiates a discussion of her weight. Ruth admits that she does not exercise, that she does not have much energy, and that she does not feel good about her weight or how she looks. I choose to focus on the behavioral dimension, but this does not exclude working with beliefs she has about her weight or her feelings about being overweight.

Drawing on behavior therapy and reality therapy, I strive to help Ruth assess the contributing factors to her concern over her weight. Once Ruth and I agree that getting involved in an exercise program is something she really wants, I function as a teacher and a consultant in helping her develop a behavioral plan. This includes teaching her about the importance of formulating an action plan, which we collaboratively devise together. We discuss how essential it is that Ruth monitor and record her progress in carrying out her plans.

1. If you are counseling Ruth and she informs you that she wants to work on concerns about her weight, how would you proceed? What behavioral methods would you use?

2. Besides working from a behavioral slant on themes such as weight and exercise, what possibilities do you see of bringing a cognitive and emotive dimension into this work?

3. What value do you see in homework and practicing outside of the session?

Session 9. An Integrative Perspective

Because Ruth is an integrated being, it makes sense to work with her from an integrative focus. I think it is important to begin with a comprehensive assessment of a client on all dimensions of human functioning. After making this comprehensive assessment of Ruth's current functioning, together she and I can then identify a number of specific target goals in different areas. It is possible to deal with a wide range of feelings, thoughts, and actions from a holistic framework. Here I find Adlerian theory most useful in providing a holistic perspective. Also useful are some concepts and techniques of both solution-focused brief therapy and narrative therapy. These approaches provide a foundation for building on Ruth's strengths and resources, as well as assisting her in revising her life story.

At this point, I encourage you to think of the process of developing a counseling style that fits you as an ongoing project. Your most challenging task will be to wisely and creatively select therapeutic procedures that you can employ in working with diverse client populations. As you take steps to develop an integrated perspective, ask yourself these questions:

1. Which theories provide a basis for understanding the cognitive dimension?
2. Which theories help you understand the feeling dimension?
3. How can you best work with the behavioral dimension?

Session 10. Working With Transference and Countertransference

Transference can be an especially useful tool in the counseling process. Clients will project a diversity of feelings, and they will oftentimes react to you as they reacted to other significant figures in their life. In Ruth's case, she saw some of her father in me. I encourage Ruth to express a range of feelings. Once she has done this, she can sort out aspects that are projections based on past experiences from real reactions. Countertransference is the other side of the coin, which needs to be monitored by the therapist if the therapy is to proceed. Of all the theories, I find the psychoanalytic approach to be the most useful in conceptualizing ways of understanding and working with transference and countertransference.

1. If you are engaged in short-term therapy with Ruth, to what extent will you be interested in exploring transference reactions? What will you do if Ruth's reactions to you trigger some of your own feelings?

2. Reality therapy and rational emotive behavior therapy pay little attention to transference. What are your thoughts about this?

Session 11. Understanding How the Past Influences the Present and the Future

The past is an important path to the here and now. I tend to pay attention to what clients report in the here and now and listen for evidence of unfinished business from the past. I am indebted to Gestalt therapy with its emphasis on how stuck points from the past tend to show up in present functioning. I don't need to ask Ruth to recount lengthy stories about her early childhood experiences to adequately understand how her past is influencing her presently. In a Gestalt manner, I ask Ruth to stay with whatever comes to her awareness and identify this. After she reports an event that happened when she was a child, I shift the emphasis from Ruth merely reporting an event to living that event. I suggest that she become the age she was and talk directly to her father (using me as her symbolic father). Ruth has many concerns from her childhood. Rather than talking about these events and the feelings associated with them, I find it much more powerful to suggest experiments in which Ruth can relive and reexperience these earlier situations. By attending to the present, salient events from the past are illuminated and provide a fruitful avenue of exploration.

1. How much interest would you have in working with Ruth's past life experiences? Her current issues? Her future aspirations and strivings? Which of these areas do you favor? Why?

2. How comfortable would you be in drawing on Gestalt interventions as a way of working with past experiences? What other theories would you find useful in linking Ruth's past and present?

3. What ideas might you borrow from both solution-focused brief therapy and narrative therapy to assist Ruth in getting a clearer picture of what kind of future she wants?

Session 12. Working Toward Decisions and Behavior Change

As we move toward the final phase of our work together, Ruth identifies some early decisions she made and becomes increasingly aware of new possibilities. Ruth has discovered a pattern in decisions she has made and how those decisions have a continuing influence in her life today. Because she has been willing to take what she has learned in the counseling office to the outside world, Ruth is able to make new decisions that are more functional. She is getting better at identifying old messages and self-defeating self-talk, and she is learning how to talk back to these critical voices. The key is not to discard early learnings, but to help clients revise early decisions.

Ruth even brings up the matter of termination, and together we begin to explore plans for where she can go from here. Therapy is a new beginning rather than an answer to all of life's problems. Here I would draw from approaches such as narrative therapy, solution-focused therapy, and existential therapy in encouraging Ruth to reflect on ways she would like to continue the process of redesigning herself and what kind of life she would like 5 years hence. Again, I would draw from cognitive behavioral approaches in helping Ruth restructure some of her basic beliefs and develop further plans as a way to reach her new goals.

1. What theories would you find useful in working with Ruth's decisions?

2. How would you intervene to get Ruth to critically evaluate some of the messages that influence what she does today? How might you help her to evaluate the degree to which her early decisions are still serving her well at this point in her life?

Session 13. Evaluation and Termination

We use the final session to review some significant points in the past 12 sessions and to discuss what was most helpful to her in her therapy. It is important that Ruth look specifically at what she learned, how she learned these lessons, and what can she do to build on these learnings now that formal therapy is over. From the narrative approach, I use the technique of writing a letter to Ruth in which I summarize many of her strengths and accomplishments that became evident in our work together. Ruth discovered that she is a person with various abilities, resources, and insights from which she can draw in dealing with both her present and future concerns. She now has increased confidence in herself and knows she can draw upon her courage and resourcefulness in dealing with future challenges. I also leave the door open so that Ruth will feel free to come in for future sessions should the need arise.

At this point, consider the partnership that you and Ruth formed, and summarize the highlights of your work together.

1. Reflect on how you might make the determination of when Ruth was ready to end therapy? How could you fully include her in this process?

2. If you were to write Ruth a letter in which you wanted to remind her of her major accomplishments, what would you most want to say to her? What value do you see in writing Ruth a letter that would give her your perspective on the changes you have noticed in her?

3. What therapeutic approaches would you rely on in assisting Ruth to bring closure to her therapeutic experience? What specific techniques are you likely to use?

Concluding Comments

Knowing the unique needs of your clients, your own values and personality, and the theories themselves is a good basis for beginning to develop a theory that is an expression of yourself. Building your personalized orientation to counseling is a long-term venture, so be patient with yourself as you continue to grow through your reading, thinking, and experience in working with clients and through your own personal struggles and life experiences.

In this brief section on the values of an integrative perspective, it is not possible to do justice to this approach. For some further reading on applying an integrative perspective in working with Ruth, see these two chapters in *Case Approach to Counseling and Psychotherapy:* Chapter 13 deals with working with Ruth from multicultural perspectives. Different contributors show how they would counsel Ruth assuming she is a Latina, an Asian American, and an African American. Chapter 14 presents integrative approaches to working with Ruth. This chapter brings the theoretical approaches together and shows how to develop your own therapeutic style. In addition, my book, *The Art of Integrative Counseling,* has as its primary purpose assisting you in thinking about ways to construct your own therapeutic style. Chapter 16 of *Theory and Practice of Counseling and Psychotherapy* deals with applying an integrative approach to working with Stan. Many of the techniques I describe in working with Stan could also be applied to Ruth's case.

QUESTIONS AND ISSUES: GUIDELINES FOR DEVELOPING YOUR PERSONAL STYLE OF COUNSELING

In reviewing the various approaches to psychotherapy, apply the following questions to each theory. Comparing your own thinking on the underlying issues with the positions of the various therapies can assist you in developing a frame of reference for your personal style of counseling.

1. Are you drawn to a particular theory because it fits your own worldview, experiences, and value system? Does your theory provide you with confirmation of your views, or does it challenge you to think about new dimensions of the counseling process?

2. What aspects of each theory are most useful to you? Why?

3. If you had to select one theory that comes closest to your thinking, which theory would this be? What is your theory of choice? Explain?

4. What theory that you have studied is most divergent from your own theoretical frame of reference? Explain.

5. Does your theory of choice account for differences in culture, gender, sexual orientation, and socioeconomic status? How relevant is this theory when it is applied to working with culturally diverse client populations?

6. What are the implications of each theory for multicultural counseling? Can you think of any ethnic or cultural groups that are likely to experience difficulties with any of the particular therapy approaches?

7. Are you open to using the methods and techniques of a particular approach in a flexible manner, especially in working with culturally diverse clients? Would you tailor your techniques to the needs of your clients, or would you be inclined to fit your clients to your techniques?

8. To what degree does your acceptance or rejection of a particular theory indicate your own biases?

9. Examine the contemporary popularity of each theory, and attempt to identify factors that contribute to this popularity or lack of it. Consider issues such as efficiency, expense, population served, time involved, and so on.

10. Which theories lend themselves well to time-limited and brief formats? Is brevity an important concern for you? Why or why not?

11. What does each theoretical approach offer you (by way of key concepts) that is most significant in terms of integrating it into your practice?

12. What are the philosophical assumptions underlying each theory? How is the view of human nature of each theoretical approach reflected in the therapeutic goals? In the client–therapist relationship? In the techniques and procedures?

13. What are some unique features of each of the therapies presented? What is the central focus of each approach? What are the significant contributions?

14. What are the limitations of each approach in terms of its theoretical concepts, the therapeutic process, and the applications of techniques to various counseling situations? What are some other limitations with respect to practical aspects such as time involved, level of training necessary, kind of population for which the therapy is effective or ineffective, settings where it is appropriate or inappropriate, and cost? What are some limitations of the approach as applied to multicultural counseling?

15. What are some common denominators among the therapies? To what degree do most approaches share some underlying areas of agreement with regard to goals, therapeutic process, and use of techniques?

16. What approaches can be combined to give a broader, deeper, and more useful way of working therapeutically with people? For example, what are the possible benefits of combining Gestalt therapy and reality therapy? Or combining the basic philosophy of the postmodern therapies with Gestalt techniques? Or combining REBT with reality therapy?

17. What are some contrasts between therapies? For example, what major differences exist between psychoanalysis and behavior therapy? Between existential therapy and behavior therapy? Between person-centered therapy and REBT? Between narrative therapy and REBT? Between reality therapy and person-centered therapy? Between solution-focused brief therapy and person-centered therapy?

18. What criteria exist for determining the degree of "successful" outcomes of counseling and psychotherapy in each approach? How specific are the criteria? Can they be measured objectively or observed?

19. Most approaches emphasize the client–therapist relationship as a crucial determinant of the outcomes of the therapeutic process. How does each approach view the nature and importance of the therapeutic relationship? What constitutes an effective collaborative therapeutic relationship?

20. What time frame does each approach emphasize: The past? The present? The future? How do the therapies that focus on the here and now account for the client's past and future?

21. How do the various therapies view the issue of the balance of responsibility between therapist and client? To what degree is the client's behavior controlled in the counseling sessions? Outside the sessions? What degree of structure is provided by the therapist?

22. What are the advantages and disadvantages of practicing within the framework of one specific theory as opposed to developing a more integrative approach made up of several different therapies?

23. State the position of each of the theoretical approaches on these basic issues:

    a. the importance of the role of interpretation

    b. diagnosis as essential or detrimental

    c. the balance between the cognitive aspects and feeling aspects

    d. transference and countertransference

    e. the importance of the client–therapist relationship

    f. a collaborative partnership in which therapy becomes a joint venture

    g. insight as a crucial factor

    h. the orientation of therapy toward insight or action

    i. the degree to which therapy is viewed as a didactic and reeducative process

    j. the issue of reality

24. For each therapeutic model assume that you are a practitioner following that approach. How would you approach your work with clients at the initial session? How would you function? What would you focus on with respect to goals and therapeutic procedures?

25. For each approach cast yourself in the role of a client to get a sense of how you might respond to the approach. What would be your goals, role, and experience in the therapy process? How might you react to some of the techniques in each of the approaches?

 ## SUGGESTED ACTIVITIES AND EXERCISES: DEVELOPING YOUR PHILOSOPHY OF COUNSELING

Early in the semester I routinely ask my students to write their philosophy of life (and counseling). At that point their views and values toward counseling are fuzzy. The exercise helps them gain a clearer focus on the basic attitudes and issues underlying counseling practice, and it typically generates thoughtful reflection. The material also can provide a variety of resources for discussion in class.

During the final weeks of the course I ask them to write a *revision* of the earlier paper. This time I ask them to integrate what they have learned from their readings in the various theories with their own basic values related to counseling. A *comparison* of the two papers provides excellent summary and integration material at the conclusion of the course, and it helps students determine what they have personally learned during the semester.

I recommend that you write your philosophy of counseling or, at the very least, develop a fairly comprehensive outline of your key ideas on that topic. Use the following questions to guide your work.

1. What is your view of human nature? How is your point of view significant in terms of your philosophy of counseling? What factors account for changes in behavior?

2. What is your definition of counseling? How would you explain to a prospective client what counseling is about at the first meeting?

3. What are some examples of goals of counseling that you view as appropriate? Can you list any goals that you consider inappropriate?

4. What are some of the most important functions of a counselor? How would you define your own role as a helper?

5. What do you think are the essential characteristics of an effective relationship between the client and the therapist? How important is this relationship as a factor for change?

6. What makes for a therapist's excellence? What distinguishes a mediocre therapist from an outstanding one?

7. What is one value you hold that you see as influencing your work as a counselor? How might this particular value influence you as a helping person?

8. How do cultural variables influence the counseling process? To what extent are you clear about the values of your culture and how they might influence your work as a counselor?

9. What life experiences of yours will help you work effectively with a wide range of clients? What struggles or crises have you effectively faced in your life, and how did you deal with them? What experiences have you had with people whose cultural values are different from your own?

10. What gives you a sense of meaning and purpose in life? How is your life's meaning potentially related to your need to help others?

11. Why are you selecting work in one of the helping professions? What is in it for you personally? What needs of yours are being met by being a helper?

12. To what degree are you doing in your life what you would want for your clients? What are you doing in your own life that will enable you to be an agent of change for your clients?

13. Now that you have studied the various theories, what steps could you take to begin to formulate your own orientation to counseling?

14. What key ethical concerns do you have about the practice of counseling? How would you go about resolving an ethical dilemma that you might face?

15. Can you think of some limitations in your own life experience that might hinder your ability to understand and relate to certain clients? How might you overcome some of your personal limitations so that you could counsel a wider range of clients more effectively?

 QUIZ ON AN INTEGRATIVE PERSPECTIVE

A Comprehension Check

Score ____%

Note: Please refer to Appendix 1 for the scoring key.

True/false items: Decide if the following statements are "more true" or "more false" as they apply to integration.

T   F   1. For decades, counselors were resistant to integration, often to the point of denying the validity of alternative theories and of ignoring effective methods from other theoretical schools.

T   F   2. As the field of psychotherapy has matured, the concept of integration has emerged as a mainstay.

T   F   3. Syncretism occurs when a practitioner, lacking in knowledge and skill in selecting interventions, looks for anything that seems to work.

T   F   4. One of the best known forms of technical integration is multidimensional therapy created by Arnold Lazarus.

T   F   5. Psychotherapy integration stresses tailoring of interventions to the individual client, rather than to an overarching theory.

T   F   6. Although clients' spiritual and religious beliefs may be important to them, it is ethically inappropriate for clinicians to address these beliefs in the context of therapy.

T   F   7. Most forms of short-term psychotherapy are active in nature, collaborative in relationship, and
integrative in orientation.

T   F   8. Therapeutic goals should always be
specific, concrete, and short term.

T   F   9. Evaluating how well psychotherapy
works is relatively simple.

T   F   10. Significant empirical research on
effectiveness has been produced for
all of the major models covered in
this book.

Multiple-choice items: Select the *one best answer* of those alternatives given.

_____ 11. _____ is best characterized by attempts to look beyond and across
the confines of single-school approaches to see what can be learned
from other perspectives.

    a. Psychotherapy integration
    b. Person-centered integration
    c. Syncretistic confusion
    d. Syncretism

_____ 12. Which of the following is NOT one
of the four most common pathways
toward the integration of psycho-
therapies?

    a. technical integration
    b. symbolic integration
    c. assimilative integration
    d. common factors approach

_____ 13. Which path calls for using techniques
from different schools without necessarily subscribing to the theoretical
positions that spawned them?

    a. technical integration
    b. symbolic integration
    c. assimilative integration
    d. common factors approach

_____ 14. Which of the following therapies
synthesize the best aspects of two or
more theoretical approaches?

    a. Dialectical behavior therapy
      (DBT)
    b. Acceptance and commitment
      therapy
    c. Emotion-focused therapy
    d. All of these

_____ 15. The _____ approach is grounded
in a particular school of psychotherapy, along with an openness
to selectively incorporate practices
from other therapeutic approaches.

    a. technical integration
    b. symbolic integration
    c. assimilative integration
    d. common factors approach

_____ 16. Support, warmth, feedback, reas-
surance, and credibility are considered _____ that have empirically
shown to be curative.

    a. common factors
    b. techniques
    c. theoretical factors
    d. symbolic factors

_____ 17. _____ will increasingly become
the organizing force for integration.

    a. Practice-based evidence
    b. Evidence-based practice
    c. Theory-based practice
    d. Theory-based evidence

_____ 18. One aspect of integration that is
particularly well-suited to taking
cultural factors into account is

    a. syncretism.
    b. symbolism.
    c. therapeutic flexibility.
    d. transference.

_____ 19. Sydney, a grief counselor, mentioned to his colleagues in a peer
supervision group that he is open to
discussing his clients' spiritual and
religious beliefs with them. What
should he say to his colleagues who
are skeptical about this practice?

    a. "My clients' spiritual and reli-
      gious beliefs are a major sus-
      taining power that supports
      them when all else fails. I think
      it would be unethical for me to
      overlook this."
    b. "I know it is unethical for me
      to raise these issues during ses-
      sions, but my clients don't seem
      to mind."
    c. "Who are you to question my
      practices? You are being com-
      pletely negligent and unethical
      by not discussing religion with
      your clients."
    d. None of these.

_____ 20. Which of the following is NOT a defining characteristic of brief therapy?

   a. clear specification of achievable treatment goals
   b. emphasis on client's deficits and unconscious dynamics
   c. here-and-now orientation with a primary focus on current functioning in thinking, feeling, and behaving
   d. clear division of responsibilities between client and therapist

_____ 21. What would both cognitive behavior therapists and reality therapists be inclined to say to their clients?

   a. "I think you are projecting anger on to me that belongs with your mother. Let's explore that."
   b. "Tell me about every part of your dream that you can recall. What do you think your dream is trying to tell you?"
   c. "What do you think about trying out the new behaviors we discussed today during the week? Can you think of opportunities you may have this week to practice being assertive?"
   d. "Why don't you tell your mother that she has a toxic effect on you every time she compares you to your sister. And feel free to tell her that your therapist thinks so too!"

_____ 22. Which of the following approaches does NOT emphasize the personal relationship as *the* crucial determinant of treatment outcomes?

   a. The existential approach
   b. The person-centered approach
   c. The Gestalt approach
   d. The behavioral approach

_____ 23. Eliza considers herself an Adlerian therapist, Julie regards herself as a feminist therapist, and Kyle specializes in cognitive behavioral therapy. What must all three therapists do regardless of their theoretical orientation?

   a. They must decide what relationship style to adopt with each client.
   b. They must decide what techniques, procedures, or intervention methods to use in each case.
   c. They must decide when to use certain techniques, procedures, or intervention methods, and with which clients.
   d. All of these.

_____ 24. Most outcome studies in counseling have been conducted by researchers affiliated with

   a. behavior and cognitive therapy and person-centered therapy
   b. narrative therapy
   c. psychodrama
   d. gestalt therapy

_____ 25. Research evidence from meta-analyses has demonstrated that psychotherapy is

   a. not effective at all.
   b. somewhat effective.
   c. moderately effective.
   d. remarkably effective.

Chapter 16

Case Illustration: An Integrative Approach in Working With Stan

AN OVERVIEW OF THEORIES: MAJOR AREAS OF FOCUS IN STAN'S THERAPY

Theory	Focus in Stan's Therapy
Psychoanalytic therapy	My focus is on the ways in which Stan is repeating his early childhood in his present relationships. I am particularly interested in how he brings his experiences with his father into the sessions with me. We attend to his reactions to me, because working with transference is one path toward insight. I am interested in his dreams, any resistance that he reveals in the sessions, and other clues to his unconscious processes. One of my main goals is to assist Stan in bringing to awareness unconscious memories and experiences that have a current influence on him.
Adlerian therapy	My focus is on determining what Stan's lifestyle is. In conducting a lifestyle assessment, I examine his early childhood experiences through his recollections and family constellation. My main interest is in identifying what his goals and priorities in life are. I assume that what he is striving toward is equally as valid as his past dynamics. Therapy consists of doing a comprehensive assessment, helping him understand his dynamics, and then collaborative working with him to define new goals and translate them into action.
Existential therapy	My aim is to be as fully present and available for Stan as possible because the relationship I establish with him will be the source of our work together. I am interested in how he finds meaning in life and whether spiritual values have been or currently are a part of his life. Although I would not impose any spiritual or religious beliefs during therapy, it is important to let Stan know that we can talk about his beliefs and values if he so chooses. We explore his existential anxiety and his fears of dying. I want to find out more about his fear of death and what keeps him alive, and I assess the risk of suicide at the outset. We also explore what quality of life he is striving for. I am interested in how Stan is dealing with freedom and the responsibility that accompanies it. Therapy is a venture that can help him expand his awareness of the way he is in his world, which will give him the potential to make changes.

Theory	Focus in Stan's Therapy
Person-centered therapy	Because I trust Stan to find his own direction for therapy, I avoid planning and structuring the sessions. My main focus is on being real, on accepting his feelings and thoughts, and on demonstrating my unconditional positive regard for him. Although Stan is only dimly aware of his feelings at the initial phase of therapy, he moves toward increased clarity as I accept him fully, without conditions and without judgments. If I can create a climate of openness, trust, caring, understanding, and acceptance, Stan can use this relationship to grow.
Gestalt therapy	My focus is on noticing signs of Stan's unfinished business, as evidenced by the ways in which he reaches a stuck point in his therapy. If he has never worked through his feelings of not being accepted, for example, these issues will appear in his therapy. I will ask Stan to bring them into the present by reliving them rather than merely talking about past events. I hope to help him experience his feelings fully rather than simply gaining insight into his problems or speculating about why he feels the way he does. I encourage Stan to pay attention to his moment-by-moment awareness, especially to what he is aware of in his body. Attending to what Stan is presently experiencing provides the direction therapy takes. My job is to intervene in ways that enable Stan to work through places where he is stuck.
Behavior therapy	Initially, I conduct a thorough assessment of Stan's current behavior, and I ask Stan to monitor what he is doing so we can create baseline data to evaluate any changes. We collaboratively developing concrete goals to guide our work, and I draw on a wide range of cognitive and behavioral techniques to help Stan achieve his goals. We may use techniques such as role playing, modeling, coaching, assertion training, carrying out homework assignments, and relaxation methods. I stress learning new coping skills that Stan can use in everyday situations. He is expected to practice what he learns in therapy sessions in his daily life.
Cognitive behavior therapy	My focus is on how Stan's internal dialogue and thinking processes are affecting his behavior. I use an active and directive therapeutic style. Therapy is time-limited, present-centered, and structured. My task is to create a form of collaborative working relationship in which Stan can learn to recognize and change self-defeating beliefs. We concentrate on the content and process of his thinking by looking for ways to restructure some of his beliefs. Rather than merely telling Stan what faulty beliefs he has, I emphasize his gathering data and weighing the evidence in support of certain beliefs. By the use of Socratic dialogue, I assist Stan in detecting his faulty thinking, in learning ways of correcting his distortions, and in substituting more effective self-talk and beliefs. We use a wide range of cognitive, emotive, and behavioral techniques to accomplish our goals.
Reality therapy	Counseling is guided by the principles of choice theory. First, I do my best to demonstrate my personal involvement with Stan by listening to his story. The emphasis is on his total behavior, including his doing, thinking, feeling, and physiology. If we concentrate on what he is actually doing and thinking and if change occurs on these levels, Stan will also change on the feeling and physiological levels. After Stan evaluates his

present behavior, it is up to him to decide the degree to which it is working for him. We explore those areas of his behavior that he identifies as not meeting his needs. Much of the therapy consists of creating specific, realistic, and attainable plans. Once Stan agrees to a plan of action, it is essential that he make a commitment to following through with it.

Feminist therapy	Stan comes to therapy with clear goals: to stop drinking, to feel better about himself, to relate to women on an equal basis, and to learn to love and trust himself and others. I build on these strengths. I focus on establishing an egalitarian working relationship to help Stan begin to regain his personal power. I spend considerable time explaining my view of the therapy process and how it works. By demystifying the therapeutic process, I am conveying to Stan that he is in charge of the direction his therapy will take. Our therapy might include a gender-role analysis so that Stan can come to a fuller understanding of the limiting roles he has uncritically accepted.
Postmodern approaches	Operating from the joint perspectives of the solution-focused and narrative approaches, I believe Stan is an expert on his life and that I am a consultant who invites and assists Stan in identifying, clarifying, and achieving his goals and preferences. I believe Stan has the internal and external resources he needs to make the kinds of changes he is seeking. I construct questions that assist Stan in discovering more choices and in accomplishing his goals, and ultimately, I assist him in reauthoring the story of his life.
Family systems therapy	Stan has identified a number of strained relationships with his mother, father, and siblings. Ideally, at least one session includes all the members of his family. The focus is on Stan gaining greater clarity on how his interpersonal style is largely the result of his interactions with his family of origin. Working individually with Stan, I emphasize the many ways in which his current struggles are related to the family system of which he is a part. Through our therapy, Stan learns to recognize the rules that governed his family of origin and the decisions he made about himself. Rather than trying to change the members of his family, we work on discovering what Stan most wants to change about himself in relation to how he interacts with them.

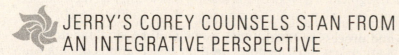

JERRY'S COREY COUNSELS STAN FROM AN INTEGRATIVE PERSPECTIVE

Session 13. An Integrative Approach to Working With Stan

This session deals with termination and takes an integrative view of Stan's work. We address what was learned in therapy and how Stan can continue to apply what he learned from the therapy experience to his daily life. Before viewing this final session, read Chapter 16 and answer the questions in the text under the heading "Follow-Up: You Continue Working With Stan in an Integrative Style."

As you watch this final counseling session, look for specific topics that you would want to address with Stan if you were his counselor. Also, imagine what reactions you might have to coming to an end of formal work with him. After viewing the session, discuss these questions:

1. What would you most want to ask Stan as a way to review what he has learned from his therapy?

2. How would you prepare Stan for the termination of his therapy with you?

3. What is one belief that Stan reports having changed?

4. What is one behavior that Stan says he has acquired or eliminated?

5. What is one example of a feeling or mood that Stan has changed?

6. The therapist asks Stan to take credit for any changes he has made during the course of his therapy. What value do you see in asking Stan to identify what he did to bring his changes about?

7. What would you most want to accomplish with Stan during the termination session?

8. What theories and techniques would you combine for an ideal integrative approach?

9. Would you encourage Stan to contact you if some future problem arises that he would want further help with or if he wanted to talk about changes he made after termination? Why or why not?

10. How would you help Stan to think of ways he might deal with stumbling blocks after the termination of his therapy?

A Suggested In-Class Activity

There are many activities that can help you integrate what you have learned in reading about Stan, viewing counseling sessions with him, and the combination of your work in small groups in your class for the semester. Let me describe one of my favorite class exercises that I have often used in conjunction with the final chapter in the text that illustrates an integrative approach in working with Stan. Time is always a consideration, especially toward the end of a course. Your instructor and the class may want to use some adaptation of the exercise below.

I ask one student who feels some identification with Stan to volunteer to play the role of Stan. Alternatively, the instructor might want to play Stan (which I typically do in my classes). Eleven students volunteer to play the role of the therapist, each student representing one of the 11 therapeutic approaches. Each "therapist" demonstrates in about 6 to 7 minutes how he or she would counsel Stan from the standpoint of a specific orientation. Then the entire class participates in a critique and discussion of the sessions. Here are some specific suggestions.

1. It is best to choose volunteers a week in advance so they can think about some aspects they want to focus on and can do some preparation in the particular therapy orientation.

2. In my classes, I prefer to have all the counselors work with Stan one after the other, without stopping to discuss each segment. The processing session is held after all the volunteer counselors have had a chance to work with Stan for no more than 7 minutes each.

3. During the time that each counselor is attempting to stay within a single therapeutic model, the other students are asked to write notes on their observations of *both* Stan and each counselor. These comments can address what they are seeing that they particularly like and find useful.

4. The volunteer therapists are asked to assume that they were watching the prior counselor work with Stan through a one-way glass. In this way, each counselor does not have to start from scratch (except for the first counselor). The idea is to build upon previous sessions and, ideally, to demonstrate how a different theoretical perspective might approach the same theme from a different angle. Volunteers can use some imagination here.

5. After all "therapists" have had a chance to counsel Stan (this generally takes a little over one hour), "Stan" is given a chance to talk about what it was like to be the client in this exercise.

6. Finally, the 11 students who functioned as separate therapists sit together (form an inner circle in the class) and share their reactions to the time they spent with "Stan."

What were they thinking and feeling? What were their reactions to Stan? And, more important, what impressions did they have of themselves as they counseled him?

AN ACTIVITY: YOU DEMONSTRATE YOUR INTEGRATIVE APPROACH IN WORKING WITH STAN

You have been reading about how different therapists would apply interventions from their respective theoretical orientations, and I hope that you have been viewing the video illustrating my work with Stan from the various theories. Reflect on how you would counsel Stan from your integrative perspective. The following questions can guide your thinking in doing this task.

1. As you anticipate meeting Stan for the first session, what might you be thinking and feeling? What will be some of your main focal points as you begin working with him?

   a. What therapeutic approaches might you draw from in helping Stan formulate goals that will guide his therapy?

   b. How might you enlist his involvement in collaboratively developing goals for therapy?

   c. What background information might you seek as a foundation for working with him? Which therapies might you draw from in doing this assessment of his current functioning?

2. Show how you might proceed with Stan by combining concepts from various theories. Give some idea of how you would work with him if you could meet with him 6 to 12 times. Attempt to integrate techniques and concepts that suit your personal style, and show how you could draw on several of the models in a balanced way.

3. Describe how you would pay attention to the factors of thinking, feeling, and doing when working with Stan. How could you develop a series of counseling sessions that would encourage him to explore his feelings, develop insight, put his problems into a cognitive perspective, and take action to make the changes he would most like to make?

4. In conceptualizing Stan's case and in thinking about a treatment plan (or approaches you might take with him), consider some of the following questions:

   a. How much direction and structuring does Stan need? To what degree would you take the responsibility for structuring his sessions?

   b. What major themes would you focus on in his life?

   c. How would you modify your interventions to fit a brief therapy framework?

   d. How much might you be inclined to work toward major personality reconstruction? How inclined would you be to work toward specific skill development and problem-solving strategies?

   e. What values do you hold that are similar to Stan's? How do you expect that this similarity would either get in the way of or facilitate the therapeutic process?

   f. Assume that Stan is a person of color. Think of the ways in which you might modify your techniques to fit with his cultural background. What special issues would you want to explore with him if he were an African American? Native American? Latino? Asian American?

   g. What ethical issues do you think may be involved in working with Stan's case?

   h. How might you structure outside-of-therapy activities (homework, reading, journal writing, and so forth) for Stan? What kinds of activity-oriented homework assignments might you suggest for him?

   i. In working with Stan, how much interest would you have in his *past* experiences? How might you work with some early childhood issues? What interest would you have in his *current* functioning? Would you have a concern about his *future* strivings and aspirations? How might you work with him on his expectations?

j. Would you be inclined to focus on his *thinking* processes and his belief systems (cognitive dimension)? His *feelings* associated with his experiences (emotional dimension)? His ability and willingness to *do* something different and to *take action* (behavioral dimension)? Which dimension do you think you would make the focus of therapy? Why?

5. In thinking about termination of Stan's therapy, show what criteria you might use to determine when it would be appropriate. Consider a few of these issues:

a. Would you, as Stan's counselor, suggest termination? Would you wait until he brought up the matter?

b. Consider each of the various therapeutic approaches. When would he be ready to stop coming in for counseling? What standards would determine his readiness for termination in each of the theories of therapy?

c. What would you do if you thought he was ready to terminate but *he* did not feel ready quite yet? What if he wanted to stop coming to sessions and you were convinced that he had many more issues to explore that he was avoiding and that he was somewhat frightened about continuing therapy?

d. What ideas do you have for evaluating Stan's overall therapy? How might you assess his level of change? How would you measure the outcomes of your work together?

Scoring Key for Chapter Quizzes

Item Number	Chapter 2 The Counselor: Person and Professional	Chapter 3 Ethical Issues	Chapter 4 Psychoanalytic Therapy	Chapter 5 Adlerian Therapy	Chapter 6 Existential Therapy	Chapter 7 Person-Centered Therapy	Chapter 8 Gestalt Therapy	Chapter 9 Behavior Therapy	Chapter 10 Cognitive Behavior Therapy	Chapter 11 Reality Therapy	Chapter 12 Feminist Therapy	Chapter 13 Postmodern Therapy	Chapter 14 Family Systems Approaches	Chapter 15 An Integrative Perspective
1	T	F	F	T	T	F	T	T	F	T	F	T	F	T
2	T	F	T	T	T	F	T	T	T	T	T	T	F	T
3	F	T	T	T	F	T	F	T	T	T	F	T	F	T
4	T	T	F	F	F	T	F	F	T	F	F	T	T	F
5	F	F	T	T	T	F	T	T	F	F	T	F	T	T
6	F	F	F	F	F	T	T	F	T	F	T	T	T	F
7	F	T	F	F	T	T	T	T	F	T	F	T	T	T
8	F	T	T	T	F	F	F	F	T	T	F	T	T	F
9	T	F	T	T	T	T	F	F	T	T	T	F	T	F
10	F	T	T	F	T	T	T	T	T	F	F	F	T	F
11	A	B	D	D	E	E	B	B	E	A	A	B	B	A
12	C	A	D	B	D	B	E	A	C	B	D	C	E	B
13	B	C	C	B	C	E	B	B	A	D	C	C	D	A
14	C	A	B	D	B	A	A	A	D	B	A	C	A	D
15	C	D	C	E	E	A	B	A	E	D	A	A	E	C
16	D	A	C	C	D	E	D	B	D	E	B	D	A	A
17	A	C	A	D	A	D	B	E	B	A	B	B	E	B
18	A	D	B	B	E	D	E	B	A	B	B	A	A	C
19	B	A	C	B	D	D	C	A	E	E	B	A	E	A
20	C	C	E	D	C	C	D	E	C	E	D	D	A	B
21	A	B	C	B	B	D	E	D	C	D	E	A	B	C
22	C	C	C	E	B	B	C	B	C	A	E	B	C	D
23	D	A	B	A	C	E	A	A	E	B	B	C	A	D
24	C	B	E	E	B	E	D	C	D	D	B	D	A	D
25	A	B	A	C	D	B	E	D	B	C	B	B	C	D